THE COMPLETE HANDBOOK OF

WOODWORKING TOOLS
AND
HARDWARE

THE COMPLETE HANDBOOK OF
WOODWORKING TOOLS
AND
HARDWARE

BY CHARLES R. SELF

TAB BOOKS Inc.
BLUE RIDGE SUMMIT, PA. 17214

FIRST EDITION
FIRST PRINTING

Library of Congress Cataloging in Publication Data

Self, Charles R.
The complete handbook of woodworking tools and hardware.

Includes index.
1. Woodworking tools. I. Title.
TT186.S4   1983   684′.082   82-19350
ISBN 0-8306-0484-7
ISBN 0-8306-1484-2 (pbk.)

Cover photograph courtesy of Shopsmith, Inc.

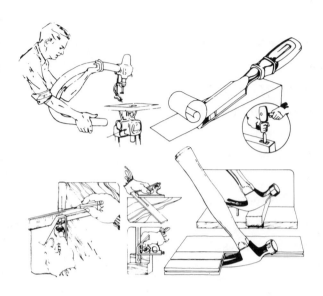

Contents

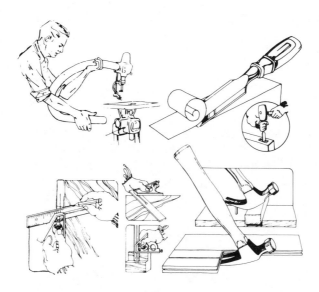

Introduction

WOODWORKING IS ONE OF THE MOST pleasant crafts known to man. But in its varied phases you'll find that it takes some settling down and some firm decisions to make sure you don't, as I have done at times, fly off in too many directions. The result of such darting about tends to be an overexpenditure on tools and little completed work.

Woodworking tools for a basic shop are not really expensive. With minimal care, most will last a lifetime and beyond. But remember one thing: The original tool is often far, far less expensive than the eventual pile of accessories you'll add to it. Certain tools such as routers, table saws and radial-arm saws readily fit this description, but many others can easily do in your bank account.

If you're a novice, begin with some of the simpler kits available and see how much you enjoy those before moving on to the acquisition of more tools, more wood, and more complex plans. Step easy when purchasing and go for quality when you purchase. As a result, you will learn many new things and complete many new projects.

This book is dedicated to Ed Benfield, manager of public information at The Stanley Works for the past 31 years, on the eve of his retirement. I hate to see anyone who does a job as well as he does leave, but I hope with all my heart that his retirement is long and enjoyable. I'm sure I'm not the only one who will miss this master of his craft.

Other TAB books by the author:

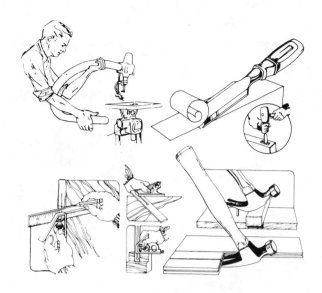

Overview

THIS BOOK IS MEANT FOR THE BEGINNING and intermediate woodworker. I hope it will also provide some information of good value for the more advanced craftsmen and craftswomen in the field. This book covers close to everything needed for woodworking, from the most basic handtool to stationary power tools, as well as hardware, nails, screws, bolts, hinges, and so on. I know of no other book that covers as many tools and their uses in detail.

Acquiring a full complement of woodworking tools can take a lifetime or a few hours of poring over catalogs and paying for the tools all at once. The acquisition of tools is something nearly everyone does. Some people need no more than a putty knife, pliers and a few screwdrivers; others require a fully equipped woodworking shop.

As time passes, you might find that your needs change and you will want to add to your tool collection. One thing never changes, though: the novice woodworker is never wise to start from the top, buying the most expensive tools first and moving down from there. If you have little or no experience in woodworking (given the prices of good-quality power tools such as lathes, radial-arm saws, and table saws) and the need for practice to become skilled in the use of tools, do not spend thousands of dollars on equipment. This could result in little more than a flat wallet, frustration, a great deal of sawdust, and no practical results. I've seen this happen to too many people. The waste is appalling because used tools fetch nothing like their original cost. Very often, such an experience will sour you on working with wood when a less expensive start would allow you to progress further with far less

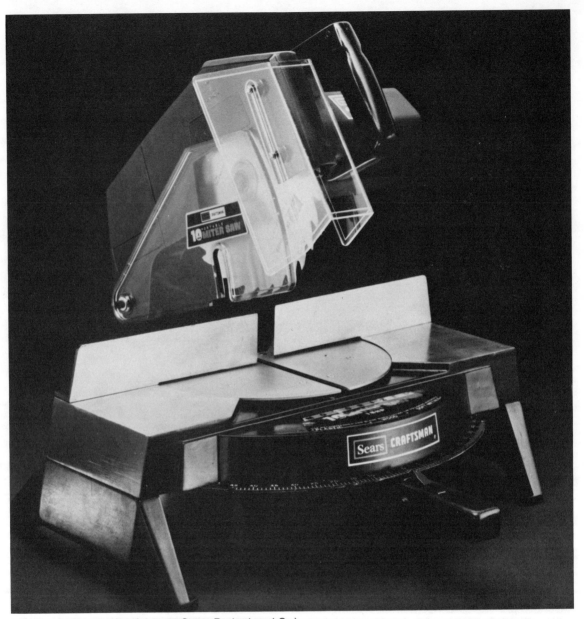

Fig. O-1. Power miter box (courtesy Sears, Roebuck and Co.).

cost and greater satisfaction and results.

I am not saying that you should not buy quality woodworking tools. A quality tool, even in the hands of a novice, is going to do a much better job than a poor tool. Tools of quality are properly designed for their particular jobs, fit the hands better, require less effort overall to use, and are generally more easily maintained in a ready-to-use state. See Figs. 0-1 through 0-18.

Fig. O-2. Electric impact wrench (courtesy Sears, Roebuck and Co.).

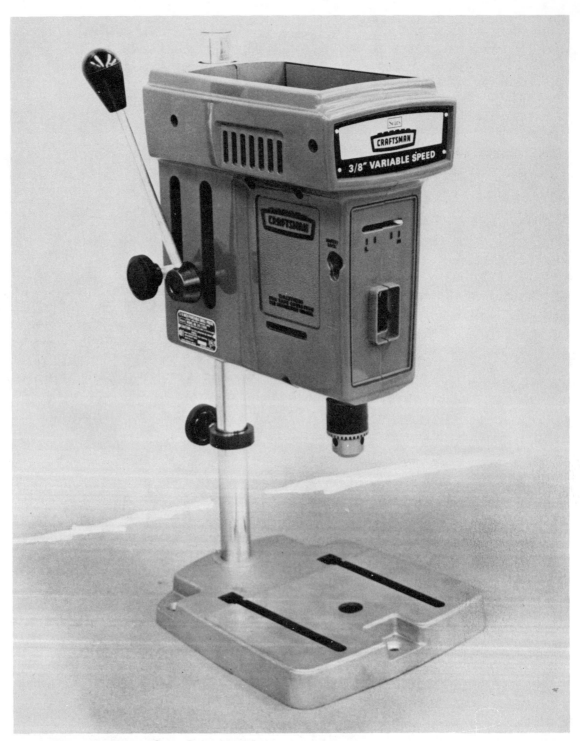

Fig. O-3. Drill press (courtesy Sears, Roebuck and Co.).

What I *am* saying is that if you have never used even a hammer or handsaw, it doesn't make sense to spend $350 for a wood lathe and another $200 to $300 for woodturning tools and accessories and then discover it will take possibly 60 or 70 or even more hours of practice to even begin to develop a proficiency level in woodturning. By the same token, if you never use, or rather buy, rough-surfaced wood, spending over $1,000 for a planer/molder is more than a bit on the wild side.

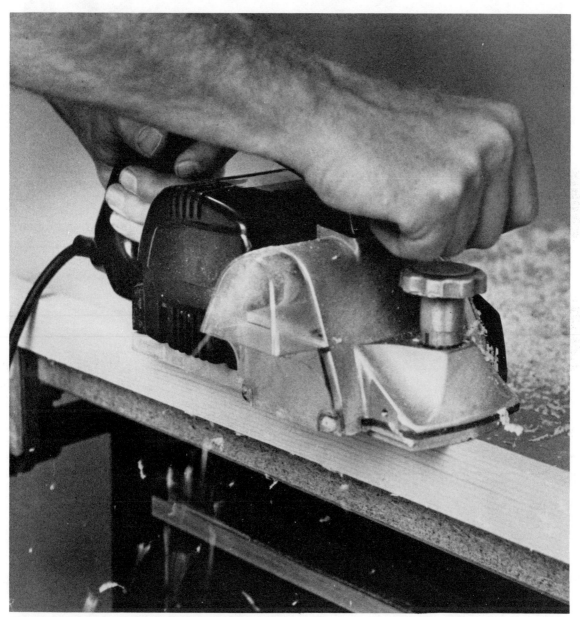

Fig. O-4. Power planer (courtesy Sears, Roebuck and Co.).

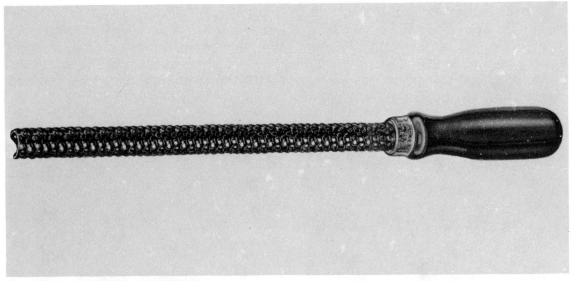

Fig. O-5. Surform (courtesy Stanley Tools).

When buying woodworking tools, take into consideration not only the expense factor, but also your current skills, overall experience, jobs to be done, and desire to either gain more skills or keep them at their present level. If you have some woodworking experience, then it will be far easier to decide where you want to go in the future, even though your skills do not yet match the most sophisticated woodworking tools. Without any experience but with a need or desire to get involved with woodworking, you

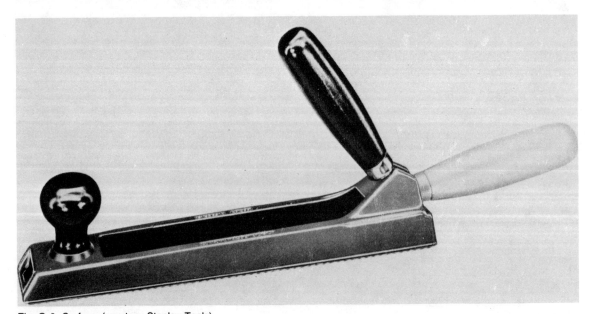

Fig. O-6. Surform (courtesy Stanley Tools).

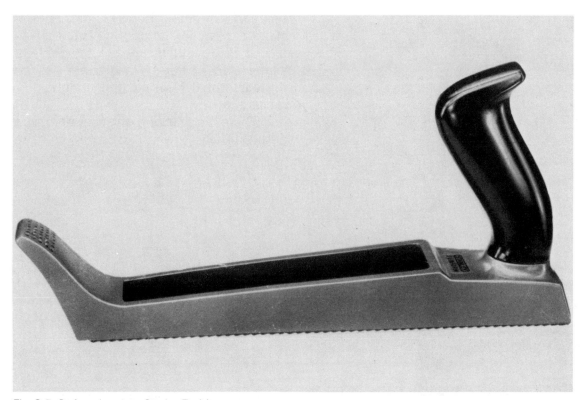

Fig. O-7. Surform (courtesy Stanley Tools).

are best off starting small in whatever field of woodworking you think will interest you most.

If simple woodcarving is your preference, start with a small set of carving tools (top-quality carving tools in a basic set will include about six tools), a book on basic woodcarving, and a sharpening stone. It is possible to spend more than $21 for a single gouge in many cases, and a few are even higher. If you then find that woodcarving suits your talents and preferences, you can purchase a more complete set of tools and possibly move on into wood sculpting.

If home carpentry repairs are all you want to do, the choice is, oddly, more complex. The reason is simple: you'll have to select a hammer that fits your strength and job needs: a saw of some kind, probably two

or three kinds; some measuring tools such as a folding rule or a tape measure; some form of square; and a marking tool. More extensive carpentry will require more tools.

No matter what tools you acquire or their cost, store them carefully and securely. Good handsaws can range in price from about $20 on up past $40. Other tools such as circular saws can be far more costly. Once they're yours, keep them locked up when they're not in use and keep them yours.

For basic cabinetry or furniture making, you are going to need hand tools and stationary power tools. Usually, you can make a good start on cabinetmaking and furniture making with a good radial-arm saw or table saw and go from there as required. In any case, the investment is not to be taken lightly

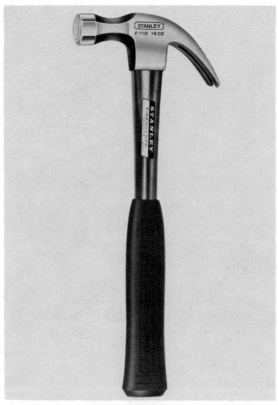

Fig. O-8. A curved-claw hammer (courtesy Stanley Tools).

be readily reduced between machines if clearance above the machine is not possible. It is obviously unwise to locate a jointer/planer where a long board pushed through would ram into the upright of a radial-arm saw.

There is a solution to the space problem and, partially, to the cost problem. The

because the least expensive, decent-quality table saw—with motor, legs and table extensions—that I've seen costs over $225 before you have it home. It is easily possible to spend well over $600 for a larger, more powerful table saw. By the same token, a good radial-arm saw will cost a bit more, something on the order of $350, and you can again go well over $600 for top-of-the-line, larger and more powerful models.

Wood turning, of course, requires a lathe, and these will cost nearly $275 with a motor and over $300 with legs added. Stationary woodworking tools not only require a considerable investment in cash, but they also expand your need for workshop space. In most home workshops, a single tool will be in use at a time. Space often can

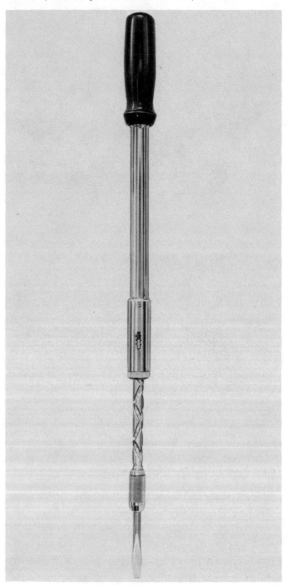

Fig. O-9. Yankee screwdriver (courtesy Stanley Tools).

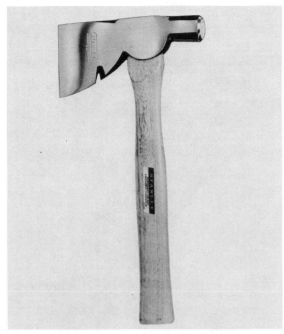

Fig. O-10. Half hatchet (courtesy Stanley Tools).

Shopsmith Mark V multitool unit (Fig. O-19) stores in about a 2-×-6-foot space. This doesn't eliminate the need for working space, but it means you don't have to allow working space for several tools. The Mark V and the standard accessory package offers a 10-inch table saw, a 16½-inch drill press, a horizontal boring machine, a 34-inch (long) lathe, and a 12-inch disc sander. The cost is about $1,200 for this package. Included is a text on woodworking operations and a self-study course. Shopsmith also offers seminars. If you find you need more tools, there is a jointer; a jigsaw, a band saw and other accessories. All of these are run by a single motor. Most use a single working table (the band saw doesn't). The basic unit weighs 198 pounds and the motor draws 13.5 amps and puts out more than 2 horsepower.

For a single-saw shop, the radial-arm

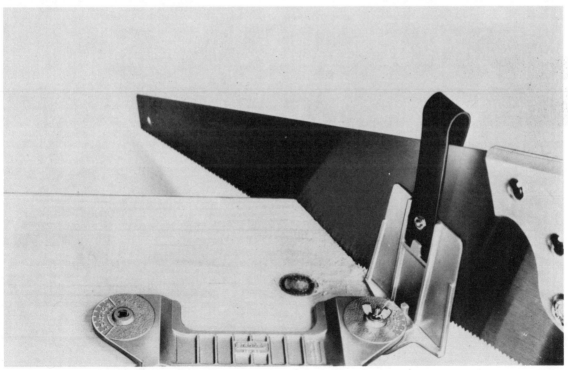

Fig. O-11. Miter guide (courtesy Stanley Tools).

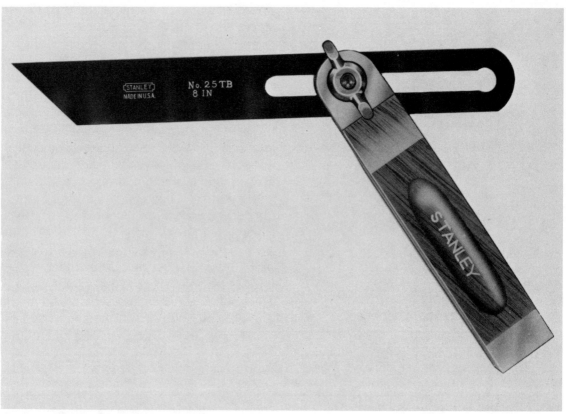

Fig. O-12. Sliding T bevel (courtesy Stanley Tools).

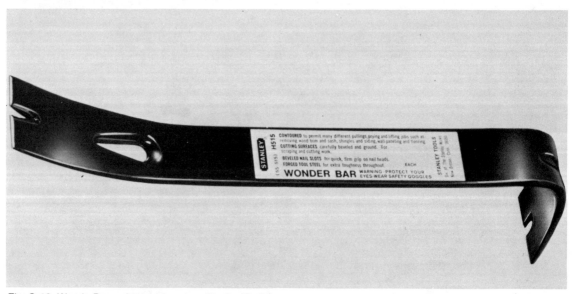

Fig. O-13. WonderBar prying tool (courtesy Stanley Tools).

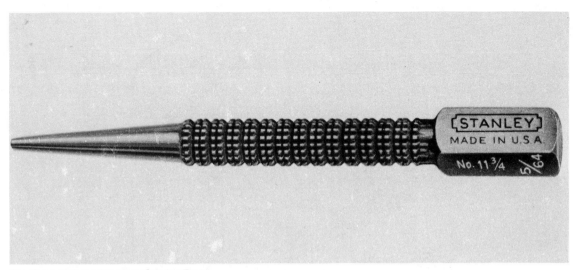

Fig. O-14. Nail set (courtesy Stanley Tools).

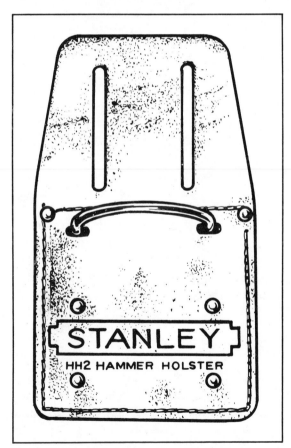

Fig. O-15. Hammer holster (courtesy Stanley Tools).

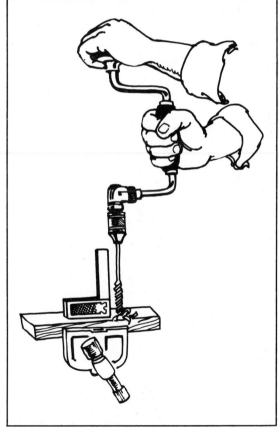

Fig. O-16. Brace and bit in use (courtesy Stanley Tools).

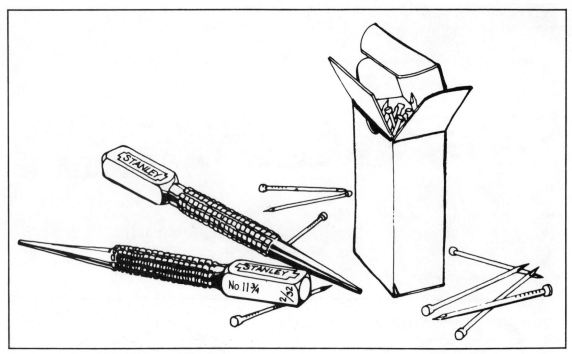

Fig. O-17. Nailsets and nails (courtesy Stanley Tools).

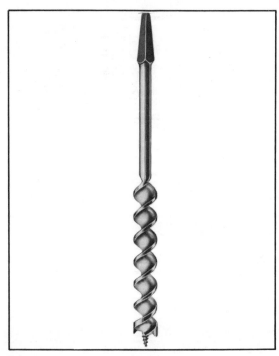

Fig. O-18. Augur bit (courtesy Stanley Tools).

saw is probably your best bet. The machine can be turned into a router, a disc sander, or a surface planer (rotary only) and still do everything a table saw is able to. I've heard some arguments over the past 25 or so years that a table saw is marginally more accurate on complex cuts than is a radial-arm saw. This might be true, but with minor exceptions I would guess the utility would outweigh the slight increase in accuracy. Actually, because the work remains stationary while the blade is moved through it, for some cuts the radial-arm saw is more accurate, and more easily used, than is the table saw.

Band saws provide the greatest depth-of-cut capacity of all stationary woodworking saws (outside a sawmill). Most people consider, and rightly so, the band saw adapted best to cutting curves where the wood is too thick for using a jigsaw. Bandsaws are

Fig. O-19. Shopsmith Mark V in use as a planer (courtesy Shopsmith, Inc.).

Fig. O-20. A 10-inch band saw (courtesy Sears, Roebuck and Co.).

handy for jobs such as cutting curves in thick or thin stock; resawing (ripping a thick board down to two thinner ones), cutting circles, and making various compound cuts. Many can also be adapted for sanding or take metal cutting blades (Fig. O-20). A 12-inch band saw, with motor and legs, rip fence, miter gauge and a small extension table, will most likely sell for very close to $400.

Too much emphasis on tool cost, though, is as bad as too little. You must also consider your needs and preferences. Always remember that you don't have to buy it all at once. Buying good quality a piece at a time is better than immediately having a shop full of junk.

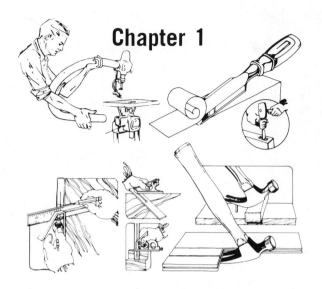

Chapter 1

Wood

WOOD IS DURABLE. WOOD USED 300 YEARS ago in Japanese temples has lost little of its original strength. Wood piles have been found, intact, after 1,000 years under the streets of Venice. Of course, some woods resist decay better than others. Fallen redwood trees have been found lying, undamaged by decay or insects, on forest floors a century or more after they'd fallen. Cedar and cypress are two other woods that naturally resist decay quite well, and, today, you find products such as Koppers Company's Wolmanized pressure-treated lumber. In many areas of the country, pressure treating lumber offers a less costly alternative to buying redwood or cedar materials. Local wood can be so treated and last almost as long as the wood nature made decay resistant and insect resistant.

Wood offers, in addition to strength and durability, a warmth in natural finish that I believe no other material can even begin to approach. It offers a wide, wide spectrum of colors and grain patterns. See Figs. 1-1 through 1-4. Think of the grain patterns, or near lack of them, of soft pine compared to the color and grain of walnut. Wood takes many types of finishes exceptionally well. You can change colors without changing or covering grain patterns or change colors and eliminate any grain pattern simply by using the appropriate stain or paint. Wood can simply be left exposed to the weather to turn a natural silvery gray with time (in such cases, you'll get better durability using a treated wood or redwood, cedar, or cypress).

Textured finishes in a great many styles are easily obtained. They can prove attractive in many uses such as for home ex-

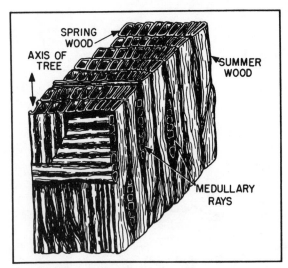

Fig. 1-1. Structure of wood.

teriors, panel fencing, walls, and other individual projects. In most cases today, textured finish wood is more readily obtained in plywoods.

Various forms of wood are most suitable for some jobs than others and are more inexpensively and readily obtainable in certain areas than other spots (this is even more true today than ever because of the always increasing costs of transportation). Cypress is expensive and hard to find no matter where you are, but unless you get involved with fancy boat or dock building, it can be replaced by other woods. The various firs and pines are easily obtained throughout the United States and Canada. Black walnut is virtually confined to the Eastern portion of the United States and above the Southern Atlantic Region and Gulf states. This fine wood is exceptionally expensive these days, no matter your locale. The base price of black walnut per board feet is so high that transportation costs have little relationship to overall costs. At present, black walnut, with no transport costs in this area, is about $5.00 a board foot.

Teak is another attractive, expensive wood. It comes from Burma and Thailand. Another expensive hardwood, mahogany comes from the Phillipines. Phillipine mahoganies have a coarser overall texture and appearance (there are actually four Phillipine species, but most are sold as Lauan or Phillipine and no distinction is often made). True mahoganies (there are three species) originate in Africa (primarily West Africa), the West Indies, and on up into Florida). The third type is Tropical American mahogany. It comes from Mexico, Central America, and Venezuela, plus a few parts of Peru.

The exotic woods available are extensive and expensive. Most of us work with the less exotic woods such as pine, oak, ash, and elm. Each has a set of features that tend to make one wood suitable for a particular job and another more suitable for a different job. Maple, for example, is a good wood (not all maples, but the heavier, harder ones such as sugar maple or rock maple) for floors and furniture. The birds'-eye grains that show up often are quite attractive.

Poplar is not really useful for furniture (some cheap furniture is made with soft, inexpensive wood), but it is fine for shelves, drawer parts and boxes. White oak is a very

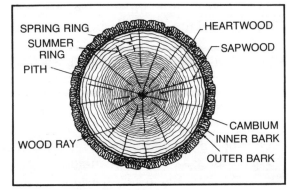

Fig. 1-2. Cross section of a tree.

Fig. 1-3. Koppers Company's Wolmanized brand pressure-treated lumber being used to construct a deck.

Fig. 1-4. The pressure treated uprights for the deck in place.

heavy, hard and strong wood with many uses. It is fairly easy to work, but tends to split and check often. It has a very coarse grain. Shrinkage is also great, but the wood is elastic, durable and so strong it is used for fence posts, in a lot of areas of boat construction, for very heavy furniture, and for tool handles (though in my opinion the best tool handles are of hickory).

Hickory is another very heavy and very tough wood. It is very, very difficult to work. Some years ago, I used a Homelite Super EZ 16-inch chain saw to cut down a dead, standing shagbark hickory that was really seasoned. The tree wasn't more than 14 or 15 inches in diameter and possibly 25 feet tall, but I had to sharpen my chain three times to get the thing cut into 2-foot firewood lengths.

Selecting the proper wood for a job is usually quite simple. See Table 1-1. For carpentry work, specifications will be presented for strength, and you need only go to the lumberyard or sawmill and explain what's needed. For furniture work, the selections are far more difficult. Selections are done on the basis of strength, appearance, and workability. If you need curves in the work, it doesn't pay to select a wood such as elm that is hard to work when you could easily use beech, ash, or even birch. Ash will provide a close, tight grain that is very hard and tough with little shrinkage and it will take a really great finish.

PLYWOOD

To make plywood, a log is placed in a huge lathe that first turns off the bark. The bark is removed for use as a garden mulch or fuel. As the log continues to turn, knives peel off

Table 1-1. Common Woods.

Type	Sources	Uses	Characteristics
Ash	East of Rockies	Oars, boat thwarts, benches, gratings, hammer handles, cabinets, ball bats, wagon construction farm implements.	Strong, heavy, hard, tough, elastic, close straight grain, shrinks very little, takes excellent finish, lasts well.
Balsa	Ecuador	Rafts, food boxes, linings of refrigerators, life preservers, loud speakers, sound-proofing, air-conditioning devices, model airplane construction.	Lightest of all woods, very soft, strong for its weight, good heat insulating qualities, odorless.
Basswood	Eastern half of U.S. with exception of coastal regions.	Low-grade furniture, cheaply constructed buildings, interior finish, shelving, drawers, boxes, drainboards, woodenware, novelties, excelsior, general millwork.	Soft, very light, weak, brittle, not durable, shrinks considerably, inferior to poplar, but very uniform, works easily, takes screws and nails well and does not twist or warp.
Beech	East of Mississippi, Southeastern Canada.	Cabinetwork, imitation mahogany furniture, wood dowels, capping, boat trim, interior finish, tool handles, turnery, shoe lasts, carving, flooring.	Similar to birch but not so durable when exposed to weather, shrinks and checks considerably, close grain, light or dark red color.
Birch	East of Mississippi River and North of Gulf Coast States, Southeast Canada, Newfoundland.	Cabinetwork, imitation mahogany furniture, wood dowels, capping, boat trim, interior finish, tool handles, turnery, carving.	Hard, durable, fine grain even texture, heavy, stiff, strong, tough, takes high polish, works easily, forms excellent base for white enamel finish, but not durable when exposed. Heartwood is light to dark reddish brown in color.
Butternut	Southern Canada, Minnesota, Eastern U.S. as far south as Alabama and Florida.	Toys, altars, woodenware millwork, interior trim, furniture, boats, scientific instruments.	Very much like walnut in color but softer, not so soft as white pine and basswood, easy to work, coarse grained, fairly strong.

Type	Sources	Uses	Characteristics
Cypress	Maryland to Texas, along Mississippi valley to Illinois.	Small boat planking, siding, shingles, sash, doors, tanks, silos, railway ties.	Many characteristics similar to white cedar. Water resistant qualities make it excellent for use as boat planking.
Douglas Fir	Pacific Coast, British Columbia.	Deck planking on large ships, shores, strong-backs, plugs, filling pieces and bulkheads of small boats, building construction, dimension timber, plywood.	Excellent structural lumber, strong, easy to work, clear straight grained, soft, but brittle. Heartwood is durable in contact with ground, best structural timber of northwest.
Elm	States east of Colorado.	Agricultural implements, wheel-stock, boats, furniture, crossties, posts, poles.	Slippery, heavy, hard, tough, durable, difficult to split, not resistant to decay.
Hickory	Arkansas, Tennessee, Ohio, Kentucky.	Tools, handles, wagon stock, hoops, baskets, vehicles, wagon spokes.	Very heavy, hard, stronger and tougher than other native woods, but checks, shrinks, difficult to work, subject to decay and insect attack.
Lignum Vitae	Central America.	Block sheaves and pulleys, waterexposed shaft bearings of small boats and ships, tool handles, small turned articles, and mallet heads.	Dark greenish brown, unusually hard, close grained, very heavy, resinous, difficult to split and work, has soapy feeling.
Live Oak	Southern Atlantic and Gulf Coasts of U.S., Oregon, California.	Implements, wagons, ship building.	Very heavy, hard, tough, strong, durable, difficult to work, light brown or yellow sap wood nearly white.
Mahogany	Honduras, Mexico, Central America, Flordia, West Indies, Central Africa, other tropical sections.	Furniture, boats, decks, fixtures, interior trim in expensive homes, musical instruments.	Brown to red color, one of most useful of cabinet woods, hard, durable, does not split badly, open grained, takes beautiful finish when grain is filled but checks, swells, shrinks, warps slightly.

Table 1-1. Common Woods. (Continued from page 19.)

Type	Sources	Uses	Characteristics
Maple	All states east of Colorado, Southern Canada.	Excellent furniture, high-grade floors, tool handles, ship construction crossties, counter tops, bowling pins.	Fine grained, grain often curly or "Bird's Eyes," heavy, tough, hard, strong, rather easy to work, but not durable. Heartwood is light brown, sap wood is nearly white.
Norway Pine	States bordering Great Lakes.	Dimension timber, masts, spars, piling, interior trim.	Light, fairly hard, strong, not durable in contact with ground.
Philippine Mahogany	Philippine Islands	Pleasure boats, medium-grade furniture, interior trim.	Not a true mahogany, shrinks, expands, splits, warps, but available in long, wide, clear boards.
Poplar	Virginias, Tennessee, Kentucky, Mississippi Valley.	Low-grade furniture cheaply constructed buildings, interior finish, shelving, drawers, boxes.	Soft, cheap, obtainable in wide boards, warps, shrinks, rots easily, light, brittle, weak, but works easily and holds nails well, fine-textured.
Red Cedar	East of Colorado and north of Florida.	Mothproof chests, lining for linen closets, sills, and other uses similar to white cedar.	Very light, soft, weak, brittle, low shrinkage, great durability, fragrant scent, generally knotty, beautiful when finished in natural color, easily worked.
Red Oak	Virginias, Tennessee, Arkansas, Kentucky, Ohio, Missouri, Maryland.	Interior finish, furniture, cabinets, millwork, crossties when preserved.	Tends to warp, coarse grain, does not last well when exposed to weather, porous, easily impregnated with preservative, heavy, tough, strong.
Redwood	California.	General construction, tanks, paneling.	Inferior to yellow pine and fir in strength, shrinks and splits little, extremely soft, light, straight grained, very durable, exceptionally decay resistant.

Type	Sources	Uses	Characteristics
Spruce	New York, New England, West Virginia, Central Canada, Great Lakes States, Idaho, Washington, Oregon.	Railway ties, resonance wood, piles, airplanes, oars, masts, spars, baskets.	Light, soft, low strength, fair durability, close grain, yellowish, sap wood indistinct.
Sugar Pine	California, Oregon.	Same as white pine.	Very light, soft, resembles white pine.
Teak	India, Burma, Siam, Java.	Deck planking, shaft logs for small boats.	Light brown color, strong, easily worked, durable, resistant to damage by moisture.
Walnut	Eastern half of U.S. except Southern Atlantic and Gulf Coasts, some in New Mexico, Arizona, California.	Expensive furniture, cabinets, interior woodwork, gun stocks, tool handles, airplane propellers, fine boats, musical instruments.	Fine cabinet wood, coarse grained but takes beautiful finish when pores closed with woodfiller, medium weight, hard, strong, easily worked, dark chocolate color, does not warp or check, brittle.
White Cedar	Eastern Coast of U.S., and around Great Lakes.	Boat planking, railroad, ties, shingles, siding, posts, poles.	Soft, light weight, close grained, exceptionally durable when exposed to water, not strong enough for building construction, brittle, low shrinkage, fragment, generally knotty.
White Oak	Virginias, Tennessee, Arkansas, Kentucky. Ohio. Missouri, Maryland, Indiana.	Boat and ship stems, sternposts, knees, sheer strakes, fenders, capping, transoms, shaft logs, framing for buildings, strong furniture, tool handles, crossties, agricultural implements, fence posts.	Heavy, hard, strong, medium coarse grain, tough, dense most durable of hardwoods, elastic, rather easy to work, but shrinks and likely to check. Light brownish grey in color with reddish tinge, medullary rays are large and outstanding and present beautiful figures when quarter sawed, receives high polish.

Table 1-1. Common Woods. (Continued from page 21.)

Type	Sources	Uses	Characteristics
White Pine	Minnesota, Wisconsin, Maine, Michigan, Idaho, Montana, Washington, Oregon, California.	Patterns, any interior job or exterior job that doesn't require maximum strength, window sash, interior trim, millwork, cabinets, cornices.	Easy to work, fine grain, free of knots, takes excellent finish, durable when exposed to water, expands when wet, shrinks when dry, soft, white, nails without splitting, not very strong, straight grained.
Yellow Pine	Virginia to Texas.	Most important lumber for heavy construction and exterior work, keelsons, risings, filling pieces, clamps, floors, bulkheads of small boats, shores, wedges, plugs, strongbacks, staging, joists, posts, piling, ties, paving blocks.	Hard, strong, heartwood is durable in the ground, grain varies, heavy, tough, reddish brown in color, resinous, medullary rays well marked.

thin sheets that will become veneer layers in the plywood. Once the log is peeled as far down as is possible, any remaining wood is cut into 2×4s.

Once the veneer sheets are ready to be used for plywood, they are called plies. The plies are coated with adhesive and joined together under pressure. If the plywood is properly made, the bond between plies will be as strong as, or stronger than, the plies themselves. (Fig. 1-5).

Plies can be laid up in many ways. Much depends on the purpose intended for the final product. In most modern plywood there will be an odd number of plies with the individual plies all having their grain running at a 90-degree angle to the plies above and below it. This is called *cross laminating* and it provides a sheet stronger in most ways than the original wood. If for some reason an even number of plies is used, say four, the two center plies will have the grain going in the same direction and the exterior plies will have the grain running at 90-degree angles to the center plywood or layer. The center layer is considered a single ply because the grain of both sheets runs in the same direction.

Modern plywood was first manufactured about 1905. By 1925, production was up to 153 million square feet a year. Today's plants can produce as much in just a few days. In 1933, uniform grade marking was introduced by the Douglas Fir Plywood Association (now the American Plywood As-

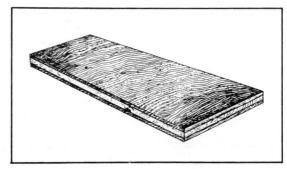

Fig. 1-5. Plywood.

sociation). A year later, waterproof glues were introduced and the use of plywood greatly increased. By 1940, plywood was used for subflooring, paneling, cabinets and many other jobs; production passed a billion square feet by the end of the year. By 1960, production surpassed 7 billion square feet. Today the figure is over 15 billion square feet (assuming "normal" times for construction industries and so forth).

At the outset, all plywood was made in the West and the wood most used was Douglas Fir. Today plywood is made in many areas and more than 70 species of trees are used to make it. With all of this development and change, many of us can easily end up a bit dizzy trying to select the correct form of plywood for a particular job. Even in construction grades, the difference in cost between one type of plywood and another could be as much as $15.00 a 4-×-8 foot sheet, it pays to use the proper grade.

While all plywood is of the flat panel type and built of plies of veneer glued under pressure, there are a great many differences in plywood types, finishes, purposes, final appearance, strength, and capability to resist weather or wetting. Waste arises when the wrong plywood is selected. That waste can come as easily from picking the cheapest grade of plywood when a more expensive grade is required as it can come from picking the most expensive when the cheapest will do.

A house can be sheathed with exterior glue CD plywood with no problems if siding is installed fairly soon. If it must stand a winter season, the plywood must be an exterior grade and not just one made with exterior glue. If the siding is plywood, only a siding or exterior grade can be used. By the same token, using plywood made with marine glues, or with furniture veneers, is exorbitantly expensive. With the furniture veneers for exterior grades, you'd have to have the plywood custom made, most likely, but that is possible at many mills. It's a waste of money to use plywood with an A (clear, sanded) surface for most types of floor underlayment.

While the American Plywood Association's grading system is far from totally simple, it is clear and can provide you with the information you need to get the proper wood for the job you must do. With so many kinds of plywood on the market, such a system of grading and marking is virtually essential.

VENEER GRADES

Plywood veneer grades start with *A*. The surface is smooth and paintable, and neatly made repairs (plugs and patches) are permitted. A natural finish can be used when a perfect surface isn't needed. Grade *B* must have a solid surface veneer that may have circular plugs and a few tight knots. Grade *C* may have knotholes to 1 inch in diameter with most limited to ½ inch or less. Limited splits are allowed. Grade C is the minimum grade allowed for use in exterior plywoods. Grade *C plugged* is a better C grade for uses where a smooth surface is needed. Splits are limited to ⅛ of an inch. Knotholes and borer holes may be no larger than a quarter by half an inch. For Grade *D* knots and knotholes may go to 2½ inches, width and, under some conditions, slightly larger (about half an inch). Some splits are allowed.

Basic plywood grades are exterior and interior. Plywood is also graded for both sides and has a rating for the inner plies. The top exterior grade is *A-A*, with both sides smooth, and interior plies of C grade. This type is useful for applications where both sides will be visible. Grade *A-B*, C interior

Table 1-2. Plywood Grades.

Interior Type

Grade Designation[2]	Description and Most Common Use	Typical Grade-trademarks	Face	Back	Inner plies	Most Common Thicknesses (inch)[3]
N-N, N-A, N-B INT-APA	Cabinet quality. For natural finish furniture, cabinet doors, built-ins, etc. Special order items.	NN G1 NT APA PS 1 74 / NA G2 INT APA PS 1 74	N	N.A. or B	C	3/4
N-D-INT-APA	For natural finish paneling. Special order items.	ND G3 INT APA PS 1 74	N	D	D	1/4
A-A INT-APA	For applications with both sides on view. Built-ins, cabinets, furniture and partitions. Smooth face: suitable for painting.	AA G4 INT APA PS 1 74	A	A	D	1/4, 3/8, 1/2, 5/8, 3/4
A-B INT-APA	Use where appearance of one side is less important but two smooth solid surfaces are necessary.	AB G4 INT APA PS 1 74	A	B	D	1/4, 3/8, 1/2, 5/8, 3/4
A-D INT-APA	Use where appearance of only one side is important. Paneling, built-ins, shelving, partitions, and flow racks.	A-D GROUP 1 INTERIOR PS 1-74 000 (APA)	A	D	D	1/4, 3/8, 1/2, 5/8, 3/4
B-B INT-APA	Utility panel with two smooth sides. Permits circular plugs.	BB G1 INT APA PS 1 74	B	B	D	1/4, 3/8, 1/2, 5/8, 3/4
B-D INT-APA	Utility panel with one smooth side. Good for backing, sides of built-ins. Industry: shelving, slip sheets, separator boards and bins.	B-D GROUP 3 INTERIOR PS 1-74 000 (APA)	B	D	D	1/4, 3/8, 1/2, 5/8, 3/4
DECORATIVE PANELS-APA	Rough-sawn, brushed, grooved, or striated faces. For paneling, interior accent walls, built-ins, counter facing, displays, and exhibits.	DECORATIVE BD G1 INT APA PS 1 74	C or btr.	D	C & D	5/16, 3/8, 1/2, 5/8
PLYRON INT-APA	Hardboard face on both sides. For counter tops, shelving, cabinet doors, flooring. Faces tempered, untempered, smooth, or screened.	PLYRON INT APA PS 1 74				1/2, 5/8, 3/4

Exterior Type

Grade Designation[2]	Description and Most Common Use	Typical Grade-trademarks	Face	Back	Inner plies	Most Common Thicknesses (inch)[3]
A-A EXT-APA	Use where appearance of both sides is important. Fences, built-ins, signs, boats, cabinets, commercial refrigerators, shipping containers, tote boxes, tanks, and ducts. (4)	AA G3 EXT APA PS 1 74	A	A	C	1/4, 3/8, 1/2, 5/8, 3/4
A-B EXT-APA	Use where the appearance of one side is less important. (4)	AB G1 EXT APA PS 1 74	A	B	C	1/4, 3/8, 1/2, 5/8, 3/4
A-C EXT-APA	Use where the appearance of only one side is important. Soffits, fences, structural uses, boxcar and truck lining, farm buildings. Tanks, trays, commercial refrigerators. (4)	A-C GROUP 3 EXTERIOR PS 1-74 000 (APA)	A	C	C	1/4, 3/8, 1/2, 5/8, 3/4

Exterior Type	Description	Grade-trademark	Veneer Grade			1/4	3/8	1/2	5/8	3/4
B-B EXT-APA	Utility panel with solid faces. (4)	BB G1 EXT APA PA 1 74	B	B	C	1/4	3/8	1/2	5/8	3/4
B-C EXT-APA	Utility panel for farm service and work buildings, boxcar and truck lining, containers, tanks, agricultural equipment. Also as base for exterior coatings for walls, roofs. (4)	B-C GROUP 2 EXTERIOR PS 1-74 000 APA	B	C	C	1/4	3/8	1/2	5/8	3/4
HDO EXT-APA	High Density Overlay plywood. Has a hard, semi-opaque resin-fiber overlay both faces. Abrasion resistant. For concrete forms, cabinets, counter tops, signs and tanks. (4)	HDO 6060 BB PLYFORM EXT	A or B	A or B	C or C plgd		3/8	1/2	5/8	3/4
MDO EXT-APA	Medium Density Overlay with smooth, opaque, resin-fiber overlay one or both panel faces. Highly recommended for siding and other outdoor applications, built-ins, signs, and displays ideal base for paint. (4)	MDO BB G4 EXT APA PS 1 74	B	B or C	C		3/8	1/2	5/8	3/4
303 SIDING EXT-APA	Proprietary plywood products for exterior siding, fencing, etc. Special surface treatment such as V-groove channel groove, striated, brushed, rough-sawn. (6)	303 SIDING 16 oc GROUP 1 EXTERIOR PS 1-74 000 APA	(5)	C	C		3/8	1/2	5/8	
T 1-11 EXT-APA	Special 303 panel having grooves 1/4″ deep, 3/8″ wide, spaced 4″ or 8″ o.c. Other spacing optional. Edges shiplapped. Available unsanded, textured, and MDO. (6)	303 Siding 16 oc T111 GROUP 1 EXTERIOR PS 1-74 000 APA	C or btr.	C	C				5/8	
PLYRON EXT-APA	Hardboard faces both sides, tempered, smooth or screened.	PLYRON EXT APA PS 1 74			C		3/8	1/2	5/8	3/4
MARINE EXT-APA	Ideal for boat hulls. Made only with Douglas fir or western larch. Special solid jointed core construction. Subject to special limitations on core gaps and number of face repairs. Also available with HDO or MDO faces.	MARINE AA EXT APA PS 1 74	A or B	A or B	B	1/4	3/8	1/2	5/8	3/4

(1) Sanded both sides except where decorative or other surfaces specified.
(2) Available in Group 1, 2, 3, 4, or 5 unless otherwise noted.
(3) Standard 4×8 panel sizes, other sizes available.
(4) Also available in Structural I (all plies limited to Group 1 species) and Structural II (all plies limited to Group 1, 2, or 3 species).
(5) C or better for 5 plies; C Plugged or better for 3-ply panels.
(6) Stud spacing is shown on grade stamp.
(7) For finishing recommendations, see form V307.
(8) For strength properties of appearance grades, refer to "Plywood Design Specification," form Y510.

Courtesy of the American Plywood Association

25

plies, can be used outdoors where the appearance of one side is of lesser importance, but still must be fairly good looking. Grade *A-C* is used where only a single side of the panel will show, such as on soffits and siding. Grade *B-C* is for use when one side must present a good appearance, but not great, and the other side is hidden. Grade B-C is very useful for farm buildings, garden sheds, and so on. Grade *C-C plugged* offers one side or face plugged and is often used as a base for tile or other type of floors subject to frequent wetting. Grade C-C is unsanded and is used where rough appearance makes no difference.

Four other grades of Exterior plywood may be of interest to the amateur woodworker or carpenter: Type 303 siding has plywood surfaces with a variety of textures or grooves or other patterns, and veneer grades are C or better. Uses extend from siding houses, to panel fences, to outdoor screening. Grade T1-11 is a special ⅝-inch thick paneling with deep parallel grooves. It is used as a finish siding with or without (usually without, but it can also be used as replacement siding) sheathing. A variety of textures are available for the surface. MDO plywood has a B face veneer, as well as a B back veneer, and is short for medium density overlay. The face forms almost an ideal base for almost all paints so this grade is useful as siding and for such things as built in cabinets and signs. HDO is similar to MDO except that the face may be either A or B grade, as may the back. The center plies will be C or C plugged and the surface is extremely hard so that no painting is required. For the amateur woodworker, the greatest utility of HDO plywood would be in cabinet building and for counter tops. See Table 1-2.

Interior plywood types offer pretty much the same grade ratings as do exterior types, but different glues are used and the internal plies are most often D grade rather than C. Grade A-A with D inner plies is for cabinet doors and furniture. Grade A-B has a solid a smooth back not quite as good looking as A grade. Grade A-D interior is the general grade rating for interior plywood types where no one will be able to see the back. Grade B-D is useful for the back parts of built-in furniture or desks where the face seldom will be seen. Unsanded C-D interior plywood is often used for subflooring. The unsanded surface provides a good "tooth" for the adhesives used with resilient floor tiles. Underlayment grade is C plugged, on the face, with a D back and C inner plies. It is used when a smooth surface is needed to get a good finished job (Table 1-3).

SPECIES

Classification by tree species should help clarify some things a bit. There are five basic tree group classifications and each is a group of trees that are closely related. Group 1 includes Douglas fir, Western Larch, Southern pines and the birches.

Group 2 has Port Orford cedar, cypress, black maple, and Western white pine. Table 1-4 shows the rest of the groups.

GLUES

Glues make up much of the difference in exterior and interior plywoods, though not quite all of it. Interior plywoods are seldom as strong as exterior panels of the same size even though exterior glues may be used to meet dampness conditions (this is in large part due to the use of D grade interior plies). If only interior grade glues are used, the plywood must not be subjected to extremes of humidity or dampness for any extended period of time (keeping them totally dry is best). Interior plywood with an intermediate

Table 1-3. Plywood Types, a Typical Trademark, and Identification Indexes for Unsanded Grades.

UA
USES,
APPLICATIONS

Use These Terms When You Specify Plywood	Description and Most Common Uses	Typical Grade-trademarks	Veneer Grade			Most Common Thicknesses (inch) (2) (3)				
			Face	Back	Inner Plies					
C-D INT-APA (1) (4)	For wall and roof sheathing, subflooring, industrial uses such as pallets. Usually supplied with exterior glue; sometimes with interior glue. Product Standard has provision for intermediate glue, but availability is currently limited. Specify exterior glue for best durability in longer construction delays and for treated wood foundations.	C-D 48/24 INTERIOR PS 1-74 000 (APA)	C	D	D	5/16	3/8	1/2	5/8	3/4
STRUCTURAL-I C-D INT APA (4) and STRUCTURAL II C-D INT-APA (4)	Unsanded structural grades where plywood strength properties are of maximum importance: structural diaphragms, box beams, gusset plates, stressed-skin panels, containers, pallet bins. Made only with exterior glue. See (5) for Group requirements.	STRUCTURAL I C-D 32/16 INTERIOR PS 1-74 000 (APA)	C	D	D	5/16	3/8	1/2	5/8	3/4
C-D PLUGGED INT-APA (1) (5)	For built-ins, wall and ceiling tile backing, cable reels, walkways, separator boards. Not a substitute for Underlayment, as it lacks Underlayment's punch-through resistance. Touch-sanded.	C-D PLUGGED GROUP 2 INTERIOR PS 1-74 000 (APA)	C Plgd.	D	D	5/16	3/8	1/2	5/8	3/4
2·4·1 INT-APA (1) (6)	"Heavy Timber" roof decking and combination subfloor-underlayment. Quality base for resilient floor coverings, carpeting, wood strip flooring. Use 2·4·1 with exterior glue in areas subject to moisture. Unsanded or touch-sanded as specified.	2·4·1 GROUP 1 INTERIOR PS 1-74 000 (APA)	C Plgd.	D	C & D	1-1/8"				
C-C EXT-APA (4)	Unsanded grade with waterproof bond for subflooring and roof decking, siding on service and farm buildings, wood foundations, crating, pallet bins, cable reels.	C-C 42/20 EXTERIOR PS 1-74 000 (APA)	C	C	C	5/16	3/8	1/2	5/8	3/4
STRUCTURAL I C-C EXT-APA (4) and STRUCTURAL II C-C EXT-APA (4)	For engineered applications in construction and industry where full Exterior type panels are required. Unsanded. See (5) for Group requirements.	STRUCTURAL I C-C 32/16 EXTERIOR PS 1-74 000 (APA)	C	C	C	5/16	3/8	1/2	5/8	3/4

(1) Can be manufactured with exterior or intermediate glue (check dealer for availability of intermediate glue in your area).
(2) All grades can be manufactured tongue-and-grooved in panels 1/2" and thicker.
(3) Panels are standard 4×8-foot size. Other sizes available.
(4) Grade-trademarked with Identification Index shown in guide below.
(5) Can be manufactured in Structural I (all plies limited to Group 1 species) and Structural II (all piles limited to Group 1, 2, or 3 species).
(6) Available in Group 1, 2, or 3 only.

Typical grade-trademark

Grade of veneer on panel face
Grade of veneer on panel back
Identification Index Designates the type of plywood — C-D
Exterior or Interior — 32/16 (APA)
Product Standard governing — INTERIOR
manufacture — PS 1-74 000
Type of glue used — EXTERIOR GLUE

Mill number

Courtesy of the American Plywood Association.

Identification indexes for unsanded grades
Panels thicker than 7/8 inch shall be identified by Group.

Thickness (inch)	C-C EXTERIOR C-D INTERIOR			STRUCTURAL I C-D & C-C STRUCTURAL II(b) C-D & C-C	STRUCTURAL II C-D & C-C
	Group 1 Group 2(a)	Group 2 or 3 Group 4(a)	Group 4	Group 1	Group 2 or 3
5/16	20/0	16/0	12/0	20/0	16/0
3/8	24/0	20/0	16/0	24/0	20/0
1/2	32/16	24/0	24/0	32/16	24/0
5/8	42/20	32/16	30/12	42/20	32/16
3/4	48/24	42/20	36/16	48/24	42/20
7/8		48/24	42/20		38/24

(a) Panels conforming to special thickness provisions and panel construction of Paragraph 3.8.6 of PS 1.
(b) Panels manufactured with Group 1 faces but classified as STRUCTURAL II by reason of Group 2 inner plies.

Table 1-4. Wood Species Used in Plywoods.

Group 1	Group 2		Group 3	Group 4	Group 5
Apitong [a][b]	Cedar, Port Orford	Maple, Black	Alder, Red	Aspen	Basswood
Beech, American	Cypress	Mengkulang [a]	Birch, Paper	Bigtooth	Fir, Balsam
Birch	Douglas Fir 2 [c]	Meranti, Red [a][d]	Cedar, Alaska	Quaking	Poplar, Balsam
Sweet	Fir	Mersawa [a]	Fir, Subalpine	Cativo	
Yellow	California Red	Pine	Hemlock, Eastern	Cedar	
Douglas Fir 1 [c]	Grand	Pond	Maple, Bigleaf	Incense	
Kapur (a)	Noble	Red	Pine	Western Red	
Keruing (a) (b)	Pacific Silver	Virginia	Jack	Cottonwood	
Larch, Western	White	Western White	Lodgepole	Eastern	
Maple, Sugar	Hemlock, Western	Spruce	Ponderosa	Black (Western Poplar)	
Pine	Lauan	Red	Spruce	Pine	
Caribbean	Almon	Sitka	Redwood	Eastern White	
Ocote	Bagtikan	Sweetgum	Spruce	Sugar	
Pine, Southern	Mayapis	Tamarack	Black		
Loblolly	Red Lauan	Yellow Poplar	Engelmann		
Longleaf	Tangile		White		
Shortleaf	White Lauan				
Slash					
Tanoak					

(a) Each of these names represents a trade group of woods consisting of a number of closely related species.
(b) Species from the genus Dipterocarpus are marketed collectively. Apitong if originating in the Philippines; Keruing if originating in Malaysia or Indonesia.
(c) Douglas fir from trees grown in the states of Washington, Oregon, California, Idaho, Montana, Wyoming, and the Canadian Provinces of Alberta and British Columbia shall be classed as Douglas fir No. 1. Douglas fir from trees grown in the states of Nevada, Utah, Colorado, Arizona and New Mexico shall be classed as Douglas fir No. 2.
(d) Red Meranti shall be limited to species having a specific gravity of 0.41 or more based on green volume and oven dry weight.

glue (IMG) has an adhesive more resistant to molds, bacteria and dampness, but it should still not be allowed to stay damp or wet too long. Interior grades made with full exterior glues are still not the equivalent of exterior plywoods and they cannot be expected to last as long under extreme weather or damp conditions (Fig. 1-6).

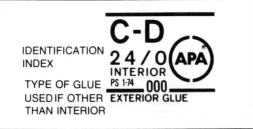

Fig. 1-6. American Plywood Association grade markings.

HARDWOOD PLYWOOD

For making your own furniture, you'll find many types of hardwood-faced plywoods available and some particle boards with a hardwood-face veneer. Most often, you'll find that exotic or expensive woods are used. There now seems almost no type of wood that cannot be obtained in plywood form, whether it's domestic white oak, Japanese ash, Carpathian elm, olive, French walnut, or ebony. In many cases, you'll find a local dealer who can supply such materials.

Just as with regular plywood, hardwood plywoods are made in interior and exterior grades, with thicknesses from an eighth of an inch up to 1 inch. Type I uses exterior glue for applications in areas where there is a lot of moisture. Type II uses a water resistant glue for moderate interior moisture areas. Type III uses moisture resistant glue for use in standard applications where a good wetting down is extremely unlikely. Type IV is also called Technical Type I and uses waterproof glue, but varies in thickness and ply design for various uses.

Hardwood appearance grading starts with Premium #1, that has only select, matched veneers with no great color contrasts. Premium #1 is the most costly of the hardwood plywood grades. Good #1 has no great color contrasts and no great grain constrasts. Sound #2 allows some surface defects of grain matching and color contrasts. Utility #3 will have some tight knots, color streaks and, possibly, some small splits. From this point, you move to back grade panels, with greater surface defects, and the SP grade that is custom made and supremely expensive.

The most important point to consider when working with hardwood plywoods is the job to be done. You can achieve greater drama in a simple chest, for example, by using Sound #2 grade plywood with its color contrasts than you can by using Premium #1, and, at the same time, save money. On the other hand, if you're building a rather fancy design—something that already has drama built into the design—the quietness of Premium #1 may be essential to a good-looking finished job.

Shelving built in a light-colored room might do very well in adding to the overall decor if the shelves are built of Utility #3 plywood. But formal shelves to house a collection of fine china, glassware or such items would look best with the dignity of, for example, Premium #1 cherry or black walnut than with Utility #3 ebony or zebrawood.

STORAGE

The storage of wood materials before use involves one or two special procedures. In general, this means nothing more than keeping already seasoned wood flat and dry. You might, after a time, decide to buy green wood and season it yourself. Many people working with fine woods and doing work on fine furniture prefer the slow process of air drying—it can take years to air dry some hardwoods—to the speeded-up process of kiln drying. There tends to be less checking and warping with the slower process. There are also claims that the resulting seasoned wood is stronger.

Lumber for carpentry can be stored outside, off the ground (usually on cleats laid every foot to foot and a half), and covered with plastic or canvas tarps. Millwork (windows, doors, moldings, etc.) and strip or parquet flooring must be stored indoors.

Lumber for furniture making must also be stored indoors, or, at least, under cover sturdier than a tarp. Such lumber should be well supported and placed on cleats so that each piece continually receives a flow of air around it. Plywood should be stored flat, on cleats set every foot, and covered well. Keep it dry and flat and you should have fewer problems with warping, cupping, and rot.

In most cases, try to have enough wood on hand for a week or more of work. In the case of furniture woods, keep enough on hand to finish the piece so that all will be at the same moisture content level when the piece is assembled.

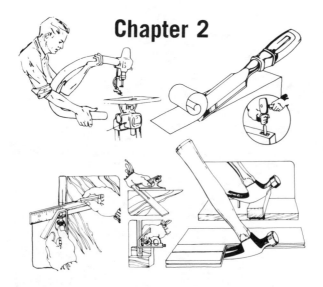

Chapter 2

Tool Quality

OVERALL TOOL QUALITY IS ALWAYS RElated, to some extent, to overall tool costs. Unfortunately, that is a truism (Fig. 2-1). You simply cannot make top quality tools with poor equipment, cheap labor, and shoddy materials. Therefore, the price of the top-of-the-line tool must be higher than the junk tool.

Is it worth it? Much depends on need and frequency of use, but at no time does it pay you to buy bottom-of-the-line tools. A cheap screwdriver, for example, is seldom ground so that the tip properly fits screws. It will chew up the screw head and mar the work surface of the wood. It might have a grip designed by an idiot to fit the hand of a monkey. Another good example is the handsaw. A poorly made handsaw will have a poorly attached, usually poorly designed, handle. It will not hold its set or sharpness for

very long (that is assuming it was even properly set and sharpened when bought). In addition, the saw blade will probably flex and it might be attached out of alignment at the start. The result would make it impossible to get a straight smooth cut, no matter how hard you work.

In many cases, the amateur needs only medium-quality hand tools. But the medium quality tools must still be good enough to do the job properly. Another cliche says a workman is only as good as his tools. That's nonsense in one manner, of course, but just for kicks sometime try to use a cheap cold chisel (for metal) to cut out a mortise in a piece of scrap lumber. It's definitely possible, but the results are going to be a lot rougher than they would be with a proper mortising chisel.

How to recognize tool quality can be a

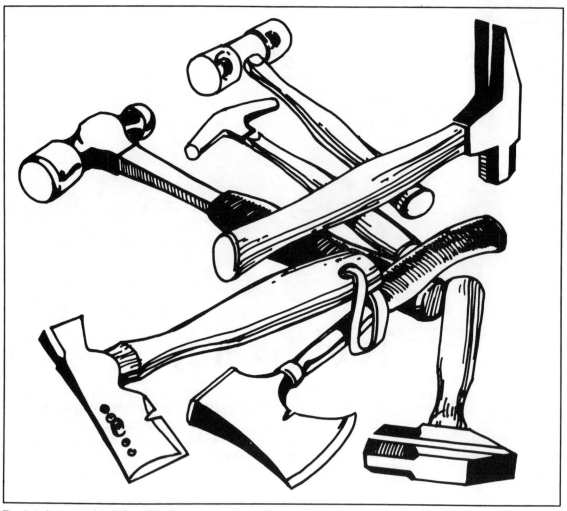

Fig. 2-1. An array of tools from Plumb (courtesy the Cooper Tool Group).

bit of a mystery. Judging handsaws is easy in most ways, but judging files and many types of wrenches is difficult. A good handsaw must have a good steel blade specially tempered to be tough enough to hold a cutting edge a long time, while remaining sturdy enough to resist buckling, and still allowing enough resilience in the metal to allow the setting of teeth and their filing when sharpening is needed. Today, most saws are taper ground from the teeth to the back. This is really impossible to see in most cases so you must take the manufacturer's word for it. The handle of a saw must be positioned properly or you're going to be wasting energy pushing in the wrong direction. The handle should be set so that the push goes directly to the sawing teeth and not to the back of the saw. Chapter 3, on handsaws, lists some checks you can make to further assure yourself of saw quality.

A file is a different matter. The file has been around a long time—not as long as the saw, probably, but at least since about 1100 or 1090 B.C. Leonardo da Vinci was the inventor of the first machine made to cut files by machine, but the first working machine didn't come about until further developments were made in 1750 by a Frenchman named Chopitel. At that time, the files were made of mild steel and the teeth were carburized to harden them. Today, a special annealed file steel is used. The process starts with file steel being cut into the near length and then rough shaped with heating and forging. It is then annealed to soften the teeth for cutting. After the teeth are cut, and the final shaping of the file, it is hardened by heating the file in a molten lead bath. The file is then placed in a quenching solution to get maximum hardness at the top of the teeth's cutting edges. It isn't as easy as it sounds and it doesn't even sound easy.

What's worse is that there simply is no way to tell whether all the steps have been carried out and no way to tell if they were carried out properly. In cases such as this, your only assurance of tool quality is the reputation of the maker of the tool or its distributor. Files manufactured by companies such as Nicholson assure you of top quality, no matter the pattern or size, while distributors such as Montgomery Ward, Sears, Roebuck and Co., and others assure you of no loss if any individual tool doesn't live up to its promise.

In that respect, I'll never forget some years ago (probably about 25 or so) breaking a ¾-inch socket from a Craftsman tool set. We took the two pieces in for replacement at our nearest Sears store. Form filling took a few seconds and then the clerk handed us a new socket. He then inquired just how on earth we had managed to break the thing. He almost doubled up laughing when we told him. We had bought some car parts from a junkyard, very inexpensively on the premise that we remove them ourselves. We took a breaker bar and the socket and got all but one bolt off. No luck, no matter how much penetrating oil. The next day, we came back with the socket, the breaker bar, more penetrating oil, and a 6-foot length of 1-inch iron pipe. Penetrating oil applied, socket on, and breaker bar in place, we slipped the pipe over the breaker bar and pushed down. No luck. Gene and I looked at each other, nodded, and leaped onto the bar where we bounced up and down as near the end of the 6 feet we could get. The bolt came loose just as the socket snapped in two pieces. We figured we'd have to hand back the new socket, but the policy on Craftsman tools was "If it breaks, bring it back and get a new one" at that time, and as far as I know it still is. It was creative idiocy treating good tools that way, of course, with over 300 pounds bouncing up and down 6 feet away from a ¾-inch socket. But the quality was there and it was reinforced by the warranty. At that time, the warranty was strongest in the tool industry and now a few other companies have followed suit.

Mistreatment of tools is never a good idea, but I tell the above story, with some embarrassment at being such a dolt at 18 or 19, to indicate the importance of reputation from the distributor of the tools. It is a prime quality in making sure you get prime quality when you buy tools. With proper care, all top-quality woodworking tools will come close to giving lifetime service. Some will do even longer service.

While it is not possible to list all the companies that supply top-quality woodworking tools, you could start with Nicholson for handsaws, circular saw blades and files, and move to Plumb for axes, adzes, hatchets, and hammers.

Then you could start on tools by The

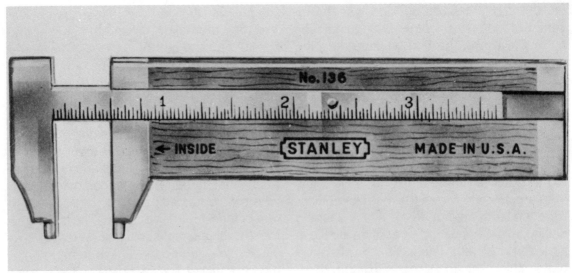

Fig. 2-2. Wood calipers (courtesy Stanley Tools).

Stanley Works where things really get complex. Stanley produces handsaws of all types, circular saw blades, levels, measuring tools, Surform tools, screwdrivers, knives, several kinds of clamps, sawhorse, brackets, hammers, axes, hatchets, drill bits for bit braces and electric drills, handsaws, router bits, planes, spokeshaves, bit braces, push drills and hand drills, doweling jigs, countersinks, miter boxes, chisels, scrapers and a long line of other products (Figs. 2-2 through 2-6).

Lufkin produces measuring tools. Boker Tree makes knife styles galore. X-Acto makes small knives and other tools for light woodwork. Crescent produces screwdrivers, pliers and wrenches of many kinds. Rockwell International makes circular saws, all-purpose saws, band saws, table saws, radial-arm saws, belt sanders, electric drills, circular-saw blades, drill presses, lathes and many other woodworking tools (Figs. 2-7 through 2-11).

Skil produces a wide variety of circular

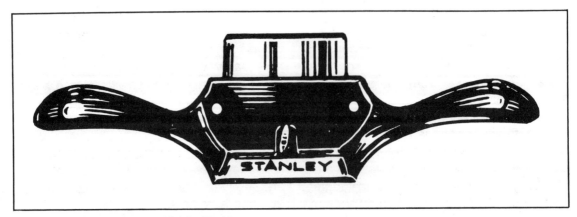

Fig. 2-3. Finish scraper (courtesy Stanley Tools).

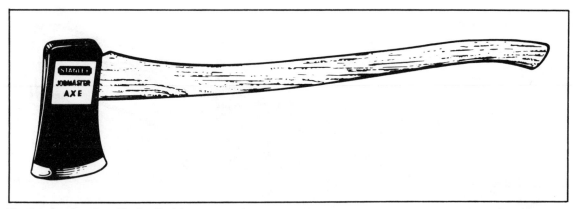

Fig. 2-4. Axe (courtesy Stanley Tools).

saws, electric drills, sanders, power planes, and electric wood tools, as does Black & Decker. Sears, Roebuck and Co., the world's largest retailer, markets a wide variety of hand tools and stationary woodworking tools under their Craftsman name (Figs. 2-12 through 2-18). Montgomery Ward markets a variety of tools under the PowRKraft name.

Garrett Wade distributes a wide line of woodworking tools of fine quality, though prices tend to be a bit on the high side for many. A quick glimpse through the latest Garrett Wade catalog provides a look at tools you probably never knew existed. As an example consider the Japanese Ryoba saw. Also consider that Continental Europe uses a different form of handsaw than we do here (ours is a British pattern). The bow or frame saw is still used in many non-British influenced areas of the world, but the Ryoba Japanese saws are special. These

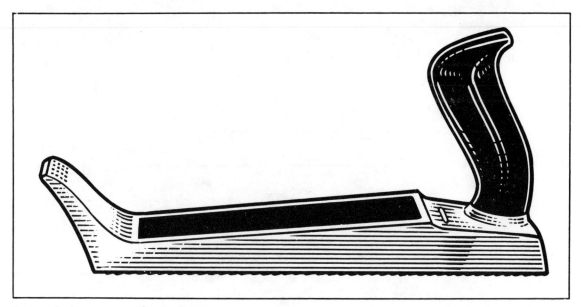

Fig. 2-5. Surform (courtesy Stanley Tools).

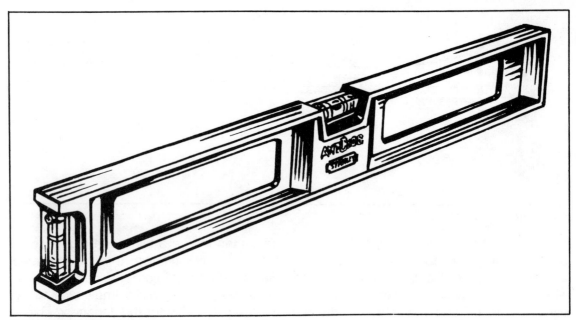
Fig. 2-6. Level (courtesy Stanley Tools).

Fig. 2-7. Power planer (courtesy Rockwell International).

straight-handled handsaws cut on the pull stroke instead of the push stroke as Western saws do. The blade is thinner and the teeth need very little set. This is said to give a very fine kerf. The blades are of forged, laminated steel rather than rolled steel. The Ryoba saw is two sided. One side is for rip cutting and one side is for cross cutting.

The Dozuki saw is similar in appearance, but it has 18 teeth per inch and is nearly impossible to sharpen. It is usually replaced when it dulls. The Anahiki saw is a rough-cut framing saw with 5½ teeth per inch on one side. It is used for both rip and crosscutting.

Garrett Wade also carries a line of electric hand tools made by Bosch in Switzerland. Of the three models they carry of the Bosch jigsaw, the least expensive is nearly $150 and the most costly is over $225. Craftsman top of the line prices are $75 and $85. I have to admit I drool more than a little when I see the Garrett Wade Swiss Master Craftsman's bench. Of European red beech, these are the last word in quality. They have two wood vises and a series of slotted holes for bench dogs. The large bench is listed now at almost $1,000, plus shipping. Their less expensive bench lines are of top quality, too, and a deluxe mahogany bench can be obtained for not too much over $220. Such benches offer ultimate in working ease when hand craftsmanship is of great importance.

In addition, Garrett carries the largest

Fig. 2-8. Routers (courtesy Rockwell International).

Fig. 2-9. Power sander (courtesy Rockwell International).

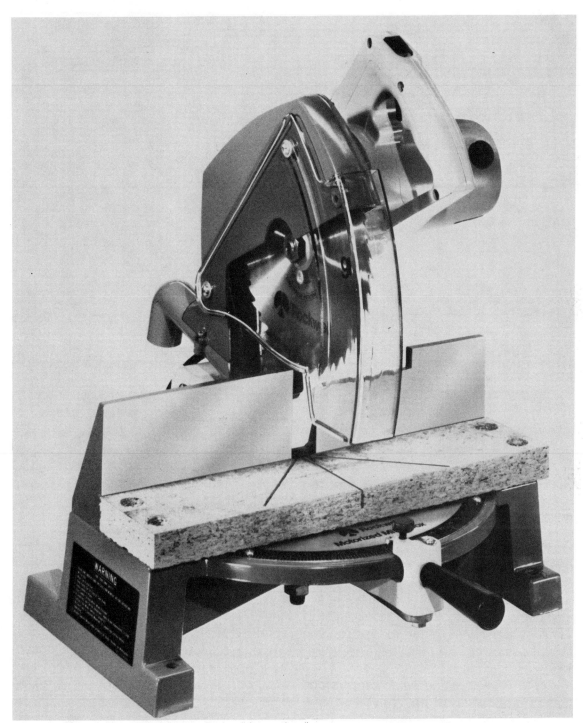

Fig. 2-10. Motorized miter box (courtesy Rockwell International).

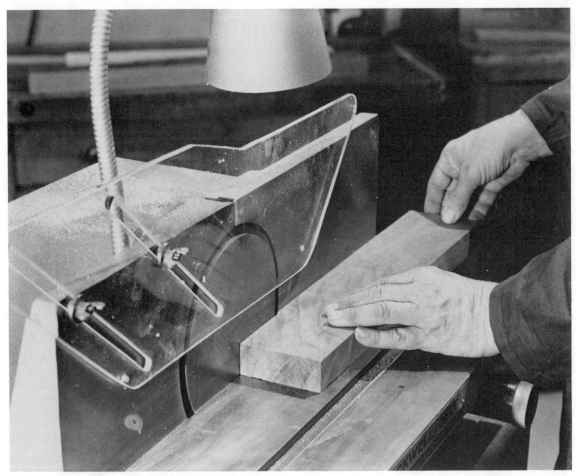

Fig. 2-11. Uniplane (courtesy Rockwell International).

array of woodcarving and sculpting tools I've ever seen. Currently, it is the only place I know of where you can readily buy a beech carpenters' mallet in two sizes (4- and 5-inch heads). They also offer lignum-vitae round head mallets; these are about double the cost of the beech mallets. (Lignum vitae is a very dense, heavy tropical wood, also used in block sheaves and pulleys for heavy lifting.)

The Garrett Wade selection of wood planes is as wide as any you'll find anywhere. If a plane is of fine quality, they carry it. That's why at least nine of their planes are

from Stanley. The line of vises and clamps (Fig. 2-19) is also very wide.

Disston makes handsaws and other handtools, including portable electric screwdrivers (Fig. 2-20). Shopsmith, Inc. makes the Shopsmith Mark V workshop. And 3M makes abrasives of many kinds. There are many other companies that make one or two good or excellent tools. Consult the *Thomas Register of American Manufacturers* at your local library for more listings.

Check catalogs and hardware stores and look through various magazines for ad-

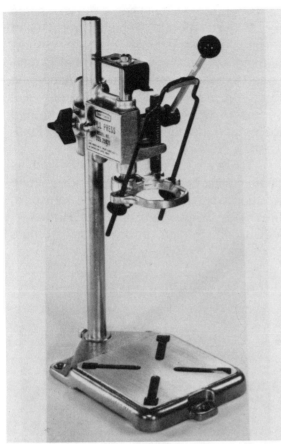

Fig. 2-12. Drill press (courtesy Sears, Roebuck and Co.).

Fig. 2-13. Radial arm saw (courtesy Sears, Roebuck and Co.).

Fig. 2-14. Route (courtesy Sears, Roebuck and Co.).

Fig. 2-15. A deluxe tool belt (courtesy Sears, Roebuck and Co.).

41

Fig. 2-16. Belt sander (courtesy Sears, Roebuck and Co.).

vertisments. New tools come out with some regularity. Recently, a company in Glen Burnie, Maryland came out with a claw hammer with a curved handle that is supposed to ease fatigue and strain. According to a friend of mine who is a form carpenter, it seems to work. The company is named Easco and the hammer is called the Hand-Tastic.

There are the rough work tools, such as chain saws, splitting mauls and splitting wedges to consider for those who want to cut firewood. Companies such as Homelite, McCulloch, Poulan, and a host of others

Fig. 2-17. Wood lathe (courtesy Sears, Roebuck and Co.).

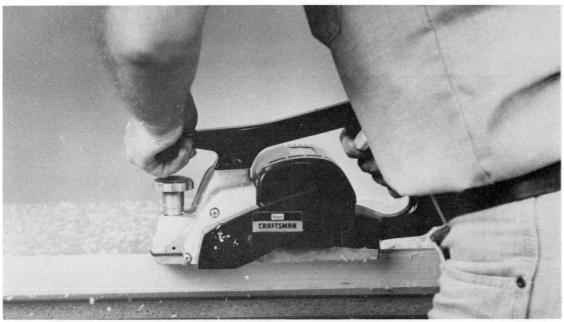

Fig. 2-18. Power plane (courtesy Sears, Roebuck and Co.).

Fig. 2-19. INCA tilting mortise table for 7- to 10-inch power saws, with a 90-degree tilt (courtesy Garrett Wade Co.).

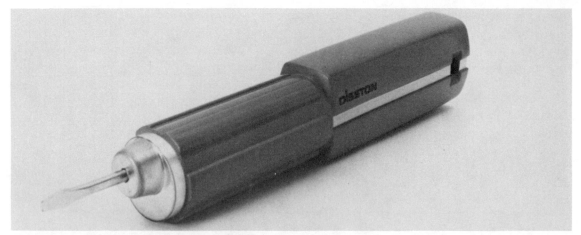

Fig. 2-20. A cordless electric screwdriver (courtesy Disston).

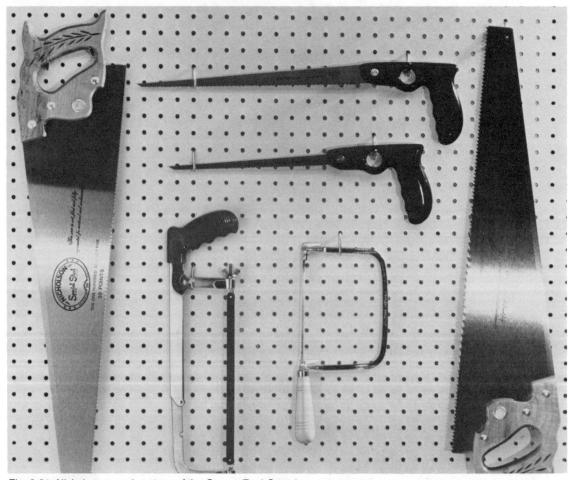

Fig. 2-21. Nicholson saws (courtesy of the Cooper Tool Group).

produce chain saws. Many of the same companies carry mauls, axes, and splitting wedges (you can get them from Montgomery Ward, Plumb, Sears, and Stanley).

Watch the company and watch the individual tool and you shouldn't go far wrong in selecting a quality tool at a reasonable price (Fig. 2-21).

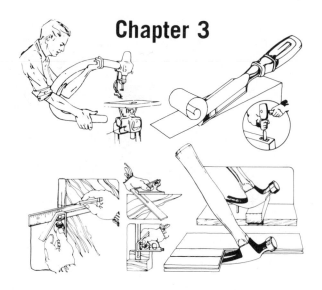

Chapter 3

Handsaws

DESIGNS FOR HANDSAWS BEGAN TO change quickly after the 1600s as the use of rolled steel allowed saw makers to give up on wooden frames. The English-pattern saw that developed is quite similar to the basic pattern of today's standard hand-saw (Fig. 3-1). A few European countries did use a pistol-grip style much like that used on our compass and keyhole saws today. The bow saw remains most popular in many European countries, but is almost never used in English-speaking areas or in areas where English influence was heavy for any length of time.

Modern metallurgy methods allow manufacturers to produce very hard-toothed saws while retaining a good deal of blade flexibility. Today's machine-cut teeth are highly efficient. Extremely accurate cuts are made possible by the accuracy of tooth alignment. Saw tooth design differs from saw to saw. For the basic handsaw, the teeth act as knives to shave out wood fibers while ripsaw teeth work as chisels.

Ripsaw teeth are filed at a 90-degree angle to the blade in order to achieve the chisel effect. Crosscut teeth are filed at about a 65-degree angle (coarser cutting crosscut teeth may reach an angle of more than 70-degrees from the blade). Tooth size is a factor in cutting speed. The larger the teeth (the fewer teeth per inch) the more rapid the cutting action, but the more coarse, or rough, the cut is going to be. The nature of the work partly determines the number of teeth per inch you'll want in your crosscut saw. For fine work, 10 or even a dozen teeth per inch will be best. For fast cutting, you might want to drop to as few as 8 teeth per inch. Ripsaws are generally in the 5-tooth-

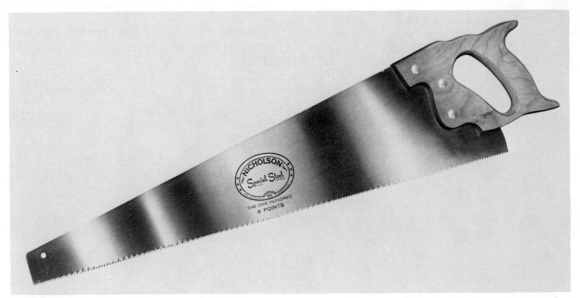

Fig. 3-1. An 8-point handsaw (courtesy Nicholson).

per-inch range; they provide a different effect on the cut in any case because of the chisel cutting style. See Figs. 3-2 through 3-4.

In addition to work style, tooth size is affected by the nature of the wood being cut.

Generally, hard and dense woods are best cut with a tooth number on the high size, with 10 or more teeth. Softer woods that are more likely to clog a saw are best cut with a slightly coarser set of teeth. My ripsaw has 5½ teeth per inch. One of my good crosscut saws has

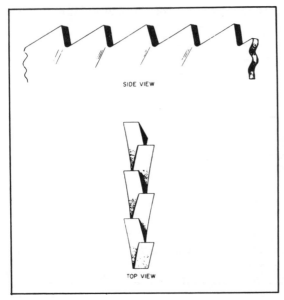

Fig. 3-2. Rip teeth.

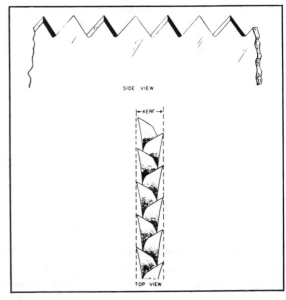

Fig. 3-3. Crosscut teeth.

48

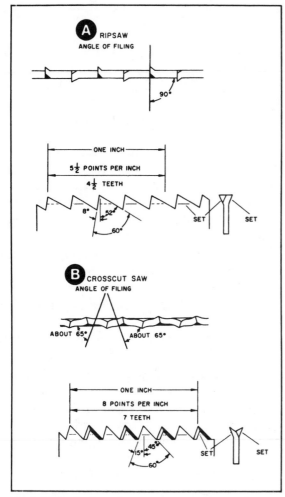

Fig. 3-4. Saw teeth angles.

the saw before finalizing the sale. In other words, if you buy by mail make sure the return policy is liberal enough so that you're not stuck with a saw that is not comfortable for you to use. Grip sizes differ considerably and what is thoroughly comfortable for one person might not be comfortable for someone with larger hands, smaller hands, longer arms, or shorter arms.

Look for at least three screws holding the handle in place. It is always best to buy a saw that has a replaceable handle should it wear out or accidentally get broken. Look for a taper ground saw. If the saw is taper ground, it will virtually always say so right on the blade.

There are several other points to be checked when buying a handsaw. First, hold the saw at arm's length in front of you and bend the blade slightly. Don't go overboard or you will warp the blade and end up buying the saw anyway. The points along the breast of the blade should all appear to be the same length. Now check along the flat side of the blade looking to see if the teeth are set uniformly. If the set is poor—too much to one side or the other—or just uneven overall, the saw will not cut straight. See Fig. 3-5. The

8 and the other a dozen. Crosscut saws are also available with 10 teeth per inch. Saws meant for particularly smooth cuts, such as back saws for miter boxes and dovetail saws, will have from 11 to 16 teeth per inch. *Note:* saw teeth are measured from the top of a tooth to the top of a tooth for an inch. That means you will actually count one *less* tooth inside that inch than the saw is listed as having.

When you're getting ready to buy a crosscut saw or ripsaw, I would seriously advise making sure you are able to handle

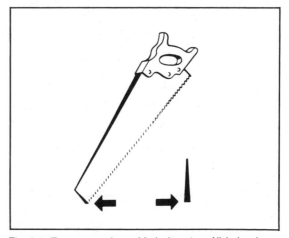

Fig. 3-5. Taper ground saw blade (courtesy Nicholson).

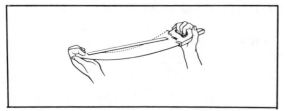

Fig. 3-6. Checking saw blade tension (courtesy Nicholson).

Fig. 3-7. Checking the saw's finish (courtesy Nicholson).

set can be corrected, as can tooth length, but there's no sense in buying a used tool as a new one, and that's what you're doing if these points are messed up.

You now need to make a tension check on the saw. To do this, hold the saw out and flex it slightly. Have someone place a straightedge across the side of the blade. The gap between the straightedge and the side of the saw should form a perfect arch if tension is correct (Fig. 3-6). If tension is not correct, the saw will be lopsided and will not give you a straight cut.

Your final saw check is the finish. A well-made saw will look well made. The handle will have nonslip carving (don't buy a saw with a plastic handle) and be well finished and solidly attached to the blade. The blade will be well finished to a high polish. There will be no nicks or roughness on either the handle or the blade. The well-done finish is not just to make you feel good at having an attractive tool (Fig. 3-7). A good hardwood handle, properly designed, and with a good finish lasts longer than a cheap and poorly finished handle. By the same token, a highly polished saw blade slips through the cut more easily and tends to resist rust better than a dull blade. A few years ago, there seemed to be some sort of passion among saw manufacturers to carry at least one Teflon-coated crosscut and rip-saw in each line. These saws generally cost a buck or two more, but it has been some time since I've heard of one being offered. I

have a feeling that carpenters and other woodworkers discovered the same thing about Teflon that housewives did earlier. The stuff is fine while it stays on the utensil or tool, but the utensil or tool is nearly useless once it begins to wear off.

Price is another indication of quality. You can buy name-brand crosscut and rip-saws for under $10.00 today. And should probably do so—assuming the overall quality is generally good—if you only use a handsaw about once every year or two. On the other hand, you could spend over $40 for each handsaw. If you're an amateur, you probably should not do so unless you've got a fair amount of extra cash to fling about. Nicholson, Stanley, Sears, Ward's, Disston and others offer fine saws for under $20, in most instances, and these will serve for virtually every job a homeowner/amateur carpenter is likely to want to do. See Figs. 3-8 and 3-9.

USE

Using a handsaw is not complicated, but it can be more than a little arm wearying until you get the hang of things. Weariness can be cut by using the proper grip on the handsaw at the start. When you use a crosscut saw, your saw, wrist, and forearm should form a straight line at an angle 45 degrees to the work surface. With a ripsaw, you need a steeper angle, about 60 degrees (Fig. 3-10).

Before beginning any cut, check the clearances. You don't want to bash your

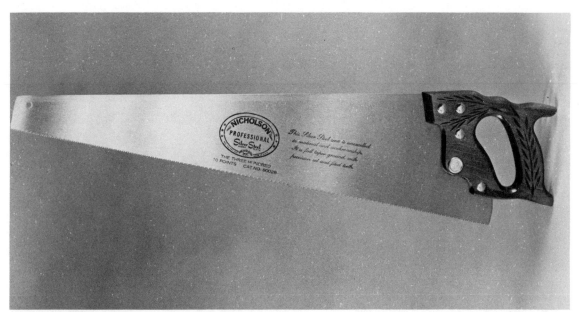

Fig. 3-8. The Nicholson Professional model 10-point crosscut saw.

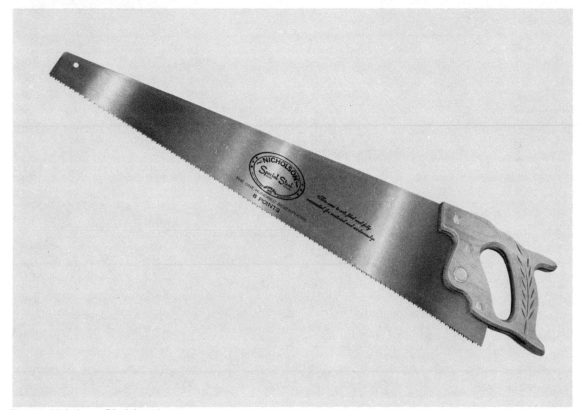

Fig. 3-9. Nicholson 175 eight-point crosscut saw.

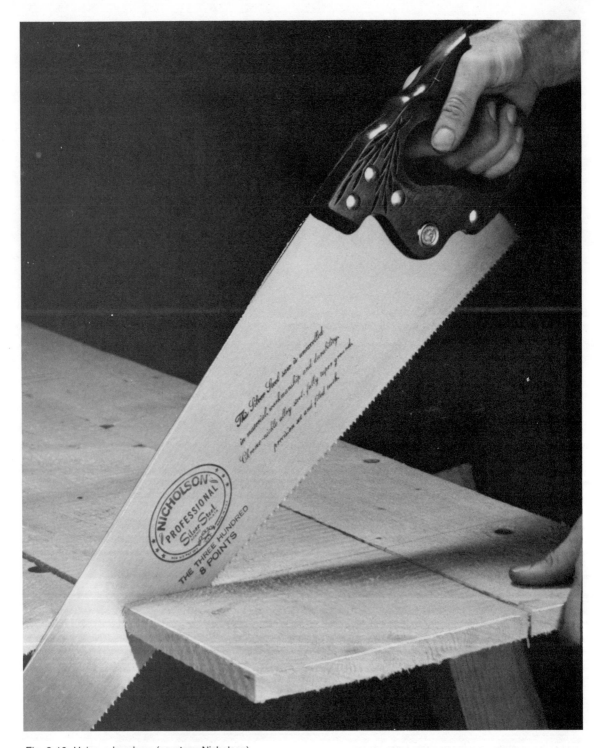

Fig. 3-10. Using a handsaw (courtesy Nicholson).

sawhorse legs with the blade or have the tip of the saw hitting the ground or any other obstruction under the wood being cut. If you're cutting scrap lumber or used lumber, check it for nails. Now, place the saw teeth just to the waste side of the marked line and steady the handle with your thumb along it. Place the thumb of your free hand down at the cut line. Just lightly brace the saw blade. Don't push the blade or you'll either cut yourself or throw the cutoff to the side (and possibly both).

Make a few short strokes to form a starting groove. While it won't matter much to amateurs, who use the saw only lightly, most professional carpenters like to vary the spot along the blade where the grooves are begun. Doing so helps prevent wear build-up in a single area. It's a pain to have to sharpen and set all the teeth on a blade because one 4-inch sector has gone dull. Think of how many teeth are on a 30-inch, 12-tooth blade!

Once you've got a groove cut, start taking full and steady strokes. Using a full stroke—virtually the entire blade length—steadily tires you a great deal less than the quick, choppy motion some people seem to

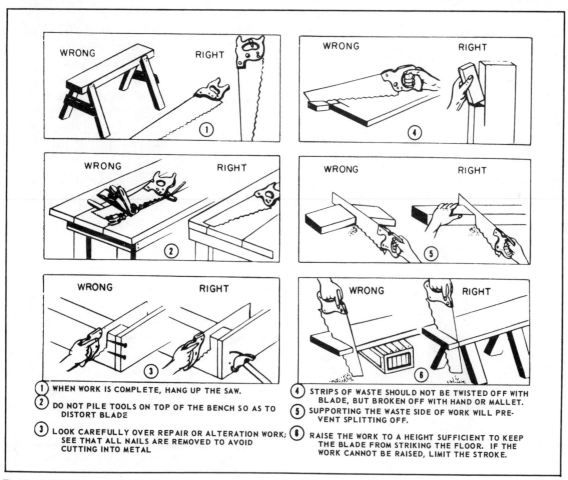

① WHEN WORK IS COMPLETE, HANG UP THE SAW.

② DO NOT PILE TOOLS ON TOP OF THE BENCH SO AS TO DISTORT BLADE

③ LOOK CAREFULLY OVER REPAIR OR ALTERATION WORK; SEE THAT ALL NAILS ARE REMOVED TO AVOID CUTTING INTO METAL

④ STRIPS OF WASTE SHOULD NOT BE TWISTED OFF WITH BLADE, BUT BROKEN OFF WITH HAND OR MALLET.

⑤ SUPPORTING THE WASTE SIDE OF WORK WILL PREVENT SPLITTING OFF.

⑥ RAISE THE WORK TO A HEIGHT SUFFICIENT TO KEEP THE BLADE FROM STRIKING THE FLOOR. IF THE WORK CANNOT BE RAISED, LIMIT THE STROKE.

Fig. 3-11. Care and use of handsaws.

develop. Don't bear down on the saw; use just enough pressure to keep the saw firmly in the kerf being opened. You'll know immediately if you're using too little pressure because the saw will chatter. If you use too much pressure, the blade will flex and might buckle and bind in the cut. When you run up on a knot, slow down the cutting speed. The harder wood should always be cut more slowly than the softer wood. (Fig. 3-11).

When you get within a couple of inches of the end of the cut, support the waste end of the cut, support the waste end of the wood with your free hand. Letting the waste end just drop off can cause the good portion of the wood to split. Never twist a saw to knock off a waste end. We've all done it at one time or another; I once ruined a good saw—knocked three teeth right out of it—doing so on a piece of oak. It's also possible for that waste end to fly into your face or a bystander's face.

When using two sawhorses or any two supports for the wood being cut, do not cut

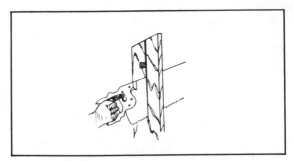
Fig. 3-13. Using wedges to keep a kerf open.

between the sawhorses. This allows the wood to sag and it will cause the saw to bind in the cut. If you have a helper, and that person is holding the waste end (particularly a good idea if the waste end is very long), he or she should apply no pressure to the board. Your helper should simply let it remain in position without much sag.

I've had a multitude of helpers who think they must raise the end of the board to help the cut. This binds the saw. That sort of treatment of wood being cut will even bind a 2½-horsepower circular saw if the lift is enough. If the work cannot be held in any other way, use clamps. I always keep two or three middle-size C-clamps around for such purposes. See Figs. 3-12 and 3-13.

CARE

Once the cutting is finished, many people—too many—take their saws in and let them drop on the workbench or toss them in a trunk. A good saw deserves proper care. With proper care, a saw will hold its sharpness and its set far, far longer than you might expect. Both of my crosscut saws have had fairly intensive use and neither has ever been sharpened, and neither needs sharpening.

First, look the saw over. If the wood you've been cutting wasn't completely dry, you'll probably find a gummy substance

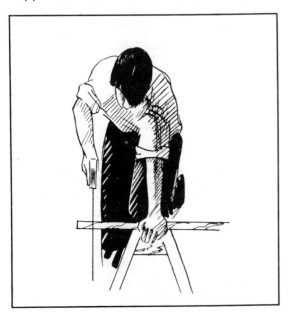
Fig. 3-12. Sawing a board to size.

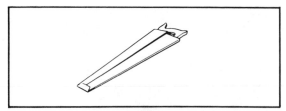

Fig. 3-14. Covering the saw after use (courtesy Nicholson).

along the blade. This gum, or resin, can be wiped away with kerosene. Use a dry rag to finish up. Once the gum is off, I use a few drops of Tri-Flon lubricant and coat the saw blade gently. This will cut down on the chance of rust. If rust should appear, take a coarse rag, soak it in oil, and give the blade a good, hard scrubbing. If this doesn't work, use fine emery cloth to remove the rust and then oil carefully. You don't want a heavy coat of oil on the blade because it would make a mess in your first few cuts the next time you use the saw.

Once the saw is cleaned and lubricated, hang it in a place where it won't get knocked about too much, if at all. Hanging a saw, by the hole near the tip of the blade, is the best way to ensure that nothing will be laid on the blade. Warping the blade would make straight cutting nearly impossible.

Most professional carpenters build a wooden box with 1-inch cleats set along the bottom to keep saws from slamming into each other. If no such toolbox is at hand, then some sort of cardboard or other sleeve should be made to keep the saw from bang-

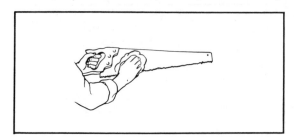

Fig. 3-15. Cleaning the saw after use (courtesy Nicholson).

ing into other tools. Such banging around could warp the blade and more often, knock the set from teeth. See Figs. 3-14 and 3-15.

BACKSAWS

Backsaws are most commonly seen mounted on miter boxes. They are used for cutting the angles needed to fit door and window moldings and to cut angles for making picture frames, mirror frames and other such projects. Backsaws are fine toothed. Virtually none of them have fewer than 11 teeth and many have a dozen or more. The saw is straight bladed, not tapering to the tip as are ripsaws and crosscut saws, and has a U-shaped band of metal at the top of the blade to prevent flexing. With the lack of flex added to the miter box guides, cutting accuracy is extremely good. When added to the fineness of the cut produced by the small teeth on the backsaw, the result is a very fine and close fitting joint. See Fig. 3-16.

Miter boxes with backsaws can be very expensive or relatively inexpensive. I know many carpenters who have never used a backsaw. They will go out and buy a rock maple miter box set with slots for 45- and 90-degree angles and use that with a fine-tooth handsaw (Fig. 3-17).

For finer work, the backsaw in a better miter box is necessary and prices can begin at a moderate $30 or so with a saw included. In such saws, the cut is usually limited to about 3 inches width (more than enough for most modern moldings), and the saw blade will seldom be over 16 inches long (Fig. 3-18). Cutting accuracy is not perfect, but it is good.

From there, you might consider miter boxes and backsaws such as the one I have. It is a middle-range Stanley model designed for the homeowner and occasional user. It gives a wide variety of angle cuts while tak-

Fig. 3-16. A backsaw (courtesy Nicholson).

ing stock up to about 4 inches wide and 4 inches tall. Clamps and guides provide good accuracy in the cuts and the cost is about $60. For those with money to burn or a need to be extremely accurate, miter boxes continue on up in price and size (Fig. 3-19). Stanley's largest model has a full 10-inch width capacity. It allows cuts from 30 to 90 degrees, with 11 positive lock positions. Listed capacities are for 90-degree-cuts. This saw will cut a full 7 inches at 45 degrees. The Stanley Professional backsaw can be purchased with a 26-inch, 28-inch or 30-inch backsaw. The longer the saw the wider the blade (thus the less the thickness of the stock that can be cut with the shorter saws). This miter box and backsaw combination lists for about $185. This is well worth it to people who need the large cut and extreme accuracy, but would be money wasted for most woodworkers. Stanley also makes more expensive miter box and backsaw combinations with smaller capacities (other features and even greater accuracy make up the price differential). The model 85-258

is priced at about $275; it has a 28-×-5-inch backsaw.

Swedish miter boxes listed by Garrett Wade (26-×-5-inch blade, and 6½-inch cut width) use a 19-tooth-per-inch backsaw and list for amost $190 (plus shipping). The largest Garrett Wade Miter Box lists for $285. It has a cut width of 9½ inches, it is made in West Germany, and it has a 11-

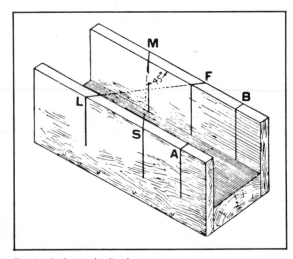

Fig. 3-17. A wood miter box.

Fig. 3-18. A small miter box (courtesy Stanley Tools).

tooth-per inch backsaw. This saw and box combination has a frame backsaw (as does the above) and blades are replaceable without having to replace the entire saw.

As you can readily see, it is easily possible to spend more than is really necessary for miter boxes and backsaws. Garrett Wade offers two of the most beautifully constructed backsaws I've ever seen for tenon and dovetail work, but the matched set costs nearly $118, plus postage.

It pays to understand capacities and to look over the type of work you expect to be doing before making any selection. Generally, it is not necessary to spend over $100 or so to get a miter box that will most likely do more than we'll ever really need. Most miter boxes under $100 offer replaceable hard-

wood or hardboard bases. Those costing $100 or more offer full metal bases, with the area of cut open. The more expensive saws will offer either greater capacity or greater accuracy. As price continues to rise, the increase in capacity is usually matched by the increase in accuracy.

Two other forms of backsaw are commonly available. They are the tenon saw and the dovetail saw. These are not used with a miter box. The wood is placed in a vise and the tenon is cut freehand on the markings (to the waste side, as always) or the dovetails are cut in the same manner. Neither is frequently used today because routers are more commonly used to cut dovetails for drawers, and, often cutting tenons for mortise-and-tenon joints as well.

COPING SAWS

The coping saw is used for making coped joints in home moldings at ceiling/wall junctions and at floor/wall junctures, and is also useful for cutting and fine shapes in a panel or other piece of light material.

Coping saws are probably not used as often today as they might be. The tools are inexpensive in comparison to most handsaws—or most other tools. Most people seem to prefer to use saber saws for the jobs best suited for the coping saw. A coping saw will make turns that no saber saw or power scroll saw can, in light stock. With its high arched back, the coping saw frame allows good clearance (mine arches over 6 inches) and a cut far deeper into material than would, say a hacksaw. Coping saws with a 4-inch arch to the back can be bought for less than $4 while Stanley's 6¾ inch arch model sells for less than $6, even with three extra blades (see Figs. 3-20 and 3-21).

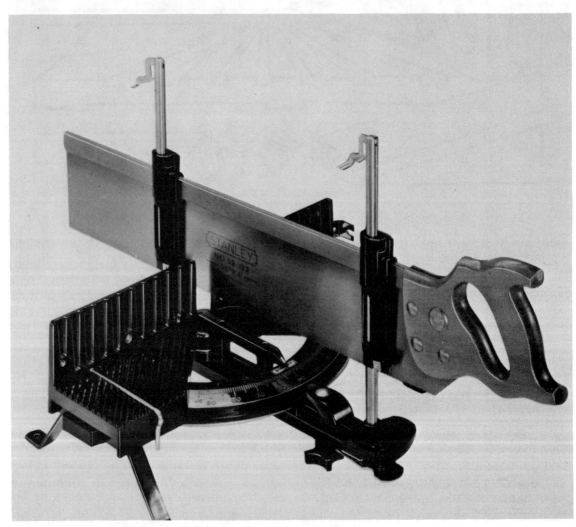

Fig. 3-19. Professional-style and quality miter box (courtesy Stanley Tools).

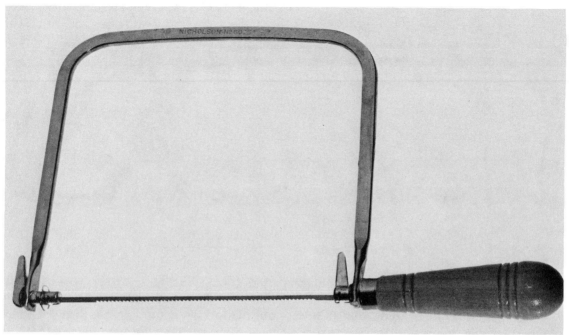

Fig. 3-20. Coping saw (courtesy Nicholson).

HACKSAWS

Hacksaws are not primarily woodworking tools. They are most often used to cut metals or plastics (Fig. 3-22). They fit in with woodworking tools because sooner or later you'll find yourself needing to cut through a nail or screw. It also pays to have one on hand along with a decent selection of hacksaw blades in varying sizes. Hacksaw blades are available in a variety of tooth sizes to fit different jobs and materials. The most common sizes are 14, 18, 24 and 32 teeth per inch. The blades with very fine teeth are used for cutting thin sheet metal and plastic. The blades with larger teeth are used for softer materials such as plastic, aluminum

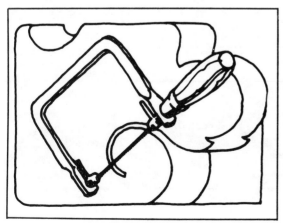

Fig. 3-21. Coping saw (courtesy Stanley Tools).

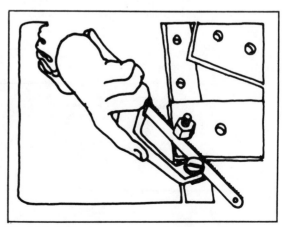

Fig. 3-22. Minihacksaw (courtesy Stanley Tools).

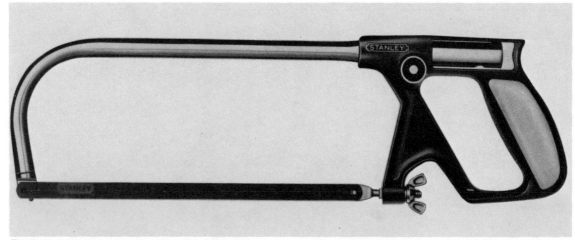

Fig. 3-23. Framed hacksaw (courtesy Stanley Tools).

and other materials that might clog the fine, small teeth (Fig. 3-23).

Minihacksaws offer somewhat greater cutting capacity and are relatively inexpensive at about $4.00 from Stanley. Full hacksaws cover a price range of about $8 to $15. Saw blades for general use should be of the type with a flexible back (these generally run around two for a dollar). See Figs. 3-24 through 3-28.

COMPASS AND KEYHOLE SAWS

Compass saws and keyhole saws use pistol grips and have blades that taper sharply to a point (Fig. 3-29). The keyhole saw is, as its name would imply, made with a more slender blade than is the compass saw. Otherwise there is little difference except that the compass blade will generally be a couple of inches longer as well as heavier. Both sell for under $10 and you can buy what is called a saw nest that will include compass, keyhole and general utility blades for under $10. That is a good bargain if you expect to be doing any inside or outside work where you need to install such items such as switch boxes, etc. Generally, a compass saw will have 8 points per inch. The keyhole saw will have smaller teeth, in keeping with its narrower

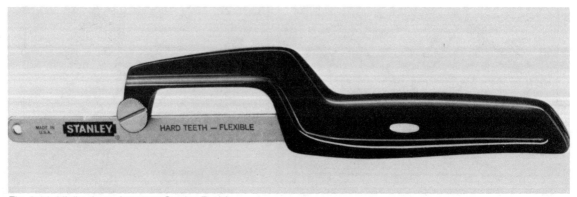

Fig. 3-24. Minihacksaw (courtesy Stanley Tools).

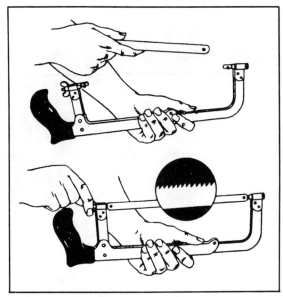

Fig. 3-25. Changing a hacksaw blade.

blade and shorter cutting radius, at 10 points per inch (Fig. 3-30).

If you expect to do any refinishing or remodelling work around a home or out-building, it makes good sense to buy a nest of saws. All that is required to make switch box cut outs, light fixture cutouts and so on is that you mark the cut, drill a hole in one corner and another diagonally opposite it, and then cut out a square hole with the compass saw. For round holes over about 5 inches in diameter, use the keyhole saw.

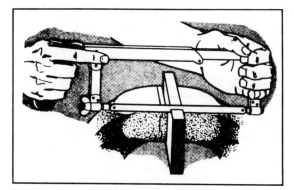

Fig. 3-26. Proper grip for using a hacksaw.

Fig. 3-27. Making a long cut near the stock's edge.

Drill at one edge and you can curve the cut on around. For smaller-diameter holes, you will need to use a coping saw or a sabre saw. Coping saws cannot readily be used to pierce and cut. Generally they are confined to use at the edges of the material being cut (Fig. 3-31).

BOW SAWS

The American bow saw is another framed model. It is a rough-toothed model suitable for removing brush, cutting tree limbs, and sawing wood to stove or fireplace lengths in lieu of a chain saw. They come in sizes from 2 feet long to 3 feet long (usually three sizes, with the central size being 30 inches).

I have a Stanley 70-087 30 inch model that serves very well when I don't have enough work to do to justify fiddling with a chain saw. It costs under $10 and replacement blades cost a little over $3. The teeth

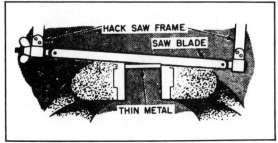

Fig. 3-28. Cutting thin metal.

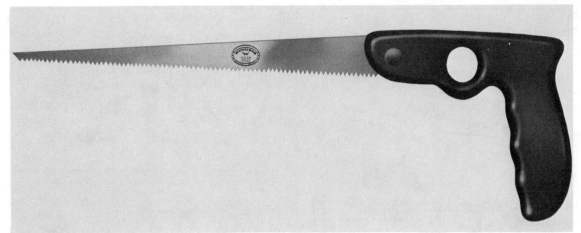

Fig. 3-29. Nicholson compass saw.

are much coarser and they are of a different design for quick, rough cutting. A quick glance shows there's barely more than 2 teeth per inch and the set is extremely wide.

Other wood-cutting saws, such as the European bow and and frame saws are readily available from companies such as Garrett Wade. These are for fine cutting. The frame limits the depth of the cut (the width of the material being cut).

One- and two-man timber-cutting saws have been around for many years. A chain saw will do the job in about one-third the time and with far less than a third the effort. So

that anyone not working on the premise of basic survival living, and using no power tools at all, would be far better off working with a chain saw. Even then, no novice should start out felling trees of a size that require much energy of any kind. Logging, of any sort, for firewood or lumber, is hard, often dirty and always dangerous work. It takes a certain amount of time and experience to know to a reasonable degree just where a tree is going to fall when it is cut down. Gathering that experience requires time, patience, and a strong instinct for self-preservation.

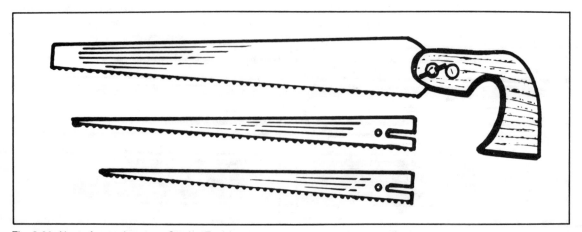

Fig. 3-30. Nest of saws (courtesy Stanley Tools).

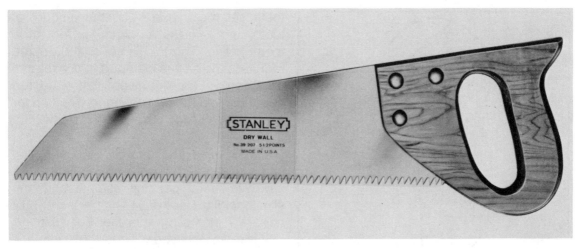

Fig. 3-31. Drywall saw (courtesy Stanley Tools).

Among his many other activities, my grandfather ran a sawmill and some logging operations around Gordonsville, Virginia. I can still see some of my uncles smile as they stare over at the present all-power operation. At one time, they had to go out into the woods with a couple of axes and two-man crosscut saws to lay down some fairly large pines and oaks. To them, the great development of the chain saw to reasonable weights and high power in the past couple of decades is something of a joke on them. Even with a chain saw used for felling trees, the work is neither easy nor exceptionally safe. See Chapter 24 on chain saws and their use.

The fret saw is a type of coping saw with an extremely high arch, often nearly a foot. The veneer saw is a handsaw with a really odd look; the blade is only about 3 inches long, serrated on both sides, and the straight handle is set at an angle to the blade. The wood-loop saw is used for cutting off tree limbs. The wood loop saw is simply a chain with teeth on one side and handles or loops at each end. It is looped around a log or branch. A log or bucking saw will do the same job with no more effort.

SHARPENING

Even the best handsaws with nonreplaceable blades will eventually need sharpening. Sharpening starts with a check of the saw teeth to see that they are all the same height. You can easily do this with a 3-foot metal straightedge. If you've hit a nail or if the saw has seen really long and hard use, the teeth might be of slightly different height. To correct this, place the saw in either a saw vise or a carpenter's vise with 3-foot long strips of 1×2 against the sides of the saw. Take a flat file and push it back and forth over the entire length of the saw blade until it just lightly touches the shortest tooth.

Once jointing is carried out, some of the saw teeth will have flattened tops and uneven gullets (the space between the teeth) and therefore must be reshaped. For this, a triangular-section taper file is needed. Hold the file level and at right angles to the blade at all times while reshaping. Use a downward pressure while filing, with a smooth, moderately light stroke (Fig. 3-32).

Once all the teeth are shaped and

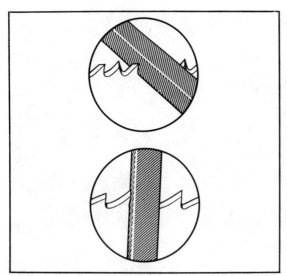

Fig. 3-32. Angles for filing teeth. The crosscut teeth are shown at the top and the rip teeth are at the bottom (courtesy Nicholson).

teeth set more than twice the amount of tooth height unless you want to crack off a tooth or two. The tool is set to the degree required, the saw is clamped in a vise, and each tooth is bent outward to the degree needed. Hold the original bend direction for each tooth and do both sides of the saw (Fig. 3-33).

File sizes and quality for sharpening crosscut saws are of great importance. For a saw with 7 teeth per inch, use a 6- or 7-inch slim taper file. For 8 or 9 teeth per inch, you'll need a 7-inch slim taper file. For 10 or 11 points to an inch, you will need a 4- or 5-inch slim taper file.

Filing is always begun at the point of the saw with the file placed in the gullet of the first tooth facing away from you. At this time, file every other tooth along the entire blade. Keep the same angle for each tooth. Reverse the process and file the teeth set in the opposite direction in the same manner, keeping to all instructions. File each tooth to a sharp point.

From the above instructions, and considering the possible number of teeth on a 30-inch handsaw blade, it is quite easy to understand why virtually everyone prefers to take the saws to a professional to have them sharpened. I can't remember the last time I sharpened a handsaw, but I have a feeling it

you've checked it with your straightedge, you can continue the job of sharpening. Crosscut saws are beveled and must be filed at an angle to the blade. According to Nicholson, the correct angle is usually 20 degrees. Blacken the teeth with a candle flame, to make it easier to see the fresh file cut, and bevel the teeth. Take it very easy while doing this job.

For ripsaws, the teeth are not beveled; they are filed at right angles to the saw. Make sure the file contacts the front edge of the tooth on your left and the back edge of the tooth on your right while doing the work. File until a sharp point is formed. Lift the file on the back stroke.

If the saw teeth need setting to prevent binding—as will happen about every third sharpening—or if saw use has been really heavy or in difficult woods, I recommend that you spend the money for a pistol grip saw set such as Stanley's 15-042 (under $35). Such tools can be adjusted to just about any amount of set. Saws should not have their

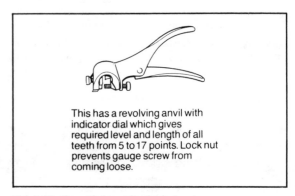

This has a revolving anvil with indicator dial which gives required level and length of all teeth from 5 to 17 points. Lock nut prevents gauge screw from coming loose.

Fig. 3-33. Saw set (courtesy Nicholson).

was before my nineteenth birthday when I was working for a Polish carpenter of great skill and Old World ideas.

I'm so lazy about sharpening any type of saw, that, unless I get caught in the woods with a dull chain saw, I prefer to pay to have them done by a professional on a machine.

The primary reason is accuracy. It takes almost daily practice to maintain the skills needed to get any saw as sharp as it was when it came from the factory. Few of us have either the time or need for that practice. Paying a couple of dollars to get out of the job is usually worthwhile.

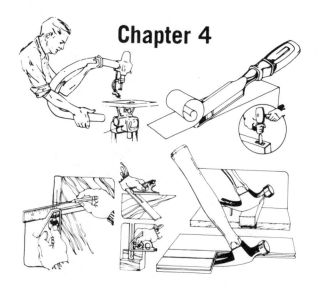

Chapter 4

Chisels and Gouges

TODAY'S SELECTION OF CHISELS AND gouges is complex. Certainly there seems to be one for virtually every wood removal job you can find; whether it's paring fine strips from a piece of lumber or gouging deep bowl shapes, to forming mortises and tenons of various sizes and styles.

Not a great deal of modern work is done with the more delicate chisels outside the amateur workshop. The same jobs can often, and usually are, done by machine. But the idea of creating a mortise and tenon joint using no more than a mallet and two chisels remains an attractive one to those who can afford the time and want to develop the skill.

Today, most work done with chisels is usually in rough form, such as cutting and lifting floorboards, ripping wood members apart, and chiseling room for pipe or wiring runs in house framing. Gouges have no real

equivalent in rough work. They are milder tools developed to provide curved surfaces. Chisels are used to form straight-faced surfaces (Fig. 4-1).

CHISELS

The basic wood chisel is also known as a *firmer chisel* and can have a wood or plastic handle. Blade widths range from ⅛ to 2 inches. This is a general-purpose, wood-cutting tool. Blades are generally about 4 inches long with a rectangular section and parallel sides. The blade is the only part of the wood chisel beveled (and that on one side only). My selection includes four chisels; ¼-inch, a ½-inch, a ¾-inch, and 1-inch. Seldom will you find that any more are needed. I did find that it pays to have on hand all steel wood chisels in 1-inch and 2-inch sizes when working on wall framing and

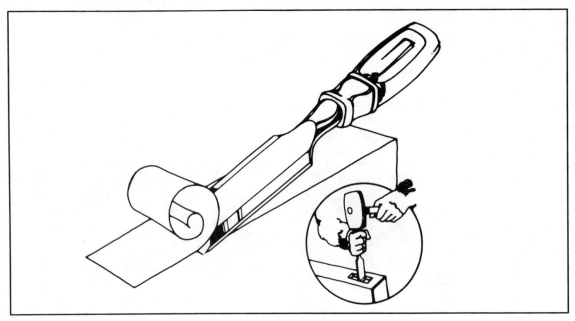

Fig. 4-1. Chisel uses (courtesy Stanley Tools).

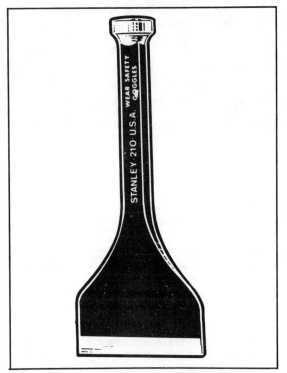

Fig. 4-2. All-metal chisel (courtesy Stanley Tools).

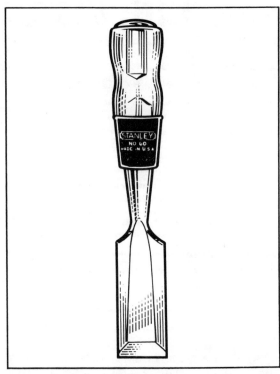

Fig. 4-3. Plastic-handled chisel with beveled blade sides (courtesy Stanley Tools).

flooring. My plastic-handled models are from Stanley and the two metal chisels are Craftsman. See Fig. 4-2.

Wood chisels are also available with beveled edges along the two top sides. All but my 2-inch all-steel wood chisel are of the beveled-edge type (Fig. 4-3). While beveling the edge does somewhat reduce the blade strength, there is otherwise no real difference. Both types of wood chisels can be lightly tapped with wood or plastic mallets if more than hand power is needed for the work. And the all-steel chisels can be driven by a hammer. As an incidental point, it is possible to use a claw hammer to tap the high-impact plastic handles on wood chisels, but not on wooden handled models. I do not like to use a claw hammer to strike any metal other than nailheads or something softer. I use a ball peen hammer when striking the all-steel chisel heads. See Figs. 4-4 through 4-6.

There are three types of mortising chisels that might be of some use to you and a fourth type that probably won't unless you intend to get into exceptionally fine work in softwoods. The basic mortise chisel comes in sizes from a half inch through an inch. They are hard to find. These are useful for cutting large mortises. They have thick blades for stiffness and handles designed to be hit by mallets. Garrett Wade carries a good line in 4mm to 12mm sizes.

The registered mortise chisel is similar to the basic mortising chisel except that the handle end is encased or wrapped in a metal ring so that tapping the chisel with a mallet does less damage. Those Garrett Wade carries are by Marple, a firm that has been making the tool for 110 years. Sizes range from a quarter inch to 1½ inches and the prices, while high, do not seem excessive for the apparent quality (from about $10 to about $20). Both of the above types of mor-

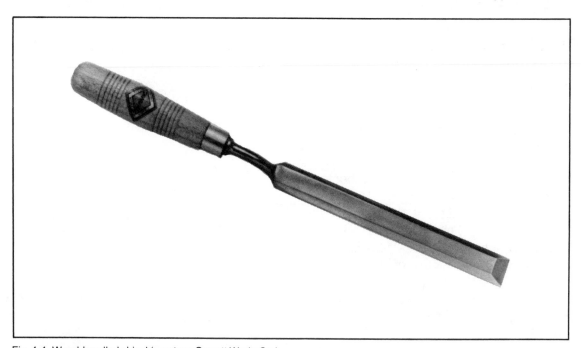

Fig. 4-4. Wood-handled chisel (courtesy Garrett Wade Co.).

Fig. 4-5. Plastic-handled firmer chisel (courtesy Stanley Tools).

are also known as *sash mortising chisels.* Garrett Wade offers Japanese mortise chisels in 3mm, 6mm, 9mm, and 12mm blade widths. These Japanese chisels are made from two layers of steel. The bottom layer has a Rockwell hardness of 65 on the C scale (which is very, very high). This would normally prove too brittle in use so a softer top layer is laminated on to prevent breakage. A line of Japanese bevel-edge chisels is also available.

When flooring has already been laid and pipe or wiring runs must be added, the *floor chisel* is the tool of choice to cut through the tongues of flooring strips. The boards can be lifted with as little damage to the surfaces as possible. The handle is usually long enough to also allow the flooring chisel to be used to pry up the floorboard after the tongue is cut through. The chisel will be all steel and have a wide blade no less than 2½ inches. The cutting edge is ground on both sides (Fig. 4-7).

Ripping chisels are for the really rough work. They usually are about a foot and a half long with a blade from 1½ to 2 inches

tising chisel have leather washers placed between the shank and the handle to absorb the shock of the striking mallet.

The lock mortise chisel looks somewhat like an offset screwdriver at first glance. It is all metal in construction. The drawer lock mortise chisel from Garrett Wade is 6½ inches long, with one end ¾ of an inch and the other end 15/16 of an inch. Another form of lock mortise chisel is the swan neck model, also from Garrett Wade, and one they have specially made in West Germany. The swan neck mortise chisels are useful for cleaning out the bottoms of mortises that other chisels just chop up. This model cleans to a depth of 6 inches. Metric sizes are used here and the three available are 6mm, 8mm, and 12mm.

Mortising chisels from a half inch down

Fig. 4-6. Plastic-handled firmer chisel (courtesy Sears, Roebuck and Co.).

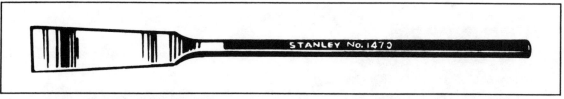

Fig. 4-7. Flooring chisel (courtesy Stanley Tools).

wide and have slots for pulling nails. Essentially, these are very similar to ripping bars, but the blades are wider and sharper. The ripping chisel is used for splitting boards, such as siding, along the grain and for pulling them off for replacement.

Wood-turning tools, both chisels and gouges, are a bit more delicately made than hand chisels simply because they are never driven. They are simply held against the piece of work being turned in a lathe. Wood-turning chisels come in a very wide variety of shapes and sizes. The basic chisel has a flat blade that is ground on both sides. The standard wood-turning chisel will be about 16½ inches long. The fine chisel or small chisel will be 3 inches shorter in length. Blade widths vary from at least ½-inch, ¾-inch and 1-inch widths.

Other shapes of wood-turning chisels include the round-nosed chisel, to make curved concavities, to V-point chisels used to make a V-shaped cut. For even fancier

work, you must use wood-turning gouges. Two lengths are available and there are a variety of blade widths. The largest is used for the first cut made in the stock, and so on down as needed, until the time comes to use the chisels for finishing. Once the finishing is completed, you pick up a *parting tool*, with a 3/16-inch blade, that has a long point on a square blade. The narrow point is used to cut a groove to part the finished turning from the waste material. For best results, stop just before the wood is actually parted and then finish the cut with a very fine handsaw. The handsaw cut is then cleaned up with a wood chisel.

CARVING TOOLS

Wood carving is a bit of an odd recreation. It can be done with nothing more than a sharp pocket knife or you can use a range of gouges and chisels. The gouges and chisels are similar to those used for wood turning, but they are slightly heavier in the handle so

Fig. 4-8. Wonder Bar (courtesy Stanley Tools).

Fig. 4-9. Wide blade all-metal chisel (courtesy Stanley Tools).

that you can lightly tap them into tough woods. Nevertheless, most smaller work is done only with hand pressure.

The blades are made of steel with wood handles (sometimes plastic) and the blades are about 4 inches long. Straight-cut and skew-cut chisels, from 1/8 to 1 inch in size, are available. Then things get complex. Gouges come in about six styles. Each gouge serves a slightly different purpose. Straight gouges are used for only convex surfaces. The curved gouge is used for working concavities that are fairly wide. The spoon-bit gouge is used to work smaller concavities. For other odd shapes, you'll find fishtail gouges and back-bent gouges. In addition, the veiner is a very fine straight-bladed gouge used for fine, detailed carving.

If you really get into the swing of things, a sculptors' adze will be a big help in starting off larger carving jobs. The adze is used with one hand and it will do a fine job of roughing in the overall outline of a moderately large to very large piece of wood sculpture. I recommend that you have at least one good foot-long, half-inch cold chisel for those times when you're tearing into something and find a nail or screw or bolt midway through and have no other tool to cut it. Essentially, the cold chisel would be necessary only if you plan to do some remodeling work in the home. See Figs. 4-8 and 4-9.

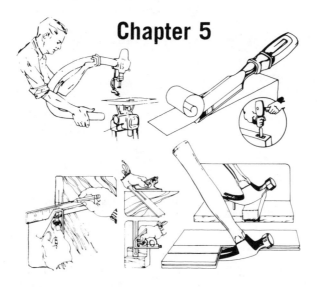

Chapter 5

Knives

FOR MOST HOME WOODWORKERS, THE need for knives will stop at one or two and seldom go further. There are also putty knives and related tools to consider. By related, I mean tools such as knives for taping gypsum wallboard joints and nailhead dimple covering. You can try this with a wide-bladed putty knife, but I can promise frustration and a poor job. The tools look identical from as close as 6 inches, but they're not. The shape of the blade and the handle are the same, but the taping knife has a far more flexible blade than does a putty knife.

Most home woodworkers find the basic utility knife the most common and useful of all knives. General-purpose utility knives come in several styles. All have easily replaceable blades. Some have retractable blades. You might not appreciate this fea-

ture until you spend some time cutting thin material and stick a hand into your carpenters' apron for a knife with a nonretractable blade. Some utility knives have snap-off blades. I can't comment on the value of these except as a time saver if you're scoring a great many sheets of wallboard and find that the blades dull.

Utility knives can be purchased with several shapes of blades for various purposes. The straight blade is fine for scoring wallboard, marking wood, and general trimming in many kinds of light materials. Hooked blades are generally used to trim resilient tile floor coverings or asphalt shingles. A very exaggerated style of hook blade is used for the larger resilient flooring sheets. Curved blades are generally used for cutting angles. For some knives, you can

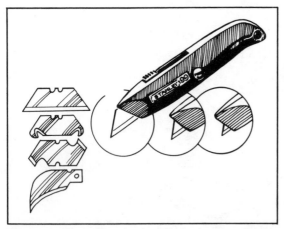

Fig. 5-1. A utility knife and various blades (courtesy Stanley Tools).

even buy serrated blades and specially shaped blades for working with plastic laminate materials (Fig 5-1).

Modeler's knives, such as those made by X-Acto, are similar to utility knives, but they are generally more finely made and have smaller blades with a variety of styles wider than those for utility knives. Blades are replaceable, usually in a chuck-style jaw, and the knives are good for a great many sorts of detailed cutting jobs in light woods.

Putty knives are generally considered as tools for puttying windowpanes in place. The most common kinds have straight blades. In most cases today, I see putty knives more often used as paint scrapers than anything else. The blades are fairly stiff and they range in size from 1 to 6 inches (Figs. 5-2 through 5-6).

Taping knives are used to fill cracks in plaster, tape wallboard joints, and so on. The knife looks exactly like a putty knife, and comes in the same sizes, but the blade is far more flexible so that the joint compound is pushed into the cracks.

Lately I've been looking for two joint-taping knives such as those I used to have. One knife was a flexible-bladed tool with a 10-inch wide blade, stiffened at its upper

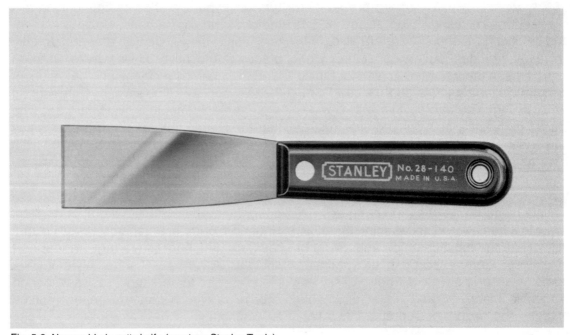

Fig. 5-2. Narrow-blade putty knife (courtesy Stanley Tools).

74

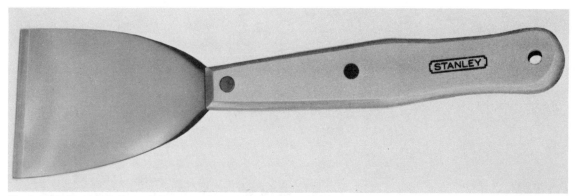

Fig. 5-3. Medium-blade burn off scraper knife (courtesy Stanley Tools).

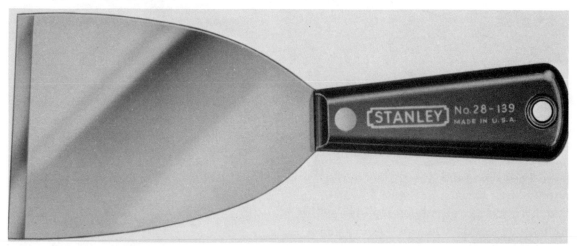

Fig. 5-4. Wide blade burn off scraper (courtesy Stanley Tools).

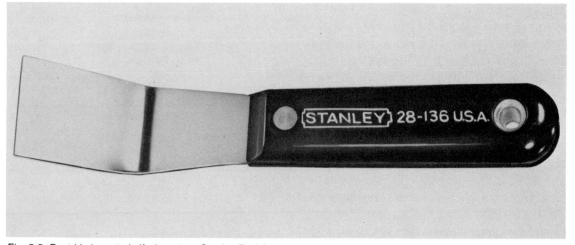

Fig. 5-5. Bent blade putty knife (courtesy Stanley Tools).

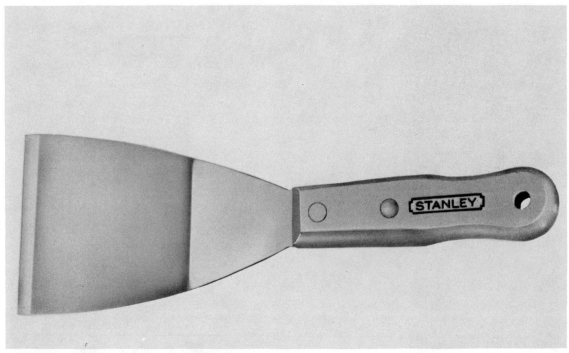

Fig. 5-6. Bent blade burn off scraper (courtesy Stanley Tools).

edge by a wood bar at right angles to the handle. This thing was great! Never more than two passes were needed to fill even the widest joints, and the job was greatly eased. Today, I make do with a 6-inch taping knife.

The other tool was more of an oddity that apparently has disappeared from the scene. It was a corner knife. Now, regardless of what anyone tells you to the contrary, taping corner joints in wallboarded rooms, neatly, with a flat-bladed knife is three chores and a half and usually sends me to the mill to buy some quarter-round molding, as I mutter under my breath. My corner knife, may it rest in peace, had a single blade bent at a 90-degree angle, thus filling both sides of the joint in one pass. Otherwise when taping corners, it's best to do one side and let it dry at least 12 hours before doing the other side (unless you do the job every day and get plenty of practice).

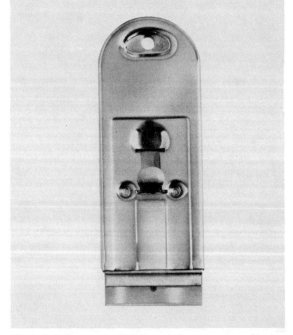

Fig. 5-7. Paint scraper knife for windows (courtesy Stanley Tools).

Fig. 5-8. Machete (courtesy Stanley Tools).

Fig. 5-9. Machete (courtesy Stanley Tools).

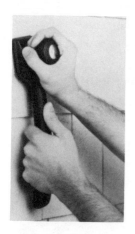  

Fig. 5-10. Paint scraper with hammer head for popped siding nails and a 12-inch handle (courtesy Stanley Tools).

Several other knives were once used for wood working. The electricians' knife is a handy item. A single sharp-leaf blade, with a sharp edged notched (for stripping wire) screwdriver blade makes the electricians' knife nearly ideal as a pocketknife. It can be used, in a pinch, as a utility knife. See Figs. 5-7 through 5-10.

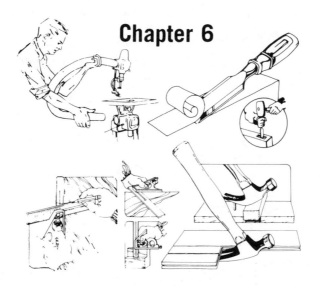

Chapter 6

Screwdrivers

WHO AMONG US HAS NOT USED AND MIS-used this everyday tool? As tools go, screwdrivers are relatively young; they first appeared about 1660. Screwdrivers are designed to drive and secure the best type of wood fasteners available: screws. Screwdriver tips are named after the types of screws they are designed to drive. The three most common types of screwdriver tips were the standard slot, the Phillips, and the Reed and Prince. Several more tips recently have been introduced.

Standard slot screwdrivers come in several tip styles: the flared tip is the most common. Its shank is flattened and flared to the sides and its edges are ground to a taper. Parallel tips are available, as is a flared tip without the sides ground down.

The Phillips screw has a crosslike slot. The Phillips-head screwdriver has flutes that end in a modestly pointed tip. The Reed and Prince, which has never been all that popular, is similar to a Phillips, but its flutes are ground square and the tip of the screwdriver has a sharp point (Figs. 6-1 and 6-2).

Today, there is a proliferation of screw-head types and screwdrivers. The Pozidriv is also a crossed-tip style but it has an added square hole at the center. Ostensibly this is so that greater torque values can be used. The Torx screwdriver is an asterisk-shaped thing that is supposed to provide a more positive fit between screw head and screw-driver tip. The Robertson is a square type that is rather like a hex key with a couple of sides missing.

The clutch-head screw is used extensively in mobile homes and has what I would call a waisted slot; the ends are moderately wide and the center of the slot is narrow (Fig.

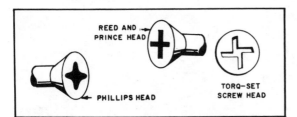

Fig. 6-1. Phillips, Reed & Prince and Torque Set screwheads.

6-3). If you ever have to work on a mobile home and don't have a clutch-head screwdriver, your best bet is to get an electric drill, with a bit just under the size of the screw shank, and drill the damned things out, replacing them with another type.

Of the seven types of screwdriver tips available, the Torx, Robertson, and Pozidriv are much more likely to be used in small engines than in woodworking and the Reed and Prince is rarely seen or used.

HANDLES

When purchasing screwdrivers, first decide on the type of handle construction you want (Fig. 6-4). You can get molded plastic handles with and without rubber grips added and one-piece wooden handles. In addition, there is a wooden-handled type in which the screwdriver blade comes right up through a two-piece wooden handle held on with

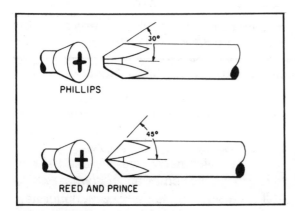

Fig. 6-2. Phillips and Reed & Prince heads.

screws or rivets. This is the strongest type of screwdriver you can find (Figs. 6-5 through 6-8).

Plastic handles can be molded into a bulb shape or fluted (most common) and could also have a rubber covering. For doing nothing but woodwork, the wooden handle is often preferred by cabinetmakers. That

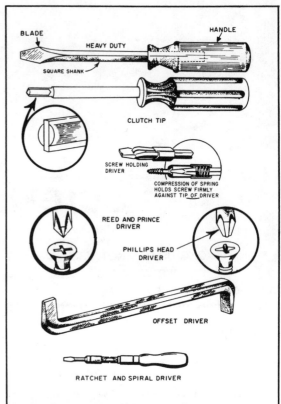

Fig. 6-3. Screwdriver types.

might simply be a basic prejudice against plastic. For any other work, and for cabinet work, a top-quality screwdriver with a plastic handle is fine. When you are working with or around electrical wiring, a plastic handle (and sometimes an insulated shaft) is a good idea. While no sane person works on a live electrical circuit in residential wiring, it is possible to be installing cabinets, for in-

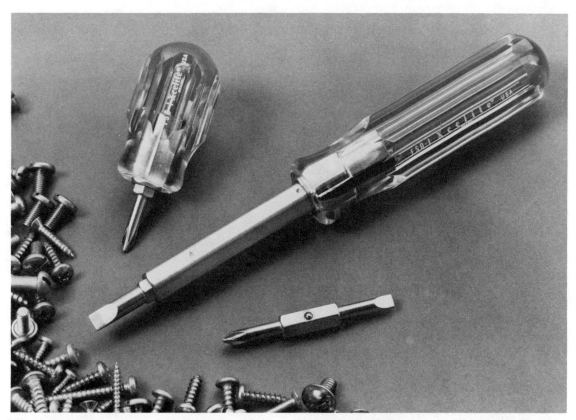

Fig. 6-4. Changeable tip screwdriver and stubby screwdriver (courtesy Xcelite).

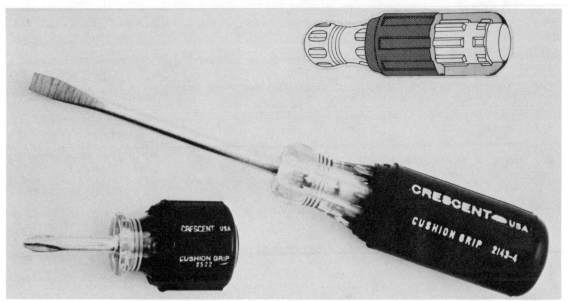

Fig. 6-5. Cushion grip screwdriver (courtesy Crescent and Cooper Tool Group).

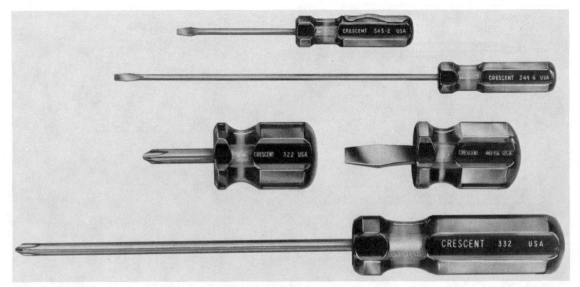

Fig. 6-6. Plastic-grip Crescent Phillips screwdriver (courtesy Cooper Tool Group).

stance, and inadvertently drive a screw into a cable. The insulation of the plastic handle is then very good to have.

When examining the screwdriver, make sure the handle fits your hand. There is a wide variation of handle sizes, but, usually, the larger the better as it will provide you with greater gripping surface and more turning power. Too small a screwdriver handle is the bane of the cheap screwdriver and not suitable for any but the most elementary jobs (Fig. 6-9).

SHANKS

Screwdriver shanks come in two styles: round and square. If you think you will someday have to attach an adjustable wrench to a screwdriver in order to get extra

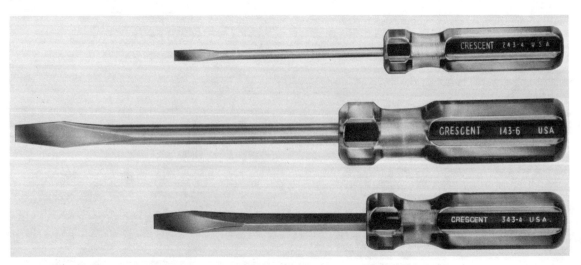

Fig. 6-7. Plastic-grip Crescent slotted tip (courtesy Cooper Tool Group).

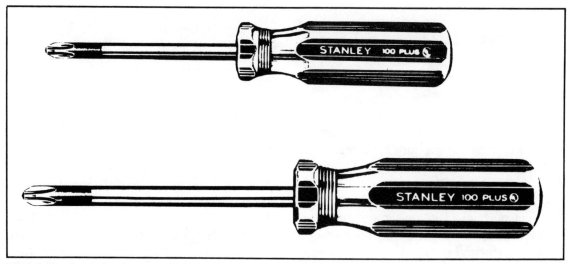

Fig. 6-8. Plastic grip Stanley screwdriver (courtesy Stanley Tools).

leverage on a stubborn screw, go for the square shank. In all other cases, the round shank is fine. The shank and blade must be made of a good alloy steel. Cheap screwdrivers tend to use cheap alloys that will allow the blade to chip or even bend under heavy stress. Name-brand quality screwdrivers will not do so unless you mistreat the tool sorely.

SPECIAL TYPES

Offset screwdrivers are made to fit into places you can't reach with even stubby-handle screwdrivers. They are generally from 3 to 6 inches long and usually available with Phillips-head tips and slotted tips. In the most common variety, it is a steel bar that is bent at both ends to a 90-degree angle (in opposite directions) with a tip formed and ground to shape. Ratcheting models are also available though I have had very little success with them. In fact, a ratcheting offset screwdriver is essential only about once every five years and generally proves very aggravating to use. Still, when it's needed, it's needed, and the cost is low (Fig. 6-9).

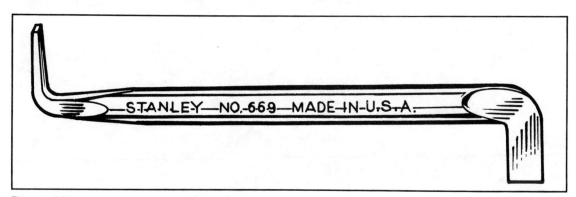

Fig. 6-9. Offset screwdriver (courtesy Stanley Tools).

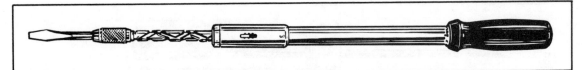

Fig. 6-10. Yankee ratcheting screwdriver (courtesy Stanley Tools).

A *ratcheting* screwdriver with a spiral shank is manufactured by Stanley Tools and sold under the tradename Yankee (Fig. 6-10). Several bits are available (I have four for mine), and the tool is, while not indispensable, surely an immense work reliever when a number of screws must be driven quickly. Essentially, you place the correct bit in the chuck and tighten it down. You then place the tip in the screw slot, with the screw ready to drive, and apply downward (or sideways or upward) pressure so that the handle moves down on the spiral. The screw goes in and when you lift the tip from the slot, the spiral shaft springs back out on the automatic return models.

There are three types of Yankee screwdrivers available: heavy duty, regular duty, and light duty. Mine is a regular duty model. It is heavily made and good for general all-purpose work. It serves well and should last many more years. Heavy-duty models are probably best left to full-time boat builders and others who must drive hundreds of screws daily. The light duty models are fine for occasional use in cabinetmaking and similar work.

When using a Yankee screwdriver to

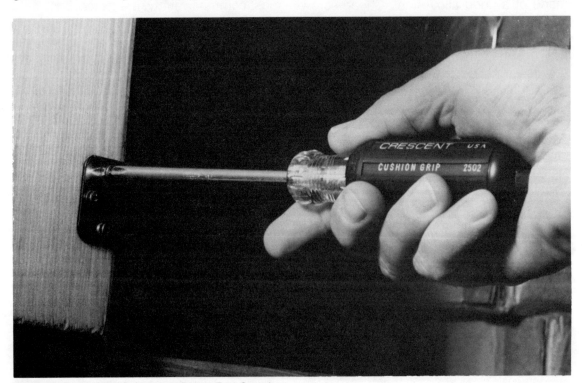

Fig. 6-11. Proper hand fit (courtesy Cooper Tool Group).

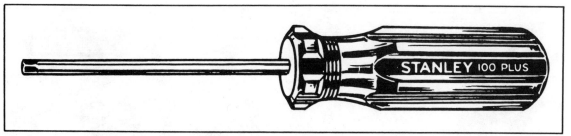

Fig. 6-12. Clutch tip screwdriver (courtesy Stanley Tools).

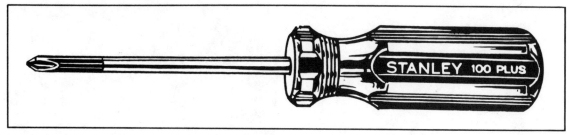

Fig. 6-13. Phillips tip screwdriver (courtesy Stanley Tools).

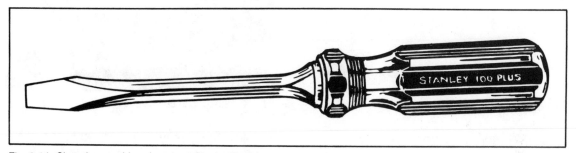

Fig. 6-14. Slotted screwdriver (courtesy Stanley Tools).

drive screws into soft wood, such as soft pine and you don't care much about the finish, you do not need to drill pilot holes. For hard woods, and for soft woods where the finish is important, you'd best drill a pilot hole. Once that screw starts to go in, the ratcheting action is fairly rapid. It is easy to slip the tip from the slot should you run into a bit of extra resistance.

The ratcheting action is reversible for screw removal or for screws threaded the reverse of normal. Also, a knurled locking ring below the thumb slide lets you lock the shaft in place so you can use the tool as an ordinary screwdriver (albeit with interchangeable blades).

SCREWDRIVER CARE

Screwdriver care is a relatively simple thing, if some consideration is given to their proper use. First, use the correct size screwdriver for the screw being driven. A screwdriver that is too large will mar the work surface around the screw. A too-small screwdriver could twist the screw slot out of shape *and* mar the work surface should it slip out of the slot.

If, for some reason, the tip of a straight-

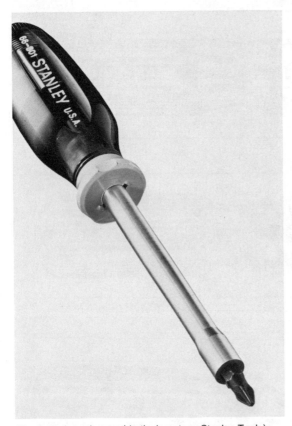

Fig. 6-15. Interchangeable tip (courtesy Stanley Tools).

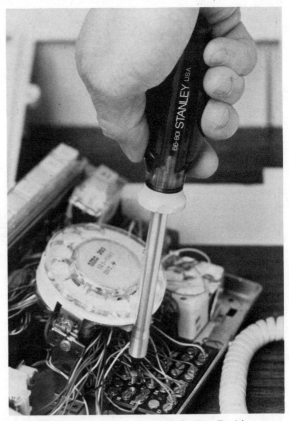

Fig. 6-16. Small tip in use (courtesy Stanley Tools)

edged screwdriver becomes damaged or shows signs of wear, you can grind the tip down on a whetstone. Keep the blade at an angle that will restore the original tip angle. You might also use a power grinder, but I prefer the oilstone because the heat produced by a power grinder could alter the temper of the blade so that it wears too quickly.

The primary reason screwdrivers wear down and wear out too rapidly is because they are too often used for jobs for which they were not designed. Many people use them as small chisels and virtually everyone opens paint cans with them. I've also seen large screwdrivers used as pry bars. Chisels are chisels. Paint cans can be opened with

an old church-key type can opener more easily, in most cases, than with a screwdriver. Use a pry bar to unstick things—including stuck windows. Beyond that, a screwdriver should need only an occasional wiping down with a dry rag to come close to outlasting its owner.

PURCHASING HINTS

Always get the best quality. The price differential between a set of cheap screwdrivers and good screwdrivers just isn't worth the trouble you'll get from the cheap tools. Choose a style handle that fits your hand and is not too small. The shank and blade should be made of a good alloy steel and the

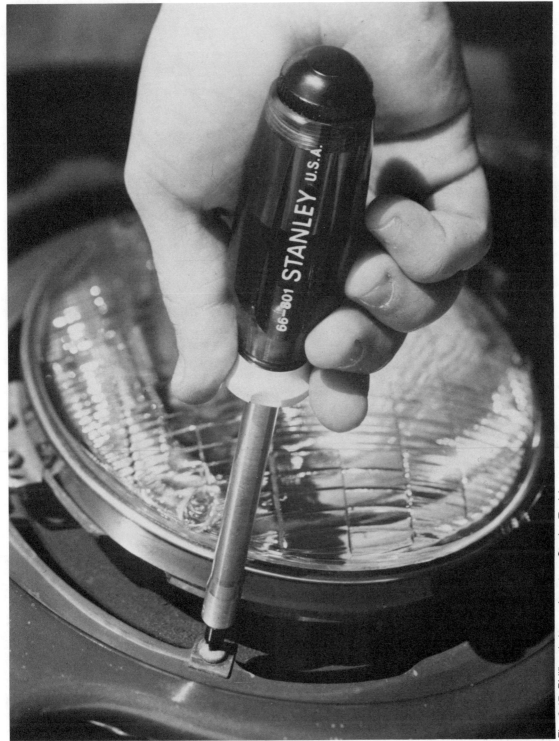

Fig. 6-17. Phillips tip in use (courtesy Stanley Tools).

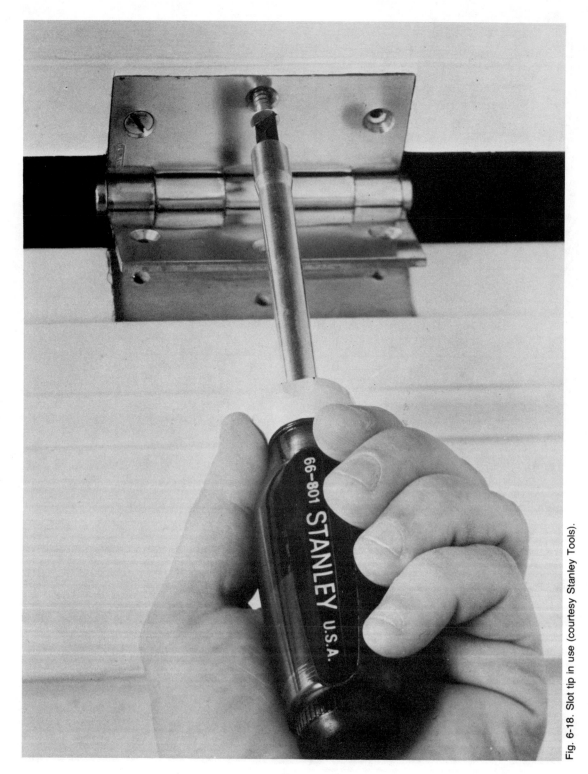

Fig. 6-18. Slot tip in use (courtesy Stanley Tools).

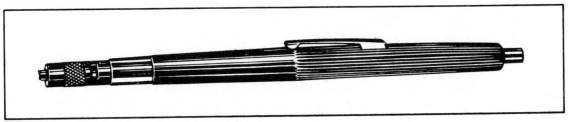

Fig. 6-19. Screw holding driver (courtesy Stanley Tools).

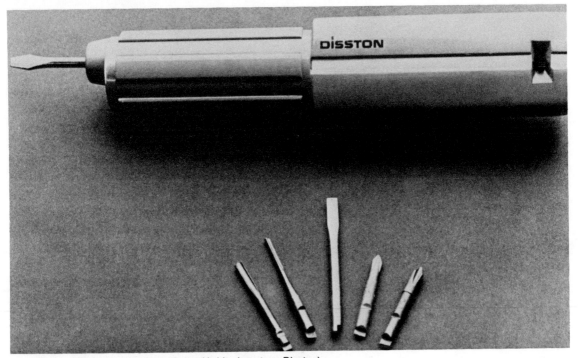

Fig. 6-20. Cordless electric screwdriver with bits (courtesy Disston).

tip should be ground clean. Most important, choose a tip that fits the screw head firmly, but not too tightly. See Figs. 6-11 through 6-20.

Chapter 7

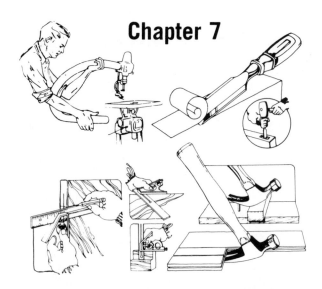

Holding Tools

THE NEED FOR HOLDING TOOLS IN WOOD-working is greater than the beginner might suppose. While the variety of such tools is not endless, it is long. You might start simple carpentry with a saw, a sawhorse and your extra hand to support the boards. When the day comes that you want to move on to planing a door's edge or to gluing some item, then you'll find the beginning of the need for clamps of many kinds, as well as vises and woodworking benches. There's nothing quite as much fun as trying to get a square, smooth edge on a large piece of lumber with a plane and having it skitter around in your helper's hands.

Such problems are readily solved with a variety of holding tools. The same is true with gluing needs when clamping is indicated and when you are working with very small pieces or holding miter boxes or other such tools to surfaces so they don't bounce around and ruin your cuts.

The basic sawhorse is the first holding tool most home craftsman will ever need. There are three ways to get a sawhorse set for use. You can buy a set of legs from Montgomery Ward, Sears, Roebuck or another company and cut off two lengths of 2×4. The legs are then simply clamped onto the cut 2×4s and you've got your sawhorse pair.

This is about as easy a way to go as any. The only easier way is to buy some of the all-metal sawhorses on the market. All-metal sawhorses do pose a problem for the woodworker. That problem arises the day you need to cut a piece that lies over the top of the sawhorse. That metal just isn't going to do your saw teeth a bit of good. Any such sawhorse used for woodwork should always

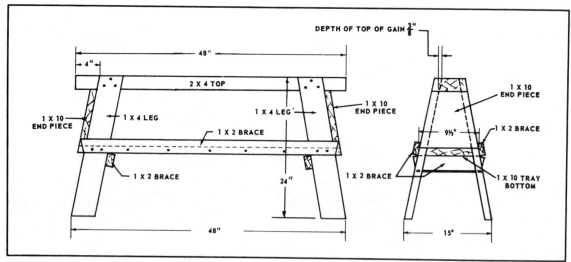

Fig. 7-1. Saw horse dimensions.

have a top piece of 2×4 screwed (with the screws well countersunk) or clamped to the top.

The second easiest method for building sawhorses is to select the joint kits made by Stanley and simply cut 2×4s to length, insert, and nail. Use screws if you're going to be doing heavy work. Both the clamp-on legs and the two types of Stanley sawhorse kits work very well and allow you to construct sawhorses in just a few minutes.

A more complex, but in some ways more satisfying, way to come up with sawhorses is to do the entire job yourself. You'll need a few pieces of 1×10s for end braces and two 4-foot long pieces if you want to add an optional tray. For a single saw horse, 10 feet of 1×2 will be needed for bracing and four feet of 2 by 4 will do for the top. Legs can be of 1-×-4 or 2-×-4 material. It depends on what use you intend for the sawhorse (Fig. 7-1).

The 2-×-4 top is the simplest. Cut it 48 inches long and make sure the ends are reasonably square. Lay it aside. Now, you have to use a framing square to lay off the

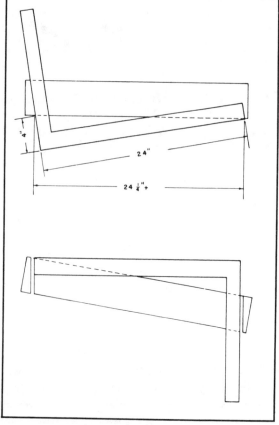

Fig. 7-2. Laying off leg end cuts.

end cuts for the legs. As the illustrations show, for 2-foot-high legs, there is little problem. With a right triangle having one leg of 24 inches and a set away (the amount the top of the leg is set in from the top bar of the sawhorse) of 4 inches, you simply set the square, as shown in Fig. 7-2, at 4 inches out on the tongue and 24 inches on the blade and mark the cut. Do the same on the top end. You'll end up with the proper angles. Start with a piece of lumber about 26 or 27 inches long to make sure that there is enough material. Don't forget to turn the square over when making the top cut (Fig. 7-3).

To set up for the side cuts (Fig. 7-4) on the legs, use 5¼ inches on the blade and, again, 24 inches on the tongue. Mark your line along the tongue, carry it across the face of the piece parallel to your previously made end cut. It's best to bevel down to this line with a plane, but you can cut it with a hand-saw or circular saw if you're very, very careful.

Now you must figure the gain at the side of the top and lay that out. Start by setting the

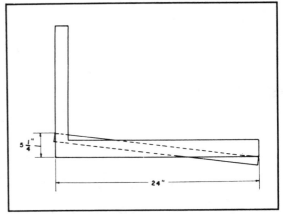

Fig. 7-4. Laying off leg side cuts.

top of a leg in place, 4 inches in from the end, and draw the lines for the sides of the gain. Score a line ⅜ of an inch in from the top edge of the leg. You can now use a chisel to cut out the gain. Do the work carefully (as shown in Fig. 7-5). For the end pieces, you will need 10 inches of width of the 1-×-10 lumber. You might have to rip this down from nominal 1-×-12 lumber. Set the framing square to exactly the same figures as for the ends of the legs (4 inches on the blade and 2 feet on the tongue) and make the first cut. Now take your sliding bevel T-square and set it to the bottom angle, move it over 9½ inches, turn it over, and mark the second cut. Make the cut and that's it for the end braces. (See Fig. 7-6).

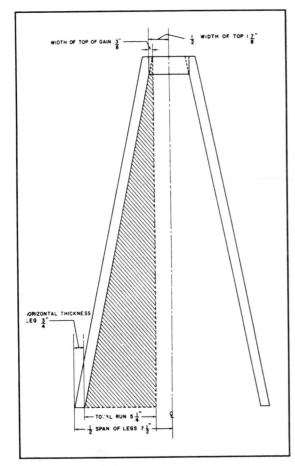

Fig. 7-3. Triangle for leg end cuts.

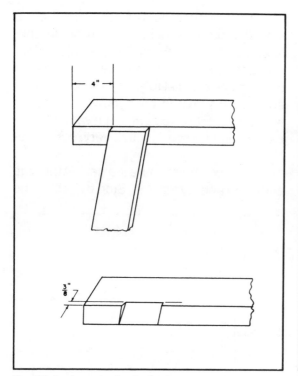

Fig. 7-5. Laying out gains for the legs.

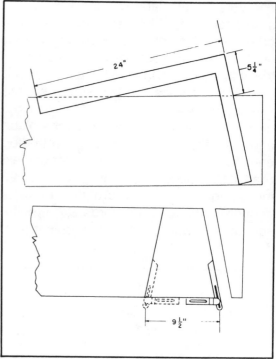

Fig. 7-6. Laying off the 1-×-10 end piece.

If you want to set in the optional tray, place the 1-×-10 material between the legs after the rest of the sawhorse is assembled, mark it, and make the bevel cuts needed to fit it tightly between the 1-×-2 supports. Do not make special cuts here unless you want to get fancy and cut to align with leg edges. The whole sawhorse should be nailed together using 8-penny galvanized nails. If the sawhorse is to be used outdoors and stored outdoors, as many are, use pressure-treated lumber, such as Koppers Company's Wolmanized brand, for longest life. Treat all cut ends with a preservative.

The foregoing sawhorse is about the most complex you can build. It is quite possible to slam together a fairly sturdy sawhorse using 10-penny nails, 2×4s, and almost no cuts. If that's your choice, fine. For rough work, truthfully, that's what most carpenters do. My idea is that the above sawhorse makes a good starting project to give you a fair idea of just how interested you are likely to become in the less rough elements of working with wood.

BENCHES

From sawhorses, the next logical step is to woodworking benches, in all their various styles. Benches now come in many styles. Woodworking benches must be the correct height for the woodworker and they must be more than fairly rigid. The need for rigidity is the reason you see the European-style woodworking benches made of heavy hardwoods (mostly beech these days, though one from Wade Garrett is mahogany), with mortise and tenon joints and, often, heavy bolts holding the joints in place.

Size variations are quite wide. A small bench might be little over 5 feet long with a working table width of less than 2 feet. Others might have benches over 8 feet long with working table widths nearly 26 inches wide. Work surface square footage can vary from as little as 6 feet up to nearly 13 square feet. The average height is somewhere between 33 and 34 inches and weights range from a light 67 pounds for a small mahogany bench to over 265 pounds for the larger benches.

On these woodworking benches you'll find, usually, one vise at an end and one on the side. The top will be pierced to take items called *bench dogs*. Bench dogs are simply protrusions that will hold work on the surface without impeding ease of removal or changing position.

Some such benches will have one or more drawers for tools and small materials, while others will have none, but virtually all have part of the work top as a tool tray. The tray will most often extend the entire length of the bench. A number have a slot as a tool rack down the back (which serves as a handy place to put saws, screwdrivers and other such tools within almost immediate reach). In essence, these are the ultimate in craftsmans' benches for woodworking. The prices indicate it. They run on up to $1,000 and seldom drop under $220.

It is possible to build such a bench yourself. The design features could be all yours. At one time or another, a study of magazines such as *Woodworker's Journal, Family Handyman, Mechanix Illustrated, Popular Mechanics* and *Workbench* will give information on who is currently making or selling the components—such as bench dogs and the large vises—that you'll need to complete the job. Sooner or later one or more of those magazines will just run a set of plans for the project.

Local materials will usually do the job. Beech or white oak are good. Rock maple or sugar maple is excellent, but will need filler. Nevertheless, it is less likely to splinter than oak.

Hickory would be a poor choice because the stuff is murderous to work. Although ash is a bit lightweight, it would be excellent. Pine, firs and hemlocks are too light. Tops are best made in what is called *Butcher-block* style. The boards are laminated and nailed or screwed together to show side grain. True butcher-block material (almost always rock maple) shows end grain, but it requires a great deal more work in lamination.

Black & Decker some years ago came out with a folding workbench that allowed clamping along its top. Sears, Roebuck and Company has a unit that comes in two versions. One has two heights and the other one is for working. Sears also offers a table-top version that should be good for light work. These workbench/vises cost about $50 to $95 and for the moderate woodworker would be well worth the investment.

In addition, Sears offers a European-style workbench made of maple. Not as massive as the master craftsman benches, it is also less expensive at $350, plus shipping. The top offers 14 pairs of holes for dogs. It has end vises, side vises, a clamping cap, and a tool tray that runs about half the length of the 70-inch long top.

In addition, Sears and others offer workbenches with metal legs and chipboard tops, as well as just leg sets, and these come

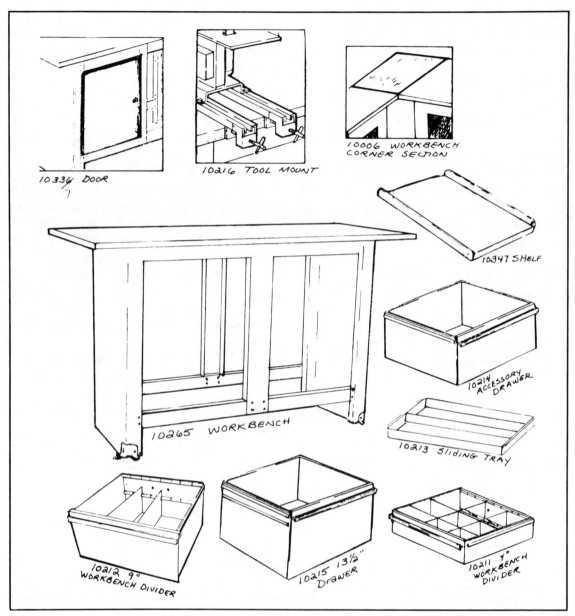

Fig. 7-7. Deluxe workbench (courtesy Sears, Roebuck and Co.).

in a wide variation of sizes and styles (Fig. 7-7). These things must be assembled by you. Much of the final rigidity depends on how carefully you tighten things down and follow instructions (which aren't always as clear as they might be).

One particular unit I do like, in concept and appearance, is set up to disappear into its own wall cabinet when not in use. The total unit costs about $200 when delivered (from Sears) and has a fold-down workbench with a 2-×-3 foot top, 20-inch wide vise jaws, and two clamping bars. The cabinet is pegboard lined to hold a fair assortment of tools. A bottom cabinet can be added (included in the price on page 98).

This sort of workbench would be good for those doing a fair amount of woodwork in a small area, such as a garage, that must serve a dual purpose. The two units hang in a space 2 feet wide by 71 inches long and only seven inches deep when closed. See Figs. 7-8 through 7-11.

CLAMPS

The variety of woodworking clamps is wide (Fig. 7-12). The most basic and probably most familiar clamp seen today is the C-clamp. C-clamps are C-shaped clamps that come in sizes ranging from as small as ¾ of an inch to a foot long to cover a good range of items to be glued or otherwise attached. C-clamps are also used in welding and other metalworking processes.

C-clamps require the use of wood blocks

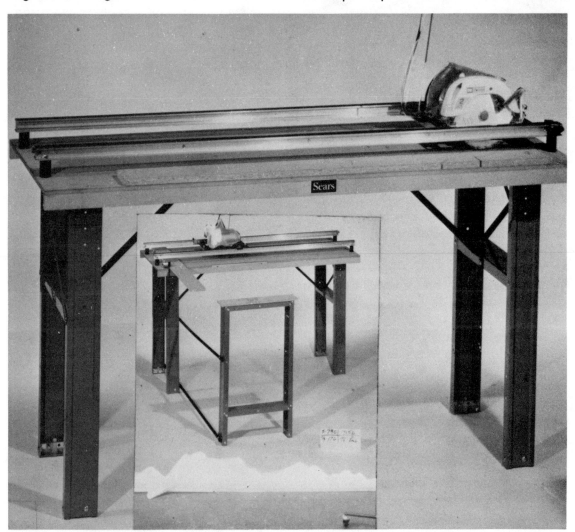

Fig. 7-8. Saw guide bench with extension shown in inset (courtesy Sears, Roebuck and Co.).

Fig. 7-9. Detail of bench extension (courtesy Sears, Roebuck and Co.).

All the C-clamps I've seen and used have a T-bar to aid in tightening the screw. Some small types of clamps have thumb screws (like those on wing nuts). When used with wood, where much pressure is needed,

between the clamp and the work in order to prevent marring. Deep C-clamps can also be found. These allow clamping in further from the edge of a work piece. See Figs. 7-13 and 7-14.

Hand-screw clamps are probably the first type of clamp to come to mind when the person knows anything of wood gluing operations. These wood-jawed clamps have two parallel screws of steel to open and close the jaws. They offer the advantage of being adjustable to virtually any angle of clamping needed to get a grip on things. These usually are found with jaw openings from 2 inches to a foot. See Fig. 7-15. One Sears' Craftsman style is made of plastic, in 2- and 4-inch sizes. Other clamps are made of hardwood.

These hardwood clamps should have the gripping surface protected from glue. It takes the fun out of a gluing job to not be able to get the clamp loose. Use a coating of beeswax or a layer of waxed paper (make sure the protection itself will not stick to the

Fig. 7-10. All-purpose workbench (courtesy Sears, Roebuck and Co.).

Fig. 7-11. General duty workbench (courtesy Sears, Roebuck and Co.).

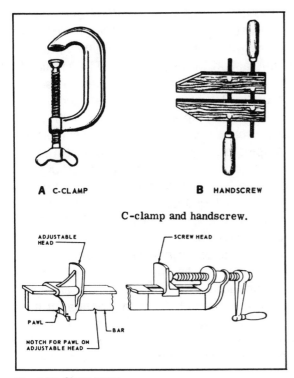

A C-CLAMP   **B** HANDSCREW

C-clamp and handscrew.

ADJUSTABLE HEAD

SCREW HEAD

PAWL

NOTCH FOR PAWL ON ADJUSTABLE HEAD

BAR

Fig. 7-12. Clamp types.

Fig. 7-14. Deep C-clamp (courtesy Sears, Roebuck and Co.).

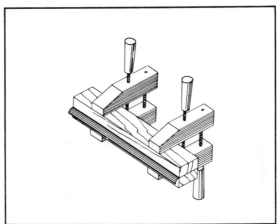

Fig. 7-15. Hand screws (courtesy Shopsmith, Inc.).

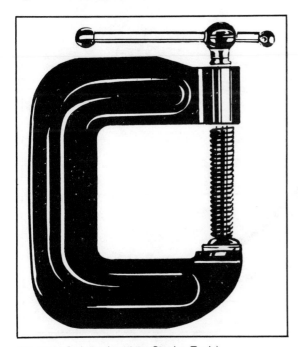

Fig. 7-13. C-clamp (courtesy Stanley Tools).

glue). Garrett Wade offers a hand-screw kit series that drops the prices of the clamps by about a third under their standard hand screws. See Fig. 7-16.

Spring clamps are small, spring loaded items that look something like alligator clips without teeth. The ones I have are from Stanley. The jaws open about 2 or 3 inches and, when released, clamp down tight. These clamps are excellent for clamping round and flat stock. They also do a fine job

101

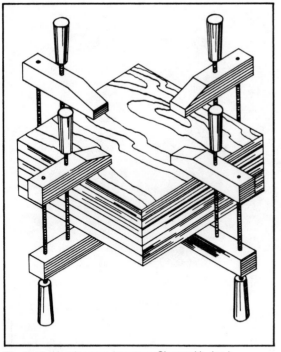

Fig. 7-16. Handscrews (courtesy Shopsmith, Inc.).

on rabbeted joints. See Figs. 7-17 and 7-18.

Fast-action clamps function in much the same manner as C-clamps, but they have a faster action in larger sizes. The smallest size generally available is 6 inches and sizes go up to 3 feet or more. In essence, the fast-action clamp is a bar clamp with a C-clamp screw added to allow fine tuning of the clamping pressure. It allows rapid closure of the major distances and then precision pressure from the screw. See Fig. 7-19.

In most cases, bar clamps have the fixed jaw attached to the screw. (Fast-action clamps have the screw attached to the sliding jaw), and come in sizes up to about 4 feet long. This makes them useful for larger clamping jobs. For really large bar clamps, the cost tends to be a bit out of line for the home craftsman. Pipe clamps are usually a better bet. Sears best pipe clamp set, to fit any ¾ exterior diameter iron pipe, costs

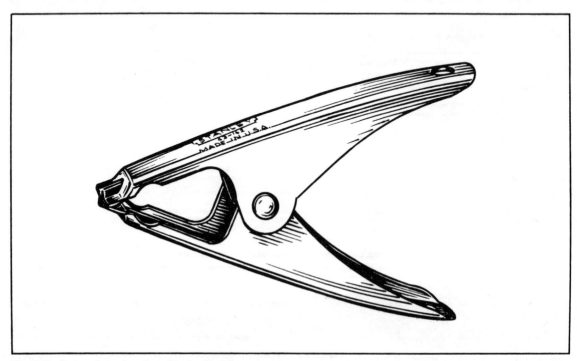

Fig. 7-17. Spring clamp (courtesy Stanley Tools).

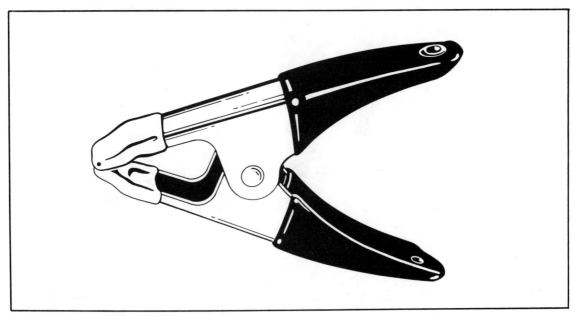

Fig. 7-18. Spring clamp (courtesy Stanley Tools).

about $10 and can be used on any length of threaded pipe.

A 2-foot bar clamp would cost about $14.

One end of the bar clamp pipe is threaded to take the fixed jaw and the other is moveable. The pipe can actually be made up in any length. For flat surfaces being glued, you might want a pair of either bar or pipe clamps. Edge gluing of wide stock can

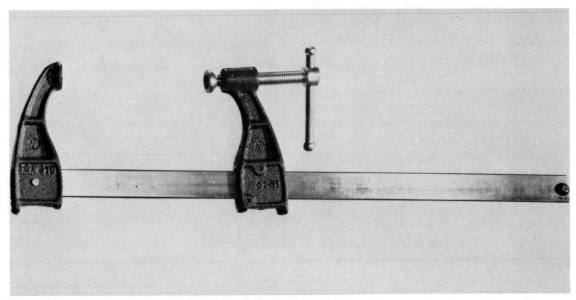

Fig. 7-19. Fast action bar clamp (courtesy Sears, Roebuck and Co.).

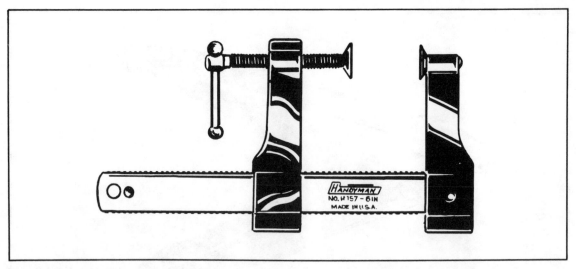

Fig. 7-20. Bar clamp (courtesy Stanley Tools).

warp the stock if only a single clamp is used. You will get best results by clamping on one side of the piece, gently, turning the piece over, and setting on the second clamp. Then do the final tightening of both See Fig. 7-20.

Web clamps and band clamps are used for clamping jobs no straightforward clamps can do. The strap, or web, is looped around the work being glued and then tightened. The particular instances that come to mind are gluing chair legs to their stretchers. Coat parts with glue, assemble, and then wrap with the web, tightening as needed. On mine, you pull on the free end of the web strap (nylon) until it is nearly as tight as it will go. Then you use a wrench to tighten up the small ratchet. It's made by Stanley. Such clamps (Fig. 7-21) can make assembling cabinet frames a lot simpler.

Also available are picture-frame clamps. They save you from having to work with four miter clamps. If you make a hobby out of making picture or mirror frames, that's about the only time the expenditure would be worthwhile.

Corner or miter clamps are another

clamp you'll probably have little use for unless you take up making frames. In most cases, if the stock being glued isn't too thin, a web clamp can do the job. If the material is thin (such as clamshell molding), you can

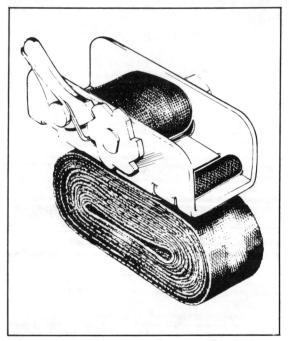

Fig. 7-21. Web clamp (courtesy Stanley Tools).

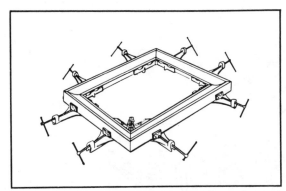

Fig. 7-22. Picture frame clamps (courtesy Sears, Roebuck and Co.).

improvise by placing two nails at adjacent corners in a board. Then use two small bar clamps to bring the other side of the frame up against those nails to form a four-corner clamp. You will have to add a nail tight to the outside edge of the side pieces not clamped. See Fig. 7-22.

VISES

Woodworking vises differ in a number of ways from metal working vises. First, the overall vise is basically lighter. It will work on two slides (in the better models) while a machinist's vise slides on one heavy bar. Most woodworking vises are designed to be screwed or bolted from underneath the bench. The jaws will allow easy attachment of hard or soft wood pieces to protect surfaces on the wood being worked. Any such lining is best left to stick up over the vise jaws about half an inch so that, if you're planing and slip, the plane blade won't be nicked.

At present, my only woodworking vise is

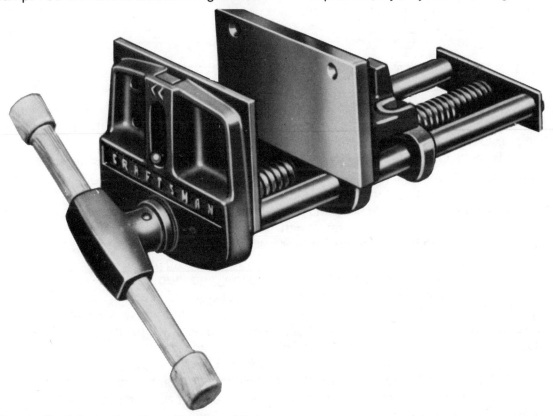

Fig. 7-23. Wood vise (courtesy Sears, Roebuck and Co.).

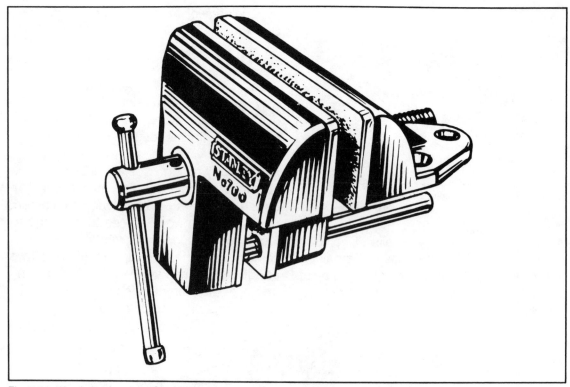

Fig. 7-24. Wood vise (courtesy Stanley Tools).

a lightweight aluminum model from Stanley that I bought about 10 years ago. It can be clamped to a bench or sawhorse and the aluminum jaws do an adequate job of holding moderate-length material for most light planing jobs, sawing curves and making cutouts. This vise has a single slide and one screw. It is tightened with a T-bar and it can be mounted so as to hold work vertically or horizontally if you're using a sawhorse (and on some benches). It is portable, light, inexpensive, and serves very well for general use with wood. See Figs. 7-23 and 7-24.

Bench vises for those who want to build their own European-style woodworking benches are another matter altogether. While the top-of-the-line woodworking vises seldom cost over $70, just the innards for a top quality shoulder vise for a workbench will cost over $105. It will have a 1¼-inch diameter screw and two thick shanks for the vise to slide on.

A slightly lighter model offers a 1-inch screw shank and overall slightly smaller size for about $65. Tail vises cost a few (very few) dollars less and are needed for the classic workbench. You can buy the screws only for about $65 a pair. After that, you supply wooden holding plates and turning bars and so on and add all this to your home-constructed workbench. Garrett Wade carries these materials as well as steel bench dogs (the bench dogs are 6 inches long with a ⅞ inch square shank) at about $20 a pair. When parts are this expensive, you can see why the completed workbench costs so much retail. You might save $500 or more building one.

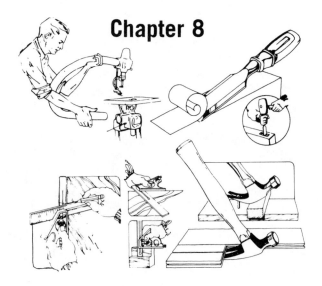

Chapter 8

Measuring Tools

T HE INCH/FOOT MEASURING SYSTEM SUR-
vives from Roman times and the metric
system is soon, supposedly, to be standard
in this country. The metric system was developed in France; by law, it is adopted there
in 1799. Essentially, it goes back to the de-
cimal system breaking everything into units
of ten, one hundred, and so on.

When someone tells me a town is 100
kilometers away, I still want to know how far
that is in "real" distance. Fortunately, the
worries over the metric system will probably
disappear with the next generation of mea-
surers. Such standardization will make
manufacturing for international sales a bit
easier or at least easier to sell.

In any case, the problem will seldom
arise in woodworking. When it does, the
equipment manufacturers will already have
it beat for you. Today, Stanley, Lufkin, Sears

and virtually all other major makers and distributors of rules and other measuring tools
make available a plethora of models that
have both English and metric sizes visible.
See Figs. 8-1 and 8-2. You won't even have
to have charts for conversions.

All sorts of metric conversion tables are
available. For $2 the federal government will
send you an eight-piece kit that includes a
metric ruler and a wallet-sized conversion
table. Included is a history of measurement
systems and a booklet of common metric
conversions (among other things). Write to
R. Woods, Consumer Information Center,
Pueblo, CO 81009.

RULES

Straight rules and folding rules are needed
for many types of woodworking. The stan-

Fig. 8-1. Preparing to take measurements.

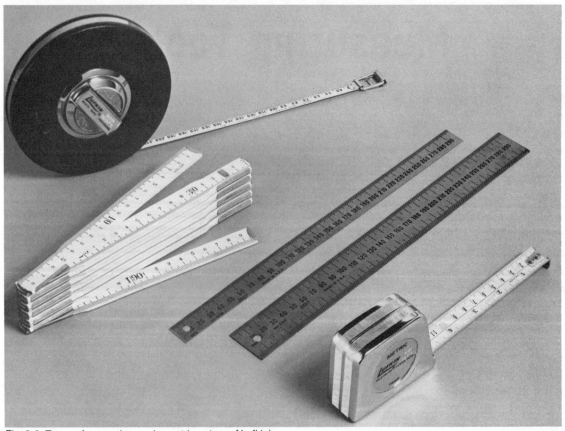

Fig. 8-2. Types of measuring equipment (courtesy of Lufkin).

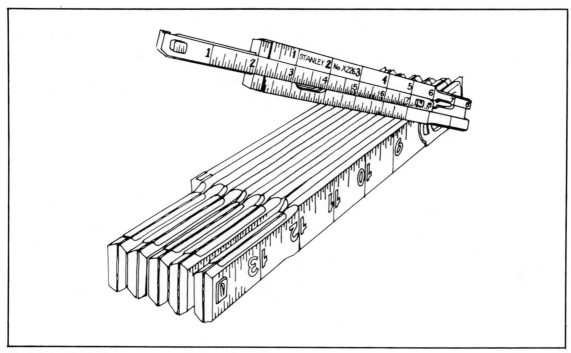

Fig. 8-3. Stanley folding rule.

dard carpenters' folding rule (Fig. 8-3) is 6 feet long and folds into about a 6-inch package a bit over 2 inches wide. Mine, from Stanley, has a 6-inch brass extension and brass couplings at each joint. It is made, as are all wooden models, of a lightweight wood with pretty good flexibility (to prevent its snapping too easily). It is yellow with black markings and 16-inch, on-center markings along it (for house framing).

Folding rules are nearly ideal for confined spaces where longer rules just won't fit. The folding feature makes them easy to carry in a carpenters' apron (Fig. 8-4 and 8-5). The extension feature makes internal readings, such as inside framework, simple because all you do is fold the rule into one length shorter than the space being measured and then slip out the extension. Adding on the length shown on the extension gives you your measurement (Fig. 8-6).

Metal rules were available at one time, but it has been some years since I've seen one around. I did have one at a period when I first started carpentry, but the thing always seemed to be bending and holding the bend (a good wood folding rule will bend a bit, but it comes back to its original shape readily) and the size variations in hot and cold weather could be more extreme than with wood rules.

Bench rules can be very handy in the shop, but in the greater lengths (mine is about 80 inches long) they tend to be more than a little unwieldy. Actually, my Lufkin bench rule is much more often used as a straightedge when I'm cutting gypsum wallboard or other material cut with a knife than when I am measuring anything. Some are made of wood, but this model happens to be of steel and it makes an excellent straightedge (Fig. 8-7).

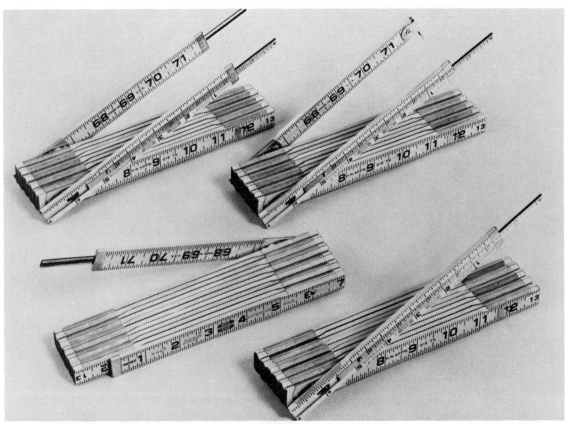

Fig. 8-4. A variety of Lufkin rules (courtesy of Cooper Tool Group).

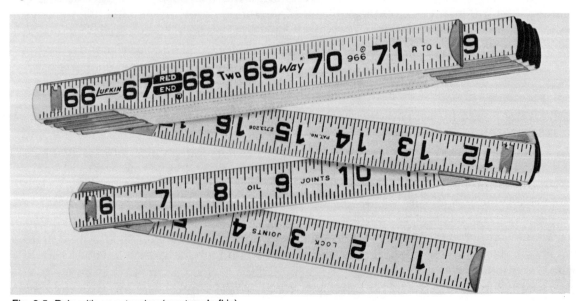

Fig. 8-5. Rule with no extension (courtesy Lufkin).

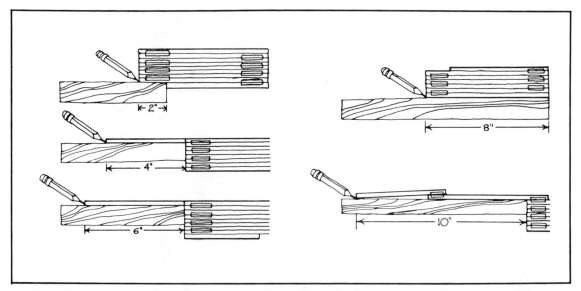

Fig. 8-6. Using the extension rule (courtesy Stanley Tools).

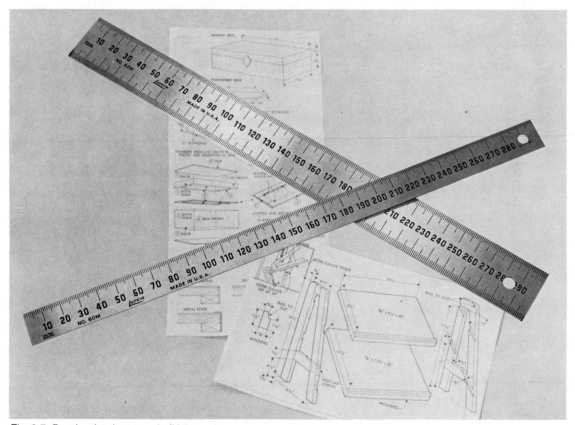

Fig. 8-7. Bench rules (courtesy Lufkin).

Fig. 8-8. Take care when measuring.

TAPES

I used to hate tape measures. Things have changed for the better. Tape measures in sizes up to 25 feet almost all have automatic returns on them and good, strong springs that last through years of hard use. Virtually, all such tape measures have a blade-locking feature so that once you take a measurement you can transfer it from the measured section to the workpiece without having the blade retract and having to be pulled out again. My recent experience with shorter tapes (two 25-foot Stanley Power lock IIs) has been excellent. These tapes (Figs. 8-8 and 8-9) have the last 7 or so feet of the blade stiffened so that you can measure fairly wide gaps without assistance.

Black on yellow has improved marking visibility in almost all brands. I know of no brand that doesn't also offer several models with both English and metric markings. Sizes range from 6 to 25 feet in retractable tapes. Blade widths will vary from a half inch to a full inch. On almost all tape measures (Figs. 8-10 through 8-16), all you need do is add the size of the case to the measurement shown on the tape to get a correct measurement.

Longer steel tapes come in a wide variety. Lufkin offers a 100-foot tape, the Banner in a 150-foot length, and the Artisan Diameter in 240-foot length. For exceptional jobs such as engineering and surveying Lufkin makes Pioneer models in lengths to 500 feet. Lufkin's Artisan tree tape has a sharp hook at the end to bite into bark and on one side converts the circumference of a tree to diameter.

No matter what type of tape you choose to use, there is always one unavoidable rule

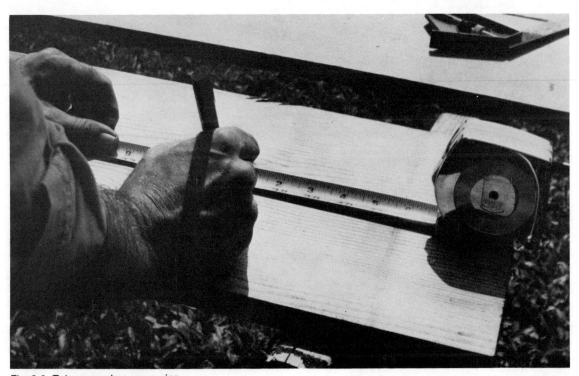

Fig. 8-9. Take care when measuring.

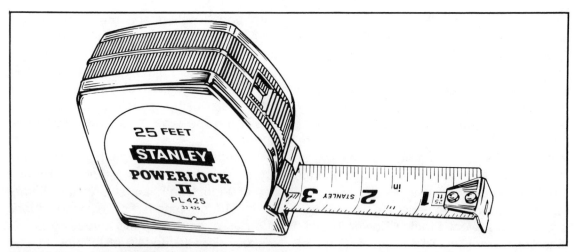

Fig. 8-10. Stanley's Powerlock II, 25 foot tape.

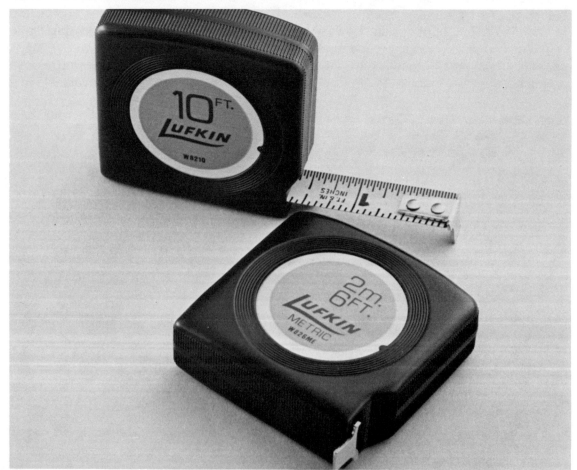

Fig. 8-11. Lufkin Economy 6- and 10-foot tapes.

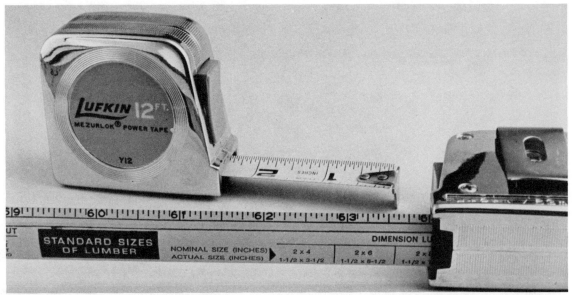

Fig. 8-12. Lufkin Mezurlok 12-foot tape.

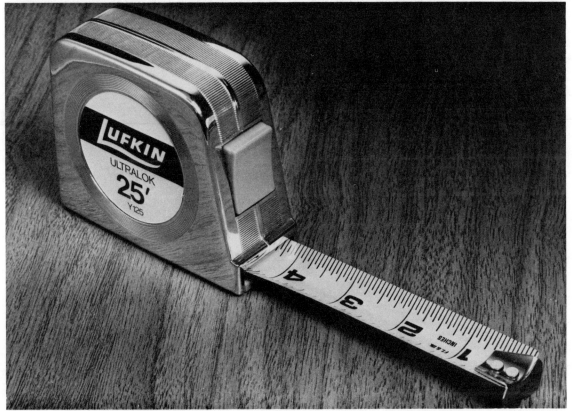

Fig. 8-13. Lufkin Ultralok 25-foot tape.

Fig. 8-14. Lufkin Economy tape in use.

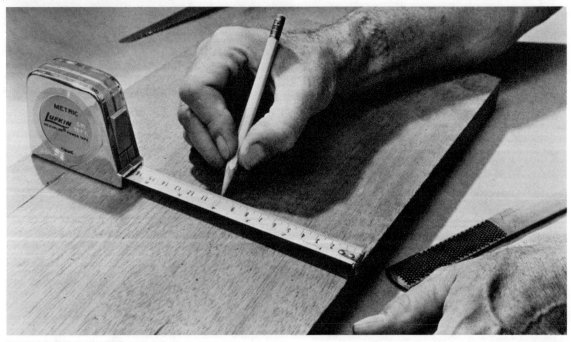

Fig. 8-15. Lufkin Mezurlok tape in use.

in taking any measurement: always take the measurement twice. If the second measurement doesn't agree with the first, check the setting of the end of the tape, or the rule, and measure a third time. Doing so can save a lot of wasted material over a period of time.

SQUARES

The try square came into existence fairly recently, around 1760 or so in England, and since then quite a number of variations on the theme have been developed. The primary carpenters' square is the try square with a blade that can range in length from 6 to 12 inches. Today, the stock might be hardwood, cast iron or, sometimes, aluminum. The stock might have a 45-degree angle for marking miter cuts or it might be set just for 90-degree cuts. The blade generally will be unmarked in any way.

The try square is used to mark a line at right angles to the edge of a board to be cut or joined. When the joint is made, the square is used to check that the joint forms an accurate 90-degree angle. The try square is also used to check work being planed square, but you'll first need to plane one true side so that it can be used as a starting point. At present, I'm using a Stanley Professional try square and I find it excellent. It has a metal handle and I can't imagine anything, short of a concrete block falling on it, knocking it out of square. See Figs. 8-17 and 8-18.

The carpenters', or framing, square is one of the handiest marking and measuring tools around. It is also one of the least likely to be found in the home workshop. All the tongue and blade markings seem to intimidate people. The squares (Figs. 8-19 and 8-20) are relatively inexpensive (generally under $20 for the best), but most home woodworkers pass them by even when they have framing work to do.

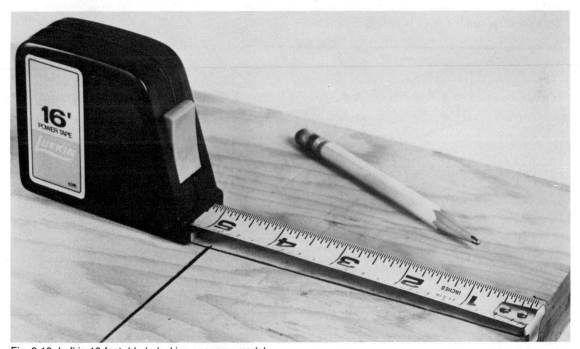

Fig. 8-16. Lufkin 16-foot, blade-locking economy model.

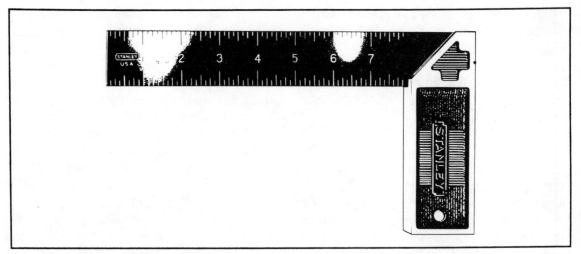

Fig. 8-17. Try square (courtesy Stanley Tools).

Basically, the framing square is used to mark rafters for framing a house, but it is also used to mark angles for building staircases. It can also be used for similar projects. The carpenters' square is also handy for checking the square of relatively large framed structures. I last used mine for checking the square of a deck I was building.

The square is of one-piece steel or aluminum. With proper care (don't hammer it or drive over it) a square should last pretty near a lifetime. Both the tongue and the blade are marked in English or metric sizes, or both, and some have various tables that are of use in working out angles and problems.

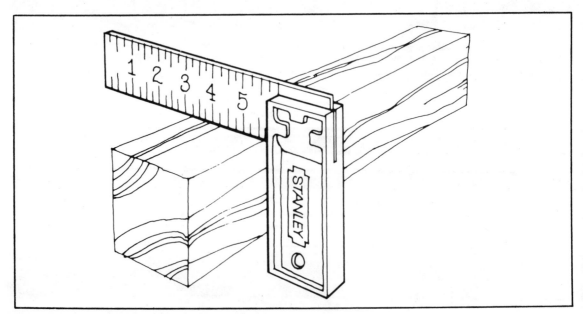

Fig. 8-18. Using a try square (courtesy Stanley Tools).

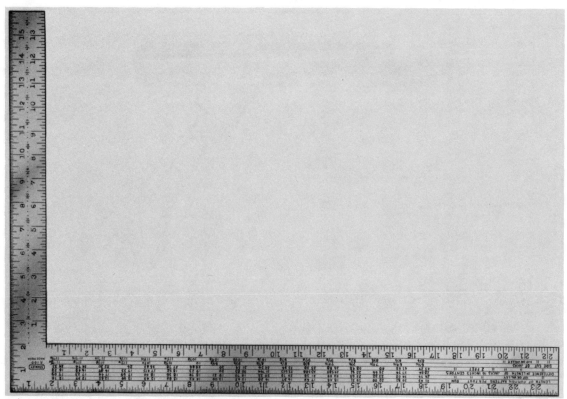

Fig. 8-19. Carpenter's square (courtesy Stanley Tools).

Inexpensive models, still accurate and good, can be bought for about $5. If you foresee putting up any kind of large frame or building a staircase, this is a tool that will probably prove indispensible.

T-bevels, or sliding T-bevels, have a blade with a slot along about half its length, and a handle (or stock) that has a locking screw passing through the slot. The T-bevel is another tool that is handy but, seldom found in the average person's home workshop. It is handy in areas such as home renovation. Should a roof rafter need to be replaced, you can take the angle off with the T bevel and transfer it to new stock without having to do a lot of complex figuring. The T bevel can also be set to a known angle by using a protractor. See Figs. 8-21 through 8-23.

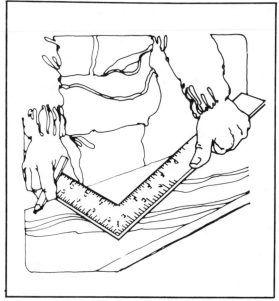

Fig. 8-20. Using a carpenter's square (courtesy Stanley Tools).

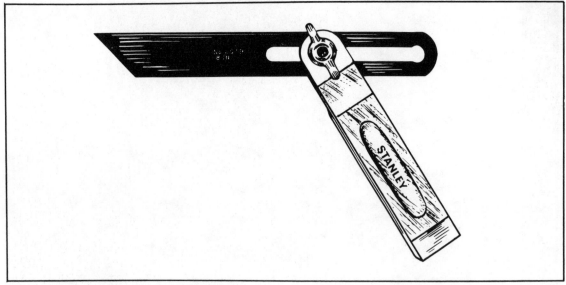

Fig. 8-21. Sliding T-bevel (courtesy Stanley Tools).

The center square is a tool that not many people use. It is used to find the center of a round wooden section or a piece of turned wood. You begin by placing the square against the wooden piece and making a mark. Move it about a third of a way around and make a second mark through the first mark. If you need to be dead accurate (as when centering something for doweling blind or for placing on a lathe for final shaping), make a third mark. See Fig. 8-24.

The combination square comes in several forms: some have grooved blades, some are slotted, and most have semiaccu-

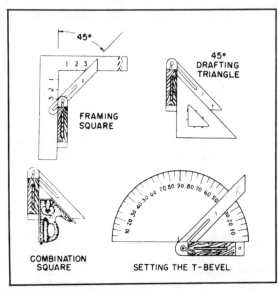

Fig. 8-22. Setting the T-bevel.

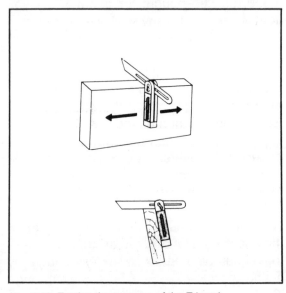

Fig. 8-23. Testing the trueness of the T-bevel.

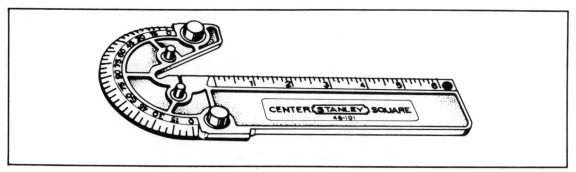

Fig. 8-24. Center square (courtesy Stanley Tools).

Fig. 8-25. Combination square (courtesy Sears, Roebuck and Co.).

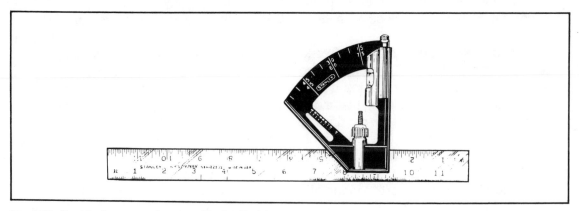

Fig. 8-26. Combination square (courtesy Stanley Tools).

Fig. 8-27. Combination square (courtesy Stanley Tools).

rate bubble levels. All of them have great utility. See Figs. 8-25, 8-26, and 8-27. In preference over most other tools, when cutting wood for framing a house, I use a combination square. The accuracy of a try square is not essential. If you're ⅛ inch out from one end of a 3-foot cabinet to another, it's likely to spoil the job. But the same miss on a 36-foot long house won't be noticeable. My mother's place is out about 5 inches overall. This is truly sloppy building, but it only becomes obvious as my brother and I installed levelled aluminum siding.

The combination square makes marking 45 degree angles easy and accurate because you can slide the handle or head

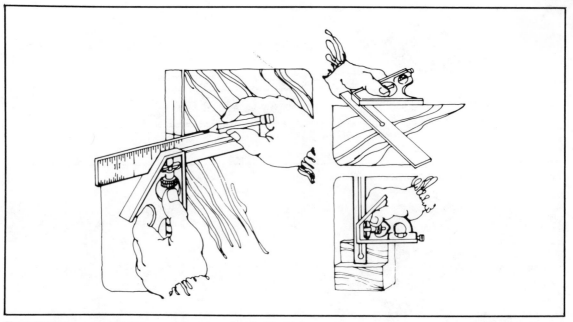

Fig. 8-28. Using a combination square (courtesy Stanley Tools).

along the blade. Although it can be used as a level, don't bet too much on real accuracy (the indication should be close in a new, quality square).

If you decide to build your own workbench and make the joints mortise and tenon, without running the mortises all the way through the stock, the sliding blade can be used to check the depth of the mortise (as can almost any rule that will fit into the mortise, in combination with a straight piece of scrap wood). See Fig 8-28.

The combination square, especially after extensive use, is not as accurate as the top quality try square. But it is accurate enough in all its aspects for general building work. You must make sure that the locking nut is tight when you use the square. I have missed on that more than once and, as a result, ended up without square cuts. It is one of the less expensive tools available. A top-of-the-line model should be in every home toolbox. Make sure that when you buy your combination square the head or handle is made of plastic. Those do not last as long and are not as accurate to start.

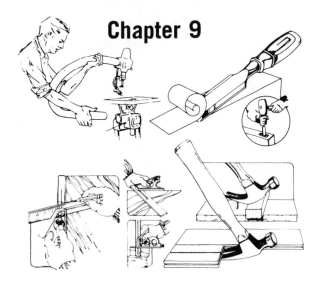

Chapter 9

Braces and Bits

ODAY'S BRACE AND REMOVABLE BIT IS THE result of about four centuries of development. Until about the turn of this century, most braces were made of wood into which a steel bit was fitted. The present chuck on the brace came into existence before that, but it took some time to catch on and a bit more time for the brace to become steel with a wooden handle.

Augur bits are generally available today in two patterns. One has a solid core, called the Irwin type, and was invented in 1884. The Jennings spiral pattern was invented 29 years earlier. Expandable bits seem to date from slightly before the turn of the century. The brace is one tool that doesn't have an extremely wide price range. The least expensive sells for about $25 and the most expensive costs under $50.

A brace is a tool that you won't need unless you plan to do a fair amount of drilling on sites where there is no electricity. When it's needed it's essential. The brace itself costs no more than a good electric drill (usually not as much), but the augur bits—if you must have a large selection—can set you back a large sum of money. Stanley's Russell Jennings double-twist set of all 13 available sizes cost nearly $170.

A brace applies torque to the bit when you rotate the frame in, usually, a clockwise direction. (Like most things, I'm reasonably certain that someone, sometime, somewhere, has made both brace and bit that work backwards. Actually, only the bit would need to be made to cut backwards because the brace can be rotated in either direction.) The offset handle on the brace frame moves through what is known as a *sweep*. The average sweep is about 10 inches. For a bit

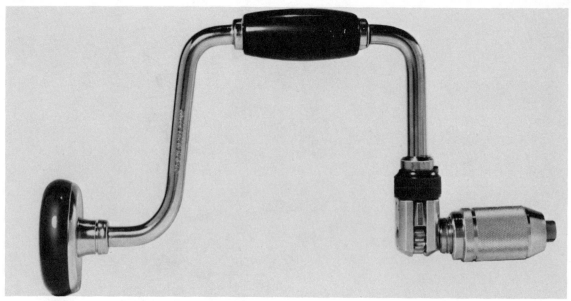

Fig. 9-1. Open ratchet bit brace (courtesy Stanley Tools).

over $54, Stanley has a 12-inch sweep brace in its Professional line. The slightly lower-quality, open-ratchet model is about $20 less in 12-inch sweep size. Stanley's least expensive model (under $20) comes with a 10-inch sweep.

Today, all braces seem to be fitted with ratchets. That means you don't have to complete the sweep if you are in a confined space. See Figs. 9-1 and 9-2.

Short sweep braces are also easily found. Garrett Wade offers one with a 6-inch sweep. Where work space is confined, you might consider using one of these. In most

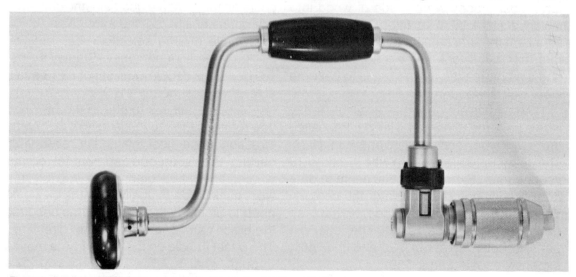

Fig. 9-2. Closed ratchet bit brace (courtesy Sears, Roebuck and Co.).

cases, a 10- or 12-inch sweep would be just fine.

The chucks on most braces are designed to fit the square-shank, low-speed auger bits made for hand drilling, Garrett Wade offers a four-jaw chuck brace that will also accept round shank bits.

Give careful consideration to frequency of use when selecting a brace. The occasional user simply does not need the built-in sturdiness of the models such as Stanley's Professional 100 Plus bit brace. It is possible to go with the Handyman Stanley brace for under $20 in such cases.

Solid-core Irwin bits cost just over half the price of the Jennings double-twist models. Because of that, they should receive first consideration for your tool box. If faster, cleaner cutting is needed, consider the Jennings pattern. Individual Irwin solid-core bits are available for just under $6 each. The individual double-twist Jennings bits cost from just over $10 to over $14.

I have half a dozen Stanley solid-core bits. If I were making a lot of cabinets or other such work, I would then feel it necessary to obtain some Jennings pattern bits. For drilling holes through joists and studs, the Irwin solid-core models are superbly helpful. See Fig. 9-3.

From this point, you might want to move to drilling holes larger than 1 inch (the maximum size available for both Jennings and Irwin styles). The expansive bit then comes into play. Stanley makes two models available; one will bore holes from ⅝ of an inch to 1¾ of an inch and the second goes from ⅞ of an inch to 3 inches. Neither of these bits is inexpensive—one is about $17 and the other about $19—but I would recommend the larger of the two if you already have a few bits. You'll probably have some that fit the sizes from ⅝ of an inch to ⅞ of an

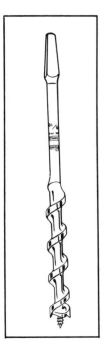

Fig. 9-3. Solid core (Irwin) bit (courtesy Stanley Tools).

inch. See Fig. 9-4.

Bits, whether for bit braces or electric drills, are no place to skip on quality. You'll want to do the job cleanly and well, with as little labor output as possible, so use the best quality bits. Countersink bits are also available. Sears offers on in ⅝-inch size and Stanley's is ¾ of an inch in diameter. See Figs. 9-5 through 9-12.

I am not a great admirer of hand drills, but at times they can serve a purpose. For drilling pilot holes, for instance, when a cabinet is being built, there is no tool that does the job better. (The hand drill, after only a bit of practice, is easier to control.) Hand drills have a gear drive, with the handle driving one large gear that will then drive one or two smaller gears that transfer the action to the chuck.

While it is possible to spend as much as $50 for a hand drill, I see little purpose in going beyond $20 unless it is for extended cabinetmaking. For occasional use, there

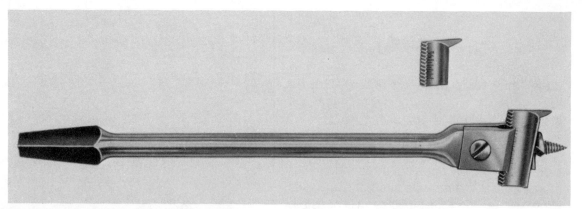

Fig. 9-4. Expandable bit (courtesy Stanley Tools).

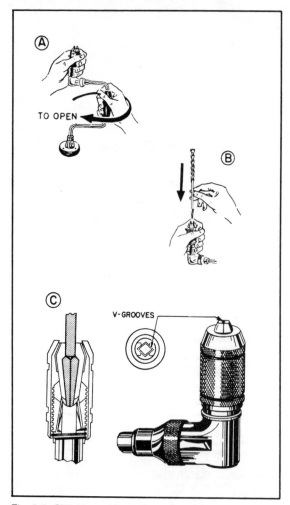

Fig. 9-5. Chucking a bit.

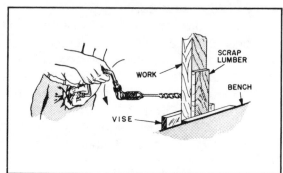

Fig. 9-6. Scrap lumber stops splintering.

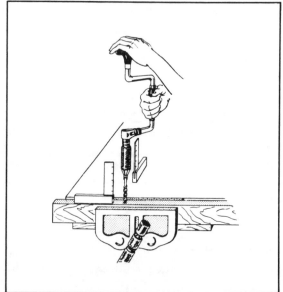

Fig. 9-7. Getting a perpendicular hole.

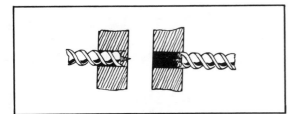

Fig. 9-8. Finishing hole from the opposite side.

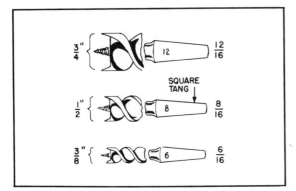

Fig. 9-9. Size markings for bits.

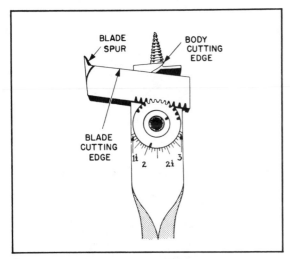

Fig. 9-10. Expansive bit size markings.

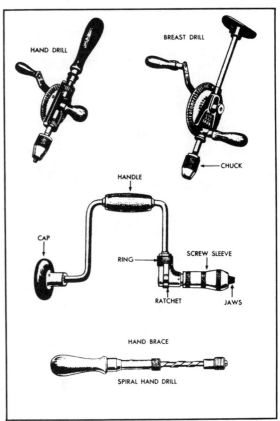

Fig. 9-11. Braces and drills.

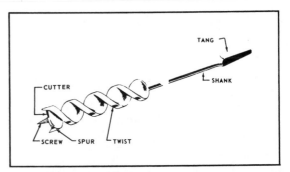

Fig. 9-12. Nomenclature of a Jennings style bit.

are hand drills available for as little as $9. In such limited-use cases, I would go with the middle range and select either Stanley's 03-222 model or Sears Craftsman 4231, both of which sell for under $20. Both include eight drills that are stored in the hollow handles of the drills and both have a ¼-inch capacity chuck. See Fig. 9-13.

Push drills are tools shown in Figs. 9-14 and 9-15. I have never been able to figure out what they can do that another tool can't do as well or better.

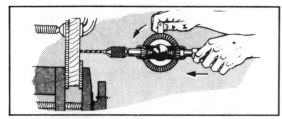

Fig. 9-13. Drilling with a hand drill.

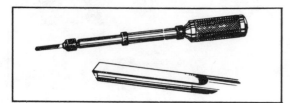

Fig. 9-14. Push drill and point.

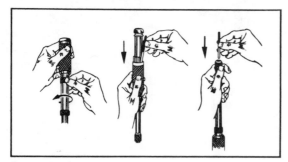

Fig. 9-15. Setting up a push drill.

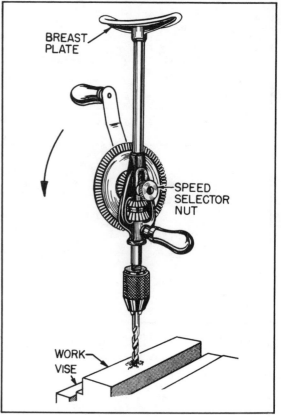

BREAST PLATE

SPEED SELECTOR NUT

WORK VISE

Fig. 9-16. Breast drill.

Using a brace and bit or a hand drill is a relatively straightforward proposition, but there are a few tips that can aid you in drilling clean, straight holes. First, make sure the bit is firmly fitted in the chuck (a slipping bit is maddening). If you're boring a vertical hole, set your try square near the hole (with a brace and bit, not so near as to slap it as you make the turns) so that you can more easily make certain the hole is being drilled at an actual 90-degree angle to the wood surface. Place pressure on the head with one hand and use your other hand to turn the handle. For horizontal drilling, where the work is low enough, place the head of the brace in your stomach. Hold it firmly with one hand, apply pressure, and twist the handle with your other hand. For higher work, you'll have to use your hand only to apply pressure to the bit and brace.

If you're drilling a deep hole, especially with solid core bits, you'll have to occasionally reverse action and back the bit out to clear the hole.

To avoid splintering of the backside of the hole when the drill bit breaks through, you can clamp on a piece of waste stock. When I do this, I like to insert a sheet of paper between the two pieces of stock so that I know when I've gotten through. Then I don't waste effort drilling on through the waste.

Keep the bits sharp and free of rust. Your drilling should go easily and quickly. See Fig. 9-16.

Chapter 10

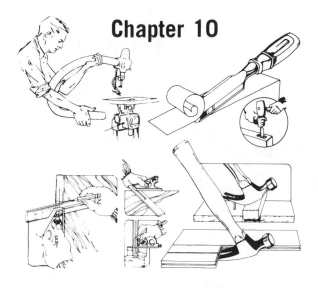

Planes

ABOUT 1860, STANLEY WAS ONE OF THE first companies to begin making metal planes. Until that time, most planes were made of wood, with metal parts as needed. At the outset, all woodworker's made their own planes. By the end of the eighteenth century, most planes were made by tool manufacturers. Today, you have a choice of wooden or metal planes in a great many styles and sizes.

Unfortunately, prices have escalated in recent years in both types. The Craftsman plane I bought for about $9 in 1963 now costs about $30, plus shipping. When a plane is needed, you have little choice but to get one and do the required job. There are jobs that planes can do that you otherwise can only do with power tools even more costly (if the work being planed isn't portable, a jointer/planer isn't of any help either).

Planes are named and sized in accordance with the jobs they are to do. Bench and block planes are designed for general-surface smoothing and squaring. The jack plane (Fig. 10-1) is primarily for smoothing with the grain, as along board edges (it is a type of bench plane). Sole length is the primary difference in bench planes. The jack plane sole length is about 14 inches, the smooth plane is a bit over 9 inches, and the jointer plane will be from 20 inches to 2 feet long.

The block plane is smaller and it is primarily used for smoothing end grains. It can be used for all small planing jobs. Block planes are usually from 6 to 7 inches long. (Figs. 10-2 and 10-3.)

Another notable difference between bench and block planes is the angle of plane iron or blade. In bench planes, the angle is

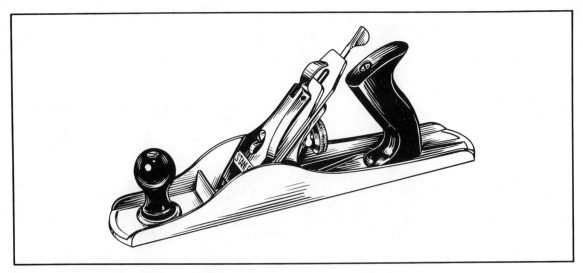

Fig. 10-1. Jack plane (courtesy Stanley Tools).

generally about 45 degrees. In block planes, the angle will be from 21 degrees down to as low as 12 degrees when a really fine finish is needed on end grains. Stanley's standard block plane uses an angle of 21 degrees. Both of Stanley's low-angle planes use the 12-degree angle.

A good Stanley smooth plane will cost a bit over $25 and a low-angle block plane will run just a bit under that price. There are plenty of other versions available.

Rabbeting planes are for use in close quarters and to cut rabbet joints. Many come with guides to aid in making rabbets. The cost is generally around $50 for a tool that is exceptionally useful in many types of cabinetmaking joinery. The bench rabbet plane is similar in construction to other planes of the bench type except that the blade goes all the way across the sole plate to allow for the cutting of rabbets. See Fig. 10-4.

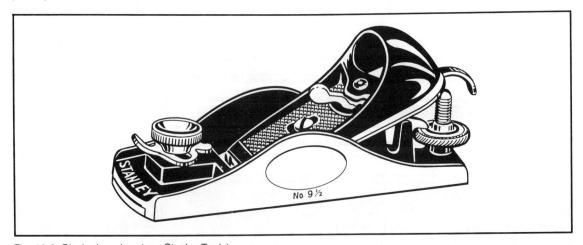

Fig. 10-2. Block plane (courtesy Stanley Tools).

130

Fig. 10-3. Block plane (courtesy Sears, Roebuck and Co.).

Toothing planes are a bit harder to find and not really as essential to the toolbox as other types. They tend to be about 8 inches or a bit longer. The blade has small ridges, or teeth, and it is set nearly upright in the plane's body. It is used to rough up wood surfaces before gluing down veneers or plastic laminates. It is not as useful as other planes simply because a variety of abrasives are available to do the job at far less cost.

A circular plane has a flexible sole and can be used on convex or concave surfaces. Look for alternative tools for working on such surfaces. The only one of these I have seen in recent years cost over $105. That is a lot of money to pay for smoothing a table edge or flattening the bottom of a bowl. See Figs. 10-5 through 10-9.

SPOKESHAVES AND DRAWKNIVES

The spokeshave can be described as a kind of two-handled plane with a very short bottom and a wide throat. It's greatest use is in smoothing irregular or curved surfaces. Most can be obtained with either straight or curved bottoms. The prices tend to be reasonable, between $15 and $20, and the cutters are about 2 inches or so wide. Stanley's 151SS has a 2⅛-inch wide cutter as does the model offered by Garrett Wade.

To use the spokeshave you hold one handle in each hand and place it on the work. Try to keep your thumbs on the back edges of the handle; this gives the best control. Push the spokeshave away from you just as

Fig. 10-4. Rabbeting plane (courtesy Stanley Tools).

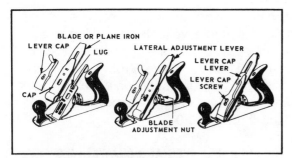

Fig. 10-5. Bench plane parts.

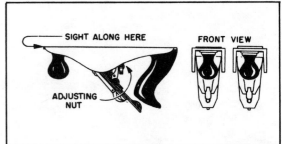

Fig. 10-7. Up and down adjustment.

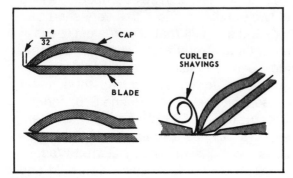

Fig. 10-6. Plane iron (blade) and cap.

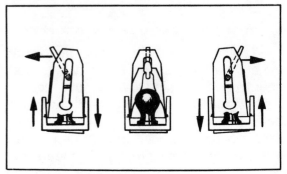

Fig. 10-8. Lateral adjustment.

you would a plane, and stop when the grain direction changes in the curve (usually about midway, but this can differ). Next, work from the other end. Staying with the grain direction in this manner helps to prevent splits from tearing away from the work (Fig. 10-10).

The drawknife is primarily used to rough shape wood to get it ready for final planing. It consists of a flat blade that has tangs bent down at each end to take wooden handles.

Blade length is usually about 10 inches, but other sizes can be found with a bit of searching.

The drawknife is used by angling it on the work to control cut depth, and then pulling it toward you. It is best to cut only with the grain and the drawknife can be used on convex and concave surfaces as well as flat surfaces. On convex surfaces keep the bevel on top. On concave surfaces face the bevel down into the work.

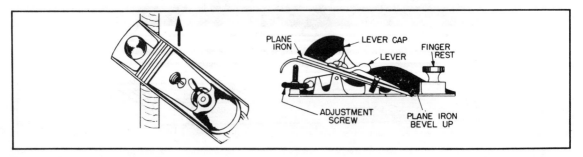

Fig. 10-9. Block plane nomenclature.

Fig. 10-10. Spokeshave (courtesy Stanley Tools).

The inshave is another version of a drawknife, but one with a curved blade that is useful for scooping out chair seats and bowls. It is used in the same manner as the drawknife, but it can only be used on concave surfaces. Inshaves cost a bit over $20. Drawknives cost about $32. Make sure you have a need for the tools.

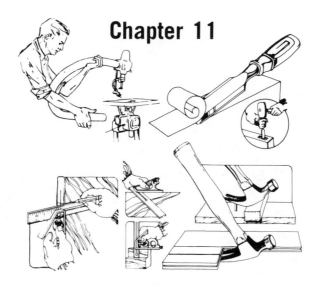

Chapter 11

Axes and Splitting Tools

AXES, ADZES, HATCHETS, AND FROES ARE all splitting or wedge-type tools (Fig. 11-1). Unfortunately, the froe, one of the tools needed for splitting wood shakes, is exceptionally hard to locate today. The only possible way to get a froe these days seems to be to make your own from an automobile leaf spring. The spring must be strongly heated and bent in a fairly complicated manner, then welded, and finally ground to an edge.

Axes are handy tools and there are a great many variations on the theme. Catalogs from Stanley, Plumb and other companies tend to show one- or two-head variations in single-bit axes. Generally, you will find head patterns in Dayton, Jersey and Michigan styles. Double-bitted axes are usually in Michigan or Western styles.

The Dayton single-bit axhead is a rela-

tively slender-head design when viewed from the side. Viewed from the top, it is a bit wider than some other designs. The Jersey design has a straight-top edge with a sort of hook back on the bottom edge. Viewed from the side, the blade and head are broader than the Dayton. The Michigan pattern is similar to the Dayton pattern, but a bit broader in side view. The double-bitted Michigan pattern has a slight concavity at the top edge and a much steeper inward slope at the bottom edge. The Western double-bitted axe curves toward the handle at top and bottom of the head only slightly and has slightly narrower blades, or bits, than the Michigan pattern.

The selection of bit style depends on the work intended. For limbing, a moderately light sharp axe with a fairly narrow poll is best. For heavier chopping and cutting

Fig. 11-1. Wedge-type tools. Splitting maul, splitting wedge, and sledge (courtesy Stanley Tools).

chores, heavier axes with thicker polls do a better job. For wood splitting, I prefer a splitting maul. Axes such as Plumb's Tasmanian-head model, at weights of from four to 4½ pounds, are best. The thicker the poll the better.

Axe handles come in straight shapes and curved shapes, and they are generally made of hickory. I tend to prefer the curved styles in a 3-foot length, but shorter people might well prefer the readily available 32-inch lengths, especially with lighter axes. Double-bitted axes come only with straight handles. In areas where hickory is hard to locate, you might find some axe handles of white oak. A few people prefer ash because its springiness is said to absorb the shock of impact better.

I've used ash, and like it, but I have never used an oak handle. I have seen, but never used, replacement axe handles of fiberglass.

Double-bitted axes serve a purpose, but there is little use for one in and around the average person's home. The two edges mean less sharpening in the woods. The logger is stopped less often, and, in addition, one edge can be sharpened for fine cutting while the other gets a thicker edge for all heavy cutting jobs. In general, the double-bitted axe (Fig. 11-2) is a bit more dangerous in the hands of the nonexpert and it isn't really needed for work that most of us do.

With a broadax, either the eye in the head is offset or an offset handle is used so that the handle can be swung in close when smoothing logs into beams. The blade is beveled on only one side. The result of using a broad axe to trim beams can be seen in many, many old homes in this country. The lighter broad hatchet is not as effective, nor is it as fast, but it can be useful for providing a rustic look to exposed beams, mantels, and other items in a house.

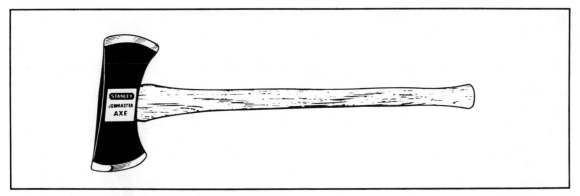

Fig. 11-2. Double bitted axe (courtesy Stanley Tools).

HATCHETS

Hatchets are nothing more than small axes used with one hand instead of two. Even the belt, or camp, axe is a hatchet. Half hatchets (those with the poll designed as a hammer) are available in many styles, with either both steel or wood handles. Plumb offers a fiberglass-handled model or two (actually one model, but different finishes). Plumb also offers a broad hatchet, lath hatchets, wallboard hatchets, shingling hatchets, box hatchets, and a car builder's hatchet (to me, it looks like a more or less common half hatchet).

Stanley offers half hatchets, an excel-lent shingling hatchet, and a rig builder's hatchet. See Fig. 11-3. The rig builder's hatchet is a version of the half hatchet. Usu-ally, it has a checkered face on the ham-merhead shaped poll. Shingling hatchets have very narrow blades (my Stanley mea-sures 2¼ inches at its widest point) and a poll that allows nailing the shingles. There is also a series of holes up the front edge of the head with a screw pin insert that allows you to determine the correct weather exposure of wood shakes or shingles. See Fig. 11-4.

ADZES

An adze resembles an axe with the head set

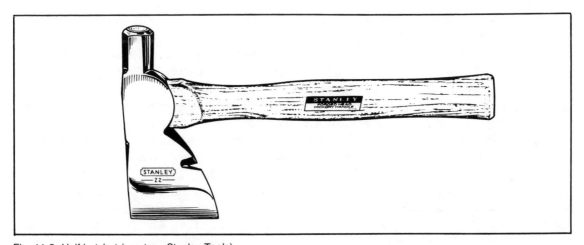

Fig. 11-3. Half hatchet (courtesy Stanley Tools).

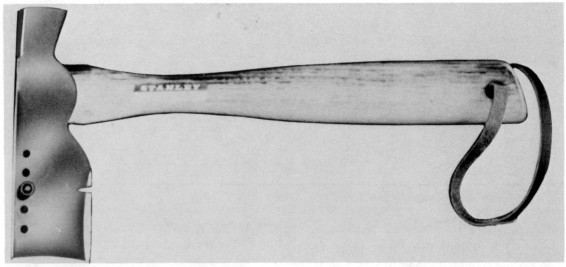

Fig. 11-4. Shingling hatchet (courtesy Stanley Tools).

at a right angle to the handle. That requires a different method of attaching the handle. The adze head has a tapered eye and the handle is inserted from above (instead of from below as with an axe). No wedges are needed to hold the handle on as the force of using the adze wedges the tapered handle end firmly into the similarly tapered adze eye.

The handle is unfinished hickory. Today, I believe the adze might be classified as more a fun or hobby tool than one most people would use seriously. Nevertheless, it could prove very handy in smoothing the top surfaces of logs if you were building a log cabin (to allow for a snug fit).

Adzes are known to old-timers as shin barkers. Stand on the log to be smoothed, and swing the adze in an arc down toward your feet using a pendulum action. There's a lot of nonsense passed about that old-time adze users could actually split the soles of their shoes—deliberately—without touching their socks, never mind their toes. That may well have been true for men who used the tool day in and day out, but anyone trying the

same thing today had better call the local shrink and see if its possible to find out why he or she has a desire to mangle the toebones.

The best method for the occasional adze user is to stand astride the work. Use a pendulum swing and use your thigh as a stop to control the depth of the swing. If you practice enough before doing any serious work, you'll be able to take off good-sized chunks or just barely shave the wood as you need.

Plumb and Garrett Wade sell adze heads and handles separately. It may well be because of the unfamiliarity of most people with the tool. Getting it in two pieces immediately indicates how it goes together. If the handle breaks, it will be far easier to get the remains out of the eye.

Sculptors' adzes are one-handed tools. They are not much less expensive than a full-scale adze. Garrett Wade offers two models; one has a straight blade and one has a curved blade. The blades are 2 inches wide instead of the 4-inch width of my carpenters' adze. The handles are 8½ inches long rather than 33 inches. Incidentally, using the carpenters' adze will usually require you to adjust the handle length. This is especially important if you plan to use the old technique of foot adzing or standing on the log being smoothed.

The sculptors' adzes are used when you're getting ready to work on a large-scale wood section and a lot of wood needs to be removed before chisels, gouges, rasps, and riffles are employed. As with the carpenters' adze, a short swing (in scale: use about a foot-long swing with the full-sized adze and possibly a bit more than half that with the smaller tools) is best. It is also best in both cases—as with most tools with sharp edges and fairly heavy heads—to let the tool do most of the work.

FROE

The froe has been around for a long time. This continued use for a couple of millenia or more because it is a lot quicker to split wood along the grain than to saw it. This funny-looking tool has a cutting edge that appears to be on the wrong side of the blade. It is an L-shaped tool with the 15-or-so-inch blade making up the bottom of the L. The cutting edge is on the bottom of the blade. The top leg of the L is the handle, usually about a foot long. A froe is used with a wooden mallet that is slammed into the top edge of the blade after the sharpened edge is placed on the wood to be split.

Billets are first cut to the length needed for your purposes. For cedar shakes, figure a weather exposure of about 8 inches for a 2-foot long shake (so billets should be cut to 2-foot lengths). Square it off with the froe. Take your time to get it as square as possible. Then split from one side in if the shakes are to be the same size as the billet (to prevent curling, it is best to keep your shakes

to 5 to 6 inches in width. You might have to trim a bit before going right on through the billet or you can later split the large shakes to smaller sizes with the froe.

Woods other than cedar can be used, where cedar is not available. But don't expect to get the same durability from, say, white pine as you would get from cedar. Any pine or fir used for shakes should be soaked overnight in a penta preservative; a week would be better.

Making a froe isn't all that difficult. An oxyacetylene torch is almost essential to the job, but you might be able to do it with a hacksaw. You'll want to find a junkyard with some loose-leaf springs lying about. Pick a spring about 2½ to 3 inches wide. Take it home and cut off a section at least 18 inches long, including the spring shackle. That's easier than heating the metal and looping it back for a handle eye. Make sure the spring is the one with the shackle eye on it.

Now, you'll need a grindstone and some patience. I would use a whetstone to keep from altering the metal temper any more than is essential. Grind the edge of the spring to about a 15-degree angle on both sides and polish things up a bit with a good whetstone. Insert a handle at least a foot long, and preferably a bit longer, in the shackle eye so that the sharp edge of the blade is on the side opposite the handle. Drive in a couple of metal axe-eye wedges and you've got your froe.

The job can be done with a hacksaw, but you can bet on hours of cutting before getting through the spring steel, which is very tough, and you'll also go through a rather large number of hacksaw blades in the process. If you haven't got welding equipment, it would be worthwhile to take the spring to a local welding shop and have them do the job.

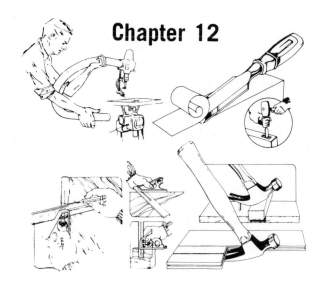

Chapter 12

Rasps and Files

FILES ARE USEFUL TO THE WOODWORK-er not just for smoothing wood, but also for sharpening various tools from chains on chain saws to drill bits and saws. Today we have really excellent, and in some cases innovative, files that can serve a variety of material-removing purposes, almost regardless of the material being worked.

In general, files are used for smoothing and shaping operations where a great deal of material needn't be removed. Some coarser rasps and tools, such as Stanley's Surform, can take off a good deal of material when such work is needed. See Figs. 12-1 and 12-2.

The most common of the metal-cutting files is the flat file used to smooth down flat surfaces. Such files, in the smaller sizes, are needed to sharpen larger circular-saw blades, axes, adzes, and other such tools.

Round files without a taper are used to sharpen chain saw chains. These are specifically designed for the purpose and they are often sold by the manufacturer of the chain saw. Chain saw tooth sizes vary with tooth pitch. For small saws, using ¼-inch pitch chain, begin filing with a 5/32 of an inch chain file. After the chain has had 50 percent of the tooth removed (don't remove it in one filing unless teeth are chipped that badly!), drop back to a ⅛ of an inch file. For ⅜ inch chain, start with a 7/32 of an inch file. After wear amounts to 50 percent, drop back to a 13/64 of an inch file. Chain designated .404 also needs a 7/32 of an inch file. The ½-inch chain (used on only the largest professional chain saws) requires a ¼-inch file. All filing should be done at an angle of about 35 degrees to the guide bar surface. It is probably best that you use some form of guide to help

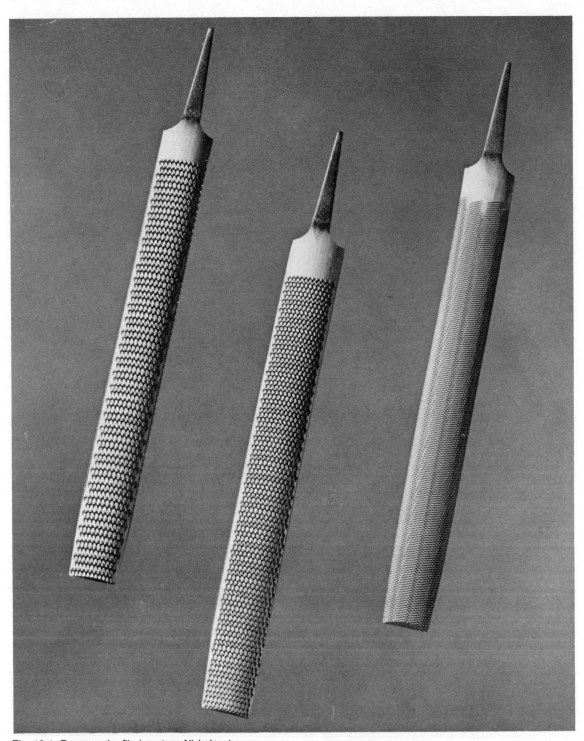
Fig. 12-1. Rasps and a file (courtesy Nicholson).

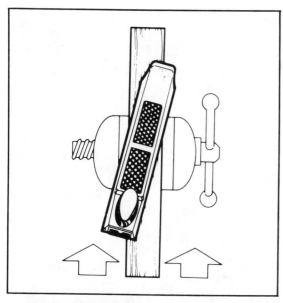

Fig. 12-2. Stanley Surform.

hold that angle unless you file chains almost daily.

Handsaws, both rip and crosscut, are sharpened with a triangular file. Nicholson (manufacturer of both files and handsaws) recommends, for a 5-tooth saw, that you use either a 7-inch regular taper file or a 6-inch heavy taper file. Five and a half teeth will need the same, while six teeth will move to either a 7-inch or 8-inch slim taper file. Seven teeth per inch on the handsaw will require a 6-inch or 7-inch slim taper file or a 9-inch double ender. Eight teeth require the same or an 8-inch double slim taper. Nine teeth per inch will require that you change to a 6-inch extra slim taper. Ten teeth per inch need a 5-inch or 6-inch extra slim taper or a 6-inch double ender.

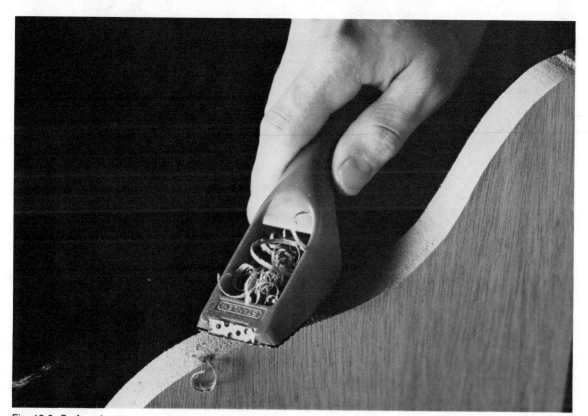

Fig. 12-3. Surform in use on wood (courtesy Stanley Tools).

Fig. 12-4. Surform in use on plastic (courtesy Stanley Tools).

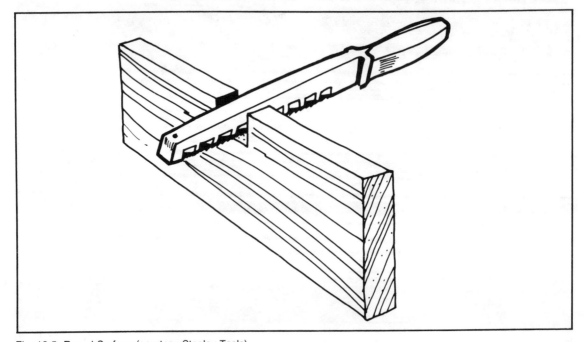

Fig. 12-5. Round Surform (courtesy Stanley Tools).

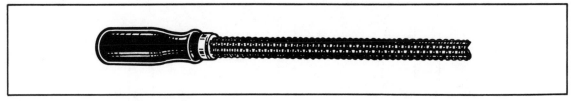

Fig. 12-6. Groove Surform (courtesy Stanley Tools).

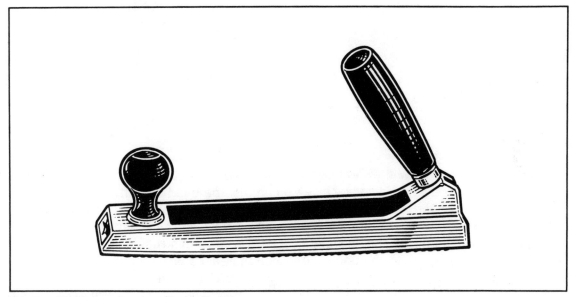

Fig. 12-7. Flat Surform (courtesy Stanley Tools).

Fig. 12-8. A Surform blade (courtesy Stanley Tools).

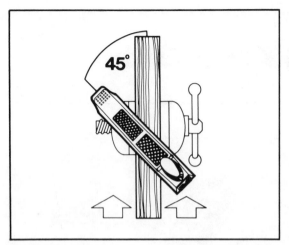

Fig. 12-9. To remove a maximum amount of material, hold the tool at a 45-degree angle to the direction of the stroke (courtesy Stanley Tools).

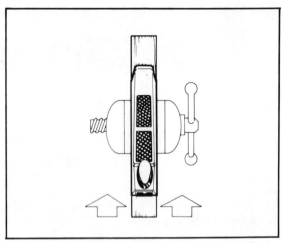

Fig. 12-11. Direct the tool parallel to the work surface (courtesy Stanley Tools).

When filing a handsaw, the saw must be held securely. If you don't want to buy a saw vise, simply clamp the saw in a regular woodworking vise between two 1×3 pieces of stock the same length as the saw blade. Keep the file dead level while sharpening the teeth.

Rasps have much larger teeth than do files, and the teeth are individually formed so

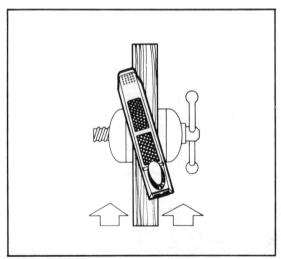

Fig. 12-10. To remove material and obtain a smooth surface, reduce the angle (courtesy Stanley Tools).

that slivers of wood are sliced off. Most rasps can also be used on soft metals. Stanley's Surform line of tools is a form of rasp, but it can be classified as a planing rasp because there is an opening behind each tooth so that soft material doesn't readily clog the blades (which are replaceable).

There are about eight models of Surform tools (I've got most of them and wouldn't be without them). For heavy duty work, where you have to take off a lot of material and use both hands, there's the model 21-296. If you only want to shave off a little material, you might consider the 21-299. For tight places and curved surfaces, consider the 21-115 Shaver. Then there's the 21-297 round model to open out holes and the 21-295 with 10-inch body for broad, flat surfaces. The Mini-File is useful in fine grooves and up at flush corners. The 21-285 has a rear handle that can be raised or lowered depending on the needs of the cut. See Figs. 12-3 through 12-8.

Unlike most standard rasps, you can get a variety of finishes with the Surform tools. If you want to take off a great deal of

Fig. 12-12. Move the tool over the work (courtesy Stanley Tools).

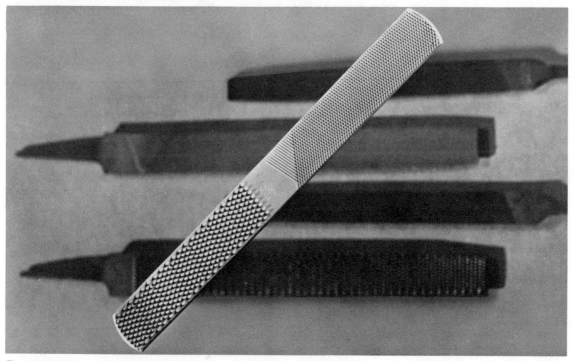

Fig. 12-13. Nicholson's four-way rasp/file (courtesy Cooper Tool Group).

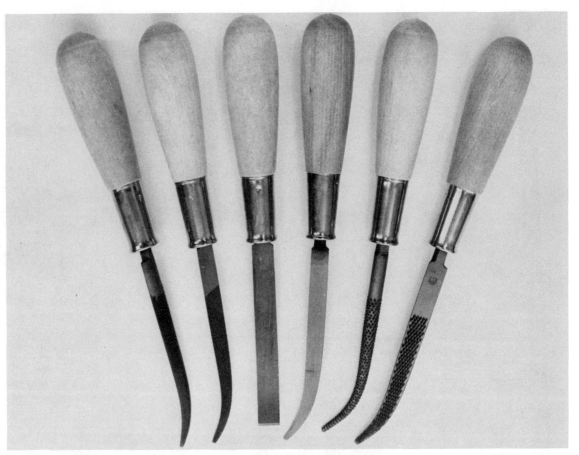

Fig. 12-14. Nicholson's riffler wood rasps and files (courtesy Cooper Tool Group).

material rapidly, use the tool at a 45-degree angle to work (Fig. 12-9). To get a slightly smoother finish and remove less material, simply reduce the angle (Fig. 12-10). For a well smoothed work surface, use the Surform parallel to the work surface (Fig. 12-11). If you want to get an almost polished effect on the work surface, use a slightly reverse angle as you move the tool over the work. See Figs. 12-12 through 12-14.

Like all other tools, files require at least a moderate amount of care to remain sharp and serviceable as long as possible. If the file teeth aren't protected, they'll loose their edge more rapidly than economy demands.

Therefore, files should be hung on a rack or stored in a drawer with wooden divisions. Keep the files away from water and grease. If a file has to be carried in a tool box, wrap it in a clean rag. The rag will serve to keep off oil from other tools and protect the teeth at the same time.

For standard files, use a file card or file brush to clean the teeth after each use. For your own safety, buy and install a file handle on every file that comes without one. Stanley's Surforms all have handles, but most standard files come without them. They generally have only a sharp tang extending from one end. That tang can really gouge a

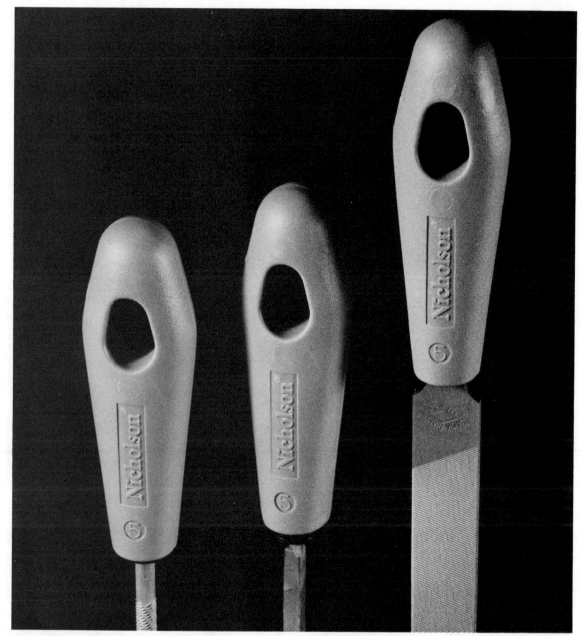

Fig. 12-15. You must use the proper-size file handles for safety (courtesy Nicholson).

chunk out of your hand if you should slip while using the file. It is even possible to get stabbed in the body with the tang. That sounds a bit more than a little odd, but I have seen it happen. Use file handles for safety. See Figs. 12-15 and 12-16.

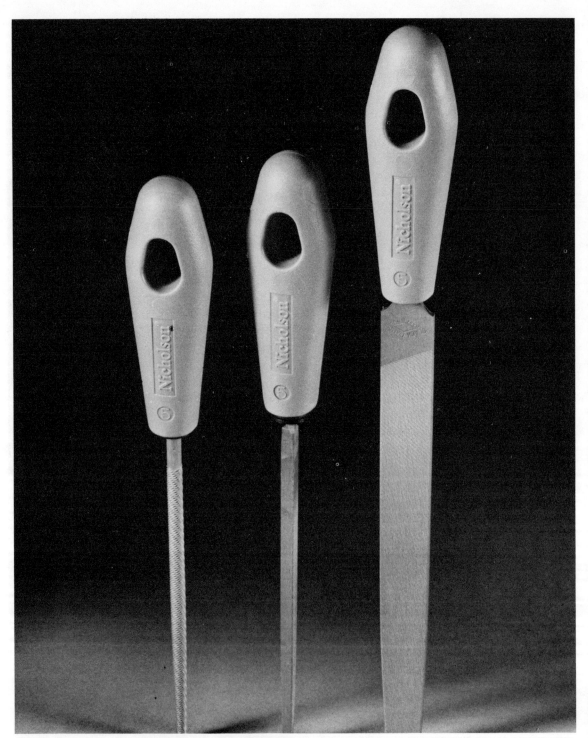
Fig. 12-16. Use the proper file handles (courtesy Nicholson).

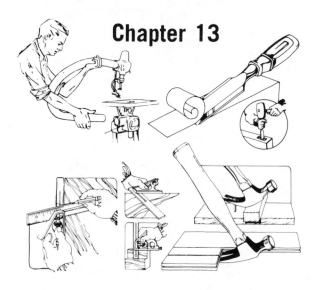

Chapter 13

Hammers

DIFFERENT HAMMERS ARE MEANT FOR DIFferent jobs, and there is little point in using the wrong hammer. While they are surely more expensive than they used to be—what isn't—even the best hammers (Fig. 13-1) aren't that costly. Prices for hammers don't seem to have escalated as much as some other tools. Some years ago, I bought a 28-ounce Craftsman framing hammer for about $10. Today, the same hammer sells for $17, plus shipping.

Most framing hammers weigh up to 22 ounces. That is more than sufficient for 99 percent of framing work. The standard 16-ounce claw hammer is overused by most people. It provides too much striking power for work such as molding and too little striking power for work such as framing and other heavy jobs. A check of Stanley's catalog shows they also carry two models that weigh 28 ounces.

Claw hammers are specifically designed for carpentry. They are made to do two jobs. Nailing is one job and the removal of partially started nails is the other. I emphasize the partially started nail. Even steel-handled hammers can be ruined if you try to yank out too large a nail that is driven nearly all the way. Nail pullers are made for that job.

The face of a quality nail hammer will be very slightly crowned with beveled edges. Some nail hammers with checked faces do not have the crown. Checked faces are handy when you are doing rough framing because they help to prevent nails from flying around due to slightly glancing blows. Checked faces are less useful for finish or

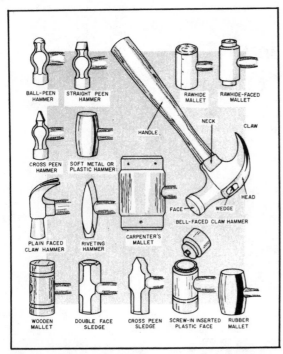

Fig. 13-1. Hammers and sledges.

lighter work because one extra shot, or a miss, with the hammer will badly mar the work surface. A standard-faced hammer might only make a slight dent (Fig. 13-2 and 13-3).

Curved claw hammers are probably the most widely used. They are more or less classified as general-purpose carpenters' hammers. Straight claw hammers are also available. They can be used for such jobs as ripping off old siding and ripping open wooden crates. Straight claw hammers are often called *ripping hammers* because of this feature (Fig. 13-4).

Handle material for claw hammers includes a choice of wood (usually hickory), fiberglass, and steel. Steel-shafted versions can have solid or tubular handles, and they are the strongest of all the materials used. They tend to transmit more shock than I like even when the handle is rubber cushioned.

Wood handles form the standard and they are most easily replaced if a handle should break.

Fiberglass is my preference for handle material. It is extremely strong and doesn't transmit shock as does steel. Steel is a good bit stronger. As with so many other points with tools, handle material choice is up to the individual. Borrow hammers with handles of all three materials, if possible, and try them out to see which you like best. In general, the least expensive hammers come with wooden handles. The most expensive are usually those with tubular steel handles. Fiberglass-handled hammers are often priced at a level with those having steel handles.

Head weight is a matter of need. For standard use, use a standard-weight, 16-ounces. The 16-ounce claw hammer is almost ubiquitous among carpenters. It is heavy enough for most general carpentry and light enough not to destroy lighter work. If you contemplate much heavy framing, I suggest that you at least consider a 20- or 22-ounce head. Not many people will need, or want, a head weight of 28 ounces. Such a hammer is absolutely useless for smaller work. It requires more than average strength and experience to use properly. When driving nails over about 20-penny size, (as in flooring a deck with 2×6s where you might use 35 or even 50 pounds of nails), that 28-ounce head comes into its own. Lighter heads are also useful. Head weights of about 13 ounces are best for trim molding around doors and windows; there you'll be using light finishing nails.

In general, for the average home woodworker's toolbox, I would guess a 16-ounce and a 22-ounce hammer would be sufficient. For anyone planning to do much molding or other light work, a 13-ounce hammer would be handy. Handle length is a

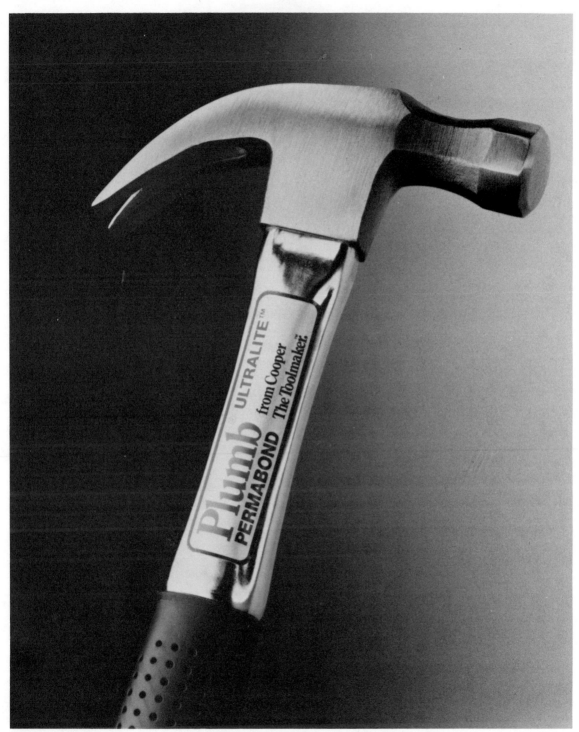

Fig. 13-2. A plumb hollow-steel, curved-handle claw hammer (courtesy Cooper Tool Group).

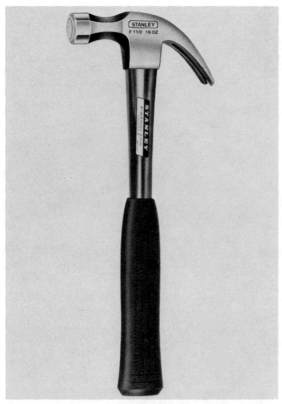

Fig. 13-3. Stanley's fiberglass, curved-handled claw hammer.

Setting the nail for a start in the above manner is particularly useful with larger nails. It can save a lot of bruised fingers because it is almost impossible to miss. Choking up on the hammer handle will tend to interfere with aiming and it adds to the work you have to do to drive a nail even when you don't bend the nail. The idea is to let the head do as much of the work as possible.

If you're driving finishing nails, stop driving when the nail is about one blow from entering the wood totally. Use a nailset to finish the job. Depending on the size of the nail, its head will be from ⅛ of an inch above the work surface to about ½ of an inch (Fig. 13-7). When nailing tongue-and-groove flooring (which is nailed through the tongue), stop driving before the hammer strikes the wood and use a nailset. Lay the nail set on its side to do the work (Fig. 13-8).

If you must pull a partially driven nail, use a block of wood under the head of the hammer to add leverage, even when working with rough framing. When working with

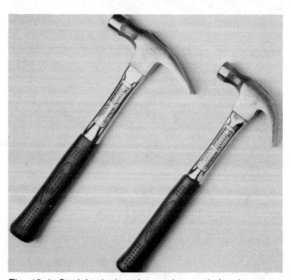

Fig. 13-4. Straight ripping claw and curved claw hammers (courtesy Plumb).

factor. My 28-ounce hammer is 17½ inches long, overall, while my 22-ounce Plumb is 15 inches long. Brands will vary in length. I think my 22-ounce Stanley is about an inch longer than the Plumb. For this reason, it is a good idea to get your hands on a hammer, even in the confines of a store, before buying it. One that suits me might not be suitable for you.

When using a carpenters' hammer, the first shot is to set the nail in place. I usually do this by placing the nail on the side of the head (as shown in E of Fig. 13-5) and striking the work. After that, the hammer is used with your hand fitting flush with the edge of the hammer as (B of Fig. 13-5) shows, and striking the face of the nail squarely (Fig. 13-6).

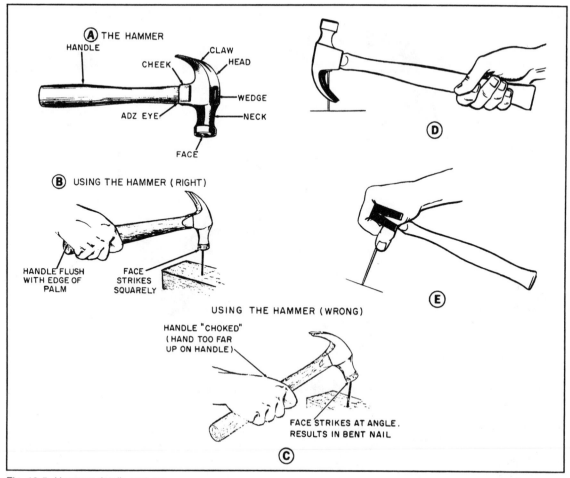

Fig. 13-5. Hammer details and use.

finished wood, use at least a scrap of wood under the head as the nail is pulled to keep from marring the wood finish (Fig. 13-9).

Most manufacturers recommend wearing safety goggles when using *any* hammer. It's a good idea because a flying nail, or a chip from either the nail head or hammer face, can cause a great deal of damage. Once a nail is set and you're ready to hammer with full force make sure your other hand is out of the way. It really isn't as funny as old cartoons make it seem when you smack a finger with your hammer. It just plain well hurts!

There are a number of other light hammers (Figs. 13-10 and 13-11) of interest and use to the woodworker. Among these, the ball peen is probably familiar to most of us because of its resemblance to the claw hammer. In place of the claw is a peen, used for shaping metal or for striking in places that the face is too broad to reach. Ball peen hammers are also used to drive cold chisels and set rivets. The selection of head weights and hammer materials is about the same as for the claw hammer, but I have worked over the years with a far smaller selection of ball peen hammers than claw hammers. For

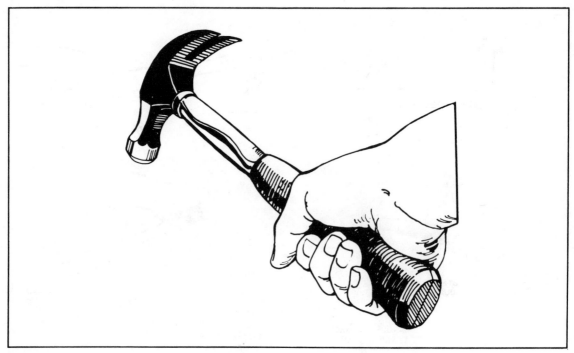

Fig. 13-6. Proper hammer grip (courtesy Stanley Tools).

moderate and light work, I use one with a 12-ounce head. For heavier work, I have a ball peen hammer with a 32-ounce head.

Soft-faced hammers are another matter entirely. If you plan to do any work that would require driving one section of wood into another or taking them apart, a soft-faced hammer becomes essential to prevent marring the work surfaces. I have two Stanley soft-faced hammers. One has replaceable plastic tips and one has solid plastic (Figs. 13-12 and 13-13). Both have hickory handles. The one with nonreplaceable faces is known as a mallet because of the width of its striking surface. It weighs 16 ounces and the other weighs 32 ounces.

Soft-faced mallets need not be made of plastic. Many are made of wood and some are made of tightly coiled rawhide (assuming you can locate one). Carvers' and sculptors' mallets are generally made with a beech

head and an ash handle. They are used to drive gouges and chisels for carving or sculpting in wood.

No matter the material, soft-faced hammers and mallets are not meant to be used with full force. The entire idea behind them is to install or remove wooden parts or other parts without damaging the material being driven. Even a plastic face will mar wood if the blow is hard enough. Beech is hard enough to mess up most other woods

Fig. 13-7. Nailset.

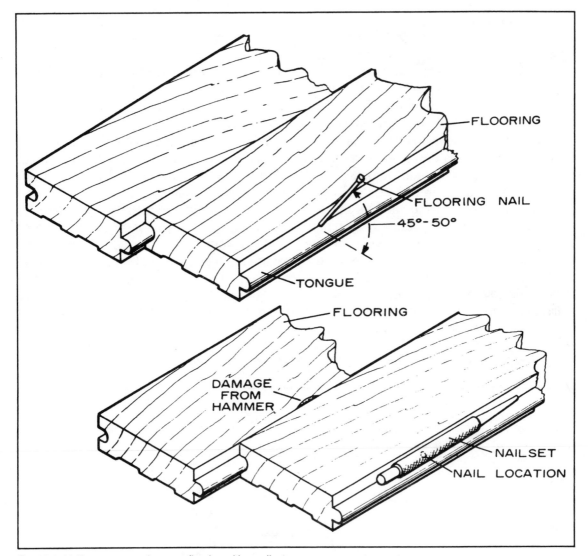

Fig. 13-8. Nailing tongue-and-groove flooring with a nailset.

so even beech-headed mallets must be used with care.

During carving and sculpting, directional control is more important than force. Removing a small amount of material is a better idea than ruining the chisel or gouge handle and splitting the wood being worked.

Rubber-headed mallets have mostly taken the place of rawhide mallets. To my mind, such mallets are more useful in au-tomobile work than in woodworking because they bounce a great deal—unless they're lead-loaded—and they are generally hard to control. Even for auto use, they're handy generally only in replacing parts that would be damaged by ball peen hammers. You might want to check TAB book No. 949, *Do-it-Yourselfer's Guide to Auto Body Repair & Painting* for further information on the subject.

At times, even heavier hammers will be needed to drive anything from fence posts to spikes, and to drive masonry nails. Hardened steel nails quickly ruin the faces of regular claw hammers and ball peen hammers. The hand-drilling hammer is an example. It is usually found in head weights of 2, 3, and 4 pounds (with hickory handles). Blacksmith hammers can also be useful at times. They come with head weights up to 4 pounds. The basic difference between the two is that the hand-drilling hammer has two more or less flat striking faces. The blacksmith's hammer has a cross peen on one side of the head. Engineers' hammers are a lot like hand-drilling hammers, but they tend to have slightly longer handles (most hand-drilling hammers are about 10 or 11 inches overall) and heavier heads. They come in weights up to 64 ounces and sometimes more. You'll seldom find a need for these hammers in woodworking, but at times associated work will require them. An example would be drilling through masonry to attach bolts for a ledger board for a porch or deck.

An even heavier hammer is the woodchoppers' maul (or go-devil). In most cases, these come in 6- or 8-pound head weights. Today, some designs go well over that. I like to use an 8-pounder with a 32-inch handle. Woodchoppers' mauls have one sharp edge, and they have a striking head that can be used to drive wedges to split wood for fires. They are my preference over axes for splitting wood, but many people don't care for them. I have noticed that the people who don't care to use go-devils also tend to drive wedges with the poll of an axe. This is a very rapid way to ruin any axe. The poll is not hardened for this use.

Very light hammers (Figs. 13-14 and 13-15) also enter the woodworking picture if

Fig. 13-9. Pulling nails with a claw hammer (courtesy Stanley Tools).

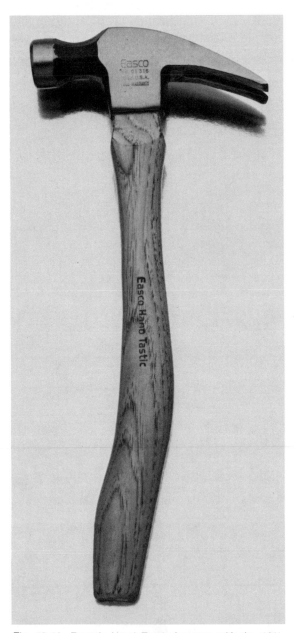

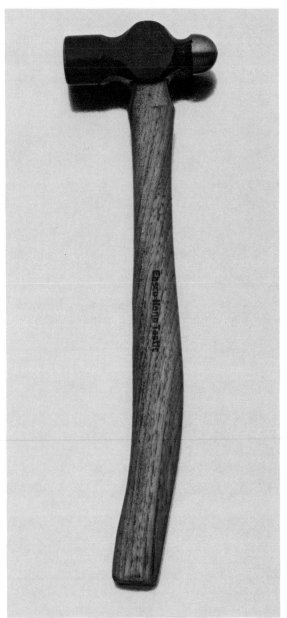

Fig. 13-10. Easco's Hand Tastic hammer with the 19½-degree curve in the handle, reportedly giving less fatigue in use.

Fig. 13-11. Easco Hand Tastic ball peen hammer.

you plan to assemble picture frames or upholster furniture. Upholsters' hammers and tack hammers come with head weights of 5 or 7 ounces, and may be magnetized. Head

designs vary depending on the manufacturer. All have a small, circular face and all are designed for work in tight spots. Handles are hickory; I've never seen or heard of any

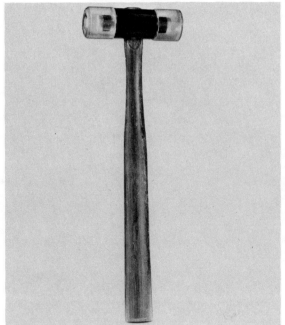

Fig. 13-12. Replaceable-tip, soft-face hammer (courtesy Stanley Tools).

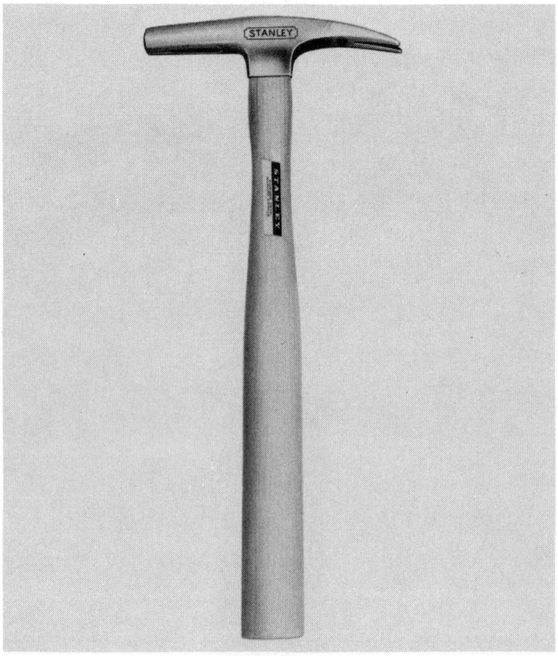

Fig. 13-14. Tack hammer (courtesy Stanley Tools).

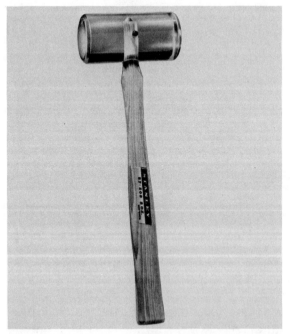

Fig. 13-13. Solid-head, soft-faced hammer (courtesy Stanley Tools).

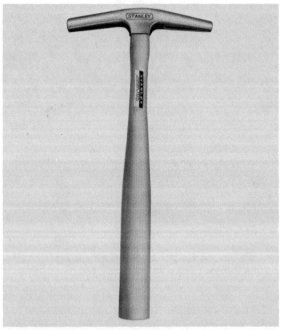

Fig. 13-15. Upholsterer's hammer (courtesy Stanley Tools).

other material being used. An essential tool for light work, the tack hammer is virtually useless if you don't do light work—very light work. Costs are reasonable so you might want to have one in your toolbox just in case. Tack hammers are handy when wall-to-wall carpeting must be pulled up and relaid.

In general with hammers, no matter the size or style, you will not save a cent by going with anything other than the best quality you can find. There is about an $8 price differential between Stanley's best 16-ounce claw hammer and its least expensive hammer. If you have extensive use for the hammer over the years, the best hammer will turn out to be far less expensive in the long run. You will probably never have to replace it and it is unlikely you'll have to replace the handle (unless you use the hammer as a crowbar or other unintended uses).

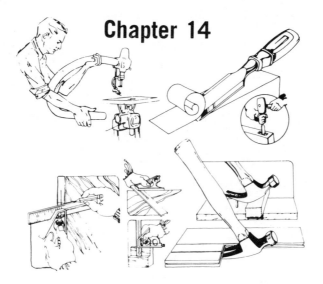

Chapter 14

Levels

L EVELS HAVEN'T BEEN WITH US AS WOOD-working tools for as long as many other devices. It was the beginning of the nineteenth century or so before spirit levels were adapted to carpentry uses and virtually supplanted the plumb bob as a tool for indicating plumb lines (vertical lines).

Today, the plumb bob is used most often as a tool for indicating a point to be marked above or below a specific point. If you must cut a hole in a ceiling so that it will fit directly over a particular spot on the floor, as you might when installing a prefabricated chimney, the shape of the chimney is marked on a piece of cardboard and the center indicated. The plumb bob is then hung from the ceiling and moved about until the point of the bob rests directly over the center marking. The basic problem with plumb bobs is that the things hardly ever are

completely still. A great deal of patience is needed.

Spirit-type levels (Fig. 14-1) are today's tool of choice for plumbing use as well as for levelling horizontal surfaces. The bubble in the fluid in the vials on a spirit level have the advantage of friction. They quickly become still and indicate the level or plumb.

The vial and its contents are the most important part of any level, but without a true frame for the level even the best-made vials will have an indication error. The vial is filled with an oil or alcohol and a bubble of air is allowed to remain. Two lines will be marked on the vial and the bubble floats freely until it comes to rest. If the bubble lies directly inside the two lines, the surface is level (plumb) (Fig. 14-2).

A *line level* is a device that is clipped to a taut line to indicate level over a long dis-

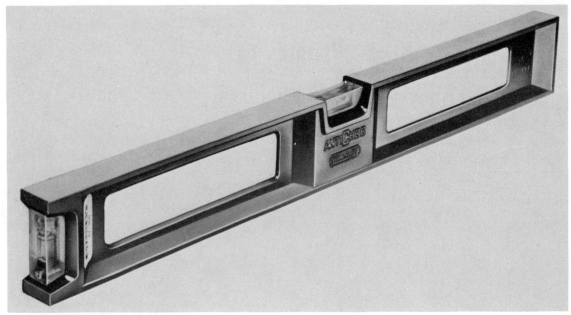

Fig. 14-1. Spirit level (courtesy Stanley Tools).

tance. The line must be strong and very tight because, although line levels weigh only a couple of ounces, any deviation in the line will affect the trueness of the indication. *Pocket levels* of about the same size as line levels are also available, but they are generally only used for rough indications of level because their approximate 3-inch length tends to be costly to accuracy. *Torpedo levels* are somewhat torpedo shaped, with the sides tapering in at each end, and they are useful for rough work jobs such as putting on furring before installing new siding where the level must be right at hand and can be carried in a carpenters' apron. Torpedo levels are about 9 inches long and can have as many as three vials. Some have one edge grooved so that they can be held on a line to give a level.

Longer levels give more accurate readings and levels with more sturdily built bodies or frames provide greater accuracy. A more or less standard carpenters' level will

be 2 feet long with an aluminum frame and two or three vials to indicate both level and plumb. My Stanley 100+ is of this type and it is a top-quality level that has seen a great amount of use over the years without losing its trueness. Such a level is an excellent tool for general purpose use. It is light and it fits on or between most surfaces.

When greater accuracy is needed, longer levels are required (Fig. 14-3). Lengths up to 80 inches are readily available from many companies, but it is usually best to hold things down a bit. Levels tend to go up in price quite quickly as they go up in length. As an indication, Stanley's magnesium levels (with three vials and a 2-foot

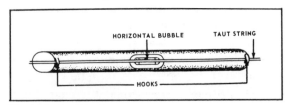

Fig. 14-2. Line level.

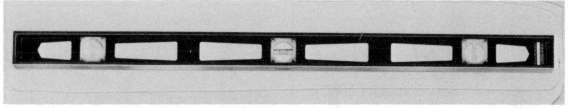

Fig. 14-3. A three-vial level (courtesy Sears, Roebuck and Co.).

length) is expensive at around $25. The 78-inch length in the same quality is well over $70.

You should not go to the bottom of any company's quality line when selecting a level for more than a single use. Lightweight levels of the type too many people buy are far too easily knocked out of true when being used or when sitting around. A knock that might not even faze a good-quality level will ruin a cheaper level. Better quality levels usually have adjustable vials so that, if the trueness is lost, all you need do is find a surface you know to be level, or horizontal, and adjust the level. In cases where adjust-

ment isn't possible, many levels have replaceable vials. A replacement vial at about a buck and a half is a lot less expensive than even an $8 level.

Wood levels, or wood-bodied levels, are also available. They are generally classified as mason's levels. Most often, the wood used is mahogany and the edges are bound in brass. The length of such levels is usually 4 feet (Fig. 4-4).

Many levels will also have a vial that reads a 45-degree angle. I've always preferred to get a plumb or level line and then use a combination square to check the 45-degree angle. One unusual level is the In-

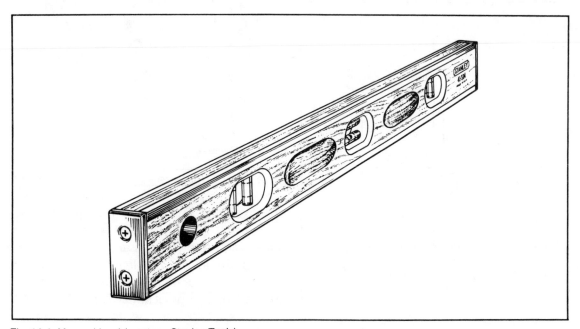

Fig. 14-4. Masons' level (courtesy Stanley Tools).

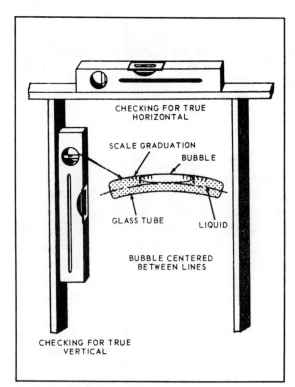

Fig. 14-5. Using a level.

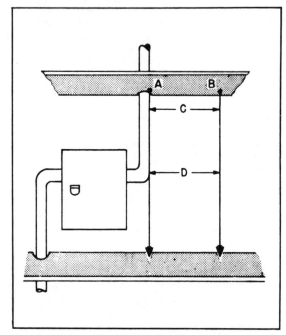

Fig. 14-6. Using a plumb bob to plumb a structural member.

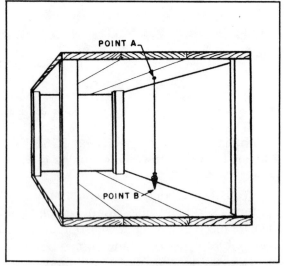

Fig. 14-7. Using a plumb bob to locate a point.

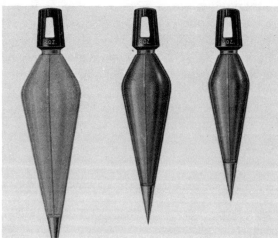

Fig. 14-8. Plumb bobs (courtesy Stanley Tools).

klinat direct-angle reading level that Garrett Wade carries. This 10-inch long level has one fixed vial and one that is in a rotating sleeve that can be moved to indicate any angle you need (angles are marked on the body of the level). The level also has open marking slots for 45 and 60 degrees. It could be used for laying out small slopes (1 degree indicates .21 inches rise per foot of run).

For general use, I recommend a tor-

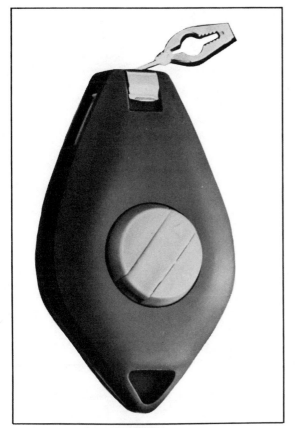

Fig. 14-9. Chalk line case can be used as a plumb bob (courtesy Stanley Tools).

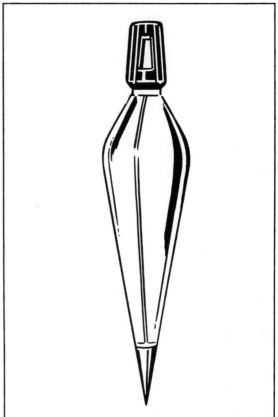

Fig. 14-10. Plumb bob (courtesy Stanley Tools).

pedo level and a good-quality, 2-foot level. The two tools in the best quality available would run you less than $35; good quality could almost halve that price. For times when doors and other long assemblies must be installed, a longer level is nice, but not essential. I use my 4-foot wood level when installing doors and checking the plumb of building corners, etc. For normal use around the home, a 78-inch level is seldom needed. These are often called door installers' levels because the length takes up almost the entire length of a standard door frame. See Figs. 14-5 through 14-10.

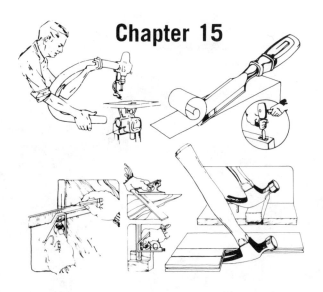

Chapter 15

Power Saws

HAND-HELD POWER SAWS COME IN THREE basic styles: the circular saw, the scroll or the saber saw, and the reciprocating saw. Actually, one could probably say the reciprocating saw is nothing more than a very heavy-duty version of a saber saw, but its uses are different.

CIRCULAR SAWS

The circular saw (Figs. 15-1 and 15-2) is the second most important small power tool for the home shop. The electric drill is the first. Sears carries five circular saws in its most recent tool catalog and an industrial model in the big catalog. The price range is from under $25 to well over $200. There also is a tremendous difference in performance. Rockwell International lists six different circular saws in its consumer tool catalog and seven in their industrial catalog (several of which overlap with those in the consumer catalog).

You'll find yourself faced with a selection of blade diameters ranging from about 5 inches (Sears' smallest saw, while Rockwell's is 4½ inches) to 8¼ inches. Most circular saws intended for use around the home or farm are 7, 7¼ or 7½ inches. The 8¼-inch saws are the most powerful and expensive, but they are also the heaviest and hardest to handle. The smallest aren't all that handy. Most will not totally cut even a nominal 2×4 at a 90-degree angle and can cut only through 1-inch stock at 45 degrees. With a weight of from 5 to 7 pounds, these smaller saws are good for working on plywood paneling where a long reach is often needed. Your arm doesn't tire as rapidly and the lighter weight generally makes the saw easier to control.

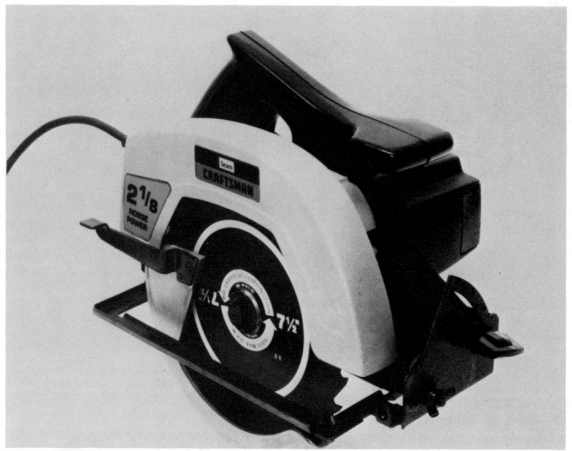

Fig. 15-1. Craftsman 2⅛-horsepower, 7½-inch, circular saw (courtesy Sears, Roebuck and Co.).

The circular saw was introduced many years ago by the Skil Corporation. For a good time they were in danger of having it become generically termed (used for all circular saws no matter the manufacturer). The trademarked name is Skilsaw. The saw is also called a cut-off saw and a utility saw, but it is not limited to such jobs.

I would guess that the circular saw was originally developed as a cut-off saw for house framers because it can zip through a 2×4 or 2×6 in seconds. Its utility has increased as the years have passed and so have the variations in size and power. Circular saws are generally rated by blade diameter, but it isn't always true that a greater diameter will give a much greater depth of cut. At one time, I had a 10¼-inch Skilsaw. It's depth of cut at 90 degrees was *not* as great as that might indicate (it would not quite cut all the way through a nominal 4×4).

There is even a variation in cut depths with the same size blade. Sears offers several 7¼-inch diameter circular saws. The least expensive of them has a cut depth of 2⅛ inches at 90 degrees. The most costly model ($30 more) will cut an eighth of an inch deeper. The major difference though is the 45-degree cut. The less expensive saw will cut wood up to 1⅝ inches thick. The more expensive models will cut wood at 2 inches thick when set for 45 degrees. This is the difference in cutting and not cutting a 2×4 at 45 degrees. You must also consider whether or not you'll be using rough or dimensioned lumber. Rough-cut lumber in 2-×-4 size is a full 2 inches by 4 inches. Dimensioned (planed and usually kiln- or air-dried) lumber is thinner, often over a quarter of an inch. If you're getting the last cut from a saw mill in rough lumber, you might find, as I have a few times, that a 2×4 (to save time) is left at 2½ or more inches thick.

Larger blade sizes might well be indicated for your work if you use rough lumber, but you should also consider that a blade that is always buried in the work almost totally will not work as efficiently as one that has a few fractions of an inch running free. Power is another consideration. The larger the blade the more power is needed to drive it when it's buried full depth in the work.

More power is needed when you are working with much rough cut lumber because the lumber will be green a lot of the time and green wood is harder to cut. With some companies, it's possible to say, for example, that a 1½-horsepower saw is underpowered for extensive heavier work (virtually all of them are), and at least 2 horse-

Fig. 15-2. Circular saw at work (courtesy Rockwell International).

Fig. 15-3. Sears' Craftsman 2-horsepower, 7¼-inch saw.

power is needed if you do much heavy framing. I burned out my 1½-horsepower Skilsaw last year doing some heavy framing.

For general to moderately heavy work, the lower-powered saw is fine. It is also less expensive. There is a price difference of about $40 between Sears' 1½-horsepower saw and their 7½-inch, 2⅛-horsepower model. It is not always sensible to go for the top of the power line because often a lighter tool with less power will serve equally well for those who never get into really heavy-duty cutting. Building such things as decks and deck-style porches, with the smallest material used being 2×4s and most being 2×6 or larger, requires a more powerful saw (Fig. 15-3).

For those who really intend to get into heavy-duty work, consideration might go to a worm-drive saw. These are, essentially, industrial-quality and they offer great torque and high durability. I've only used one, in 6½ size, and the smoothness with which it cut was impressive. Its weight was almost equally impressive (it weighed just about as much as my 10¼-inch saw). In sizes up to 8¼ inches, worm drive saws are available from several sources, including Skil, Sears, Roebuck and Company, and Montgomery Ward. Sears' Craftsman line seems to be the

Fig. 15-4. Craftsman 7½-worm gear drive circular saw (courtesy Sears, Roebuck and Co.).

least expensive at about $200 delivered for the 7¼-inch, 2 1/3-horsepower model (Fig. 15-4). (There is also a 6½-inch model with 2⅛-horsepower and an 8¼-inch model with 2¾-horsepower). It isn't often a homeowner will need such a saw. Nevertheless, I'd like to have one.

Other companies don't list horsepower on their heavy-duty saws, but you can judge power from the amperage drawn. Rockwell's 7¼-inch, 2-horsepower saw draws 10 amperes. In almost all cases, amperage will be under 15—usually no more than 13—so that a standard lighting circuit can be used to run the circular saw. If the saw drew over 15 amperes, you would have to use an appliance circuit capable of 20-ampere loading. If the saw actually drew 15 amperes, the start-up surge would probably blow your circuit breaker every time.

When selecting a circular saw, decide on the size and power you need for anticipated work. It might be better to go up in size or power a little bit to make sure future needs are met. Going too high is not a good idea because the lighter tools are easier to handle and more economical. Then see if it's possible to handle a sample of the tool and, if possible, actually make a few cuts. Most of today's circular saws are designed for efficient handling, but some brands feel better than others to different people. That is one important consideration when making a purchase. Any electrical tool bought should be double insulated, listed by Underwriters Lab, or three wire and UL listed.

Once your circular saw is home, a bit of practice will make you proficient in basic cuts. Check the saw over to make sure that the blade guard retracts easily and snaps back into place quickly. Set up some scrap pieces of various kinds of lumber and practice making cuts to get used to the feel of the blade. Remember that on a circular saw the cut is made as the blade rotates up, toward you, so that splinters are lifted off the top surface of the work. This simply means that when you make a cut you should place the "good" side down. In other words, with finished paneling, keep the finished side down. Handsaws cut on the down stroke so the finish side should be up.

As with all sawing, make your cut to the waste side of the stock, just touching the marked line with the side of the kerf. It's impossible to tell you how fast to run the saw through a cut. The speed with which you feed the saw is determined by blade type, saw power, and the type of material being cut. You must work by feel. For really accurate cuts, clamp a guide strip to the work. This is a waste of time in most framing work but, for finer work when no table saw is available, it makes for greater accuracy than does working freehand.

It is best to make all cuts with both hands on the saw, though you won't always find this possible, and always make sure the front edge of the shoe, or base plate, is firmly on the work before the blade makes contact.

173

This last item is a commonly overlooked precaution, but it assures a better start of the cut. Even with guard-protected blades, it's best to stand so that any kickback of the saw won't bring it into contact with your body. This isn't always possible. Maintain a firm grip. The weight of the saw should be on the larger, best-supported portion of the work if you want accurate cuts. See Figs. 15-5 and 15-6.

BLADES

Today, virtually all circular saws come from the box with what is called a combination blade. The combination blade (Fig. 15-7) is good for moderately fine to rough work whether you must make crosscuts, rip cuts, or need to make miters. It is a compromise. The planer blade also does all three kinds of cutting, but leaves a bit smoother edge for finer work (Fig. 15-8).

Plywood-cutting blades have a lot of fine teeth and they will give you the smoothest possible, and nearly splinter free, cuts no matter the direction of the surface veneer. Plywood blades are also useful when cutting plastics and aluminum (in light gauges). See Fig. 15-9.

Flooring blades are made of a special steel and are meant for applications where

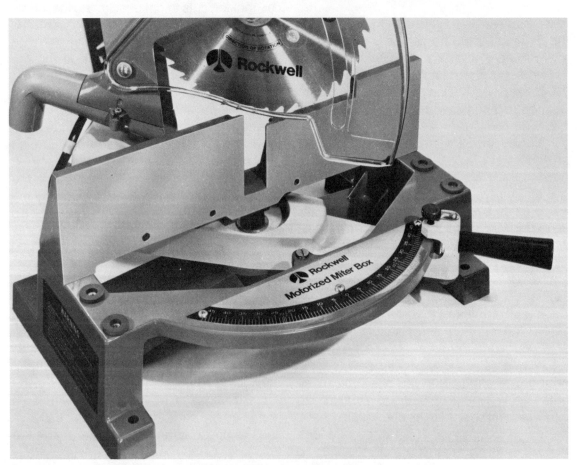

Fig. 15-5. Rockwell motorized miter saw (courtesy Rockwell International).

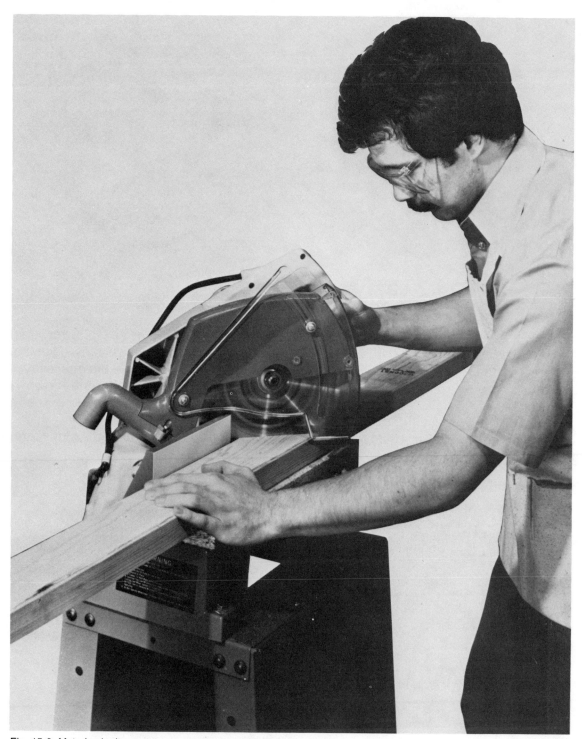

Fig. 15-6. Motorized miter saw in use (courtesy Rockwell International).

Fig. 15-7. Combination blades (courtesy Nicholson).

you might well hit nails, such as cutting used lumber and opening up floor areas.

Rip blades look very much like combination saw blades, but they don't have a bevel on the backs of the teeth. Therefore, a smoother cut is produced (Fig. 15-10).

Abrasive blades (Fig. 15-11) are used for cutting masonry or metal. I've never been particularly fond of these blades because the arbors almost always are not sturdy enough to hold up for long. With the masonry styles, the amount of dust created is absolutely incredible.

Tungsten-carbide tipped blades are

Fig. 15-8. Planer blades (courtesy Nicholson).

Fig. 15-9. Plywood blades (courtesy Nicholson).

claimed, depending on who does the claiming, to last from 15 to 50 times as long as standard steel-saw blades. Sears claims only a 5-time durability increase. I feel even that may be extending things a bit. In any case, the price is at least two times that of a standard blade. Any problems you have (touching a nail for instance) means the blade life is over. Tungsten carbide-tipped blades cannot be resharpened and the blade type selection is somewhat more limited. It is plenty wide if you don't mind paying about $30 for a planer blade.

Contractors' blades come in packages

Fig. 15-10. Rip blade (courtesy Stanley Tools).

Fig. 15-11. Masonry cut off wheel (courtesy Stanley Tools).

of from 1 to 50. They cost much less than similar-style blades that are not considered disposable. Most are combination style, but some companies make a plywood-cutting type. These can be bought individually instead of packaged. It might make sense, if you're doing an extreme amount of framing, to consider a package of these because you can usually get five blades for about a buck more than a single combination blade would cost. When the blade dulls, you simply remove it and recycle it.

SABER SAWS

Saber saws, compared to circular saws, are very underpowered and have much less cutting accuracy. Instead, they offer a great deal of versatility in cutting shapes and different materials. The saber saw can be used to cut even such materials as rubber and leather, with the proper blades in place. Modern versions, with modern blades in a profusion of types, offer different speeds as well as the capability to cut curves and make piercing cuts (Figs. 15-12 and 15-13).

Some brands have a scrolling attachment that allows you to turn the blade, thus the direction of the cut, without turning the body of the saw. Sears has a couple of automatic scrolling versions that are interest-

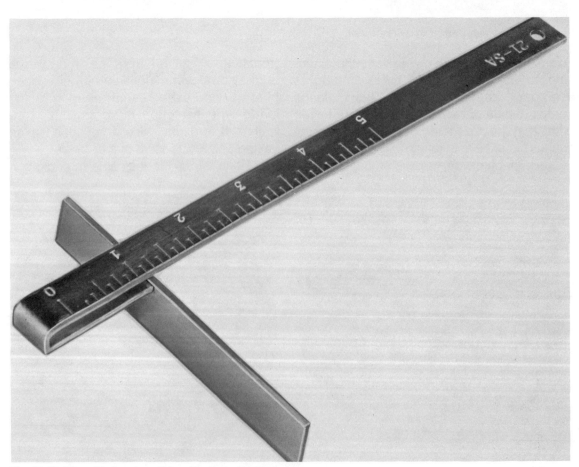

Fig. 15-12. Rip guide (courtesy Sears, Roebuck and Co.).

Fig. 15-13. Rockwell saber saw (courtesy Rockwell International).

ing. As you move the saw forward, you get a straight-line cut. When you move the saw sideways, the blade pivots to cut in that direction. It will also pivot to the rear when the saw is moved backwards. As saber saws go, these 1/3- and ½-horsepower models are more powerful and more expensive than most models. They do offer more features. See Fig. 15-14.

For a little more than $12, you can get a 1/6-horsepower saber saw. Prices begin to rise as power and features are quickly added. Top-of-the-line models can cost very close to $100. The Craftsman automatic ½-horsepower scrolling saber saw lists for about $85, plus shipping and tax.

Speed control is a feature that helps when different materials are to be cut. The

Fig. 15-14. Rockwell saber saw (courtesy Rockwell International).

harder the material the lower the speed you want to use when cutting. Some saws, such as the Rockwell 4310, offer two speeds. Stroke length varies from a half inch in the lighter models to 1 inch in the more powerful tools. The greater stroke length and added power mean you can slice through heavier material. Rockwell's Professional bayonet saw No. 348 doesn't list it's stroke length, but at 3500 strokes per minute, it will cut through 2½ inches of wood, ¾ of an inch of aluminum, and ⅛ inch steel. Virtually all the middle range models now on the market will cut through 1½-inch wood (the less powerful will take some time to do so). See Figs. 15-15 and 15-16.

For the greatest use with any saber saw, you should check and make sure the base plate will tilt 45 degrees, right and left.

Remember that, like the circular saw, the saber saw blade cuts on the up stroke. Whenever possible, the good surface of the wood should be turned down when cuts are being made. If this isn't possible, make the cuts about ⅛ to ¼ inch inside the waste line and use a Surform tool to finish the opening edges. See Fig. 15-17.

BLADES

The blade variety for saber saws can get a little confusing. Rockwell offers 11 different blades specifically for cutting wood or composition materials, four more special-purpose blades for woodworking, and four more for metal cutting and plastics. That's in their universal blade line for just about all saber saws. They go on to offer several more lines to fit their specific saws. Sears

Fig. 15-15. Saber saw starting a rip with guide in place (courtesy Sears, Roebuck and Co.).

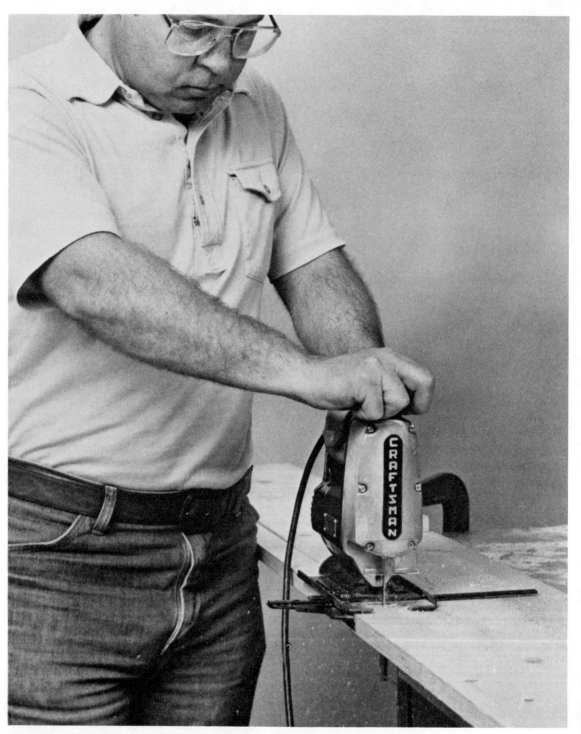

Fig. 15-16. Moving along the rip (courtesy Sears, Roebuck and Co.).

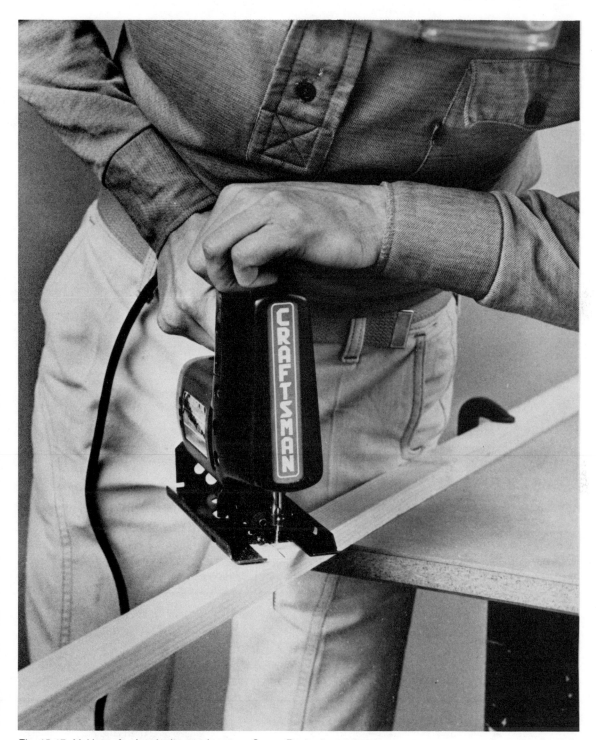

Fig. 15-17. Making a freehand miter cut (courtesy Sears, Roebuck and Co.).

kicks in with a line of a dozen different blades for use on wood, metal, leather, and so forth. Stanley offers 11 blades for various purposes.

In selecting saber saw blades (whether it is called a saber saw, scrolling saw or jigsaw), you need to make sure any blade chosen will fit your machine's chuck. Some are easier than others, but it pays to take at least the shank of the old blade along when getting a new one. Then choose the blade with the correct number (or total lack) of teeth for the job intended.

Metal cuts are made with 24 and 32 teeth per inch. The 32 teeth per inch are used for mild steel rod and so forth. The slightly coarser 24 teeth are used for non-ferrous metals such as brass, copper, and aluminum. From there, you move down to 20 teeth per inch for finish cuts of woods and plastics up to ¾ of an inch thick. Ten teeth per inch will handle finish cuts in heavier materials. These, as well as 12 teeth per inch blades, are available in a variety of blade widths so that you can make gentle and fairly sharp curves when cutting. Knife edge blades are used for cutting rubber, leather, and wallboard. Sears carries a 3-teeth-per-inch blade, 6 inches long, meant for saws with at least a 1-inch stroke. It will make angle cuts in wood up to a bit over 4 inches thick.

The lighter your saw the shorter is the limit for blade length. A 7-teeth-per-inch blade will do very well in a saw with a 1-inch stroke and ½ horsepower, but it will probably just bog down in a lighter saw. In the more powerful saw, it will cut material up to 4 inches thick. Special blades are made for flush cutting right up to walls or joints. These will usually have 5 to 8 teeth per inch.

A list of the blades you have on hand is just about a list of the jobs you can do with a saber saw. Wide blades for straight cuts. Narrow blades for curved cuts. Really narrow blades for tight curves. Wood cutting blades. Metal cutting blades. Knife-edge blades for leather and rubber. It begins to sound, when you consider the cost of circular saw blades, that to get full use from your saber saw you would need to spend hundreds of dollars just on blades after buying the tool.

Fortunately, there is a lot less metal in a saber-saw blade. Sears has a 50-blade assortment, with 10 blades of each of five types (non-ferrous metal, special purpose, scroller, finishing, and regular), in a plastic case that sells for about $22, plus tax and shipping. Packages of 10 blades range from about $4 on up to about $7, depending on blade type. Single blades are seldom sold, but packages of two seldom run over $1.50 or $2. See Fig. 15-18.

When using a saber saw, your steadiness is going to have a strong influence on the final cut. Rip guides are available for straight cuts, but cutting curves requries a good eye on the mark and a steady hand. Feeding slowly is the best bet.

One great feature of the saber saw is that you don't really have to drill a hole to start a cut. A plunge cut can be made to take care of that. Plunge cuts are made by tilting the saw so that the tip of the base plate rests on the work surface, and then presenting the teeth of the blade to the work.

Start the saw and *gently* feed it into the work. Keep a tight grip to prevent chattering (which will break a blade if it gets too bad), and very *slowly* tilt the tool back. The initial contact cannot be between the tip of the blade and the work. This is what causes chattering. The first part of the plunge cut is the forming of a groove that allows more and more teeth to come in contact with the wood

Fig. 15-18. Saber saw blades (courtesy Nicholson).

as the tool is tilted back, until you get through the wood. Practice this on waste material first.

It also doesn't pay to try to make a plunge cut with a scrolling blade. Make the plunge cut with a regular blade and then change to a scrolling blade if one is needed. Scrolling blades are exceptionally fine and easy to break. Changing blades takes only a few seconds after the plunge cut is made.

RECIPROCATING SAWS

Reciprocating saws (Fig. 15-19) are also known as bayonet saws and one or two other names. This type of saw is a coarser, more powerful version of the saber saw.

With a saber saw, the blade moves up and down, but a reciprocating saw is usually used in a position where the blade moves back and forth on a horizontal plane. It's really the same motion; its just on a different plane most of the time. Stroke length is usually a minimum of 1 inch, with some going to 1¼ inches or thereabouts, and the blades range in length from 6 inches to a foot. Single-speed, 2-speed and variable-speed reciprocating saws are available. I would avoid the single-speed models as they are extremely limited in application (wood only).

Reciprocating saws (Figs. 15-20 and 15-21) can be used to cut through logs (up to about 10 inches thick), but they are most

185

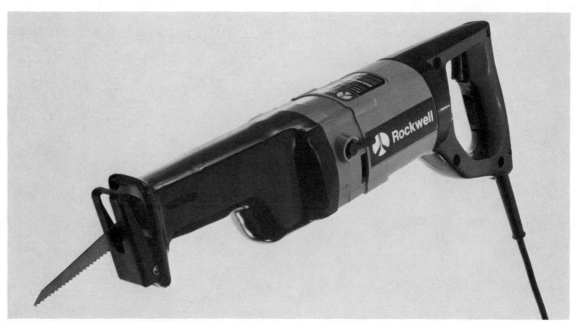

Fig. 15-19. Reciprocating saw with short blade (courtesy Rockwell International).

Fig. 15-20. Reciprocating saw with long blade (courtesy Rockwell International).

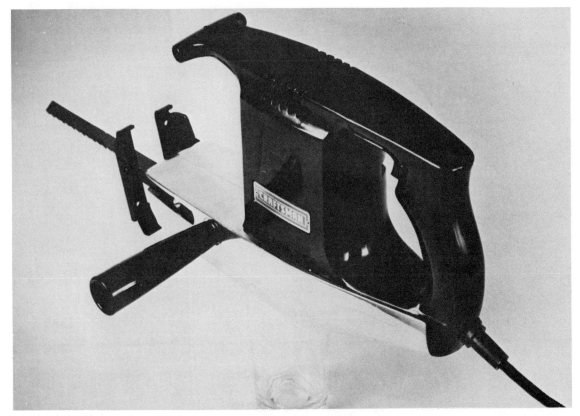

Fig. 15-21. Craftsman reciprocating saw (courtesy Sears, Roebuck and Co.).

often used when removing flooring and joists or when sawing through a wall, ceiling, or roof. The blades on most can be turned in different directions. The blade clamp can be easily rotated in order to allow for flush cuts.

Blades for the reciprocating saws will have from 6 to 32 teeth per inch. This allows the saw to be used as a power hacksaw (among other things). Several blades are available that are designed for cutting through wood where nails are expected to be in the way (Rockwell offers three of these). There is even a blade made for cutting through plaster backed by metal lath. Rockwell also offers shorter blades for cutting nail-embedded wood. There is a wavy knife edge for cutting leather and rubber and a narrow scroll cutting blade.

Chapter 16

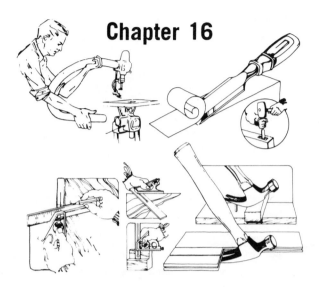

Electric Drill

ANYONE WHO HAS ANY INTEREST IN WORK-ing around a house or apartment owns at least one electric drill (Fig. 16-1). It is probably the single most versatile tool available for the home workshop. It has been for years the most widely sold power tool on the market because of that versatility. As the range of accessories opens up even more, the sales of the basic drill should remain stable.

When I bought my first drill, you had a choice: ¼-inch, ⅜-inch, or ½-inch chuck. Single speed. No reverse. A price of about $20 to $25 for the smaller models. Today, the choices could make your head spin right off. The simplest single-speed, ⅜-inch Craftsman drill should arrive on your doorstep for about $15. There are also less expensive ones on the market.

If that's not suitable, you can move to a more powerful and reversible variable speed drill and still spend less than $35. For a ⅜-inch drill, with a ⅜-horsepower motor and a 0 to 1200-rpm-speed range, you're going to spend about $70. But that's Craftsman's top-of-the-line model with ball and roller bearings instead of needle bearings.

If you want to hammer on some masonry, with a ⅜-inch chuck, expect to spend at least $85. The Craftsman 1811 offers ball, roller and sleeve bearings, and will produce as many as 25,000 impacts per minute to drill through brick, concrete, or stone. A top-of-the-line drill with a chuck capacity of half an inch will run about the same as the hammer drill, but the motor develops ⅞ of a horsepower instead of ⅜. The tool will drive much larger drill bits or other accessories.

Fig. 16-1. Rockwell's heavy-duty electric drill line.

Fig. 16-2. Lightweight cordless drill (courtesy Rockwell International).

Consider the Rockwell's No. 730 professional spade handle ¾ inch chuck drill. The drill weighs almost 25 pounds naked. I used a drill of this size some years ago and when I jammed it in the work it proceeded to lift me from my feet!

Generally, today it has become hard to find drills with quarter-inch chucks. The reason is simple; the ⅜-inch chuck offers greater versatility. And for some reason prices have stabilized pretty much (not totally, but far better than in other areas). The cost of a ⅜-inch drill today is lower than the cost of a smaller drill two decades ago.

It's probably volume sales and a lot of development, but those old drills had no

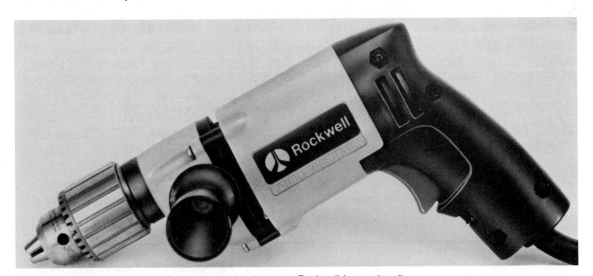

Fig. 16-3. A good combination of power and price (courtesy Rockwell International).

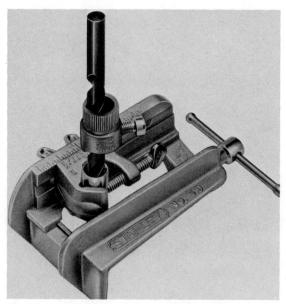
Fig. 16-4. Dowelling jig (courtesy Stanley Tools).

safety features such as double insulation or triple-wire plugs. They were prone to burn out at 6-month intervals. They seemed to like to hit the week after the warranty wore off and just go up in smoke. Usually the windings. And no cure.

In the past decade, I've only burned out one electric drill and that was a cordless model from the early days. I still can't say I'm impressed with cordless drills. They lack power and endurance and don't provide much speed. Extra power packs are now generally available, so I guess you could go out into the field with three or four charged power packs and come close to getting a days work from a cordless drill (Fig. 16-2). Unfortunately, the power packs cost over $20, and they are generally only offered to fit top-of-the-line cordless drills anyway. A brace and bit, or even a hand drill, makes more sense.

Chuck size is of great importance when selecting an electric drill. The larger the chuck size the larger the drill bit, or acces-

sory, that you can drive with the drill (assuming the drill has enough power). Obviously, the harder the material the smaller the size drill bit you can use. About the largest readily available metal drill bit for electric drills (with ½-inch chuck capacities) is 1 inch in size.

Wood drilling is another matter entirely. Wood can be pound-for-pound stronger than steel, but it's nowhere near as dense a material. Wood drill bits are readily available in sizes to one and a half inch, and even for drills with chuck sizes down to a quarter of an inch. See Fig. 16-3.

Special bits can be found to drill out up to 2⅛ inches (Stanley's 04-034 lock set bit). There are hole saws to cut out to 2½ inches. The Wood Hog goes to 4⅝ inches in diameter, but requires a drill with exceptional power and a ¾-inch chuck in the extreme sizes (smaller sizes are made for lighter drills). Some hole saws will cut to a 6-inch diameter, (cutting to 1⅛ inches of depth and up to 3⅜ inches cutting to 1⅞ inches).

Drill bits and hole saws are just the tip of the iceberg for electric drill uses. Paint removal with these metal limbed contour sanders is a rapid, easy job. They are also available—handier for woodworking—with replaceable abrasive strips now instead of just metal arms that flap. Dowelling jigs allow you to line dowel holes and to get a nice, straight hole (Fig. 16-4). Right-angle attachments allow work in hard-to-reach places (Fig. 16-5). Sanding discs and polishing bonnets can be fitted. Sanding drums in diameters to 2 3/16 inches supply smooth surfaces to inside curves. Screwdriver and socket-bit sets make the installation of otherwise time-consuming fasteners a lot quicker and easier. I can remember putting in a long stovepipe run one winter by drilling and inserting sheet metal screws,

Fig. 16-5. Right-angle attachment (courtesy Rockwell International).

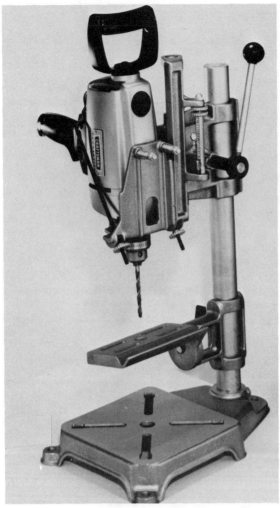

Fig. 16-6. Heavy-duty drill stand (courtesy Sears, Roebuck and Co.).

Fig. 16-7. Plug Cutter (courtesy Stanley Tools).

three to a junction. A couple of years later, I got a socket to fit the heads on the screws and used up less than a quarter of the time and probably a tenth of the energy on the same job.

Nail spinners can be used to set finishing nails without any worry about cracking light molding materials. Drill guides, such as the Portalign from Sears, make sure you get a vertical hole no matter what kind of stock you're working on or what angle you have to hold the drill at. Drill stands come close to giving you drill-press accuracy with hand-held drills. You can even buy an impact drill attachment to fit both ⅜- and ½-inch drive sockets for auto work. See Fig. 16-6.

Wire brushes, counter sinks, plug cutters (for covering countersunk nails with the cut plug) (Fig. 16-7), Surform rotary rasps, and the list of other accessories goes on and on. Suffice to say that in virtually every case where a woodworking shop of any kind is

Fig. 16-8. Countersink (courtesy Stanley Tools).

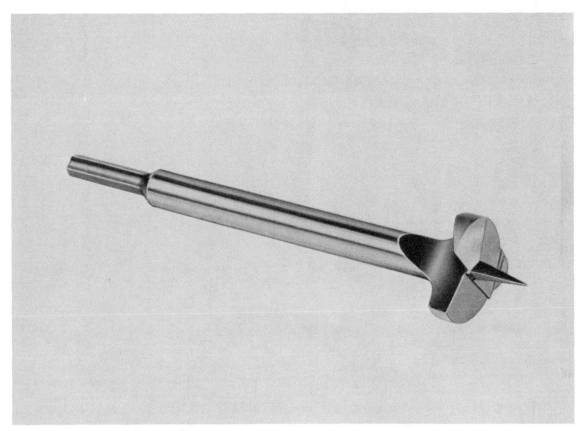

Fig. 16-9. Expandable bit (courtesy Stanley Tools).

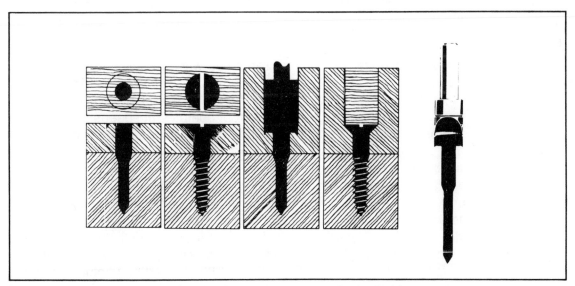

Fig. 16-10. Combination countersink/pilot hole/counter bore (courtesy Stanley Tools).

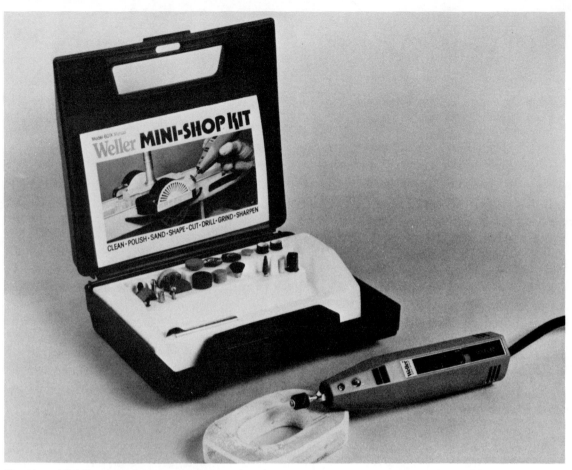

Fig. 16-11. Mini-Shop outfit (courtesy The Cooper Tool Group).

contemplated, you will have an awfully hard time doing without an electric drill (Figs. 16-8 through 16-10).

In addition, you might want to consider some accessories and you might want to have more than a single drill. A good, middle- or top-range ⅜-of-an-inch electric drill is much lighter than a half-inch model. It is also easier to use while doing work on cabinets and so forth.

For the heavier jobs of boring holes in joists to run electrical wiring or pipe, the half-inch drills have the smaller ones beat all the way. You might want to have two or even three if you want a really fine job of drilling done. An example is Weller's Mini-Shop Kit 651K variable-speed drill (Fig. 16-11). This small tool operates at speeds from 5000 to 28,000 rpm. It does everything its big brothers can do, but on a smaller scale. This 46-piece outfit comes in a plastic case. Included are wire brushes, sanding discs, abrasive bands, a filt wheel, a ball cutter, a cylinder cutter, seven grinding wheels and points, and a ⅛-inch drill wrench. There is also an engraving tip. For a price of between $75 and $80, it could be useful for the fine woodworker.

Chapter 17

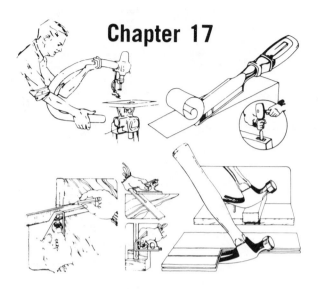

Routers

IN A SENSE, A ROUTER CAN BE CONSIDERED an expert woodworkers' tool because, to really get the most out of it, it takes a great deal of practice and patience. Recently, accessories to add to its uses and to make its basic uses simpler have been arriving in something of a flurry on the market. Not a particularly impressive-looking hand tool, the router (Fig. 17-1) to me resembles an electric drill someone forgot to finish. The tool is not really complex. The motor sits on top. There is a baseplate with a frame coming up to the motor and holding two handles. The bit extends below the base and is set in a chuck. The motor is a high-speed type, and the easiest and best work is done with a high-powered router. You can often do the same jobs with a smaller router, but it will take more passes (thus reducing your chance at great accuracy).

As an example of high speeds, all four Craftsman routers have a no load speed of 25,000 rpm. The three made by Rockwell International kick over at 22,000 rpm. Looking at the features on the inexpensive Craftsman 1735 versus the top of the line 1743, you can see what generates the $60 price difference. First, the motor triples in power from one-half to 1½ horsepower. The inexpensive model has depth gradations in 32nds of an inch. The more accurate 1743 has its gradations in 64ths. An auto shaft lock on the 1743 makes bit changes easier and faster. A zero reset feature makes setting up for repeat cuts simpler with the 1743. The built-in worklight behind two chip deflector shields aid freehand work a great deal. In addition, a dust pick-up on the top-of-the-line model keeps about 80 percent of the mess off full-surface cuts (Fig. 17-2).

Fig. 17-1. Model 630 router (courtesy Rockwell International).

What does all this mean? Well, a router is often thought of as a tool that routs out material to form decorations on kitchen cabinet doors and other such decorative work. It does that well. But it can also pierce wood, cut dados, grooves and rabbets, and it is the best tool around for trimming (Fig. 17-3) laminates on countertops.

The router itself is not really complex, but the jobs it can do—especially with some of the new accessories on the market—are complex. It is a tool that should be treated with respect because it has a lot of starting torque. Hold it firmly and don't start it with the bit resting on the work surface. The router is not an exceptionally expensive tool un-

Fig. 17-2. Craftsman router (courtesy Sears, Roebuck and Co.).

Fig. 17-3. Router used for trimming (courtesy Rockwell International).

Fig. 17-4. Straight bit (courtesy Sears, Roebuck and Co.).

Fig. 17-6. Ogee-end cutting bit (courtesy Sears, Roebuck and Co.).

less you buy one of the professional models that retail for several hundred dollars. Most models should arrive at your home for about $100 to $125. The smaller hobby models can be bought for something on the order of $45. Where the expense starts to arrive is with the bits and other accessories.

Router bits *must* be of high-speed steel and they must be made with a shank that will fit your particular router's chuck. Today, most bits come with a ¼-inch shank. Most routers will take those no matter the style of chuck they have. Router bits are available in many shapes and styles. They are even available with carbide tips. A ½-inch dovetail cutter in high-speed steel is a little over $5 while the same bit with carbide tips runs over $13.

I have 40 bits, about 25 of which have never been out of the case, and I recommend that you start a little more slowly. The 40-bit Craftsman set now sells for something

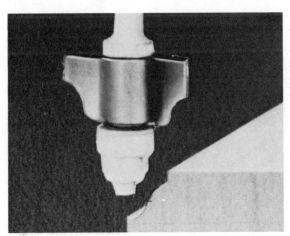

Fig. 17-5. Roman ogee bit (courtesy Sears, Roebuck and Co.).

Fig. 17-7. Ogee-end cutting bit when only a single side is used (courtesy Sears, Roebuck and Co.).

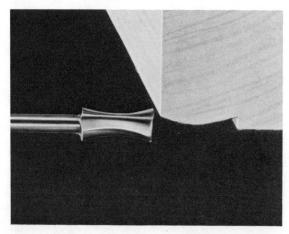

Fig. 17-8. Edge rounding bit (courtesy Sears, Roebuck and Co.).

like $135. Decide what you want to do and buy the individual bits for those jobs. If you're not going to be installing spline grooves, for example—to join pieces of wood or add T-moldings to counter edges—a slotting bit is about useless to you. I don't do either and I have two of the things. If you plan to install laminates on countertops, however, the special laminate bits are invaluable (this bit has to be carbide tipped).

Bit styles are diverse (Figs. 17-4 through 17-14), but straight (making a straight-sided flat bottomed groove) bits, V-grooving bits, chamfering (beveled edges) bits, and cove bits are among the most popular. You'll also find veining bits that produce a vertical-sided, concave-bottom slot, rabbeting bits, and bits for making bead and quarter-round moldings. Dovetail bits provide a slot with a flat bottom and sides that slant in towards the top of the slot.

Dovetail joints have for a long, long time been the sign of quality in furniture with drawers. Dovetails can be cut in many ways. They were, of course, first done by hand. Now with the correct dovetail bit in your

router, and a dovetail jig on the workpiece, you can cut drawers up to a foot deep and do them with either flush or rabbeted dovetails, in much less time and with great accuracy.

These jigs are not inexpensive. If you decide to use ¼-inch instead of ½-inch dovetails, you must add the price of the adapter template. All in all, the foot-deep drawer capacity, with both sizes of template, is going to run approximately $55. An 8-inch deep capacity unit would drop off about $25 from that price. If you decide to do much cabinet work, the kit is of great use and the cost will seem minimal in time. See Fig. 17-15.

For general-purpose edge and counter guiding, and to cut out circles up to 2 feet in diameter, another rig is handy. Fastened to the baseplate of your router, the multipurpose guide keeps you straight on edge cuts, guides along contours, allows accurate laminate trimming and serves as a trammel point for cutting circular designs. The cost is moderate, at under $20, and very likely worthwhile for anyone doing much work with a router.

Another template kit that might prove

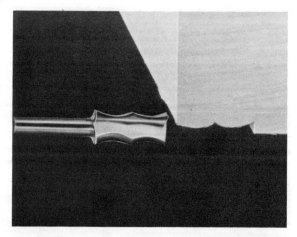

Fig. 17-9. Double-bead edging bit (courtesy Sears, Roebuck and Co.).

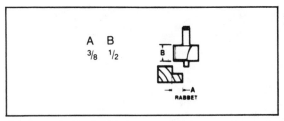

Fig. 17-10. Rabbeting bit (courtesy Stanley Tools).

A	B
3/8	1/2

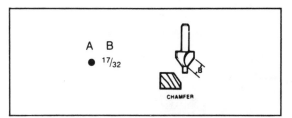

Fig. 17-11. Chamfering bit (courtesy Stanley Tools).

A	B
●	17/32

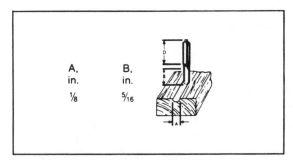

Fig. 17-12. Veining bit (courtesy Stanley Tools).

A, in.	B, in.
1/8	5/16

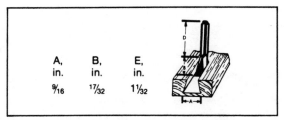

Fig. 17-13. Dovetail bit (courtesy Stanley Tools).

A, in.	B, in.	E, in.
9/16	17/32	1 1/32

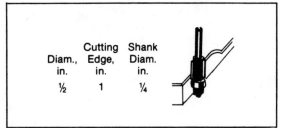

Fig. 17-14. Flush trimming laminate bit (courtesy Stanley Tools).

Diam., in.	Cutting Edge, in.	Shank Diam. in.
1/2	1	1/4

handy for some, and be useless for others, is the template clamp setup for mortising doors and jambs to take hinges. The setup is simple and fast and the cutting goes quickly, but the price (over $55) makes it an unlikely accessory for anyone not getting into door installation. Something of the same holds true for door and panel decorating kits that provide guide rails, clamps and template corners for routing designs on panels up to 3 feet by 3 feet. The price puts it up for grabs if you don't plan on doing a lot of kitchen cabinet building because it comes to over $75 delivered.

Further use for the router comes in making signs in different styles. There are two kits to aid you in this work. The simplest—a set that has the full alphabet and 10 numeral templates, as well as a template holder—costs about $15. For greater speed in sign making, Sears' Rout-A-Signer offers a far greater chance at creativity. Your router is attached to the unit, with the appropriate bit in place, and the wood is placed against a fence. The template is then inserted in the letter frame and the character height and slant (22 to 35 degrees right as preferred) are set. Character height is then set (from ¾ to 4½ inches). The template is traced with the stylus and the router follows and cuts the letters in a board from 2 to 10 inches wide and ½ to 2 inches thick. Price is about $40 delivered. It is similar to a pantagraph. See Figs. 17-16 and 17-17.

Another tool that is available for increasing router versatility is a pantagraph. A pantagraph is simply a device that allows you to trace a design in one area while reproducing it in another. In this case, the reproduction is carried out on wood with the

Fig. 17-15. Dovetail template (Rockwell International).

router cutting the design with the bit of your choice. The $35 delivered kit has five different lettering styles with full upper and lower case alphabets and numeral set in each style.

Other accessories include a router table that holds the router and turns it into a jointer of small size—giving greater cut accuracy than does freehand work—and an edge crafter for making piecrust table tops and other fancy-edge designs up to 30 inches in diameter. One that seems an oddity, though

Fig. 17-16. Sign kit (courtesy Sears, Roebuck and Co.).

Fig. 17-17. Deluxe sign kit (courtesy Sears, Roebuck and Co.).

possibly a handy oddity to me, is the router/crafter. This tool takes a workpiece up to 3 inches square and 3 feet long. It also allows you to attach the router and crank a handle moving the router and cutting rather intricate designs. It essentially turns the router into a lathe where the chisels are powered and the headstock is not. See Fig. 17-18.

Craftsman has come up with an accessory for the router called the Router-Recreator. It is fairly costly at over $100 delivered, but it is essentially a three-dimensional pantagraph. You can use your router, on this unit to make carvings up to 8 inches in diameter and 8 inches tall. See Figs. 17-19 and 17-20.

Essentially, one of the special bit set (extra) is installed in the router after the baseplate of the router is removed. The

Fig. 17-18. Router-Crafter. (Courtesy Sears, Roebuck and Co.).

205

Fig. 17-19. Edge routing (courtesy Sears, Roebuck and Co.).

Fig. 17-20. Laminate trimming (courtesy Rockwell International).

router is then placed on the Recreator and the rough stock is mounted. Next, the master is mounted. The router is started and the master is traced with a stylus bit that transfers its tracings to the rough stock (which is cut into a duplicate of the master). This tool combines all the qualities of the pantagraph and the sign-making tool along with many of the router-crafter features. Signs and even gunstocks can be carved on the machine with some movement of the material as work is done.

Routers can also be used to make cutouts for inlay work. Strip inlays are very easy to do. Simply select a straight bit that is the same size as the strip to be inlaid. Make the cut using a clamped guide or the multipurpose router guide. Fancier inlays should be set in position and the design marked before making the cuts. Always make sure the depth gauge on the router is not set deeper than the thickness of the inlay piece or it will be a subsurface inlay and not very attractive.

If you do decide a router is of interest, consider, freehand routing. Make your own designs and work on them on scraps of wood until you gain full control over the router's moves. You can create all kinds of designs such as house signs and carvings to hang on walls.

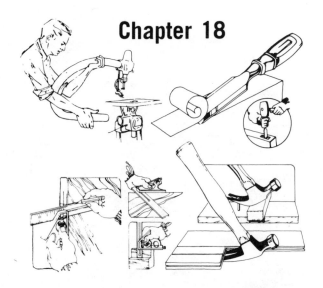

Chapter 18

Sanders and Planes

POWER SANDERS ARE NOT ESSENTIAL TO A finishing job, but they surely can cut the time and work you must do to complete finishing of projects. There are several varieties, some more suited for professional use than others, but even small finishing sanders of the oscillating type can cut a large amount of time from finishing a cabinet or other piece of work. Larger belt sanders make the finishing or refinishing of floors a relatively carefree job when properly used. Power planes are another matter. Although not overwhelmingly expensive, they are handiest when you expect to do a lot of changing of lumber dimensions of the sort that cannot be done with a saw. Often they are not needed at all in a home workshop.

Sanders. There are two basic wood sanders (Fig. 18-1 through 18-4) of general use for the home workshop: the pad sander and the belt sander. The pad sanders are virtually all finishing sanders. Belt sanders are used for large, heavy material removal jobs such as refinishing floors. A belt sander would be very inappropriate for such jobs as finishing cabinets or tables. A pad sander would lack the power and capacity to sand a floor in anything much over the size of a closet. Not that a pad sander wouldn't eventually get the floor sanding job done, it would, but both you and the sander would be worn out by the time the job was completed.

Pad sanders, or finishing sanders as they are probably more often called today, are most useful for final, fine smoothing of already sanded material. They are also useful for putting the final sheen on highly polished wood surfaces. The more expensive and powerful of them can be used, in a pinch, for moderately heavy removal of

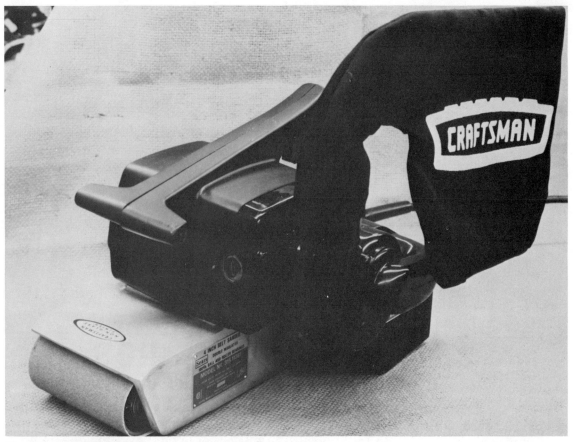

Fig. 18-1. Craftsman belt sander (courtesy Sears, Roebuck and Co.).

material. Too much such use will shorten the life of the sander.

Pad sanders come with two types of actions, or pad movements, that move the abrasives over the surface being smoothed. The broad pad allows you to keep a more level surface than you would be likely to obtain by hand sanding (though you can,

Fig. 18-2. Rockwell's belt sander line.

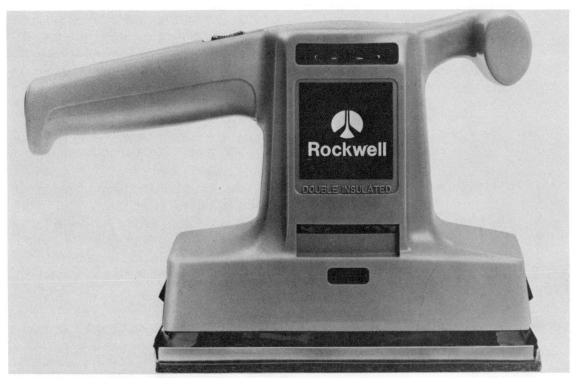

Fig. 18-3. Pad sander (Rockwell International).

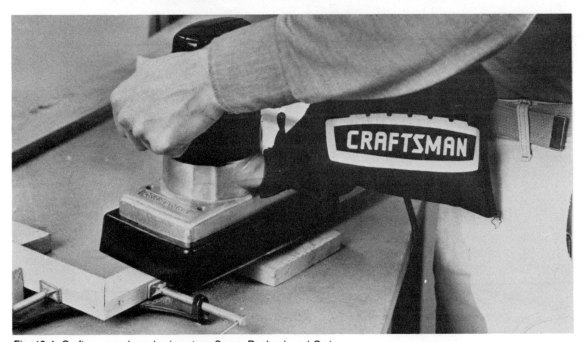

Fig. 18-4. Craftsman pad sander (courtesy Sears, Roebuck and Co.).

Fig. 18-5. Craftsman dual action sander (courtesy Sears, Roebuck and Co.).

down on swirl marks against the grain. Even the least expensive of them will probably have an orbital speed of at least 9000 per minute. The Sears Craftsman 11635 is the lowest-priced finishing sander they offer (at under $20); it has 9200 orbits per minute. Rockwell's No. 4401 has 10,000 orbits per minute. Rockwell's heavier duty No. 4420 uses ball bearings; it has 12,000 orbits per minute as a no-load speed.

Sears moves from orbital sander to dual action sanders after the 11635. Their lowest-cost, dual-action model offers a 4000-stroke or orbit per minute no-load speed. The point of dual-action sanders having a lower speed is the use of the orbital action for first material removal—and then the use of the straight line action to gain a finish that is very smooth—so that a very

with care and a great deal of effort get an extremely fine finish with hand sanding by using sanding blocks). Orbital machines need to have a high no-load speed to cut

Fig. 18-6. Finish sander (courtesy Rockwell International).

Fig. 18-7. Model 330 block sander (courtesy Rockwell International).

Fig. 18-8. Finish sander equipped with dust collector (courtesy Sears, Roebuck and Co.).

high-speed orbital action is not required. All four of the Craftsman dual-action sanders offer the same 4000 strokes or orbits per minute. Horsepower ratings vary widely, as with most electric tools, with the smallest orbital Craftsman producing 1/16 horsepower. The largest dual action turns out 1/2 a horsepower. The difference is also evident in pad size. The smaller sanders take a third of a sheet of sandpaper and the larger ones take half a sheet (Figs. 18-5 and 18-6). The same holds true for the line from Rockwell International. Their professional Speed Bloc sander (No. 330) takes a quarter of a sheet (4½×5½ inches from the standard 9-×-11-inch sandpaper sheet). See Fig. 18-7.

Sanders are generally available with or without dust pick-ups. If you have extensive sanding jobs, I readily recommend that you get such an accessory. It's only after a few dozen days' work in heavy sanding conditions that you realize the utility of the dust collector. Not only does it help protect your lungs (you should still wear one of 3M's inexpensive dust masks if you're doing a lot of sanding in an enclosed area), but the clean up is a lot less arduous afterward. Sawdust is one thing to get up, but sanding dust is so fine that you can find traces even after two or three vacuumings of a shop or other room. This is especially true with the very, very fine dust raised by finishing sanders. See Fig. 18-8.

Using a finishing sander is far from difficult, but the tool won't do all the work for you. Make sure that the sheet of sandpaper is firmly attached in the designed manner (most have a lever-action clamp at both ends of the sheet). The felt pad on the sander is fine for many woods, but if you work often with woods, such as fir that have a hard and soft grain pattern, you'll require a harder backing surface to keep the finish from being grooved along the grain lines. You can accomplish this quite easily by cutting a 1/16-inch thick piece of hardboard to fit the pad under the abrasive sheet. Don't go with a thicker hardboard or you'll probably find difficulty getting the abrasive sheet to be held firmly. You can also make a softer shoe by cutting ⅛-inch thick foam rubber to fit the pad. This soft shoe is particularly effective if you are fine sanding between coats of finish.

Today, virtually all good finishing sanders meant for one-third or larger sheet use will have knobs for two-handed operation. Using two hands is best for the job whenever possible. Bearing down, when you're working on horizontal surfaces, is seldom needed with a finishing sander. The few pounds of sander weight (ranging from about 4 to 9) will provide all the pressure needed. Any extra pressure, especially with orbital sanders, will cause scratching you will then have to get out.

Try always to work with strokes that are parallel to the grain. If you must work cross the grain, do the work slowly and use an even finer abrasive grit to keep down scratching as much as possible. Most all finish sanders have one side that will allow you to approach any wall or vertical surface flush. This is most often the side opposite the one with the levers for clamping the paper in place. Obviously, you'll know if you try to get in flush with the wrong side. Many also allow flush or near flush sanding with the forward end of the sander.

Wool-polishing bonnets are available for finishing sanders in both one-third and one-half sheet sizes. These are excellent for bringing out the final sheen on a piece that has been sanded and finished. They also do a good job on fairly flat waxed surfaces. They do not take the place of rotary polishers for work with automobiles and other things that have many curved surfaces. Finishing materials such as tung oil benefit especially from this final buffing. United Gilsonite Laboratories, for their ZAR tung oil, recommends a polish using #0000 steel wool before final buffing to give what they call an "eggshell" effect.

Belt sanders are for primary sanding. The heavy-duty workshop tool and as such are more powerful; they have larger abrasive surfaces than pad sanders. Belt width and length varies a lot, but most machines will take either a 3-inch or 4-inch wide belt and provide from 6 to 7 inches of sanding surface length. Belt speed in most cases will be around 1300 feet per minute. Power can range from about ¾ horsepower up to over 1½ horsepower. Sander size is usually stated in belt width and length (such as 3 by 21 inches, 4×24 inches and so on).

The 3-×-21-inch size is more or less standard, but belts are offered in 2×21 inches, 2½×21 inches, 3×24 inches, 3×27 inches, 4×24 inches, and 4×27 inches as well. Sears also offers belts in 4-×-36-inch and 6-×-48-inch sizes for very large sanders.

It is almost senseless to buy a belt sander without a dust-collecting attachment because these machines, especially with a coarse grit abrasive belt, remove a lot of material very rapidly. On a sander such as the Sears' Craftsman 1178C, the bag is standard equipment (this is Sears largest, most powerful belt sander).

Belt sander adjustments are important. The rear drum on belt sanders is powered, while the front drum is not, and is the point

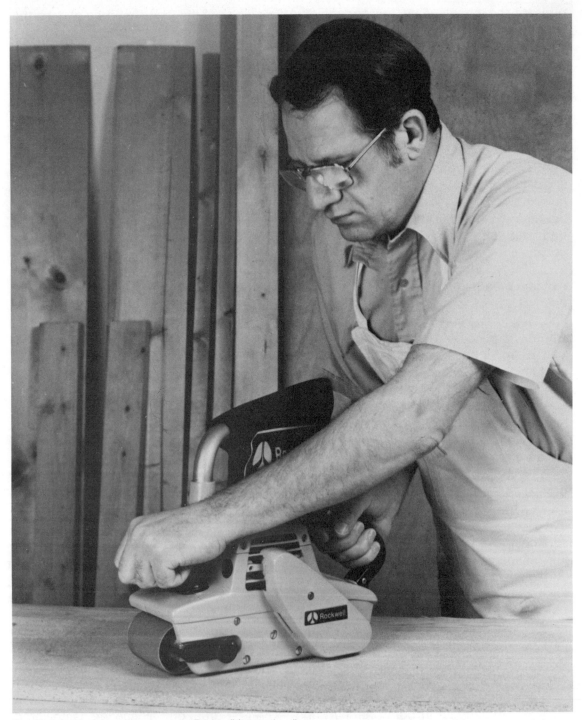

Fig. 18-9. Belt sander in use (courtesy Rockwell International).

Fig. 18-10. Sanding belts (courtesy Rockwell International).

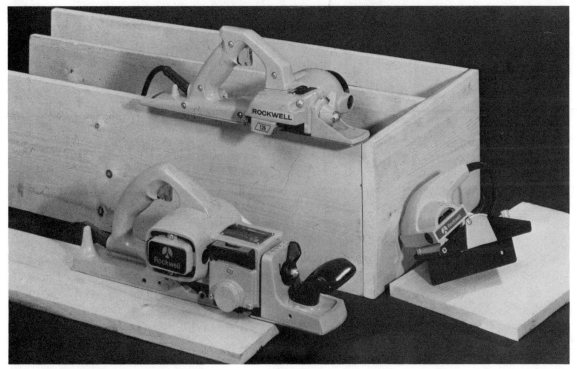

Fig. 18-11. Rockwell's power planer line.

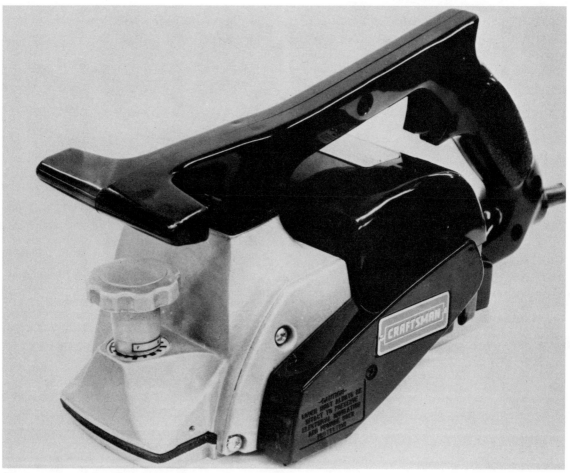

Fig. 18-12. Sears' Craftsman power planer.

where adjustments are made. Belts must first be mounted correctly. There will be an arrow pointing in the direction of rotation on all belts. All belt sanders that I've seen run in a clockwise direction. Tracking is adjusted by a knob that moves the front drum so that the belt is running straight (otherwise it might slip off the drums).

Belt sanders are started before contact is made with the work surface. Otherwise they just move themselves along the work without doing any material removal. Keep the belt sander moving once you make contact with the work surface. Letting it idle will

cut depressions in the surface. These depressions can be murderous to smooth cut. Try to work parallel to the grain and overlap strokes moving back and forth as you do. Don't use an extreme sideways motion for the overlap. This would effectively have you sanding across the grain and causing scratches that aren't necessary, and must be removed.

Cross-grain sanding is handy in some instances. If a floor is in very bad shape, with a lot of wear, you may want to quickly take off a great deal of material to get a nearly level surface before going with the grain sanding

218

for a finish. Use just enough pressure to keep the abrasive cutting, no matter which direction you're sanding, and make sure the sander is flat on the work (Fig. 18-9). As with a finish sander, the belt sander weight will usually provide all the pressure needed. Exceptions are those cases where a great deal of material must be taken off.

Abrasive selection is important with a belt sander. Because of their power, they do remove material quickly, but some materials are more readily handled than others. When you're working on old finishes, such as painted or varnished floors, you'll want to use an open coat abrasive that will not clog easily. If the paint or varnish has been worn thin, you need less of an open coat.

When the belt starts to clog in such work, keep your eyes open. Checking evey few minutes will allow you to take a stiff bristled brush and clear the belt of much of the material clogging it. With today's belt costs, you don't want to use any more than you have to (the more or less standard 3-×-21-inch belt runs a bit under $1.50 at present, while the 4-×-24-inch belt for Sears largest sander is almost $2. Packages of 10 are available. If you have a great deal of sanding to do, you will save some money (about 10 percent). See Fig. 18-10).

Besides dust collectors, about the only accessory available for belt sanders is a finishing stand. The belt sander is clamped to the stand to become a very accurate finishing sander. The stand allows small pieces needing heavy material removal to be more easily handled than with the freehand sander (small pieces must be clamped when a belt sander is used). Such stands are readily available in a price range of some $40 to $60.

Planes. Power planes are not really essential tools for the home woodworking shop. Nevertheless, they can serve some purposes of the belt sander and the router as well as doing simpler planing jobs such as

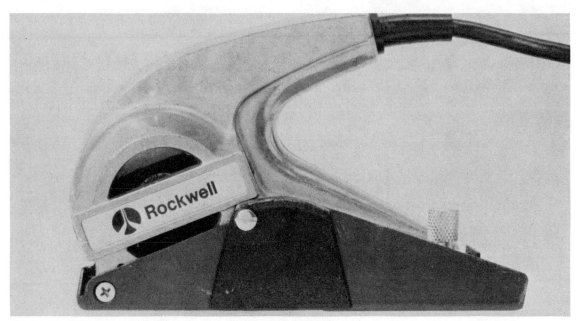

Fig. 18-13. Rabbetting power planer (courtesy Rockwell International).

Fig. 18-14. Rabbeting planer in use (courtesy Rockwell International).

Fig. 18-15. Edge beveling with a power planer (courtesy Rockwell International).

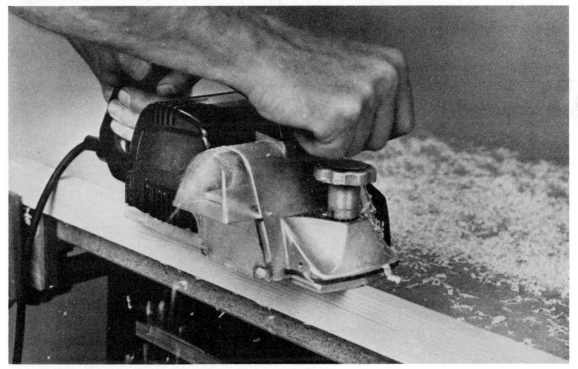

Fig. 18-16. Smoothing an edge (courtesy Sears, Roebuck and Co.).

cutting down the edge of a door. The cutter on a power plane rotates. The better ones will be high-speed models with speeds ranging from 15,000 to about 22,000 rpm. The primary advantage of a power plane (Fig. 18-11) is its ability to remove wood to a set depth for the entire length of a work surface. A belt sander is apt to cause some problems if you are not absolutely certain to apply equal pressure all the way along the surface.

Sears Craftsman 1732 will plane to a width of 3⅝ inches. That is enough to face a 2×4s' wide side in a single pass and will remove as much as 1/16 of an inch of material in a single pass. The base plate is also grooved so that the planer can be used to bevel edges at a uniform 45 degrees. A rabbeting guide allows you to rabbet to 11/32 of an inch wide and 15/64 of an inch deep in a single pass. See Figs. 18-12 through 18-16.

Chapter 19

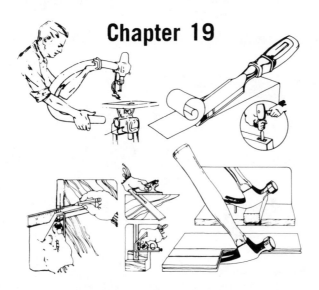

The Smithshop Mark V

THERE ARE A NUMBER OF STATIONARY POW-
er tools and many in the field are exceptionally good, versatile tools that will do a
number of jobs exceptionally well and accurately. For versatility one tool stands out.
The Shopsmith Mark V is nearly a complete
woodworking shop in itself.

The basic Mark V (Fig. 19-1) includes a
table saw, a vertical drill press, a horizontal
boring machine, a lathe, and a disc sander.
The standard Mark V package includes: a
lower saw guard; an upper saw guard—with
anti-kickback feature and kerf splitter; a
miter gauge safety grip; a miter gauge; a rip
fence; a 10-inch combination saw blade; a
sanding disc; an extension table; a lathe
tailstock; a lathe tool rest; a lathe drive
center; a lathe cup center; chuck and key;
1¼-inch saw arbor; arbor wrench; Allen
wrench for changing from one tool to

another; a self-study course; a woodworking
book, sandpaper, safety goggles, and a
push stick. The package sells for approximately $1200, but that will probably, as does
everything, increase in the future.

The following tools can be added to any
Mark V: a band saw with a 10½-inch cutoff
capacity; a jointer with a 4-inch capacity; a
6-inch belt sander (table size is 6×9 inches);
an 18-inch jigsaw that will cut to 2-inch thick
stock; enough saw blades, jointer blades,
chisels, clamps, drill bits, routine bits, mortising jigs, sanding accessories, and other
items to make you really stand up and take
notice. Adding these accessories does
greatly increase the cost of the basic
machine. Shopsmith offers what they call
the ultimate accessory package that runs
nearly $4,000. It includes the band saw,
jointer, jigsaw, belt sander, and probably

Fig. 19-1. Shopsmith Mark V (courtesy Shopsmith, Inc.).

100 other items—from sanding belts to drill bits and dado blades.

The basic Shopsmith Mark V is a 12-square-foot package (6 feet long by 2 feet wide), with a 13.5-ampere motor developing over 2 horsepower. Motor speed is variable from 700 to 5200 rpm, infinitely within that range, and tool weight is 198 pounds. The drill chuck size is ¾ of an inch. Saw arbors of 1¼ inches, ½ inch and ⅝ inch can all be used. Permanently lubricated ball bearings are used throughout.

Speed is dial adjusted. The table can be raised or lowered on a rack-and-pinion setup and locked in at the height you want. The extension table can be mounted at either end of the machine. The table saw provides a miter range from 30 to 120 degrees in both directions for greatest utility.

Over the years, the Shopsmith has been produced in Mark 10ER, Mark VII, Mark II, and the currently available Mark V model. The Shopsmith catalog (if you want one, send $1 to Shopsmith, Inc., 750 Center Drive, Vandalia, OH 45377) is coded to show what accessories will work with the machine you happen to own.

CONVERSION

Converting from one tool to another sounds

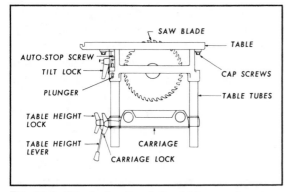

Fig. 19-2. Principal parts of the table saw (courtesy Shopsmith, Inc.).

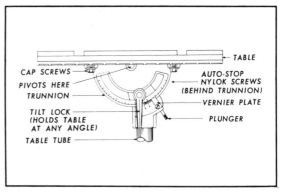

Fig. 19-4. Parts of trunnion and saw tilt mechanism (courtesy Shopsmith, Inc.).

as if it might be quite a hassle, but the Mark V was specifically designed to be convertible while sacrificing as little accuracy, size, and power as possible when compared to conventional single-unit power tools. The first step is to always unplug the machine. Though the start switch has safety wings to make it difficult to turn the machine on accidentally, there's no point in taking chances.

You begin by loosening the carriage lock on the casing at the table side just below the first rail. Now set the saw blade in its lower guard and slide the saw arbor onto the spindle. Use the Allen wrench supplied to lock the guard on the quill while making sure the post on the bottom is resting firmly

against the way tube. Align the arbor set screw with the puttied-over screw on the spindle collar so that the set screw is over the flattened, tapered spot on the spindle when the screw is tightened.

Now, unlock the table with your right hand and use the table height lever to bring the table up to the point you hear clicks. This means the table is in its highest position. Use your left hand to hold the table lever in position and reach between the way tubes to grasp the carriage with your right hand, pushing it toward the headstock stops. This automatically centers the blade in its table slot.

Now use the table handle to lower the

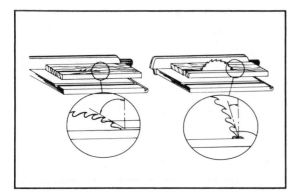

Fig. 19-3. Improper blade projections: use ½ to ¾ of an inch (courtesy Shopsmith, Inc.).

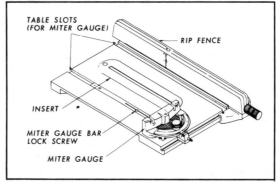

Fig. 19-5. Parts must be parallel for accurate cuts (courtesy Shopsmith, Inc.).

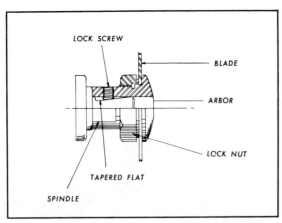

LOCK SCREW

BLADE

ARBOR

LOCK NUT

TAPERED FLAT

SPINDLE

Fig. 19-6. Lock arbor securely on tapered flat (courtesy Shopsmith, Inc.).

table to get the desired blade height. Lock the carriage and headstock. Move around to the back of the tool and hold the upper saw guard and splitter in your left hand. Slip the keyhole slots over the screws in the lower blade guard, align the guard over the blade, and tighten the screws. Now, place the miter gauge in its table slot, place the rip fence on the extension table, and turn its lock knob to secure it. See Figs. 19-2 through 19-6.

That's one tool. It sounds fairly complex, but it really isn't. The idea is to make changes as easy as possible and as quick as possible. Table height setting is simply done. The handle is a butterfly type that is clearly marked for its use. All the other adjustment necessities are easily reached. The only tool needed for the changeover is the Allen wrench (supplied with the Mark V). In any case, when the saw is first set up, and then if use is continuous, it is a good idea to check to make sure that everything is square and that all items are operating as they should.

With just the basic table saw and no special accessories, a number of cuts can be readily made (Fig. 19-7). The simple crosscut can be made with greatest accuracy of virtually all woodcutting tools. Compound miters, compound rip bevels, kerfing, rabbeting and other cuts can also be done. Molding and dado heads and blades for the table saw enable you to begin producing a great many other types of cuts. This greatly increases the number and style of projects you might want to attempt. Fingerlaps, done with a dado head, can be used in place of dovetails to join drawer sides and backs (though the joint is not quite as strong), and the dado head can also be used for cutting tongue-and-groove setups (Fig. 19-8).

Certain features go with all cuts made on any table saw, whether the Shopsmith Mark V or a free standing single unit. The work is placed against the miter gauge for crosscutting and advanced past the blade. All guards must be in place. If short stock is being cut, you always use a scrap of wood or other material such as plastic to advance the material into the blade. Even with guards in place, at no time should your fingers ever be in a position to even come near the moving saw blade!

New hold-down rods—developed not too long ago by the makers of multipurpose tools—can, in many cases, eliminate the need for a wood pusher stick. The free hand is never used to shove against the free end of the work. This will almost certainly bind the cut and can cause kickback. The free hand should be nothing more than a guide. In addition, the free hand is never used to pick up any cut free pieces until after the saw blade stops turning.

The clothing worn when using power tools is of some importance. It should be comfortable, but not billowing. Sleeves should be buttoned or rolled above the elbows and ties should be left for office and church wear. If you prefer to wear a shop coat, use heavy rubber bands to hold the

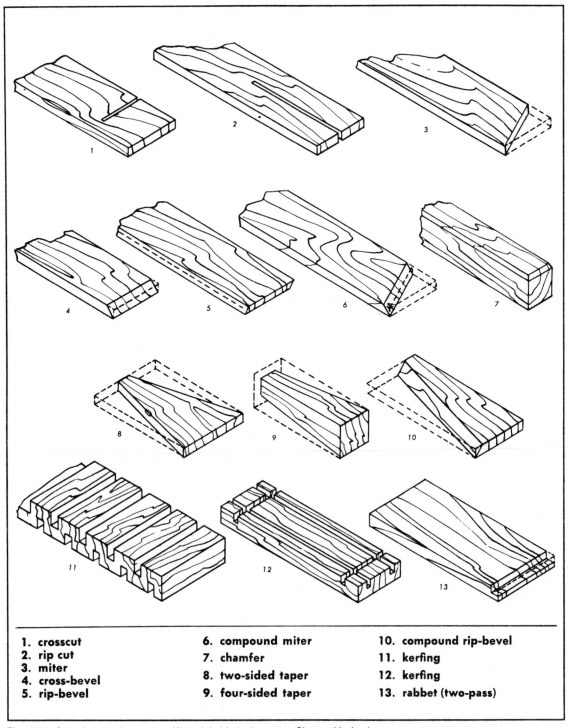

1. crosscut
2. rip cut
3. miter
4. cross-bevel
5. rip-bevel
6. compound miter
7. chamfer
8. two-sided taper
9. four-sided taper
10. compound rip-bevel
11. kerfing
12. kerfing
13. rabbet (two-pass)

Fig. 19-7. Cuts that can be made with a plain blade (courtesy Shopsmith, Inc.).

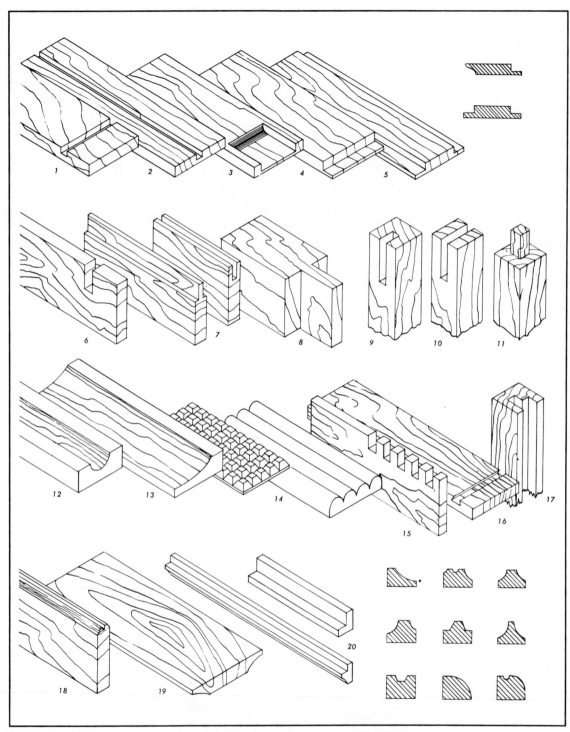

Fig. 19-8. Cuts with dado (1 to 13, 15, and 17), molding head (14, 18, 19, 20), and drill press (16). Courtesy Shopsmith, Inc.

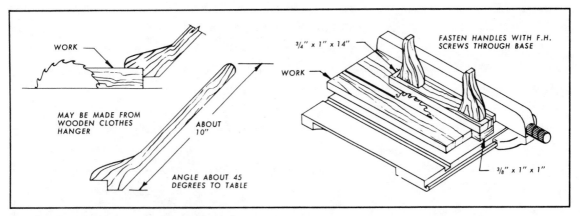

Fig. 19-9. Push sticks (courtesy Shopsmith, Inc.).

sleeves tight at the wrists. Wear comfortable shoes with nonslip soles. Most important of all don't rush things. Take your time and you won't forget either the safety rules or how to make good cuts.

Rip sawing is the time when you are usually making narrow strips and the time when the push stick is most likely to come in handy. As Fig. 19-9 shows, it is a simple thing to make and it should always be used before your fingers are within half a foot of the blade.

Mitering can be useful for many projects, and each project might require a different angle setting on the miter gauge. For a hexagon, you would use a 30-degree setting (six sides) while an octagon requires a 22½-degree setting. Essentially, the setting is easy to figure because what you'll need to do is simply divide the number of sides into 180 degrees (you'll be making twice as many cuts as there are sides on bevel mitering, so the total number of degrees will be 360).

Furniture making and cabinetmaking is fun. It can be a good way to get better looking, better lasting and less expensive wood furniture than any store can supply today. For such work, a dado blade is invaluable as

it helps to provide a number of cuts that are extremely handy in joinery of any type of wood. Actually, dados can be cut with a standard combination blade, but the number of passes needed becomes ludicrous when dado heads can make single pass cuts up to 53/64 of an inch wide (with the Mark V dado blade set and table insert (Fig. 19-10). Figure 19-11 shows some of the common woodworking joints you can readily make with either a standard saw blade or a dado set. You can readily cut tenons and full mortises are simple, but you can't mortise in the center of a piece of stock without using either chisels or a router.

Molding heads are another feature that can be used with table saws. They allow you to cut many molding designs either on strips to be used as molding or right on the panels to be used. A molding head is of steel or aluminum and locks to the spindle of the tool. It takes any of the variety of cutter shapes, which are interchangeable, and usually the head itself will be about 1 inch wide. This means a dado table insert must also be used.

Figures 19-12 and 19-13 show some of the shapes possible with molding heads. The job of using it is fairly simple, but there

229

Fig. 19-10. Dado blade in use (courtesy Shopsmith, Inc.).

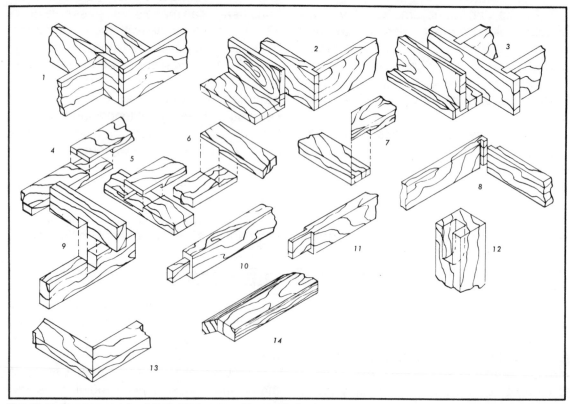

Fig. 19-11. Common woodworking joints (courtesy Shopsmith, Inc.).

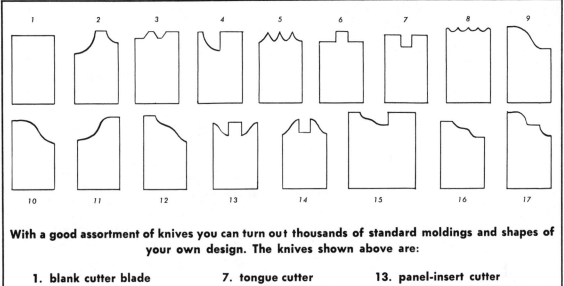

With a good assortment of knives you can turn out thousands of standard moldings and shapes of your own design. The knives shown above are:

1. blank cutter blade
2. ¼", ½" quarter round
3. glue joint, ½" stock and up
4. cabinet-door lip
5. "V"-flute molding
6. groove cutter
7. tongue cutter
8. four-bead molding
9. ogee molding
10. ogee molding
11. ogee molding
12. reverse ogee
13. panel-insert cutter
14. panel-insert (cope) cutter
15. 1⅜" sash cutter
16. 1⅜" sash cope cutter
17. bead-and-cove molding

Fig. 19-12. Table saw knives (courtesy Shopsmith, Inc.).

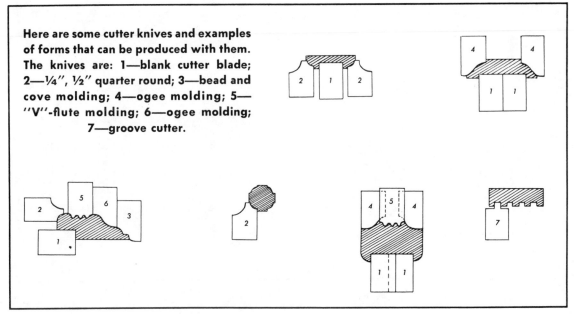

Here are some cutter knives and examples of forms that can be produced with them. The knives are: 1—blank cutter blade; 2—¼", ½" quarter round; 3—bead and cove molding; 4—ogee molding; 5—"V"-flute molding; 6—ogee molding; 7—groove cutter.

Fig. 19-13. Table saw knives and forms (courtesy Shopsmith, Inc.).

are a couple of things it pays to remember. First, it takes practice to become really good. Make your first half a hundred molding cuts on scrap wood. Second, learn to feed the material slowly. Excessive feed speed is the primary cause of problems when using a molding head. If the work chatters, you're feeding too fast. Finally, make the cross grain cuts first and the most slowly (Fig. 19-14).

Jointers are, in a sense, funny tools. A jointer is little more than a rotary cutter to plane edges smooth and square. In addition, the jointer can also shape stock to provide some of the varied shapes shown in Fig. 19-15.

Setting up the Mark V jointer is not extremely difficult. You begin by placing a straightedge on the outfeed jointer table so that it juts out over the cutter head. Turn the cutter head, by hand, until one knife is set at the top point of the cutting circle. The knife should barely scrape the straightedge. If the knife lifts the straightedge, it is set too high. If it doesn't touch the straightedge it is set too low. Three Allen screws hold the blade retention wedges; these are loosened if adjustment is needed. The two screws on which the knives rest are adjusted up or down depending on whether the knife is too high or too low. Check once more and tighten it up again (Fig. 19-16).

Fig. 19-14. Cutting thick stock (courtesy Shopsmith, Inc.).

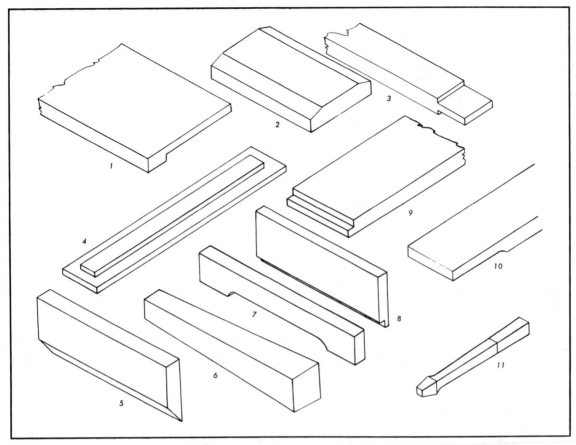

Fig. 19-15. Typical jointer cuts: 1, wide rabbet; 2, chamfer; 3, stud tenon; 4, raising; 5, bevel; 6, tapers; 7, recessing; 8, edge rabbet; 9, end rabbet; 10, surfacing; 11, varied shapes. Courtesy Shopsmith, Inc.

The forward edge of the knife should extend about 1/16 of an inch beyond the rabbeting ledge so that the work will clear the outfeed table during a rabbeting cut. Each wedge is locked in place with three Allen screws. Figure 19-17 shows what the results are if the knives are not adjusted properly and the cutter is not positioned correctly.

To adjust for depth, turn the hand knob clockwise to lower the infeed table. To raise the infeed table, you just reverse the procedure. Check scale accuracy by making a cut at a setting of 1/8 of an inch. Measure the cut. If the cut isn't correct, raise or lower the table until it is. Then set the scale pointer at

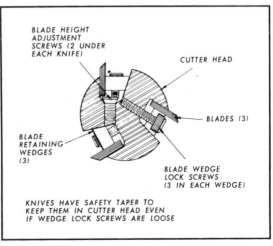

Fig. 19-16. Knife adjustment (courtesy Shopsmith, Inc.).

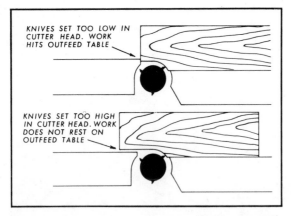

Fig. 19-17. Knives too low and too high (courtesy Shopsmith, Inc.).

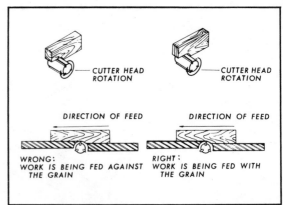

Fig. 19-19. Cut with the grain (courtesy Shopsmith, Inc.).

exactly ⅛ of an inch. That sets the full range of the scale accurately. (See Fig. 19-18).

Jointers are used only with the grain of the wood—never against. In the few cases when a cut against the grain is essential, make the cut with a very, very shallow depth and feed very slowly. The odds are still good the surface will not be as good as a with the grain cut, but splintering should be reduced. In most cases, don't cut more deeply than ⅛ of an inch. See Figs. 19-19 through 19-21.

Rabbet cuts can be made on the edge or the face of a board. Tongues can be formed by making two rabbet cuts, as may tenons. Tenons might require several pass-

es on each side because they are longer. Lightweight tenons can be made with a single pass on each side of the tenon. Therefore, two passes, one on each side, will give you a stud tenon, while four passes will give you a full tenon. If rabbets are cut across the end grain of a board, use a pusher to hold the board down. The pusher should be a board that is almost the width of the board being rabbeted, with a handle attached with screws or nails and glue. See Figs. 19-22 through 19-24.

Bevel cuts are readily made by tilting the fence. Taper cuts are made in a slightly more complicated manner. The need for

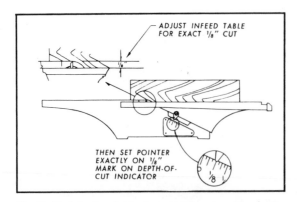

Fig. 19-18. Adjusting depth of cut scale (courtesy Shopsmith, Inc.).

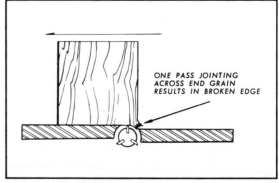

Fig. 19-20. Cutting against the grain (courtesy Shopsmith, Inc.).

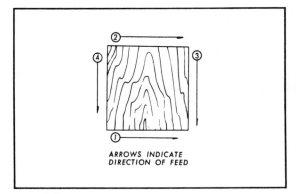

Fig. 19-21. Sequence for jointing four edges (courtesy Shopsmith, Inc.).

stop blocks at the distance the taper is to run (blocks clamped for say a 10-inch taper would be 10 inches from the cutter head). The piece is then moved to the mark where the taper is to start, and that is placed over the cutter head. It is lowered on and the taper is made.

Chamfering is nothing more than a bevel cut that doesn't remove all the stock on the edge of a board. It is accomplished by setting the fence to the angle desired and making the number of passes needed to get the chamfer. To make an octagonal shape (Fig. 19-25), you set the fence at a 45-

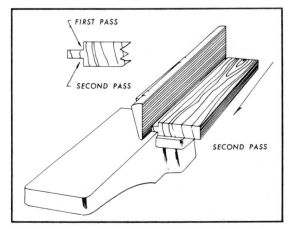

Fig. 19-22. Two rabbet cuts form tongue (courtesy Shopsmith, Inc.).

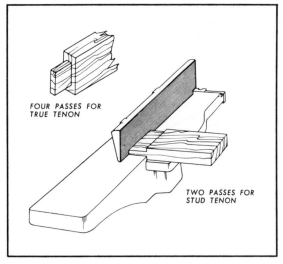

Fig. 19-23. Four cuts form a tenon (courtesy Shopsmith, Inc.).

degree angle. Using a piece of material that has already been trued up along all four edges, make the four passes as shown in the illustrations.

DRILL PRESS

Drill presses for home workshops have been underrated for years, because of their cost and because so many people had no idea how many jobs could be done with them. There is a bonus on the multipurpose Mark V because the drill press can also be used as a horizontal boring bar. All drill presses begin in the same way. A power driven steel rod holds a device at the end that, in turn, is used to hold a drill bit.

Today, the three-jaw chuck is the most common form of holding device, but router bits and dovetail cutters require specialized chucks. The basic advantage of the Mark V drill press, in a vertical position, is the weight of the head. In some cases, use in a horizontal position will be easier. The quill (the sleeve in which the spindle rotates) feeds 4¼ inches, and returns to its original position because of a coil spring in the headstock.

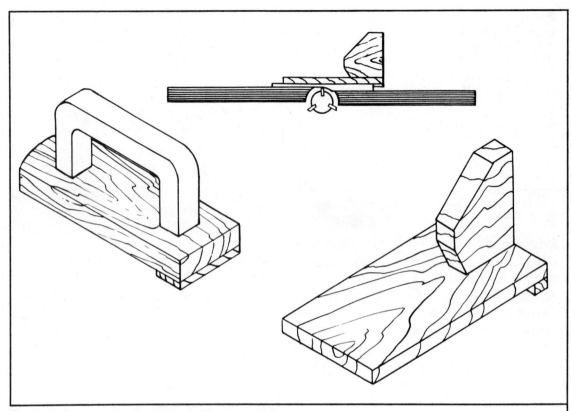

Fig. 19-24. Scrap wood pusher (courtesy Shopsmith, Inc.).

The spring is adjustable so that you are easily able to maintain a smooth, shockfree return. See Figs. 19-26 and 19-27.

To adjust the return spring, use the Allen wrench to loosen the screw on the forward end (or top) of the headstock. Extend the quill until it disengages from its pinion gear. Turn the feed lever for the quill in the same direction while the quill is disengaged. This increases spring tension. To decrease tension, turn the quill feed lever a small amount in the opposite direction. Hold the spring tension you want with the quill feed lever. Push the quill back until it engages (the rack teeth engage the pinion gear). Make sure the keyway on the top of the quill is aligned with the screw in the top of the headstock. Now bring the quill back to its

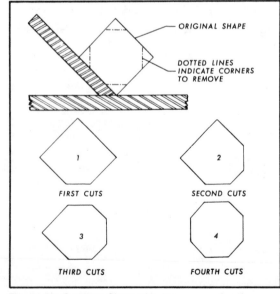

ORIGINAL SHAPE

DOTTED LINES
INDICATE CORNERS
TO REMOVE

1
FIRST CUTS

2
SECOND CUTS

3
THIRD CUTS

4
FOURTH CUTS

Fig. 19-25. Courtesy Shopsmith, Inc.

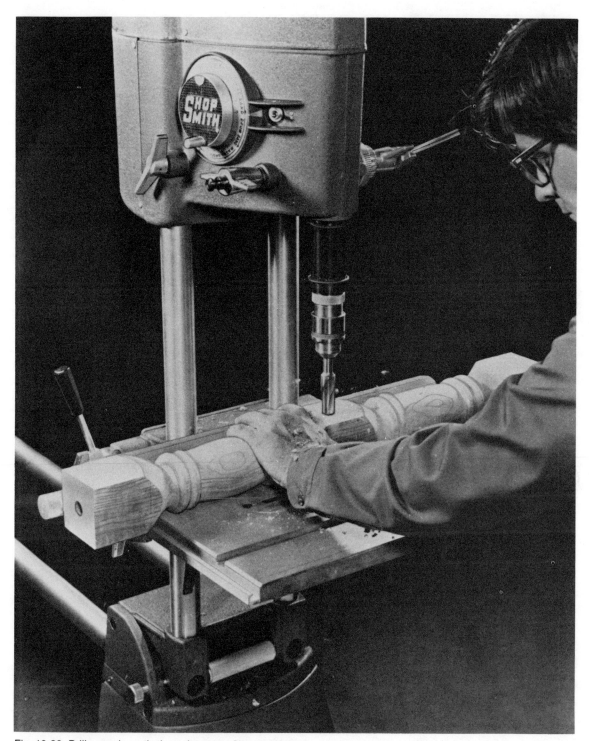

Fig. 19-26. Drill press in vertical use (courtesy Shopsmith, Inc.).

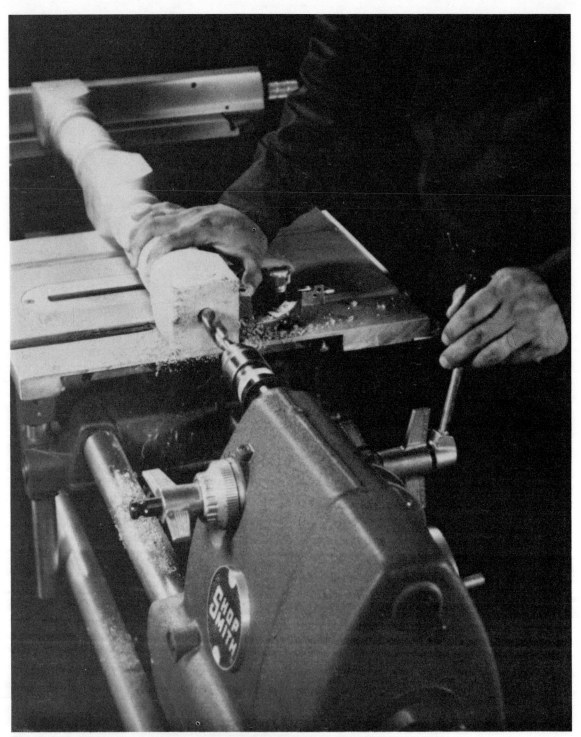

Fig. 19-27. Drill press in horizontal use (courtesy Shopsmith, Inc.).

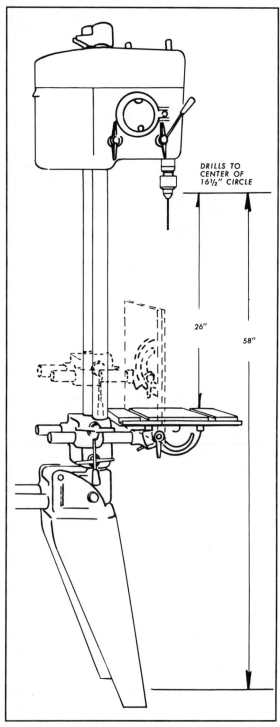

DRILLS TO
CENTER OF
16½" CIRCLE

26"

58"

Fig. 19-28. Drill press capacities (courtesy Shopsmith, Inc.).

nonextended position and tighten the set screw just enough to engage the keyway in the quill. Don't over tighten the set screw or the quill will bind.

The saw table is used as the drill press table. This leaves you with the miter gauge, rip fence, and all hold downs, stops and supports for use with the drill press as well.

To figure drill press capacities, consult Fig. 19-28. The Mark V drill press will drill to the center of a 16½ circle and allow an up and down adjustment of 26 inches. The horizonal boring position gives an unlimited—or limited only by your shop size—capacity in length and width.

Most of the tools that can be used with the electric hand drill can also be used with the drill press (as Fig. 19-29 shows). Various speeds are best for particular jobs, (see Fig. 19-30. Feed speed varies with the work being done and the material worked. Large drills in thick hardwoods obviously will have to be fed more slowly than will smaller drills in softwoods. Accuracy in drilling depends on careful measurement and layout (Figs. 19-31 and 19-32).

When a piece of work, such as a cabinet, requires a large number of drill holes, often two or three operation drill holes, a drill press is faster than a hand drill and gives more accurate work. In cabinetry, screws usually require a body hole for the screw shank and a lead hole for the thread. Body holes equal the gauge of the screw and go right on through the first piece. The lead hole should be about half the length of the threaded portion of the screw and somewhat smaller than the screw's threaded portion. Countersinking requires a countersink equal in diameter to the screw's head. Counterboring—where a dowel will be used to plug the hole—should be at least the equal of the screw head in size (Fig. 19-33).

239

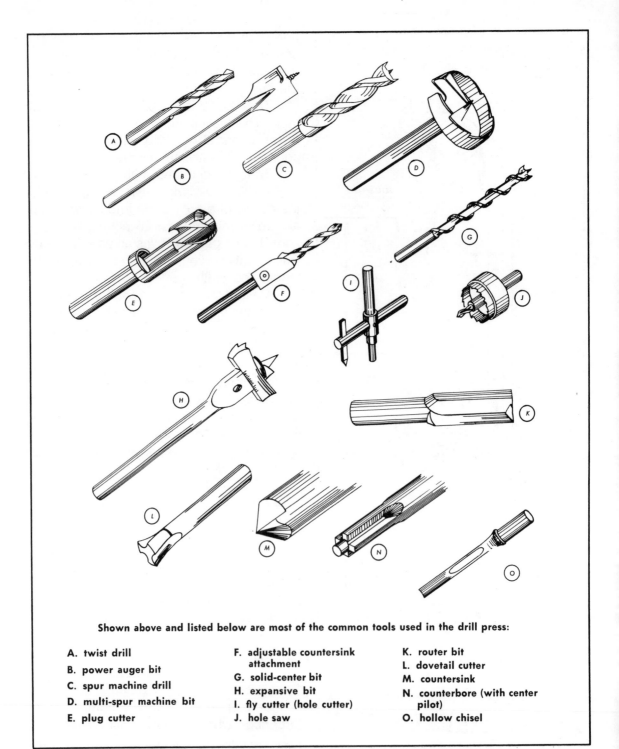

Shown above and listed below are most of the common tools used in the drill press:

A. twist drill
B. power auger bit
C. spur machine drill
D. multi-spur machine bit
E. plug cutter

F. adjustable countersink attachment
G. solid-center bit
H. expansive bit
I. fly cutter (hole cutter)
J. hole saw

K. router bit
L. dovetail cutter
M. countersink
N. counterbore (with center pilot)
O. hollow chisel

Fig. 19-29. Accessories (courtesy Shopsmith, Inc.).

Keeping the same distance between screw holes can prove a real problem, but a simple jig can be made to do the job, using the fence, an auxiliary fence, and a couple of clamps (as shown in Fig. 19-34). Clamp the auxiliary fence to the regular fence and slip the dowel into the guide block. The dowel slips into the hole already drilled in the work and positions it for the next hole to be drilled. To use the same guide block and dowel for all sizes for work, simply place a small pin in the dowel and drill pilot holes to mark locations, going afterward to full-size holes.

Mortising can also be done on a drill press. You'll need a mortising bit and still need a chisel to clean out the bottoms of the

MATERIAL	OPERATION	SPEED (rpm)	SPEED-DIAL SETTING
wood	drilling—up to ¼″	3,800	S
wood	drilling—¼″ to ½″	3,100	P
wood	drilling—½″ to ¾″	2,300	M
wood	drilling—¾″ to 1″	2,000	K
wood	drilling—over 1″	700	Slow
wood	using expansion or multi-spur bit	700	Slow
wood	routing	4,000-5,000	Rout-Shape
wood	cutting plugs or short dowels	3,300	Q
wood	carving	4,000-5,000	Rout-Shape
wood	using fly-cutter	700	Slow
wood	using dowel-cutter	1,800	J
hardwood	mortising	2,200	L
softwood	mortising	3,300	Q
metal	fine wire-brushing	3,300	Q
metal	coarse wire-brushing	1,000	D
wood	coarse wire-brushing	2,200	L
soft metals	buffing (cloth wheel)	3,800	S
hard metals	buffing (cloth wheel)	4,700	U
plastics	buffing (cloth wheel)	2,300	M
metal	using fly-cutter	700	Slow
metal	grinding—3″-4″ cup wheel	3,100	P
glass	drilling with metal tube	700	Slow

Fig. 19-30. Speeds (courtesy Shopsmith, Inc.).

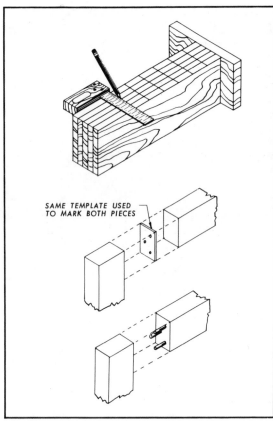

Fig. 19-31. Layout (courtesy Shopsmith, Inc.).

mortises and the corners, but the work will go a lot more rapidly than by hand. Now there is a special mortising attachment so that little or no chiseling is required.

Essentially, Shopsmith has designed a drill bit that is surrounded by a chisel. The chisel is clamped (it is square) while the bit spins freely inside it. There is also a special hold-down jig to keep the work from leaping around while the tools do their jobs. The whole setup isn't inexpensive; the half inch bit and chisel runs about $35, the mortising attachment is $26, and the mortise hold down is $17. Still, considering the fact that the mortise and tenon joint is about the strongest going for large furniture pieces, the cost can't be considered too high. I would

guess, for blind mortising, the bottom of the mortise would still have to be cleaned out with a chisel, though I'm not sure.

Dovetail joints are also possible with the drill press and special bits. This is about the strongest joint possible and is especially good in drawers that receive a lot of use because the only way the joint doesn't resist stress is the direction in which the tenons are inserted. The special routing bit for the Mark V makes the job fairly simple and allows you to form the types of joints shown in Fig. 19-35. Dovetail tenons require two passes of the bit; the mortise needs a single pass.

Dowelling is another job for the drill press and it is one good way of strengthening a joint without going to the complexity of mortise-and-tenon or dovetail work. A hole spacing jig, such as the one shown in Fig. 19-36, is of very great help when dowelling. Fasten the jig to the ways and it automati-

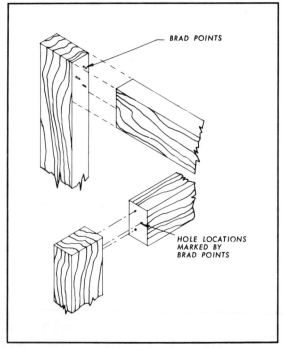

Fig. 19-32. Hole marking (courtesy Shopsmith, Inc.).

SCREW GAUGE	BODY HOLE	LEAD HOLE	SCREW GAUGE IN INCHES
0	53	—	.060
1	49	—	.073
2	44	56*	.086
3	40	52*	.099
4	33	51*	.112
5	1/8	49*	.125
6	28	47	.138
7	24	46	.151
8	19	42	.164
9	15	41	.177
10	10	38	.190
11	5	37	.203
12	7/32	36	.216
14	D	31	.242
16	I	28	.268
18	19/64	23	.294
*In hardwoods only.			

Fig. 19-33. Counterboring (courtesy Shopsmith, Inc.).

cally positions the work for the next hole when a dowel peg engages the first hole.

Drill presses, along with a few short pieces of dowel, can be used to form joints that are as strong as dovetailed joints, yet far easier to make. Simply place the two pieces to be joined in a clamp, drill the proper size and depth holes, insert glue, and slip in the dowels. The horizontal boring bar action of the Mark V makes this job even easier because the lower section can be placed on the table, against a stop. The upright section is held against it, while the boring bar is used to drill the holes, without clamping. This is handy to make drawers and some types of furniture. The dowel pegs can be used as design details. In such cases, the dowels can be sanded flush with the overall surface or rounded and left to extend a slight bit above the surface. See Fig. 19-37.

You can form your own dowels from scrap stock, using a plug cutter, of a wood type not commonly available as dowels. The plug cutter is simply run to its capacity into the work. The table saw is then used to cut the work, which frees up the dowels. This is useful in work where you want to, for example, use dowels contrasting in color with the overall finished surface or when dowels are hard, or impossible, to locate in the correct wood.

The drill press attachment, with router bits, can be used (as Fig. 19-38 shows) to do edge trimming or to form edge grooves. With a template (as shown in Fig. 19-39), it is useful for grooving curved sections on their edges or on the surface. See Figs. 19-40 through 19-42.

THE LATHE

Lathes were originally turned by hand, then by foot treadles, and today they are turned by electric motors. Lathes are tools with two adjustable centers along a common horizontal plane. The material is held between the centers and rotated as it is worked. The principle hasn't changed since ancient times despite the complexity of some rather

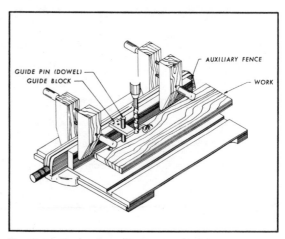

Fig. 19-34. Jig to control distances between holes (courtesy Shopsmith, Inc.).

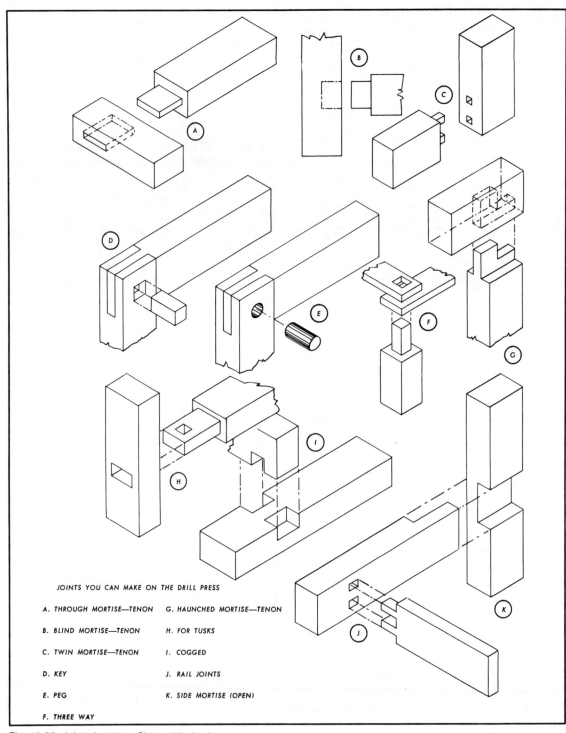

JOINTS YOU CAN MAKE ON THE DRILL PRESS

A. THROUGH MORTISE—TENON   G. HAUNCHED MORTISE—TENON

B. BLIND MORTISE—TENON   H. FOR TUSKS

C. TWIN MORTISE—TENON   I. COGGED

D. KEY   J. RAIL JOINTS

E. PEG   K. SIDE MORTISE (OPEN)

F. THREE WAY

Fig. 19-35. Joints (courtesy Shopsmith, Inc.).

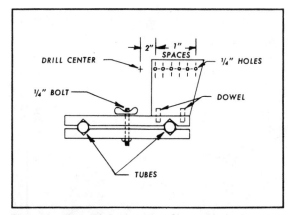

Fig. 19-36. Doweling jig (courtesy Shopsmith, Inc.).

spectacular modern metal-working lathes which are virtually completely automated.

The Mark V conversion to a lathe requires about 32 seconds after you've gained a bit of practice. Shopsmith conversion charts show that converting from lathe to saw to sander to horizontal drill to vertical drill to lathe requires a total of under 3 minutes for all processes, once the tool user gains a bit of practice. The Mark V will take stock up to 34 inches long between centers. It has a 16½ inch swing that allows you to complete good-sized jobs. Before starting any lathe job, you should check to make sure the drive and cup centers are in perfect alignment. See Fig. 19-43.

Check drive alignment by bringing the headstock all the way to the right of the tubes. Now, extend the quill until its spur point almost touches the cup point. A visual check will now show if the two are aligned correctly. If not, loosen the cup center-mount screw and turn the cup center to bring it in line with the drive point. Lock the cup center mount, recheck alignment, and you're ready to begin work. As you get ready to do the work, consider that while the drive center turns, the cup center does not. This could cause the wood held on the cup center to

bind or burn so that some lubrication is necessary.

Under no circumstances should you ever use oil for this lubrication because the wood will absorb the oil and become discolored. A bit of beeswax or, if that's not available, a bit of bar soap will provide lubrication without discoloration of the wood. For those who want to work metal, a tailstock live-cup center is available to replace the standard dead, or nonturning, center. The live-cup

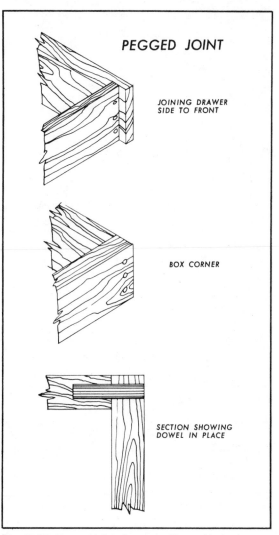

Fig. 19-37. Pegged joints (courtesy Shopsmith, Inc.).

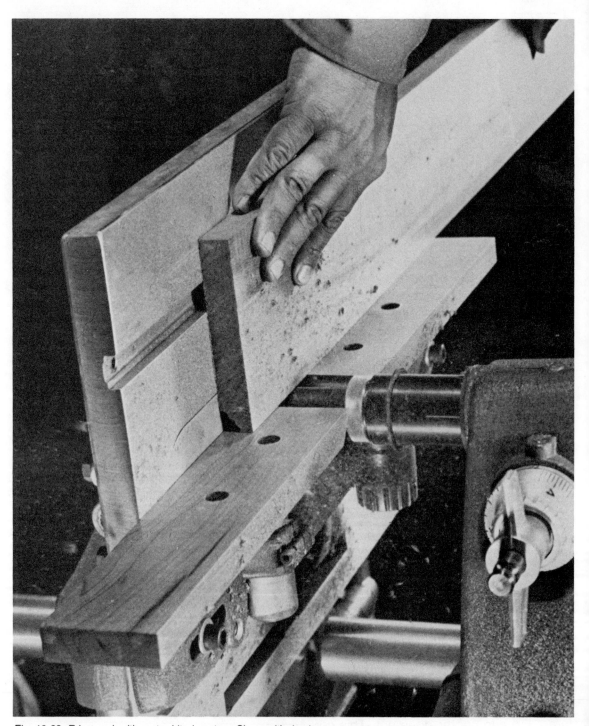

Fig. 19-38. Edge work with router bits (courtesy Shopsmith, Inc.).

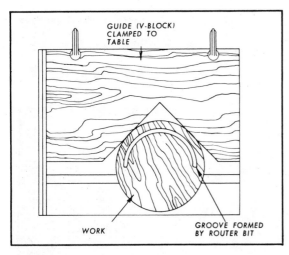

Fig. 19-39. Circular grooves (courtesy Shopsmith, Inc.).

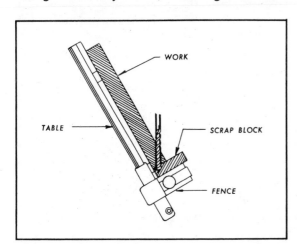

Fig. 19-40. Setting up to drill angular screw hole pockets (courtesy Shopsmith, Inc.).

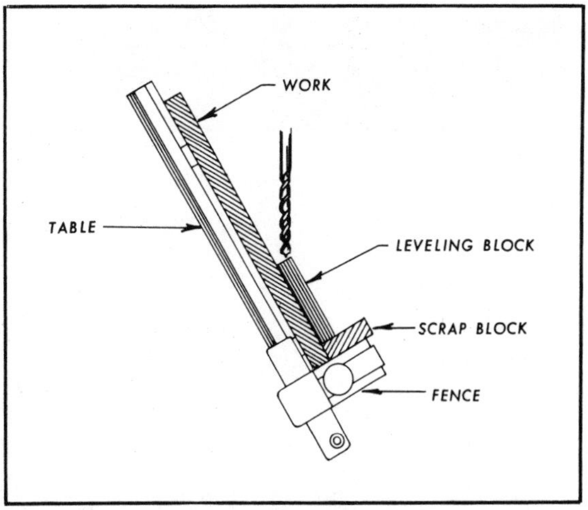

Fig. 19-41. Setting up to drill angular screw hole pockets at extreme angles (courtesy Shopsmith, Inc.).

center is also handy when working large jobs with woods that are hard to work, but it is essential to metal working.

The location of the work center is not difficult. You simply draw lines on square stock from each corner to the diagonally opposite corner. Where the lines cross you have the center. More time consuming, though not really much, is finding the center of octagonal, hexagonal and other work. Finding the center on round work is fairly difficult. Shopsmith offers an inexpensive center finder that will do the job on circles up to 8 inches in diameter and on hexagons up to 5¾ inches across. See Fig. 19-44.

Once the center is found, you set the drive center with a soft mallet (Shopsmith offers about the only rawhide head mallet I've seen in years, or you can use a plastic mallet). Mount the work in the spindle and adjust the tool rest with the widest edge of the work ⅛ of an inch from the tool rest. You'll have to keep moving the tool rest in as the work is reduced in size to maintain the correct distance. Adjust as needed to provide maximum support to your chisels as you cut. I would recommend that you don't let the distance increase much over ⅜ of an inch for greatest stability. The work should have its centerline about ⅛ of an inch below the tool rest edge. See Fig. 19-45.

Table 19-1 shows lathe speeds for different materials. Note that the speeds change as you go from the rough cutting to

Fig. 19-42. Drilling screw hole pockets (courtesy Shopsmith, Inc.).

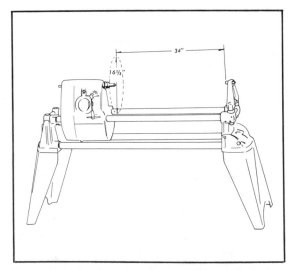

Fig. 19-43. Lathe dimensions (courtesy Shopsmith, Inc.).

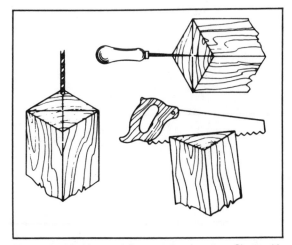

Fig. 19-44. Marking work for mounting (courtesy Shopsmith, Inc.).

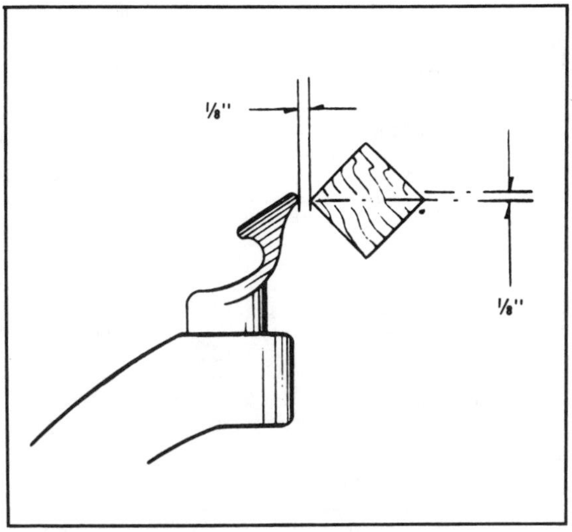

Fig. 19-45. Adjusting tool rest (courtesy Shopsmith, Inc

the finish cutting. Much higher speeds are used to provide a smooth finish. With the Mark V, only nonferrous metals may be turned (and then only up to 3 inches in diameter). The speed adjustment is made with the vernier dial, as shown in Fig. 19-46. No matter the stage of work, large pieces of material should be turned more slowly than small. The centrifugal force of a rapidly turning foot diameter workpiece could too

easily cause it to fly out of the centers. That is not a happy situation. It is very dangerous. See Fig. 19-47.

Chisels for lathe work are typically skews. It's a good idea to get both right- and left-hand skews, a roundnose, a ¾-inch gauge, and a ¼-inch gauge. In addition, a parting tool is usually included. It's possible to use an ordinary butt chisel in place of the square-nose lathe chisel.

When positioning the tool, one hand will hold it firmly on the tool rest about a half inch back from the tool's tip. The other hand should hold firmly at the end of the tool handle. In my case, the right hand holds the tool handle and gives the movement and control of the cut. The chisel is fed slowly and steadily into the work. Make sure it is not jabbed or forced into the wood. Jabbing the tool into the work is a good way to have it yanked out of your hands (which is not safe). Once you've got the tool in position on the tool rest, advance it slowly until it makes contact with the turning wood (Fig. 19-48).

You'll find that lathe tools work in one of three ways. It depends on the angle at which

Table 19-1. Lathe-Speed Guide.

MATERIAL AND DIAMETER	ROUGHING CUT		SHAPING CUT		FINISHING CUT	
	Speed-Dial setting	revolutions per minute	Speed-Dial setting	revolutions per minute	Speed-Dial setting	revolutions per minute
wood up to 2″	C	910	N	2,590	T	4,250
wood 2″ to 4″	B	810	M	2,375	Q	3,380
wood 4″ to 6″	SLOW	650	J	1,825	M	2,375
wood 6″ to 8″	SLOW	650	F	1,200	J	1,825
wood 8″ to 10″	SLOW	650	C	910	D	1,025
wood over 10″	SLOW	650	SLOW	650	SLOW	650
plastics up to 3″	L	2,200	P	3,125	S	3,875
plastics over 3″	D	1,025	F	1,200	I	1,680
non-ferrous metals up to 3″ (with carbide-tipped tools)	SLOW	650	G	1,300	P	3,125

they are held. Scraping is the best method to use for a start. It is the easiest and the least likely to be dangerous. It is also the slowest. Many experts never bother with the other two cuts because, in spite of the small amount of material removed at any one turn, the results are easily controlled and bad cuts are thereby reduced.

Cutting calls for lowering the handle of the tool. This cuts off more stock in a single pass. Slow, slow feed of the tool into the work is *very* important when using the cutting action. You can have the tool jerked from your hands by too fast a feed. At the least, you'll take a large uneven chunk out of the wood in such a case. If you decide to use the cutting action, get a good amount of practice using the scraping action first. Shearing action is usually done only with the skew or the gouge. It is a cutting action with the edge of the chisel moved parallel to the work. Become proficient with the cutting action before moving to shearing because this

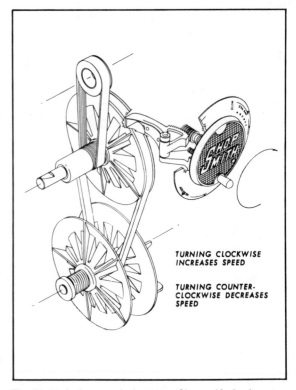

TURNING CLOCKWISE INCREASES SPEED

TURNING COUNTER-CLOCKWISE DECREASES SPEED

Fig. 19-46. Lathe speeds (courtesy Shopsmith, Inc.).

Fig. 19-47. Using the lathe (courtesy Shopsmith, Inc.).

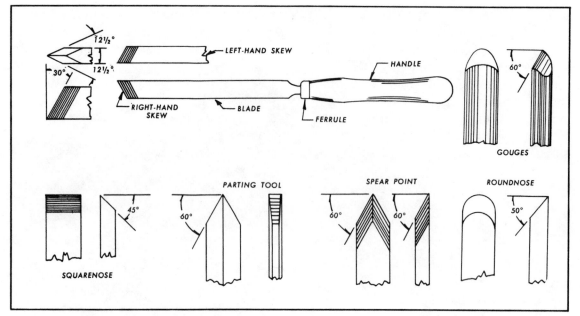

Fig. 19-48. Lathe chisels (courtesy Shopsmith, Inc.).

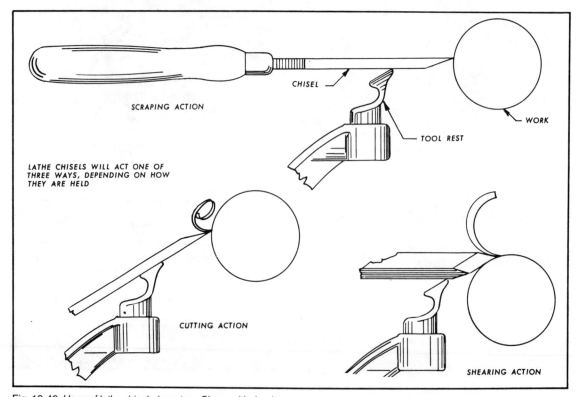

Fig. 19-49. Uses of lathe chisels (courtesy Shopsmith, Inc.).

is a very advanced form of lathe work (Fig. 19-49).

Using the gouge is using the most versatile of the turning tools on the lathe (Fig. 19-50). The gouge is the only chisel used to remove material when you're rough shaping. After practice, this is most quickly done with a shearing action, holding the tool on its side and moving it parallel to the work. Start your roughing cut along the length of the work and not at the end (see E of Fig. 19-50).

The skew is most often used in a scraping action. It is useful for making tapers, squaring stock ends, and so forth. It is also useful for smoothing down cylinders (see H of Fig. 19-51), but though this requires a shearing action and a great deal of practice. The skew can also be used to cut stock to length (as in F of Fig. 19-51).

The roundnose chisel is used with a scraping action and it can be used in form-

ing, small cove making, large cove making and hollowing (Fig. 19-52).

The parting tool is most often used with a scraping action. It can be used for making narrow shoulders, cutting narrow V's on tapers, cleaning work ends, sizing cuts and grooves, and cutting stock to length (Fig. 19-53).

Butt or square-nose chisels are used with a scraping action. They are used for smoothing, squaring a shoulder, forming short tapers, and smoothing convex surfaces—among other things (Fig. 19-54).

The spear point chisel is used for squaring during trim cuts, light chamfering, and forming V's (Fig. 19-55).

Planning and marking the work can be done as shown in Figs. 19-56 and 19-57. The use of a template makes repeating the exact dimensions—for, say, table legs, or chair legs—a great deal easier. Circular

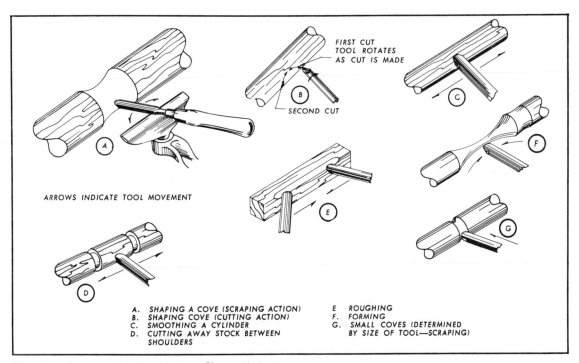

A. SHAPING A COVE (SCRAPING ACTION)
B. SHAPING COVE (CUTTING ACTION)
C. SMOOTHING A CYLINDER
D. CUTTING AWAY STOCK BETWEEN SHOULDERS
E. ROUGHING
F. FORMING
G. SMALL COVES (DETERMINED BY SIZE OF TOOL—SCRAPING)

Fig. 19-50. Gouge applications (courtesy Shopsmith, Inc.).

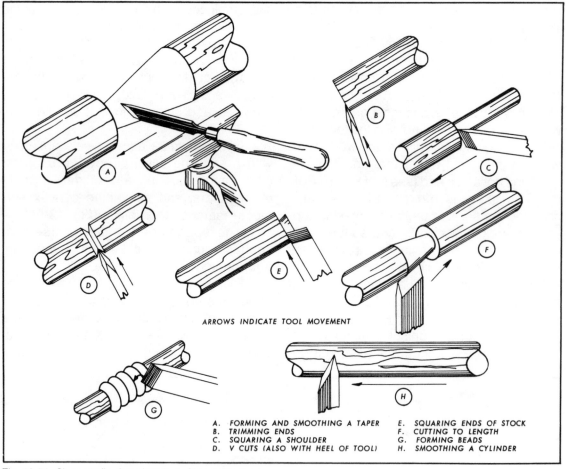

ARROWS INDICATE TOOL MOVEMENT

A. FORMING AND SMOOTHING A TAPER   E. SQUARING ENDS OF STOCK
B. TRIMMING ENDS   F. CUTTING TO LENGTH
C. SQUARING A SHOULDER   G. FORMING BEADS
D. V CUTS (ALSO WITH HEEL OF TOOL)   H. SMOOTHING A CYLINDER

Fig. 19-51. Skew applications (courtesy Shopsmith, Inc.).

stock is also worked with a template during faceplate turning (Fig. 19-58).

There are a number of procedures for turning wood, metal, or plastic. Figures 19-59 and 19-60 give an indication of the types of work that can be done.

JIGSAW

Jigsaws make ideal saws for the small workshop and allow quite an expansion of types of work that can be done. In the case of the Mark V, the jigsaw converts the rotary motion of the spindle to an up and down move-ment, using a crankshaft. Jigsaws are used primarily to cut curved lines, but they will provide reasonably good straight lines in moderately light stock. Because the thin blade allows you to cut very short radius turns, and the saw kerf is quite narrow, you can easily apply the jigsaw to find scroll designs, the shaping of furniture legs, bevel cutting, and the cutting of material to be inlaid. The Mark V jigsaw has an 18-inch-deep throat that allows you to cut to the center of a 3-foot piece of wood. It will cut wood up to 2 inches thick. See Figs. 19-61 and 19-62.

Much as any other saw, the correct blade selection will determine just how well, or poorly, the jigsaw works (in addition to your own skill and experience). This is the easiest to use of all woodworking power tools and probably the safest. Table 19-2 provides some common blade sizes and types. Getting the correct tension on the blades is important. Fine blades need more tension than do heavier blades, but too much tension will make the fine blades snap. Unfortunately, the only method I know of determining the correct tension is judgement. You'll snap some fine blades while gaining this judgement, but fortunately, they're far from extremely expensive (half a dozen will cost under $4.00). Extremely fine jeweler's saw blades cost about $5.00 per half dozen. See Fig. 19-63.

Once the jigsaw blade is in place (Figs. 19-64 through 19-67) you'll want to lay out the work you're doing. You can enlarge small designs by squares (as shown in Fig. 19-68) when designs are small. Careful pre-planning of cuts needed will help to eliminate much waste. See Fig. 19-69.

It pays to remember that a jigsaw is not a saw that cuts rapidly. It is primarily for fine work and the feed of material should be slow and steady. Working this way, you can even

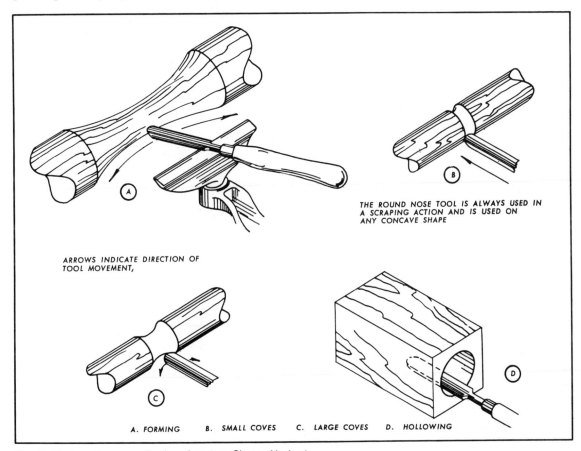

THE ROUND NOSE TOOL IS ALWAYS USED IN A SCRAPING ACTION AND IS USED ON ANY CONCAVE SHAPE

ARROWS INDICATE DIRECTION OF TOOL MOVEMENT,

A. FORMING   B. SMALL COVES   C. LARGE COVES   D. HOLLOWING

Fig. 19-52. Round nose applications (courtesy Shopsmith, Inc.).

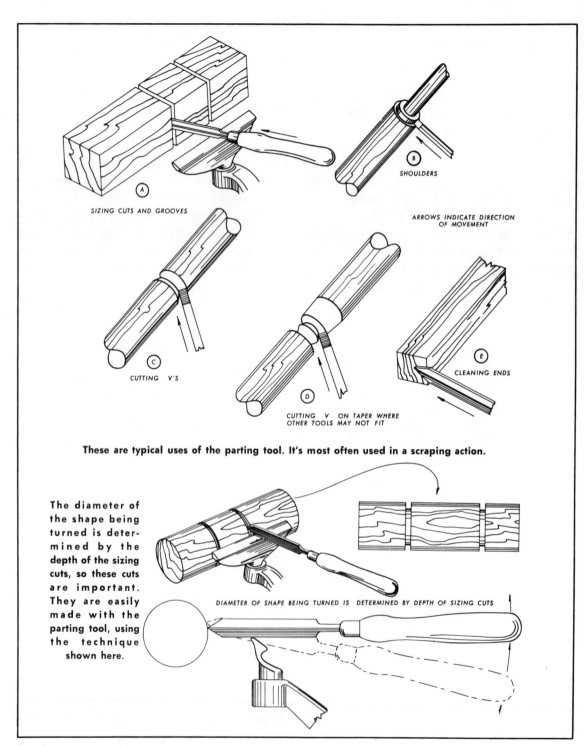

SIZING CUTS AND GROOVES

B SHOULDERS

ARROWS INDICATE DIRECTION OF MOVEMENT

C CUTTING V'S

D CUTTING V ON TAPER WHERE OTHER TOOLS MAY NOT FIT

E CLEANING ENDS

These are typical uses of the parting tool. It's most often used in a scraping action.

The diameter of the shape being turned is determined by the depth of the sizing cuts, so these cuts are important. They are easily made with the parting tool, using the technique shown here.

DIAMETER OF SHAPE BEING TURNED IS DETERMINED BY DEPTH OF SIZING CUTS

Fig. 19-53. Parting tool applications (courtesy Shopsmith, Inc.).

256

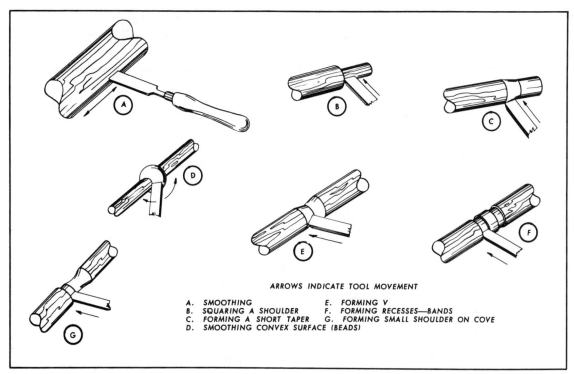

ARROWS INDICATE TOOL MOVEMENT

A. SMOOTHING
B. SQUARING A SHOULDER
C. FORMING A SHORT TAPER
D. SMOOTHING CONVEX SURFACE (BEADS)

E. FORMING V
F. FORMING RECESSES—BANDS
G. FORMING SMALL SHOULDER ON COVE

Fig. 19-54. Square nose applications (courtesy Shopsmith, Inc.).

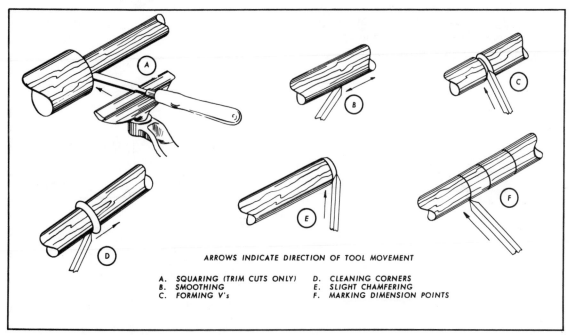

ARROWS INDICATE DIRECTION OF TOOL MOVEMENT

A. SQUARING (TRIM CUTS ONLY)
B. SMOOTHING
C. FORMING V's

D. CLEANING CORNERS
E. SLIGHT CHAMFERING
F. MARKING DIMENSION POINTS

Fig. 19-55. Spear point applications (courtesy Shopsmith, Inc.).

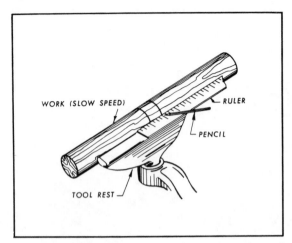

Fig. 19-56. Mark dimension lines with a ruler and pencil (courtesy Shopsmith, Inc.).

produce inside square corners (Fig. 19-70) as well as circles and other designs (Fig. 19-71). Bevel cuts can readily be made. The table tilts, from 1 to 10 degrees, to allow for such cutting. Jigsaw cutting is done precisely on the line and not on the waste side as with virtually all other saws.

The jigsaw can also be set up (Fig. 19-72) for saber sawing. This allows you to do piercing work, but on heavy work it's a

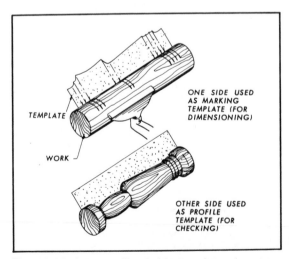

Fig. 19-57. Layout will provide templates (courtesy Shopsmith, Inc.).

good idea to use a blade insertion hole. Saber sawing is done using only the heaviest jigsawing blades and can also be done with saber saw blades for portable saber saws. The feed must be slow and steady for good results and to keep from breaking blades.

THE BAND SAW

The band saw is an accessory for later addi-

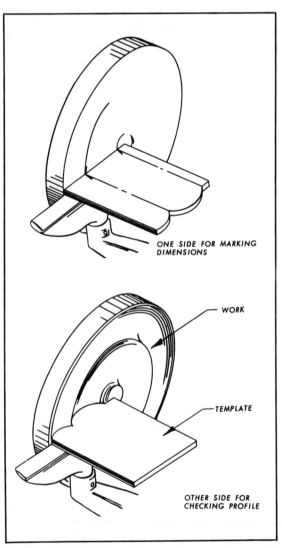

Fig. 19-58. Faceplate template use (courtesy Shopsmith, Inc.).

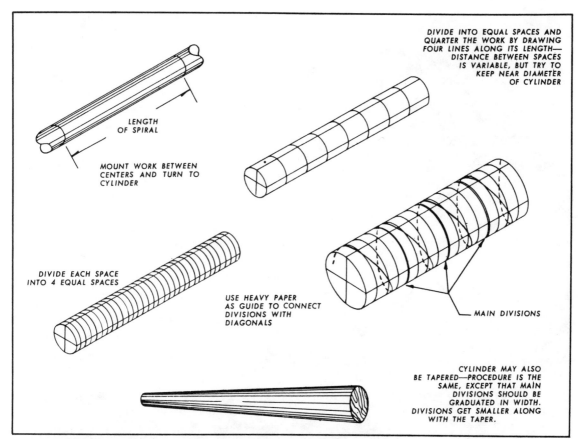

DIVIDE INTO EQUAL SPACES AND
QUARTER THE WORK BY DRAWING
FOUR LINES ALONG ITS LENGTH—
DISTANCE BETWEEN SPACES
IS VARIABLE, BUT TRY TO
KEEP NEAR DIAMETER
OF CYLINDER

LENGTH
OF SPIRAL

MOUNT WORK BETWEEN
CENTERS AND TURN TO
CYLINDER

DIVIDE EACH SPACE
INTO 4 EQUAL SPACES

USE HEAVY PAPER
AS GUIDE TO CONNECT
DIVISIONS WITH
DIAGONALS

MAIN DIVISIONS

CYLINDER MAY ALSO
BE TAPERED—PROCEDURE IS THE
SAME, EXCEPT THAT MAIN
DIVISIONS SHOULD BE
GRADUATED IN WIDTH.
DIVISIONS GET SMALLER ALONG
WITH THE TAPER.

Fig. 19-59. Forming a spiral from a cylinder (courtesy Shopsmith, Inc.).

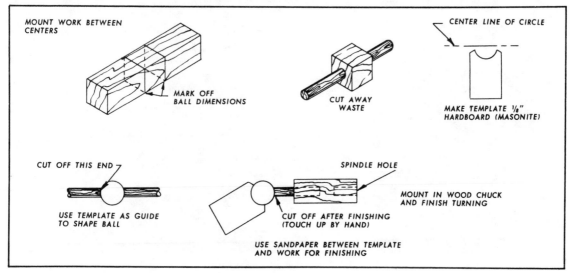

MOUNT WORK BETWEEN
CENTERS

MARK OFF
BALL DIMENSIONS

CUT AWAY
WASTE

CENTER LINE OF CIRCLE

MAKE TEMPLATE ⅛"
HARDBOARD (MASONITE)

CUT OFF THIS END

USE TEMPLATE AS GUIDE
TO SHAPE BALL

SPINDLE HOLE

MOUNT IN WOOD CHUCK
AND FINISH TURNING

CUT OFF AFTER FINISHING
(TOUCH UP BY HAND)

USE SANDPAPER BETWEEN TEMPLATE
AND WORK FOR FINISHING

Fig. 19-60. Forming a round ball (courtesy Shopsmith, Inc.).

Fig. 19-61. Mark V mounted jigsaw used as a saber saw (courtesy Shopsmith, Inc.).

Fig. 19-62. Freestanding Shopsmith jigsaw.

Table 19-2. Common Blade Sizes and Types.

BLADE	BLADE DIMENSION			OPERATION				R.P.M. AND SPEED-DIAL LETTER
	THICKNESS INCHES	WIDTH INCHES	TEETH PER INCH	STOCK THICKNESS (Inches)	CUT RADIUS	KERF	BEST FOR	
5	.028	.250	7	1/4 & up	large	coarse	soft & hard wood—pressed wood	745-A
3	.020	.110	15	1/8-1/2 in metal, 1/8 & up in other material	medium	medium	metal—wood—bone—felt—paper	1175-F
1	.010	.040	18	1/16-1/8	small	very fine	wood—bone—plastics	1600-I
6	.012	.023	20	up to 1/8	very small	fine	plastics—bone—fiber—comp. board	1050-E
7	.020	.070	7	up to 1/4	medium	medium	plastics—bone—hard rubber	1400-G
8	.010	.070	14	1/8-1/2	medium	very fine	wood—plastics—bone—hard rubber	1525-H
2	.020	.110	20	1/16-1/8	medium	medium	aluminum—copper—mild steel	940-C
4	.028	.250	20	3/32-1/2 (1/4 max. in steel)	large	coarse	aluminum—copper—mild steel	830-B

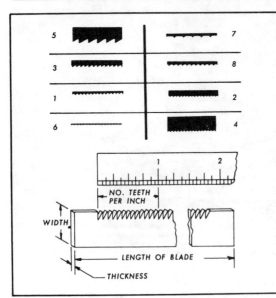

Fig. 19-63. Appearance of common blades (courtesy Shopsmith, Inc.).

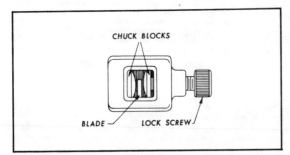

Fig. 19-64. Top end of the blade locks in the upper chuck (courtesy Shopsmith, Inc.).

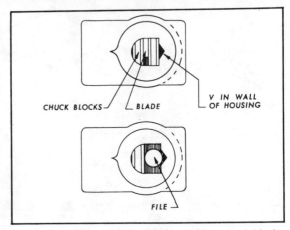

Fig. 19-65. Bottom blade end locks between chuck blocks (courtesy Shopsmith, Inc.).

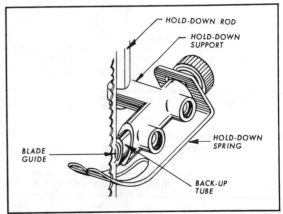

Fig. 19-66. Blade guide adjustment (courtesy Shopsmith, Inc.).

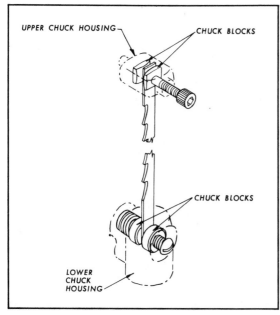

UPPER CHUCK HOUSING

CHUCK BLOCKS

CHUCK BLOCKS

LOWER
CHUCK
HOUSING

Fig. 19-67. Blade in place (courtesy Shopsmith, Inc.).

tion to the Shopsmith Mark V, but for any serious woodworker a band saw is nearly essential. It does many kinds of work but it is often considered the tool for cutting curves in heavy stock and then forgotten. That is a mistake. First, a band saw will cut through stock up to 6 inches thick. That is something no other home workshop tool can do. There are certain straight-line cutting jobs the band saw can obviously do that may make it important in a workshop. It also retains its usefulness as a tool for cutting curves and irregular patterns.

Band saws can be used for resawing (making two thin boards from a single thick board), reducing stock thickness in particular areas of a workpiece, and other jobs. The chance of using a blade only ⅛ of an inch wide allows you to cut curves nearly as tight

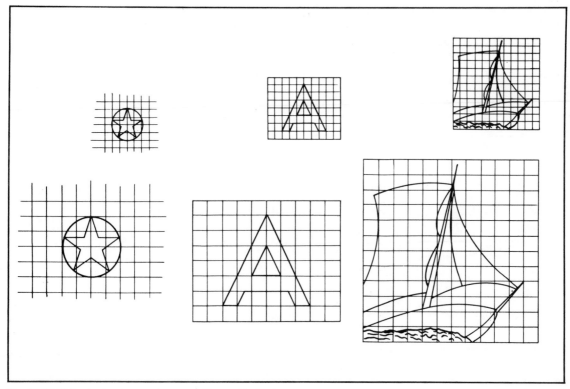

Fig. 19-68. Enlarging by squares (courtesy Shopsmith, Inc.).

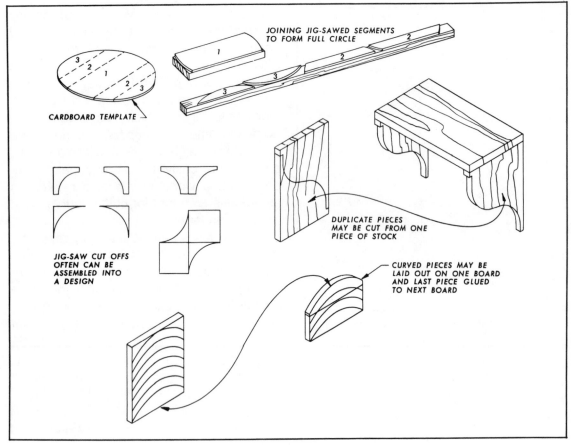

Fig. 19-69. Preplanning reduces waste (courtesy Shopsmith, Inc.).

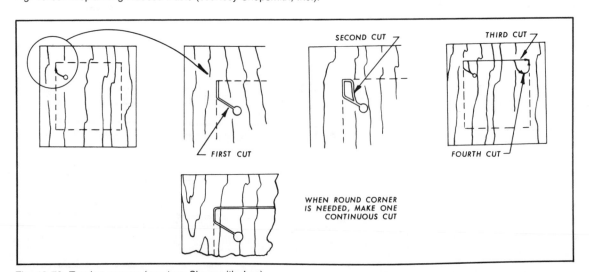

Fig. 19-70. Turning corners (courtesy Shopsmith, Inc.).

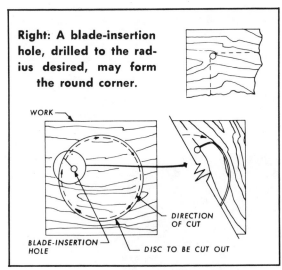

Right: A blade-insertion hole, drilled to the radius desired, may form the round corner.

WORK

DIRECTION OF CUT

BLADE-INSERTION HOLE

DISC TO BE CUT OUT

Fig. 19-71. Cutting circles (courtesy Shopsmith, Inc.).

as those you can obtain on a jigsaw. The jigsaw is the only workshop tool that will let you make internal cut outs easily, but the band saw is the only tool to cut through extremely heavy material (remember, the jigsaw is limited to 2 inches of material thickness).

The band saw comes in three styles, but the only one of interest to the home workshop owner is the band-scroll saw for cutting curved and irregular shapes, for basic straight-line sawing, and for resawing. The Mark V cut-off capacity (from the blade to the throat) is 10½ inches, but with the blade offset, you can cut to any depth in stock up to 3⅞ inches wide. The depth of cut is 6 inches, maximum, and the 11¾-×-12-inch table offers you a table tilt of 5 degrees to the left and 45 degrees to the right. Speed range is from 700 to 1100 rpm, and the tool will take blades for 3/16 to ½ inch wide (Fig. 19-73).

Little setting up is needed on the Mark V band saw, but blade changing routines are very important. First, loosen the latch and remove the table insert and front cover. Use the Allen wrench to loosen the blade tension screw (Fig. 19-74). The present blade can now be slipped off. If you are changing from a wide to a narrow blade, move the guide blocks back before mounting the new blade. After the blade is mounted, adjust the blocks to it. Hold the new blade with the teeth facing you and the points of the teeth on your right and slanting down. Slip it through the table slot and position it on the wheels. Turn the tension screw until you get the correct reading for the blade you're using (Fig. 19-75).

Too much tension will shorten blade life. Shopsmith has tested these settings to make sure they give optimum performance and life. In any case, never add tension beyond ¼ inch for a 3/16-inch blade, ⅜ inch for a ¼-inch blade and for ⅜- and ½-inch blades do not go beyond setting on scale. Now replace the cover, alignment latch, and table insert.

As with all other power saws, using the correct blade will give you the best job. Figure 19-76 shows several types of blades available for the band saw. The combination

TUBE-ARM LOCK SCREW

Fig. 19-72. Removing jigsaw arm for saber sawing (courtesy Shopsmith, Inc.).

Fig. 19-73. Band saw in use (courtesy Shopsmith, Inc.).

Fig. 19-74. Tension screw is turned with the Allen wrench (courtesy Shopsmith, Inc.).

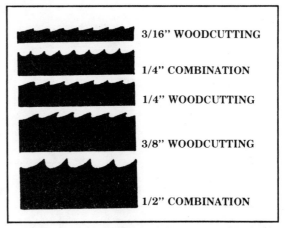

Fig. 19-76. Common band saw blades (courtesy Shopsmith, Inc.).

blades can be used to cut nonferrous metals as well as wood. As Fig. 19-77 shows, the width of the blade will determine the radius of any curves you can cut. Trying to get a tighter radius from a wide blade twists the blade, burns the inside of the kerf, and shortens blade life badly. If you're having trouble with binding or burning and using the correct blade width for the radius you're turning, try rubbing a bit of beeswax on the blade as a lubricant.

General sawing with a band saw requires using the left hand as a guide while your right hand feeds the work into the blade. If you stand slightly to the left of the blade, you'll probably find it easier to work. Always make sure you never apply forward pressure

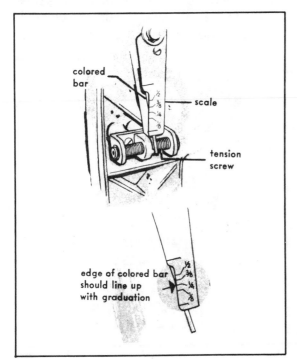

Fig. 19-75. Correct settings are required (courtesy Shopsmith, Inc.).

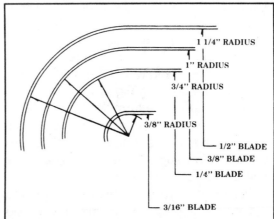

Fig. 19-77. Turning radii and blade width (courtesy Shopsmith, Inc.).

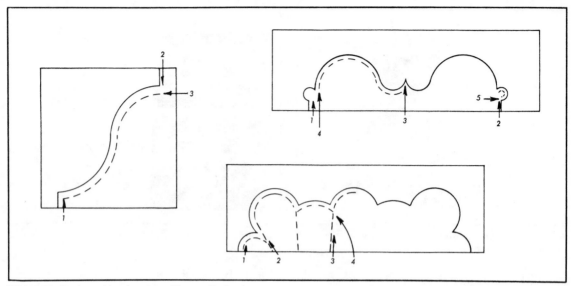

Fig. 19-78. Back tracking (courtesy Shopsmith, Inc.).

with your hand when the hand is directly in line with the blade. Should you slip, your hand might go into the blade.

When using a band saw, you should try to imagine how you'll make the cut most efficiently. Think of the turning radius needed and where to start to make the cut in a single pass—whenever possible. When a single pass won't do the job, you'll have to use a technique known as *backtracking.* Make the shorter cuts first (as Fig. 19-78 shows). Backtrack with care because the procedure might pull the blade from between the guide blocks. Relief openings and turns that cannot be made within the blade radius are done as shown in Fig. 19-79.

The miter gauge from the Mark V table saw can also be used with the band saw as a miter gauge and as a fence. Extensions are added to the gauge as needed. The three most useful sizes are shown in Fig. 19-80.

Crosscutting is done, with or without the miter gauge, very slowly on a band saw. Too much speed tends to give you a curved cut. Rip cuts also require a very slow feed to

keep the cut from curving. Resawing is an operation also requiring a slow feed. Stock over four inches thick being resawed is best done with the half-inch, all-purpose blade. If you force the feed during resawing, that

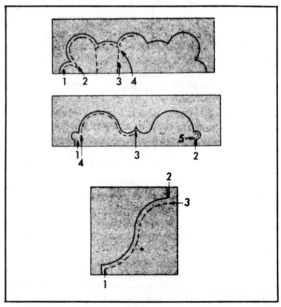

Fig. 19-79. Cutting relief openings (courtesy Shopsmith, Inc.).

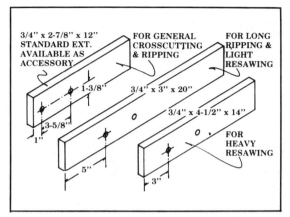

Fig. 19-80. Miter gauge extensions (courtesy Shopsmith, Inc.).

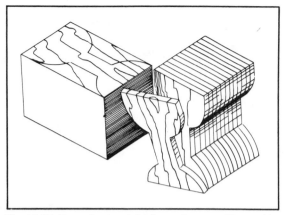

Fig. 19-81. Resawing to get duplicates (courtesy Shopsmith, Inc.).

flexible band saw blade will tend to follow the lines of internal grain patterns in the wood.

If you need to cut off material greater in length than the saw's throat will accept, you can offset the blade by reversing the blade guides. This allows you a cut off without throat interference, but limits the cut to 3⅞ inches (though flipping the stock can increase this to 7¾ inches).

There are two methods of cutting multiple parts on a band saw. As in Fig. 19-81, you can use a solid block of wood, cut it to shape, and then resaw to get the individual parts. Or you can nail the stock together in a pad (making sure the nails are in waste stock where the blade will not hit) and saw the patterns. This is known as *pad cutting* (Fig. 19-82).

DISC SANDER

Sanding is usually the last, or nearly the last, step in getting ready to apply a finish to a project. The final appearance of the project will depend on just how well the sanding is done and whether or not it is done with proper abrasive material. Your first consideration should be choosing the proper abrasive(s). There are three points to ponder when choosing abrasives. First, do you need an open or closed coat abrasive? Open coat abrasives are more useful for rough sanding when a lot of material is to be removed and the material might clog the abrasive coating. Closed-coat abrasives have the abrasive particles much more closely spaced so that a more complete surface is offered and the sanding is lighter and the finish smoother.

Next, you need to select an abrasive material. I'm not going to cover emery. That is almost exclusively used for metals, but you still have a choice of four materials. Flint is the least expensive abrasive available, but

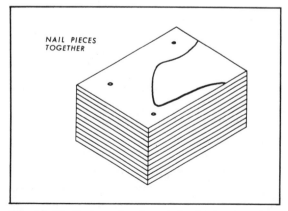

Fig. 19-82. Pad sawing to get duplicates (courtesy Shopsmith, Inc.).

Table 19-3. Abrasive Qualities.

ABRASIVE	USE	GRIT			REMARKS
		ROUGH	MEDIUM	FINE	
aluminum oxide	hardwood aluminum copper steel ivory plastic	2½-1½ 40 40-50 24-30 60-80 50-80	1/2-1/0 60-80 80-100 60-80 100-120 120-180	2/0-3/0 100 100-120 100 120-280 240	Manufactured, brown color, bauxite base, more costly than garnet but usually cheaper to use per unit of work
garnet	hardwood softwood composition board plastic horn	2½-1½ 1½-1 1½-1 50-80 1½	1/2-1/0 1/0 1/2 120-180 1/2-1/0	2/0-3/0 2/0 1/0 240 2/0-3/0	Natural mineral, red color, harder and sharper than flint
silicon carbide	glass cast iron	50-60 24-30	100-120 60-80	12-320 100	Manufactured, harder but more brittle than aluminum oxide, very fast cutting
flint	removing paint, old finishes	3-1½	1/2-1/0		Natural hard form of quartz, low cost, use on jobs that clog the paper quickly

it doesn't last as long as garnet. Garnet is not only harder, but it is also sharper. Aluminum oxide is a manufactured abrasive tougher than garnet; it has wedge shaped crystals. It is very good for power sanding. Silicon carbide is the hardest of all the abrasives (and the most expensive). It is good for sanding between finish coats, but not really needed in other woodworking sanding operations.

You will need to think about the size of the grit used on the abrasive you select. The finer the finish needed the finer the grit required. Tables 19-3 and 19-4 show some of the qualities and uses of the four major woodworking grits.

The disc sander on the Mark V is quite large—1 foot in diameter. It is best mounted with the headstock all the way at the right of the way tubes. For sanding the ends of extra-long work, you might want to turn the headstock to the left and use the extension table (Fig. 19-83). Keep the work table no more than a half inch below the centerline of the sanding disc for best results. Use a speed of no more than 1800 rpm. Adhesive keeps the abrasive disc on the metal disc, but you must make sure the sheets are firmly and flatly attached. Even small bumps will mess up a smooth finish and might well ruin an otherwise well-done project.

Do all sanding on the down side of the sander. If you work on the up side, the work will be lifted from the work table. See Fig. 19-84. No excessive pressure is needed to get the work done. Work is kept flat and fed into the disc squarely. If the work is curved, it is revolved in with a sweeping motion. Keep the feed light and smooth (Fig. 19-85) at all times. This might require you to make several passes. Too much pressure and too fast

Table 19-4. Abrasive Classes.

TYPE	VERY FINE	FINE	MEDIUM	COARSE	VERY COARSE
flint	4/0	2/0-3/0	1/0-½	1-2	2½-3½
garnet	6/0-10/0	3/0-5/0	1/0-2/0	1/2-1½	2-3
aluminum oxide and silicon carbide	220-360	120-180	80-100	40-60	24-36

	8/0 = 280	3/0 = 120	1½ = 40		
	7/0 = 240	2/0 = 100	2 = 36		
	6/0 = 220	0 = 80	2½ = 30		
	5/0 = 180	½ = 60	3 = 24		
	4/0 = 150	1 = 50			

Fig. 19-83. Using the disc sander on ends (courtesy Shopsmith, Inc.).

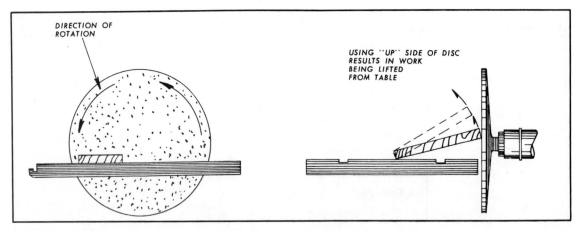

Fig. 19-84. Always use the down side of the sander (courtesy Shopsmith, Inc.).

a feed can burn the edges of the work. In cases where the work is longer than the disc radius, it can cause an uneven surface.

BELT SANDER

The belt sander is another Mark V accessory. It is similar in many respects to a hand-held belt sander. For sanding with the wood grain to get the smoothest possible finish, the belt sander is far better than the disc sander. The Mark V uses a 6-inch-×-4-foot belt, with a table 6×9 inches. The belt sander operates best at speeds from 915 to 1830 surface feet per minute. See Fig. 19-86.

You'll do the best surface sanding with the unit in a horizontal position. The table can be used as a stop or set down parallel with the belt for sanding long pieces. When using the belt sander, you move the work being sanded against the belt's direction of rotation. You must keep the work moving. Keep your left hand lightly on the top of the work and guide it with your right hand. The hands almost always are used for guiding only because the weight of the piece being sanded should provide sufficient pressure

for the abrasive surface to do its job. See Figs. 19-87 through 19-90.

SHAPER

Adding a shaper fence to the vertical drill press, and using various cutters, can give you many options in edge finishing that might well improve a great many of the possible projects. The shaper also goes beyond mere decorative possibilities because it can be used for rabbeting, jointing, and forming drawer joints. The speed used for shaping is

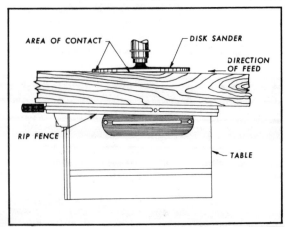

Fig. 19-85. Keep the feed light and even (courtesy Shopsmith, Inc.).

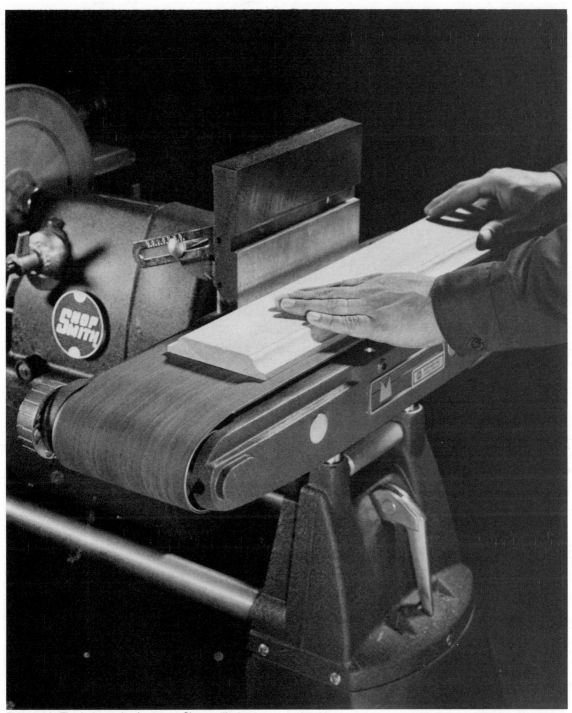

Fig. 19-86. The belt sander (courtesy Shopsmith, Inc.).

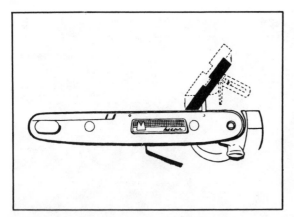

Fig. 19-87. Tilting table (courtesy Shopsmith, Inc.).

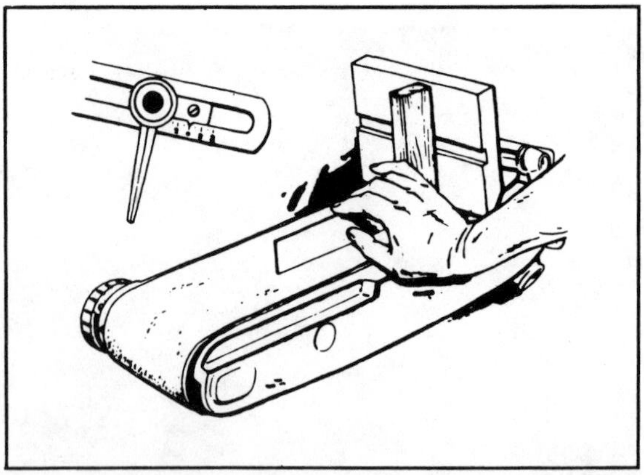

Fig. 19-89. Squaring table to the belt (courtesy Shopsmith, Inc.).

quite high (no lower than 4000 rpm and with 5000 rpm preferred).

Whenever possible, you should work against the shaper fence and the work should be fed into and against the rotation of the cutting tool. That way you get the smoothest work, but also it tends—if you lose your grip—to fling the work piece away from you. As always, keep your fingers away from the cutting tool by using a form of pusher. Feed slowly and steadily. Never allow your hands to pass above the cutter. If the work should split, your hands could drop into the blades.

Shopsmith makes what they call a Universal Hold Down as part of their Maxi-Clamp set. This is a great aid in keeping your hands away from the cutters during fine work and when working with small pieces. There are 22 cutter shapes available. Each has a specific purpose (Fig. 19-91) such as the drop-leaf, table-edge cutters. Actually, you can locate a great many more shapes if you want to try, but you'll probably never need more than a dozen or so. It is best to select them as the need for them comes up. The drop-leaf cutters (a set of two) now costs about $22.00. Other cutters cost $10 to $11

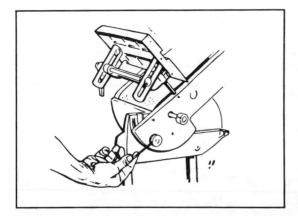

Fig. 19-88. Locking table in position (courtesy Shopsmith, Inc.).

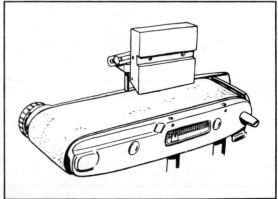

Fig. 19-90. Table parallel to sanding belt (courtesy Shopsmith, Inc.).

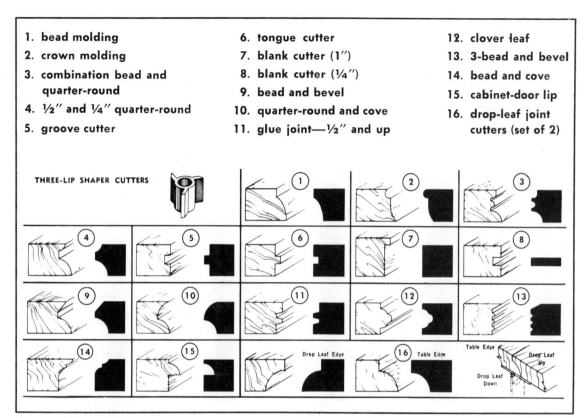

1. bead molding	6. tongue cutter	12. clover leaf
2. crown molding	7. blank cutter (1″)	13. 3-bead and bevel
3. combination bead and quarter-round	8. blank cutter (¼″)	14. bead and cove
4. ½″ and ¼″ quarter-round	9. bead and bevel	15. cabinet-door lip
5. groove cutter	10. quarter-round and cove	16. drop-leaf joint cutters (set of 2)
	11. glue joint—½″ and up	

THREE-LIP SHAPER CUTTERS

Fig. 19-91. Cutter shapes (courtesy Shopsmith, Inc.).

each. Figure 19-92 shows the methods of working with the fence in place and working up against it. This emphasizes the need for properly adjusted fences when an entire edge is removed.

Shaping is another action that should, whenever possible, be done with the grain. But often you'll need to make cuts against the grain. When that's necessary, you should slow the feed down even more and make sure that meeting cuts with the grain are made last.

For freehand shaping, or shaping against collars, for circular work, you cannot use the shaper fence. Special collars are used to control the depth of cut and you can even work on the inside of a circular cutout (Fig. 19-93). Fulcrum pins (Fig. 19-94) are used as supports so you can cut against a collar without the work kicking back. Figure 19-95 indicates the need for making sure that there is enough bearing surface on the workpiece. Narrow pieces worked against collars should be backed up by a larger piece (later cut off on a table saw).

SHARPENING

Dull tools are an abomination. A blunt edge won't cut well (if it cuts at all). Force is needed and this makes the job dangerous because using force in woodworking can cause your hands to slip and bring them in contact with sharp edges. Dull saw blades increase the danger of binding and kickback.

Sharp, clean tools are easier and safer to use. They inevitably produce better re-

275

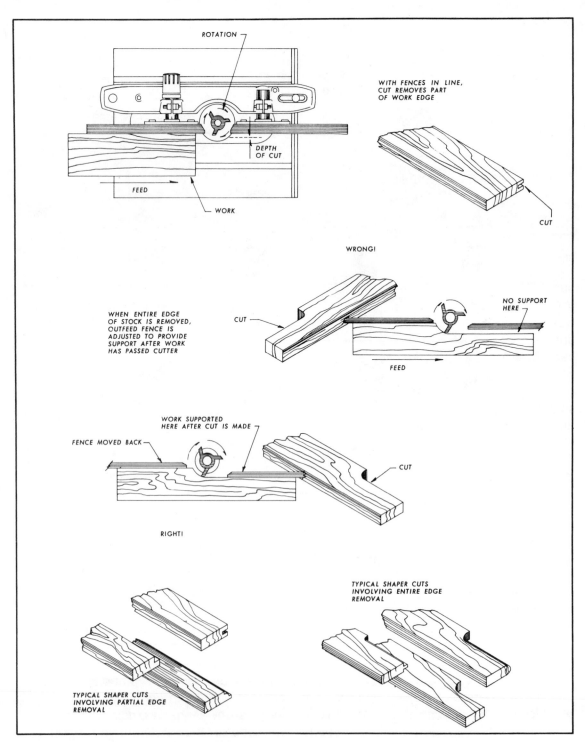

ROTATION

WITH FENCES IN LINE, CUT REMOVES PART OF WORK EDGE

DEPTH OF CUT

FEED

WORK

CUT

WRONG!

WHEN ENTIRE EDGE OF STOCK IS REMOVED, OUTFEED FENCE IS ADJUSTED TO PROVIDE SUPPORT AFTER WORK HAS PASSED CUTTER

CUT

NO SUPPORT HERE

FEED

WORK SUPPORTED HERE AFTER CUT IS MADE

FENCE MOVED BACK

CUT

RIGHT!

TYPICAL SHAPER CUTS INVOLVING ENTIRE EDGE REMOVAL

TYPICAL SHAPER CUTS INVOLVING PARTIAL EDGE REMOVAL

Fig. 19-92. Working the shaper (courtesy Shopsmith, Inc.).

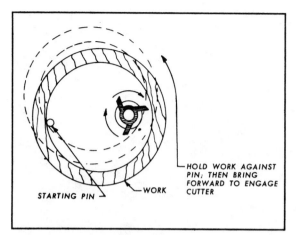

Fig. 19-93. Shaping inside a circular cut out (courtesy Shopsmith, Inc.).

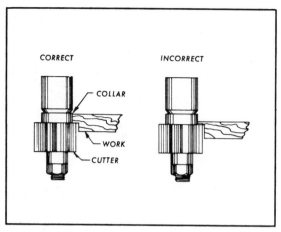

Fig. 19-95. Make sure you get enough bearing surface when shaping (courtesy Shopsmith, Inc.).

sults. To use a grinding wheel on your Mark V, you need to form a guard to fit over the way tubes and protect them from dropping grit. This is done as shown in Fig. 19-96. You can also build a guard to keep flying grit from your face and eyes.

Use the lathe tool rest as a tool rest for sharpening against the grinding wheel (a rubber-bonded grinding wheel of about a 60-grit is best for all round sharpening). Work high-speed steels dry, but don't use excessive pressure against the grinding wheel. Dip the tools in water every minute or

two to keep from over heating the metal and ruining its temper. Anytime you apply so much pressure to the metal it turns blue, then you are drawing the temper and ruining the cutting edge.

Chisels can be held square to the grinding wheel with the jig shown in Fig. 19-97 and honed to a finish on a fine oilstone (Fig. 19-98).

I feel it is usually more sensible to have circular-saw blades and other saw blades sharpened professionally. The time and energy saved is well worth the cost. Machine

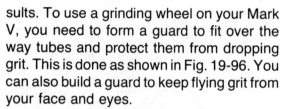

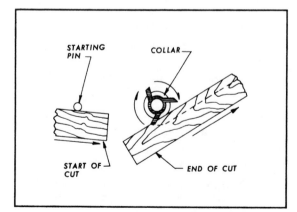

Fig. 19-94. Fulcrum pin prevents kickback (courtesy Shopsmith, Inc.).

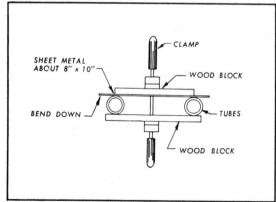

Fig. 19-96. Make a dust shield for the tubes (courtesy Shopsmith, Inc.).

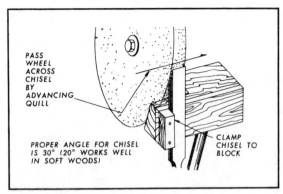

Fig. 19-97. A guide for sharpening chisels (courtesy Shopsmith, Inc.).

sharpening is usually more accurate than hand sharpening.

Shopsmith's Mark V requires the same attention to safety practices as do all stationary power tools (Fig. 19-99). Always wear safe clothing. Wear no ties, watches or rings. Short sleeves are best.

When getting ready to plug the machine in, check to make sure that the switch is off. Always unplug the Mark V before making any major adjustments. It's a good idea to make it a habit of turning the machine off and then pulling the plug when you're finished for the day or evening.

Check the machine to be sure all locks are tight before you turn it on. Turn the machine over by hand before turning it on. Before switching it on, make sure no pieces have been left in or around moving parts.

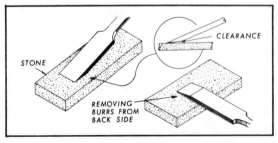

Fig. 19-98. Final honing is needed (courtesy Shopsmith, Inc.).

Fig. 19-99. Drum sanding with the Mark V (courtesy Shopsmith, Inc.).

Keep alert. If you're too tired to be alert, you're too tired to work on a project. Never, under any circumstances, work with power machinery if you've been drinking or taking any drug that could have an affect such as drowsiness. Tranquilizers and antihistamines are probably among the worst offenders here. Keep your hands in sight and well clear of moving parts. Never reach across any machine when it is running.

Don't push the free end of work and don't pick up cutoff pieces while the machine is still running. Don't attempt to slow down or stop a tool after switching it off by grabbing the work or a tool or by jamming a piece of wood against, for example, a saw blade.

Keep all tools sharp and keep the saw

blade just high enough for the job being done. Use the saw guard and splitter unless such use is absolutely impossible. Use pusher sticks and hold-downs to keep your fingers away from saw blades or cutters.

Use correct tool speeds. In cases where you're not certain of the speed, use a lower speed. Never force the work. Take your time on the job. Oddly enough, too much hurry tends to slow woodworking down and it can be dangerous. Whenever you can, stand to one side of a cutting tool instead of in line with it.

Keep the shop floor clean. Sawdust or chips underfoot can be very slippery. Following every safety precaution in the book isn't going to help if you let this one go and slip into the machinery.

Chapter 20

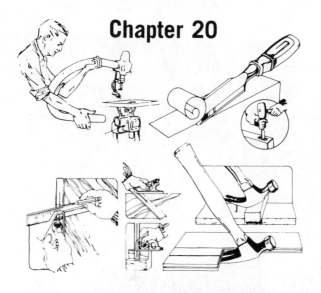

Table Saws

THE TABLE SAW, ALSO KNOWN AS THE BENCH saw, is a precise wood-cutting tool. It gives a great gain in accuracy over almost any form of hand woodcutting. Production is increased and labor needs drop because the saw is motor driven. See Fig. 20-1.

You might consider the table saw the basic saw in a woodworking shop for straight-line cutting operations. It is, in its primary functions, not at all that difficult to operate. Ripping and crosscutting are the primary operations, of course, and the other four basic cuts can be rapidly learned. The other four cuts are the bevel rip, the bevel crosscut, the miter, and the bevel miter. Once you have the six basic cuts down reasonably pat, you can think about combining them to produce some really complex wood figures or structures.

Table saws for home workshop use come with blade diameters ranging from about 8 inches to 12 inches. Commercial saws of greater size are available, but even contractors stick to a 10- or 12-inch saw these days. Depth of cut is a variable depending at least in part on blade diameter. Rockwell International's Model 34710 will give a cut depth of 2 9/16 inches at 90 degrees. Their Model 34-310 contractors' saw gives a cut depth of 3¼ inches with the same diameter blade. Sears' Craftsman 2525N, with 12-inch blade, offers a depth of cut of 3 9/16 of an inch at 90 degrees. Their 10-inch blade 29814N offers a depth of 3⅜ inches. Even selecting the largest-diameter saw blade possible doesn't always assure you'll get much more in the depth of cut.

Today's table saws are reasonably simple in operation. A motor is connected to the threaded arbor shaft by a belt and pul-

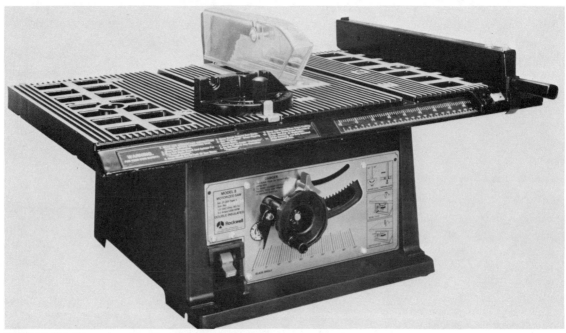

Fig. 20-1. Bench saw (courtesy Rockwell International).

leys and the blade is attached to the arbor shaft, which is driven by the motor. From here things get a bit more complex. The table of the saw is slotted so that the blade comes through. There are several grooves in it so that a miter gauge can be moved across the top to guide wood through the blade. The miter gauge is used when making crosscuts. A rip fence is usually attached to rails along the sides of the table and is used to guide wood in all ripsawing operations.

Protective devices are standard on table saws today; most have three. There is the blade guard that should always be in place when the saw is running, the antikickback fingers, and a kerf splitter or spreader. The last mentioned is simply a piece of metal directly behind the sawblade that keeps the kerf open and prevents the saw blade from binding. It is especially important to keep the kerf spreader on the saw and in use during ripsawing operations. The

spreader will have a series of small metal fingers that also add to kickback protection.

Arbor speed for woodworking is not crucial. You'll probably find a range of from about 3450 rpm to no more than 4000 rpm. All Sears' Craftsman saws appear to come with 3450 rpm motors. Most of the Rockwell International models also turn at that speed. Belt and pulley arrangements are used to raise arbor rpm to 3800 and 4000 rpm in a couple of Rockwell's models.

Power is of more importance. You should expect a 10-inch diameter table saw to have a motor of at least 1 horsepower. The range goes up to about 3 horsepower for the top-of-the-line, heavy-duty models. A home-duty, 12-inch diameter saw will need at least 2 horsepower and a 9-inch diameter saw can get by with about ¾ of a horsepower.

Shop wiring is a point to be considered when you think of buying any large power tool. You should never operate a table saw of any size off a lighting (15-ampere, 110-volt) circuit. A small appliance (20-ampere) circuit is needed to get the most efficiency from the motor. In the case of larger saws, such as the Craftsman 12-inch model, you'll have to use 240-volt wiring, allowing for at least a 20 ampere loading. If you run more than one power tool off the same line, you won't really run into problems unless you have two tools running at the same time. Any shop lighting circuits should be entirely separate from tool circuits. You can't believe how dim a light bulb can get when you kick the start button on an electric motor drawing 13.5 amperes. It is quite possible that one or two large light bulbs on a 20-ampere circuit

could cause—with the motor's starting surge—the circuit breaker to pop.

When you get ready to buy a table saw, the first check is the easiest. Check all the controls to see that they fall easily to hand. Carefully check to make sure that the on/off switch is easily reached in an emergency, without a lot of messing around (Fig. 20-2).

Most good, modern table saws will have a pull-for-on, push-for-off switch to make the operation safer. A great many will have some form of simple lock to keep unauthorized fingers from starting the motor. This lock is seldom more than a metal rod that slots in to allow you to complete the circuit. While it might sound a pain, most people simply wire the key within a couple of feet of

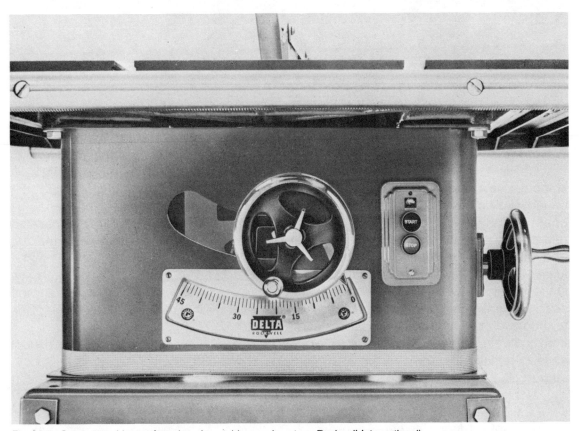

Fig. 20-2. Good control layout for a bench or table saw (courtesy Rockwell International).

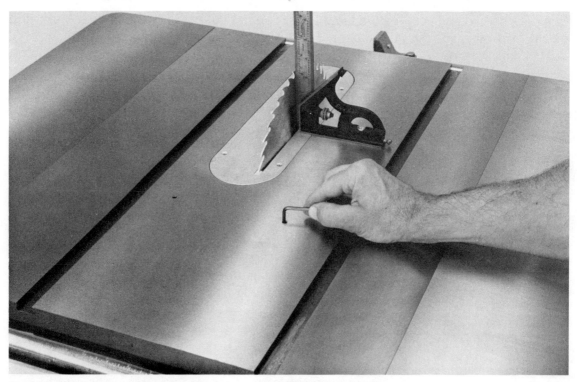

Fig. 20-3. Checking the blade for cut accuracy (courtesy Rockwell International).

the switch. Then they don't have to worry about either losing the key or having children turn on the tool when they're not supervised.

Check to see that the saw's table is smooth. Use a straightedge. Move the miter gauge and rip fence to make certain they operate easily and smoothly. Take a short rule and measure the width of the blade slot. The narrower the better. Run the blade to a full 45-degree tilt. Make sure that it doesn't strike the edges of the slot. Too wide a blade slot allows splinters or narrow pieces of work to drop into the opening. Those pieces can then come zinging back into your face. If you have to remove the insert to get a full 45-degree tilt, that's even worse.

The table saw should have a rip capacity of a full 24 inches so that you can cut to the center of a 4-foot wide panel of plywood or other material. With the blade raised only 1 inch above the surface of the table, make sure there's at least a foot of table in front of the blade so that you can support 1-inch-×-1-foot wide stock crosscutting. Actually, the larger the table the better. Wider tables make for ease in using wider pieces of wood cut from plywood sheets. Make sure that the saw has enough capacity to cut a 2×4 at a full 45-degree tilt. Virtually any saw will have this because today's 2×4 is more on the order of 1⅝ inches than it is 2 inches. See Fig. 20-3.

When checking the blade guard, except to get one of the newer plastic models, usually in orange plastic, and make sure the kerf splitter and antikickback fingers are included. Check the underside of the table to see that it is cast with enough ribs to make

Fig. 20-4. Good maching, general finish and ease of operation are all indicated here at the rip fence (courtesy Rockwell International).

for sturdiness and long life. A table that starts to flex causes an extreme loss of accuracy, and thus usefulness, in the saw. See Fig. 20-4.

Once you're satisifed that the saw you're looking at meets all your needs, consider the installation in your workshop. I've seen some absolutely fine table saws installed in areas that vastly limit their usefulness. There's not much point in having a table saw that will cut to the center of a 4-foot wide panel if you don't have the 8 feet of backspace on both sides of the table that panel is almost sure to require. Actually, you need more like 10 feet because you will require some standing space.

If you expect to be ripping very long pieces of wood, even more room will be needed. For crosscutting operations, you must consider lengths from the side of the saw blade. At a minimum, you will need 10 feet of clearance on each side of the table saw. That doesn't mean you can't have anything in that space—though you can't if you must use the space to walk a panel into the saw blade—but whatever you have in that space must be lower than the saw table height.

Saw table height is another consideration. Rockwell's table saws packaged with stands come at 32-inch and 33 1/3-inch heights. Sears doesn't state table height on

285

their saws. In any case, the table top is best at an inch or so below waist height. See Figs. 20-5 and 20-6.

As you're setting up the table saw, make the same alignment checks covered in Chapter 19 for the Shopsmith Mark V table saw. Check blade alignment, the miter gauge, and the rip fence. Each manufacturer's saw will have adjustments in slightly different ways. You'll need the owners' manual for the particular saw to figure most of them.

When you get ready to cut, set the stock to be cut next to the blade and run the blade up or down until just about a quarter of an inch projects above the stock surface. If you're doing rough work and need a lot of pieces, extending the blade to its maximum

will provide the fastest cutting. It will also increase chipping. It decreases the chance of burning because there is less friction on the rim of the blade. Start the motor and let the blade reach full speed before you begin to make your cuts. Stand to one side of the blade and use both hands to hold the work.

Wide stock is classified as 4 inches or more. When ripping work any narrower, you must use a push stick instead of your fingers to guide it through the cutting process. As usual, waste stock remaining on the table is never touched until after the blade has stopped turning. You start using your push stick, on narrow stock, just after the end of stock (still uncut) goes over the end of the table. See Fig. 20-7. You can make the push stick described in Chapter 19 or a less fancy

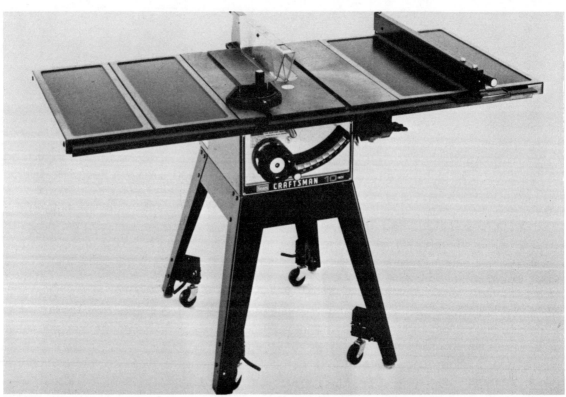

Fig. 20-5. Craftsman's 10-inch table saw with stand and locking wheels. Note the heft of the locks (courtesy Sears, Roebuck and Co.).

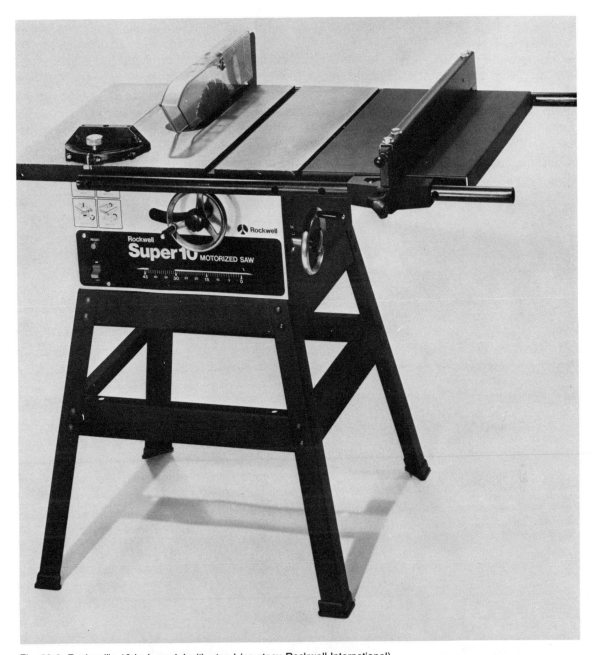

Fig. 20-6. Rockwell's 10-inch model with stand (courtesy Rockwell International).

model that is nothing more than a piece of 1-×-2-inch stock a foot or so long with an inch deep notch cut in the stock holding end. The push stick will work better if the top edge of the notch is about twice as long as the bottom edge.

Dado heads are available for regular table saws. See Fig. 20-8. Adjustable dado heads are the easiest to use because you don't have to take the entire unit apart to add chippers when a wider dado is needed. You simply dial in the size and, in most cases, you can dial in a new size without taking the dado head off the arbor. The Craftsman adjustable dado head offers this feature, as well as a dado width up to 13/16 inches with a depth of 1½ inches maximum (Fig. 20-9).

In addition, triple cutting molding heads and sanding wheels are also available. All add to the versatility of the basic table saw. With both the dado head and the molding head, you must remember to buy the correct table insert because the blade insert is far too narrow to permit use of these accessories. Fortunately, in most cases these inserts cost less than $10 or just a bit more.

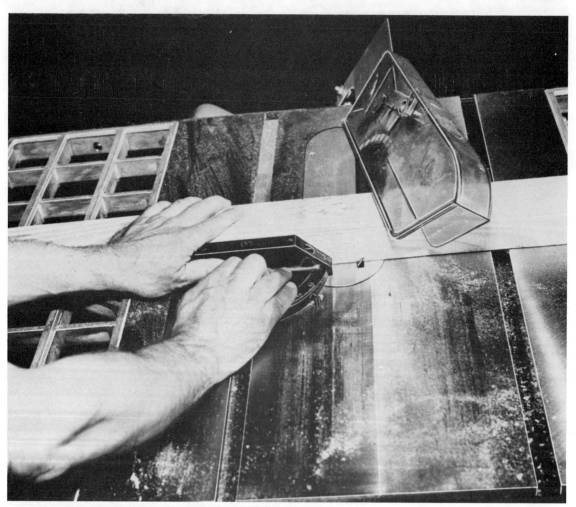

Fig. 20-7. Making a bevel miter cut (courtesy Rockwell International).

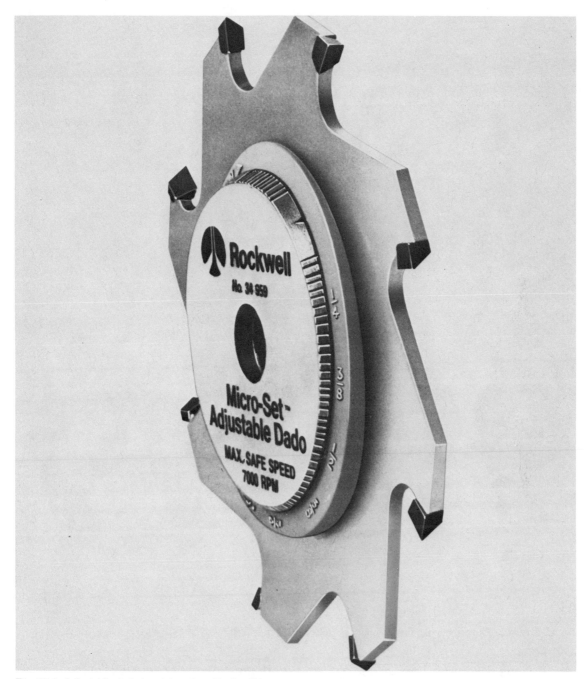

Fig. 20-8. Adjustable dado head (courtesy Rockwell International).

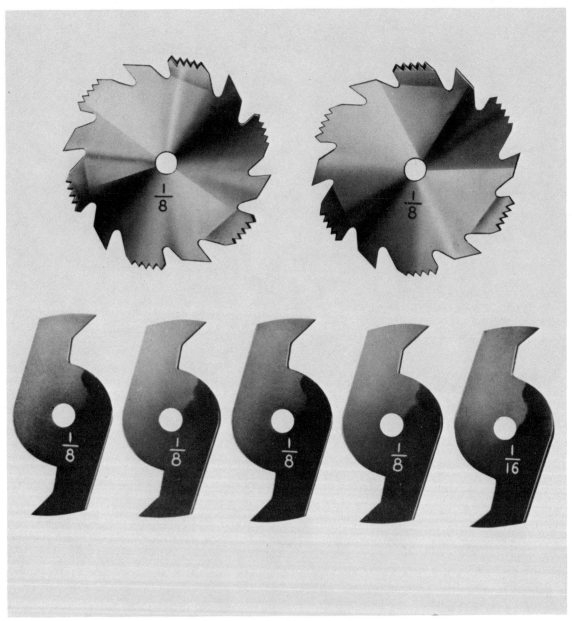

Fig. 20-9. Standard adjustable dado head (courtesy Rockwell International).

Various extensions and extension tables are available for table saws. They aid cutting by adding support under larger work pieces. In cases—both for rip sawing and for crosscutting—where a really long piece of work must be cut, roller support stands can be used. You can buy these, though they tend to be rather expensive, but it's generally easier and less expensive to build your own.

The simplest method is to build a stand

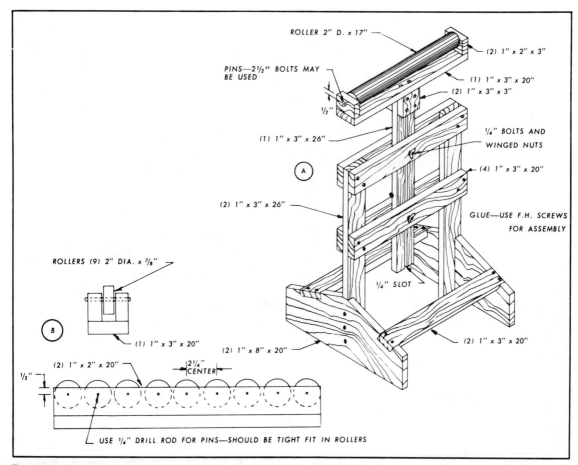

ROLLER 2" D. x 17"

PINS—2½" BOLTS MAY BE USED

(2) 1" x 2" x 3"

(1) 1" x 3" x 20"

(2) 1" x 3" x 3"

½"

(1) 1" x 3" x 26"

¼" BOLTS AND WINGED NUTS

A

(4) 1" x 3" x 20"

(2) 1" x 3" x 26"

GLUE—USE F.H. SCREWS FOR ASSEMBLY

ROLLERS (9) 2" DIA. x ⅞"

¼" SLOT

B

(1) 1" x 3" x 20"

(2) 1" x 8" x 20"

(2) 1" x 3" x 20"

(2) 1" x 2" x 20"

2¼" CENTER

½"

USE ¼" DRILL ROD FOR PINS—SHOULD BE TIGHT FIT IN ROLLERS

Fig. 20-10. Roller extension stand for table saws (courtesy Shopsmith, Inc.).

of 6-inch nominal lumber, 1 inch thick, and about ¾ of an inch lower than the height of your table top. You can insert a crosspiece of 1×6 to brace the stand and then back or front it with peg board (which becomes a handy place to hang other accessories). Obtain a dozen or so ball-roller glides of the type meant for hassocks and other small furniture.

Attach the glides to the top 1×6 on the stand and you have an extension roller table that can be positioned any distance from the saw you need. This particular form of roller is useful for rip and crosscutting. Most commercial designs (at around $100 to $125) seem most suitable for rip sawing only). See Fig. 20-10.

The table saw, as you gain experience, will become a great source of enjoyment as you learn to make taper cuts, beveled and mitered cuts for poly-sided figures, bend wood using kerf cuts (called *kerfing*), cut wedges, and use both the dado head and molding cutter to full capacity. The versatility and accuracy of a properly used table saw will surprise you—quite pleasantly, I believe.

Fig. 20-11. Dadoing (courtesy Rockwell International).

Fig. 20-12. Dadoing (courtesy Rockwell International).

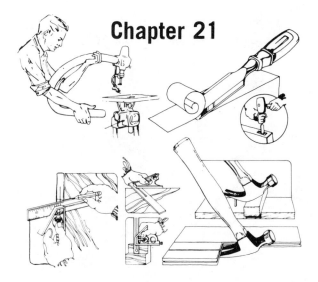

Chapter 21

Radial-Arm Saws

T HE RADIAL ARM SAW, ONE OF THE SINGLE most versatile tools any woodworking shop can have, is a somewhat odd looking tool to those unfamiliar with woodworking shops. Originally, the radial-arm saw was a contractor's tool. It remained so for a number of years and then began finding its way into professional woodworking shops and home workshops.

The radial-arm saw is virtually ideal for on-site work that involves cutting off ends of stock square (no matter stock length) and making miter after miter on long stock—whether from the right or left of the blade. By turning the head on the yoke, rips of any length can be made to a depth of 2 feet with some radial arm saws. Rockwell's version cuts to 24 inches. The Craftsman 12-inch, Sears' top-of-the-line model, cuts to 26 inches. So does the Craftsman top-of-the-

line 10-inch radial-arm saw. Even the least expensive Craftsman will rip to 24 inches.

Crosscut depth, or width, is related to rip, but it is usually quite a bit less. The small Sears' model crosscuts to 12 inches. The next up the line crosscuts to 15½ inches. Rockwell's Model 10 crosscuts to 12¾ inches. Depth of cut varies with saw power and blade diameter. The Rockwell Model 10 gives a 3-inch depth at 90 degrees. The Craftsman 1977N also has a 3-inch cut depth. Both of these have 10-inch diameter blades. The 12-inch Craftsman 1979N, with its extra size, gives a 4-inch depth of cut. In general, radial-arm saws offer greater cut depth for a particular blade diameter than do table saws. If that's important to you, it becomes another favorable feature of the radial-arm saw. See Figs. 21-1 and 21-2.

For really giant-size work, you might go

Fig. 21-1. Rockwell radial-arm saw (courtesy Rockwell International).

wild and consider something like Rockwell's industrial model 18-inch, radial-arm saw. This tool provides a 7⅛-inch depth of cut, a 2-foot crosscutting capacity, and a rip sawing capacity of 38½ inches! The shipping weight is almost 800 pounds. That is more than four times the weight of the Craftsman 12-inch, radial-arm saw.

There is some competition between radial-arm saws and tools such as the Shopsmith Mark V. The radial-arm saw can accept router bits, rotary surface planes, sanding drums and discs, dado heads, and molding heads. There is often a second spindle running at a different speed and it can accept flexible shafts to run light grinding tools.

The primary difference as a saw between the table saw and the radial-arm saw is demonstrated by looking at a crosscut. On a table saw, you hold the work piece against the miter gauge and move it into the blade to make the cut. On a radial-arm saw, you hold the work against the fence and pull the blade to you to make the cut. Some people claim the moderately long column, or neck, that holds the radial arm and its yoke allows more flexibility and thus cuts down on accuracy over the table saw. Others feel that being able to hold the work piece stationary gives slightly greater accuracy in certain angled cuts. I've gotten exceptionally accurate cuts with both kinds of saws. See Fig. 21-3 and 21-4.

Overall, radial-arm saws are quite similar in appearance. Such details as the

Fig. 21-2. Craftsman radial arm saw (courtesy Sears, Roebuck and Co.).

method of adjusting the miter stops, turning the power head in the yoke for rip cuts, and the position of the on/off switch can differ markedly. The radial-arm saw blade always rotates away from the operator. This helps hold the work against the fence as you make the cut. As with virtually all woodworking tools, the speed at which you feed the blade into the work is crucial. The slower the speed the smoother the cut.

For rip cuts, the power head is swiveled 90 degrees, placing it parallel to the fence. For ripsawing, you do not move the head; instead you feed the work to it. The work is fed against the blade's rotation. This tends to cause the blade to fight the feed. Therefore, the antikickback fingers are essential to safe ripsawing with a radial-arm saw.

All radial-arm saw blades cut into the table. Most tables are of composition material. When the time comes, they can be readily replaced. If you're going to be doing a lot of odd-angle mitering as well as regular-angle mitering and crosscutting, you might want to place a ⅛-inch piece of plywood or hardboard over the table to keep it from being worn out before its time. Otherwise there is not any need to worry about the cuts through the table and fence.

Keeping the penetration of the table to a reasonable amount is the surest way of making certain you don't have to replace it too frequently. The blade must cut the table to complete the cuts, but it should be set so that no more than ⅛ to ¼ of an inch of penetration occurs. Miter cutting tears up fences pretty rapidly, but this is simply a piece of straight wood, varying in size depending on the saw, and you can replace it in about five minutes on most radial-arm saws.

As with most saws, all cuts are made on the waste side of the cut line. The work is lined up for crosscuts on the guide cut in the fence. The saw is positioned so that the blade is behind the fence. If the work piece is large enough, use your left hand to hold it in place. Slowly and steadily draw the saw yoke toward you. If the workpiece is too minute to be held with safety, you can either use a nail through the waste portion (don't drive it all the way in) or a clamp if it runs close enough to a table edge. Keep your hand out of the way.

In any case, make sure that you keep your left hand well away from the cut line. As the saw blade is drawn to you, it becomes easy to ignore possible danger to the left hand with a radial-arm saw. Don't. Always make sure it is well out of the way of the cut line before making the cut. That's a good reason for drawing a line all the way across the work piece even though only an edge mark is really needed to line up with the fence cut used as a guide.

Ripping cuts are made by setting the head and blade parallel to the fence. The antikickback fingers should be adjusted (they're normally on a rod that is held in place with a clamp and set screw) so that they are just resting on the surface of the work. Set the fingers too tightly and the work will be hard to get through the saw. Set them too loosely and you get some kickback. Don't set them at all and you'll almost surely get kickback.

When work is being ripped too narrowly for the safety of your fingers, you must use a push stick. But you can't use quite the same push stick you would for a table saw. If the thing slips, you're in trouble. A deep notch in the end of the stick is needed. Rather than making the stick a foot long, make it about 18 inches to 2 feet long so that the blade isn't near your hand at any time.

Some kinds of work are more easily

done with a radial-arm saw than with a table saw (V grooving is a good example). Such cuts can be made with a table saw. But because the blade is under the work, you are in essence, cutting blind. The cut is made from the top on a radial-arm saw so it is easier. Set the saw blade for a rip bevel, or a crosscut bevel, to the depth you want and make the first cut. If your first cut is in the board's center, then you can simply flip the board and make the second cut. If the V is anywhere else on the board, you'll have to reposition the blade angled from the other side to match the first cut.

Molding heads, sanding discs, sanding drums, and other accessories—such as router bits and dado heads—add greatly to the capabilities of any radial-arm saw. With

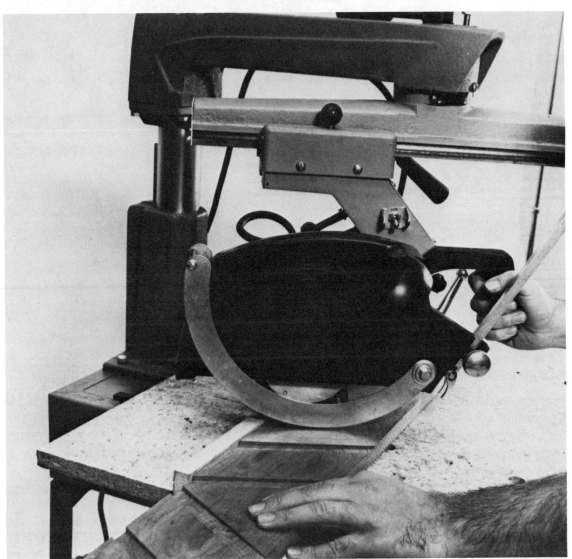

Fig. 21-3. Pulling the saw through the work (courtesy Rockwell International).

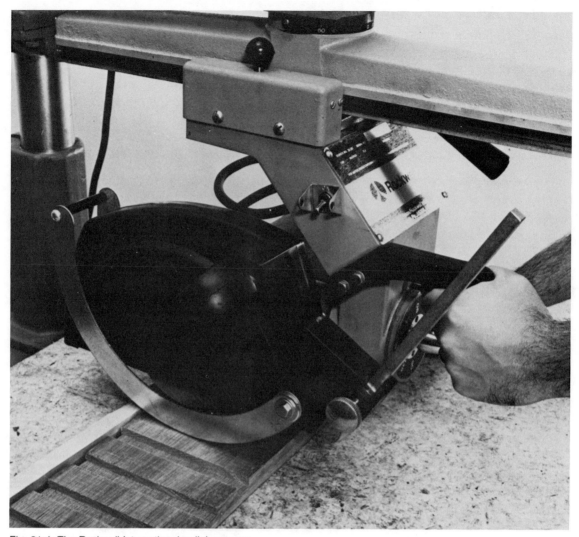

Fig. 21-4. The Rockwell International radial-arm saw.

practice, you might even want to go beyond things and do such work as making circle cuts or even saucer cuts (which generally use the blade more as a scraper, but can be used to make quite large concavities). Pierced cuts are done either with the saw blade or the dado head by making one cut and then flipping the work over and coming in from that side, going just a hair more than half the depth of the stock with each cut. The dado head can be used to form circular tenons or tapered legs almost as if you had a lathe. Some types of drilling and even horizontal drilling can also be done. Grinding operations are also possible, by mounting a grinding wheel, but make absolutely sure the saw doesn't turn too fast for the grinding wheel you use.

All in all, the radial-arm saw is a most versatile tool and one that can increase in versatility over the years as you add accessories and gain experience.

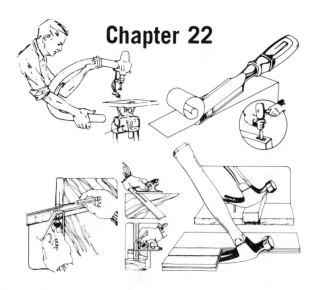

Chapter 22

Lathes

FOR WOODWORKING TOOLS, THE LATHE IS moderately priced in comparison to some top-of-the-line radial-arm saws and table saws. The Craftsman 12-inch lathe can be set up on stands in your shop for under $350. That includes a steel-legged stand with a solid top, and a ½-horsepower motor. See Fig. 22-1.

The motor turns at 1725 rpm, but stepped pulleys offer final speeds of 875 rpm, 1350 rpm, 2250 rpm, and 3450 rpm. A disc sander attachment is available using a 9-inch disc and having a table that will tilt to 45 degrees.

You must, when thinking of getting a lathe, remember that it is one of the few woodworking tools capable of starting a job and finishing it without ever removing it from the head and tailstocks. You can begin a piece with nothing but a 4-inch square of wood and come out the other end with a complete, and complex, project ready for its final coat of varnish or whatever finish you choose. It's possible for you to turn out quite nice bowls, for instance, with no other tool. See Fig. 22-2.

Basically, two types of work are done on a lathe. The spindle turnings are those that are mounted between the headstock and the tailstock, while faceplate turnings are mounted only at the headstock (Fig. 22-3). For work too small to be mounted on the faceplate, use screw centers. I've seen some very nice miniatures done on lathes.

The basic speed rule applies here. For large work, use slow speeds and use the higher speeds for smaller jobs. Roughing in work requires much slower speeds than does final finishing no matter the size of the job being carried out. Operations are just

Fig. 22-1. Craftsman wood lathe (courtesy Sears, Roebuck and Co.).

about identical to those described for the Shopsmith Mark V.

One consideration, for both spindle and face plate work, you might want to think about is the use of molding knives to design and cut special projects. With the wide array of such knives on the market—if you already have a molding cutter head for your table or radial-arm saw, and a few of the cutters—you can lay the cutters directly on your template design sheet and make the design tracing around them.

300

After that, it's simply a matter of making handles for the molding cutters and using them in place of lathe chisels to do the actual work. Probably the easiest way to make such a handle is to get hold of some half-round maple or other nonsplintery hardwood (stay away from oaks) and a piece of aluminum bar stock at least a quarter inch thick (and the same width as the half round hardwood) and drill four holes through the molding and bar stock. Let the bottom section of molding and the bar stock extend past the top section of molding enough so that a hole drilled in the bar stock and bottom piece of molding will allow your particular brand of molding knife to butt its blunt end against the top piece of molding. Use countersunk wood screws to join the three pieces or use screws and nuts. Make sure the nuts are also countersunk (this last is the best way, but you must countersink the nuts or the tool will be quite uncomfortable to hold for any period of time).

A machine screw is then run through the bottom piece of molding and a nut is run down to attach the molding knife. The mold-

Fig. 22-2. A four-speed lathe from Rockwell International.

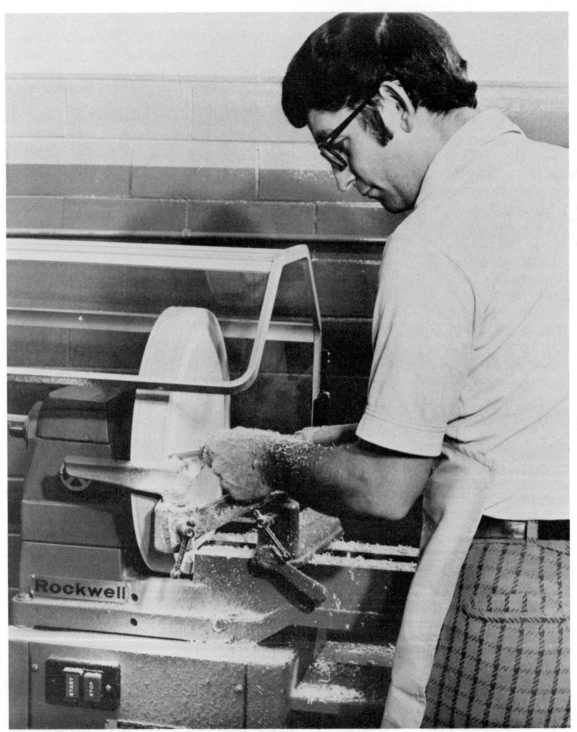

Fig. 22-3. Face plate turning (courtesy Rockwell International).

Fig. 22-4. Lathe headstock (courtesy Rockwell International).

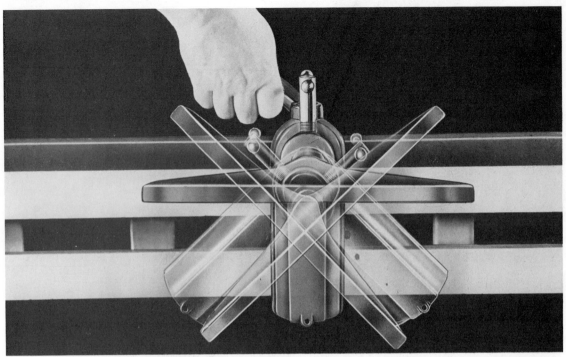

Fig. 22-5. Adjustable tool rest (courtesy Rockwell International).

Fig. 22-6. Lathe and headstock, minus tailstock and showing bed rails (courtesy Rockwell International).

Fig. 22-7. Headstock with cover off to show drive belts (courtesy Rockwell International).

ing knife should extend over the end of the bar stock from 1/4 to 3/16 of an inch and no more. This tool is always used with scraping action and you should remove particles not much heavier than those you would get using a medium-coarse sandpaper grit.

Stanley's Surfor rasps are also good matches for a lathe and will remove material quickly. Sandpaper strips can be used for final finishing while the lathe continues to turn the work. This takes almost all the work out of sanding small round pieces. Use care because if you've designed a piece with sharp edges a lathe turning at even a slow 875 rpm will allow sandpaper to quickly round those sharp edges and mess up your job. See Figs. 22-4 through 22-9.

Fig. 22-8. Lathe controls (courtesy Rockwell International).

305

Fig. 22-9. Tools can be fashioned to fit job needs (courtesy Rockwell International).

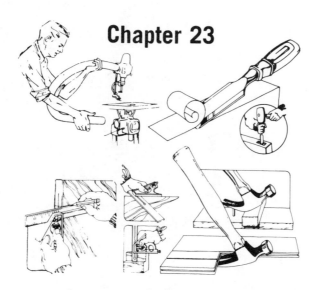

Chapter 23

Other Stationary Tools

THERE ARE FREESTANDING POWER TOOLS that are useful to extremely serious woodworkers. Generally, they are of little interest to the average person. This is mostly due to the cost. You can't get a large-size planer/molder for much less than $1,300 (delivered). Such a tool is appropriate only for someone wanting to do very specialized jobs such as air drying rough-cut green lumber and then planing it to size and shape.

BAND SAW

Freestanding band saws add various capacities to a shop that no other saw can. They can cut really thick stock (up to 6 inches in most cases, unless you go to industrial machines that will cut to over a foot) and at the same time give the capacity for cutting curves and all kinds of odd shapes and not

so odd shapes (Fig. 23-1). Simply replacing the band-saw blade with a sanding belt gives you a sander that is virtually an ideal tool for working with the intricate shapes you can cut out with the saw.

The Craftsman band saw (Fig. 23-2) has a 6-inch-×-1-foot cutting capacity. Accessories available include a rip fence, a miter gauge, an extension table, sanding belts, and circle-cutting attachments (for up to 12-inch diameter circles, this unit speeds set up and operation). You can also get a speed reducer (to drop speed to 135 feet per minute). The speed reducer allows the use of the bandsaw in metal cutting operations. The Craftsman 2434N bandsaw uses 80-inch blades in widths from 1/8 of an inch to 1/2 inch. Therefore, you get a good selection of curves to choose from.

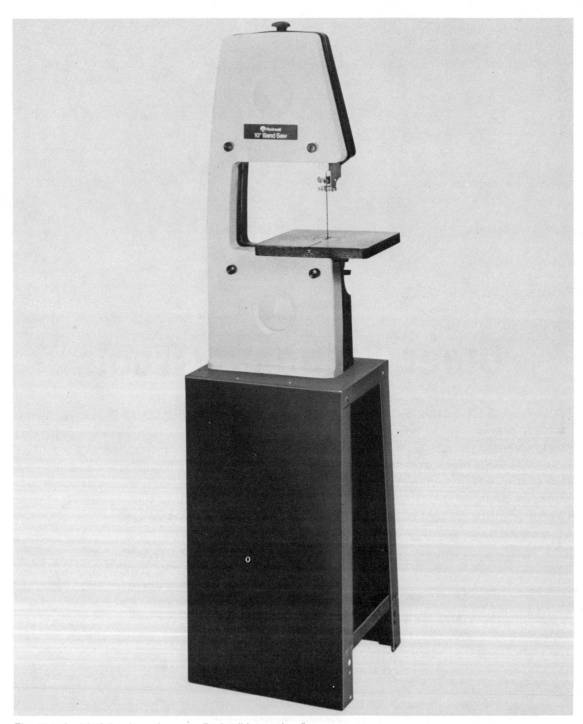

Fig. 23-1. A 10-inch band saw (courtesy Rockwell International).

used as a saber saw and it has a 15-inch throat depth. See Fig. 23-3.

For larger jigsaws, the Rockwell industrial model has a 2-foot throat depth. The table is almost twice the surface area, tilts 45 degrees right and 15 degrees left, and also adds a 45-degree tilt to the front. The Rockwell comes in a Delta 4-speed with 610, 910, 1255 and 1725 cutting strokes per minute. The variable speed model has speeds from 650 to 1700 cutting strokes per minute. It also converts easily and readily to a saber saw. This machine has its own splash system for lubrication with a refillable reservoir. See Figs. 23-4 through 23-9.

BELT SANDER

Stationary belt sanders are readily available as freestanding tools. The Sears' Craftsman 2476 is a compact unit with an overall size of 11 by 10 by 15 inches high. It uses a 1-×-30 inch sanding belt and gives much the same sanding performance as a band saw (naturally, at less speed, and with lower capacity).

The belt moves at about 2700 feet per minute and a pulley setup lets you change from internal to external sanding. In addition, the tool has a 5-inch sanding disc on its right side; it spins at 4400 rpm. The plate is removable on the belt sander to allow for flexible sanding of irregular shapes. The disc sander allows a 45-degree table tilt and includes a miter gauge. See Figs. 23-10, 23-11, and 23-12.

Larger stationary belt sanders are available in several designs. Craftsman offers one tool that has a full 100 square inches of sanding area with a 6-inch-×-4-foot sanding belt and a disc sander on the side. The disc sander is 9 inches in diameter. The sanding belt runs over a drum at one end that is open for use and 3 inches in diameter

Fig. 23-2. A Craftsman 12-inch band saw (courtesy Sears, Roebuck and Co.).

JIGSAW

Sears calls their Craftsman 2472C a scroll saw/sander. It has been designed to fit on top of a bench. It is light, at under 17 pounds, but fast, at 3450 strokes per minute, with a table that will tilt 45 degrees for bevel cuts. An accessory kit offers a flexible shaft attachment, as well as sanding discs, drum sander and extra bands, grinding wheels and some other components useful with flexible shaft tools. This saw can also be

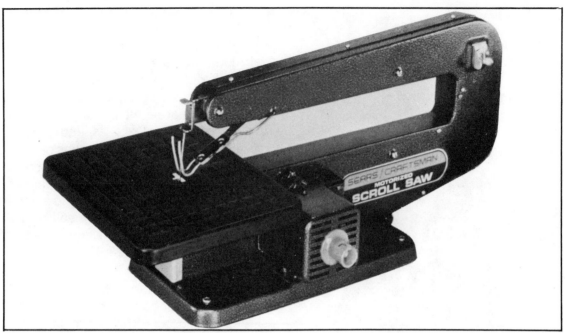

Fig. 23-3. Craftsman jigsaw (courtesy Sears, Roebuck and Co.).

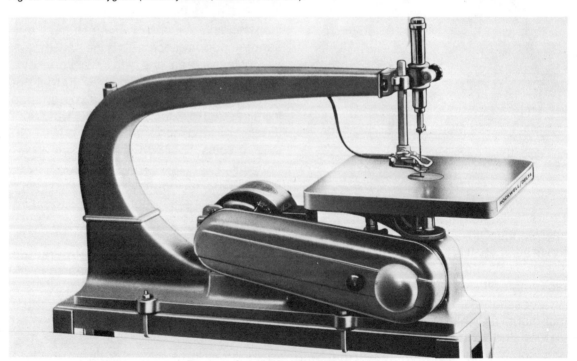

Fig. 23-4. Rockwell jigsaw without stand (courtesy Rockwell International).

Fig. 23-5. Jigsaw with stand (courtesy Rockwell International).

Fig. 23-6. Upper chuck (courtesy Rockwell International).

for sanding 1½-inch or larger radius curves. The sanding belt tilts up from the horizontal to make end finishing of assembled small projects easy. The disc has a table that tilts to 45 degrees for sanding bevels (Fig. 23-13).

Craftsman's smaller disc/belt sander offers a table-top setup and a much lower cost. The sanding capacity is reduced to a 4-inch-×-1-foot belt table. The 6-inch disc sander has a table that tilts 45 degrees, as well as miter gauge, and would be an excellent tool of choice for anyone not wanting to spend the over $300 for the larger unit (this

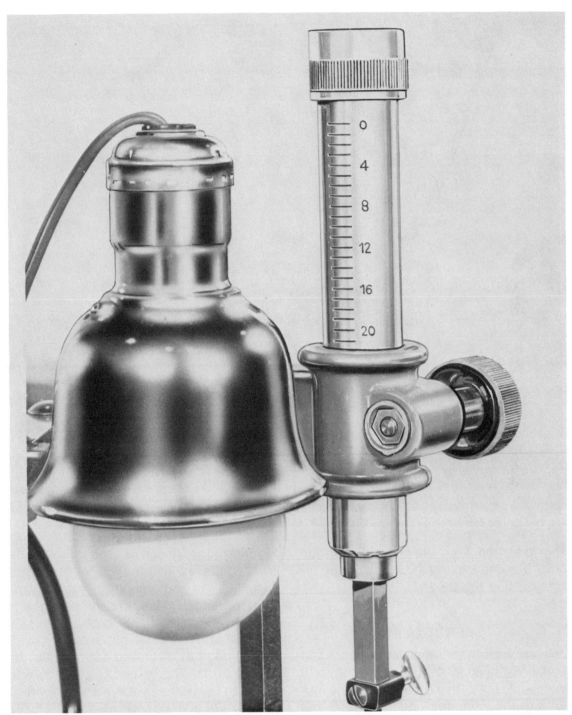

Fig. 23-7. Gauge (courtesy Rockwell International).

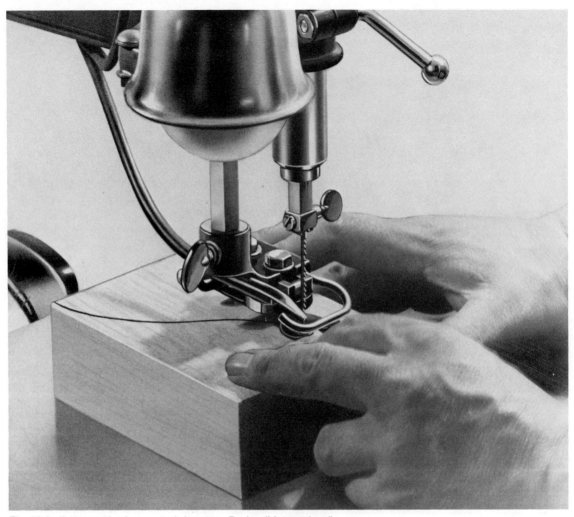

Fig. 23-8. Jigsaw cutting heavy stock (courtesy Rockwell International).

should be about half the price). In addition, belts are less expensive because they are smaller. See Fig. 23-14.

JOINTER/PLANER

Jointer/planers as freestanding tools generally cost over $400 by the time they're in your workshop. They do offer great utility in letting you chamfer edges. The 6-inch capacity Craftsman model offers a 6-inch wide cut for planing rough surfaces and squaring edges. It can be used to make sure joint edges are tight when you have to have a flush fit. The ½-horsepower motor turns 3450 rpm and depth of cut is up ⅛ of an inch. The knives make 12,900 cuts per minute. The cast-iron fence has positive stops at 45 and 90 degrees. A built-in scale shows the degree of tilt. This is not a light tool; with motor and legs, the jointer/planer will weigh close to 170 pounds set up. See Fig. 23-15.

Sears also makes a bench-top jointer planer. This tool has a 4½-inch capacity and it will actually plane to 4 inches wide. There is a ⅛-inch maximum cut depth. The detailing is not so fancy and the fence is calibrated, but without positive stops. It should do quite well for a great many people who have no room for the larger tools. See Fig. 23-16.

PLANER/MOLDER

For the totally dedicated woodworker, the Craftsman planer/molder can be bought with either a 2- or 5-horsepower motor. It will plane or mold wood up to a foot wide and 6 inches thick. The automatic power feed will run material through at a dozen feet per minute. As it planes the flat surfaces of the board, it can also be cutting shiplap, tongue-and-groove, or other designs in the sides of the board.

You would only need the 5-horsepower motor if you planned on running the thing continually over a long period of time. For even the most serious home woodworker, the 2-horsepower motor would be more than sufficient. Still, by the time the unit is installed in your shop and you've bought the molding cutters you want, you're staring at quite a bill. Delivered, the 2-horsepower planer/molder is unlikely to run much under $1350 with any selection of molding cutters

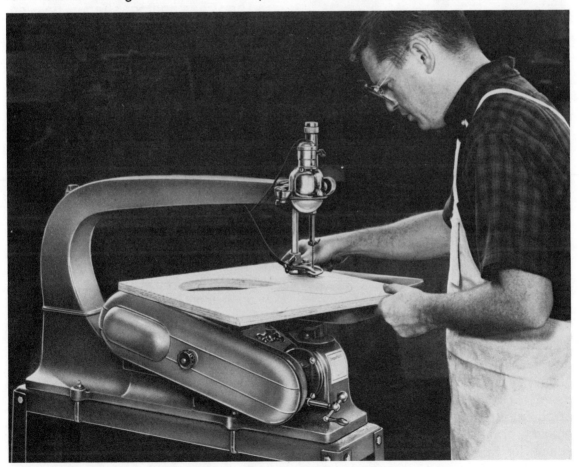

Fig. 23-9. Jigsaw cutting an intricate design (courtesy Rockwell International).

Fig. 23-10. Light duty belt sander (courtesy Rockwell International).

at all. Local sawmills have these units—usually diesel driven—and that's fine for them. Unless you really intend to get serious about storing and working with large amounts of very expensive lumber, you can search for wood to use at the local lumberyard. See Figs. 23-17 through 23-26.

SHAPER

A freestanding shaper will produce tongue-and-groove edges, shiplap edges, and drop-leaf beads, as well as various decorative designs in wood edges. The Craftsman shaper has a cutter head that revolves at 9000 rpm and an open work ground cast-iron table of good size with a groove for a miter gauge (not included). The open-grid table is very handy because it allows the chips to fall out of your way quickly so you can readily see how the work is proceeding. It will accept cutters up to 2½ inches in diameter on a ½-inch bore, and the spindle adjusts ⅞ of an inch.

The freestanding shaper has no obstructions—as you find on a drill press with shaper fence and cutters mounted—above the fence to limit work size and shape. Fence adjustment is the same. When the cutter removes a part of the work edge, the fences on both sides of the cutter are set in line. When the entire edge is removed, the outfeed fence must be moved out to support the work after it passes the cutters.

As with all shapers, the work is fed against the rotation of the cutters. In most cases, you should feed with the grain of the wood. That always gives you the smoothest possible cuts. Keep up a slow but steady feed. When you must feed a cut across the grain, make sure you still keep it steady, but slow up to about half the speed or less even than you would use for with the grain work. Cutting across the grain will almost always be smoother if you do the work in several lighter passes instead of in a single large pass. See Figs. 23-27 through 23-29.

ROUTER ARM

The Shopsmith router arm is designed to hold a Shopsmith router or most other brands of router. In essence, the router arm

Fig. 23-11. Belt sander in use (courtesy Rockwell International).

Fig. 23-12. Inside sanding (courtesy Rockwell International).

Fig. 23-13. Craftsman belt/disc sander (courtesy Sears, Roebuck and Co.).

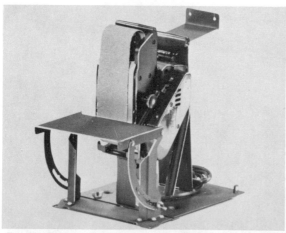

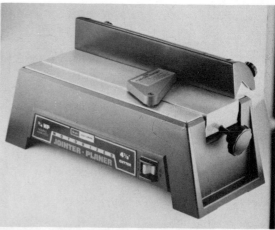

Fig. 23-14. Stand for hand belt sanders (courtesy Sears, Roebuck and Co.).

Fig. 23-16. Bench top planer (courtesy Sears, Roebuck and Co.).

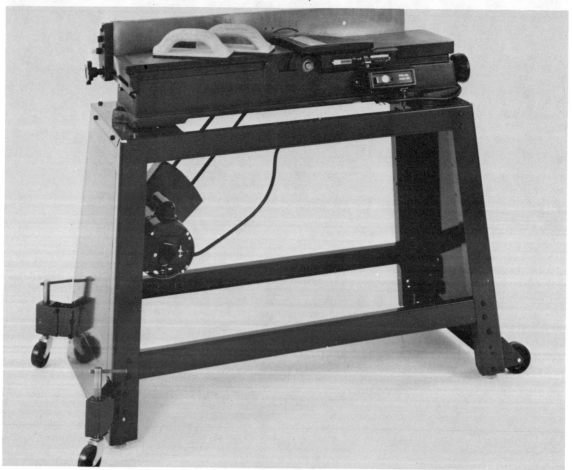

Fig. 23-15. Planer on stand (courtesy Rockwell International).

Fig. 23-17. Uniplane (courtesy Rockwell International).

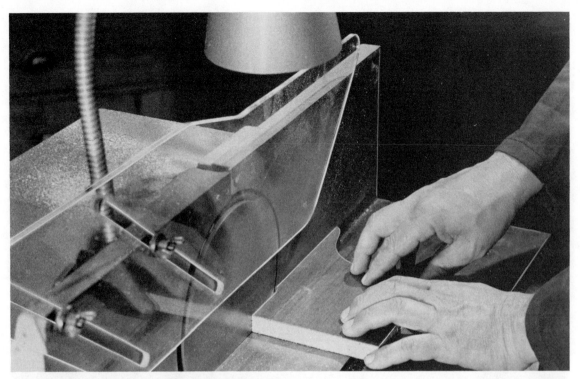

Fig. 23-18. Uniplane in use (courtesy Rockwell International).

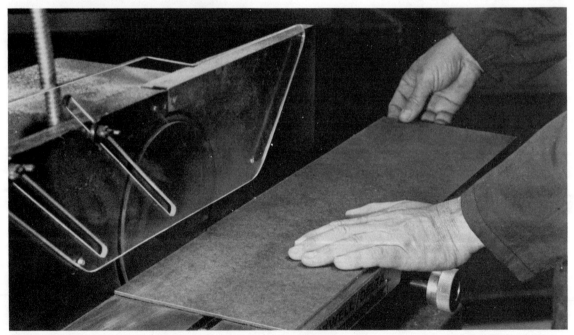

Fig. 23-19. Uniplane with thin stock (courtesy Rockwell International).

Fig. 23-20. Uniplane beveling corners (courtesy Rockwell International).

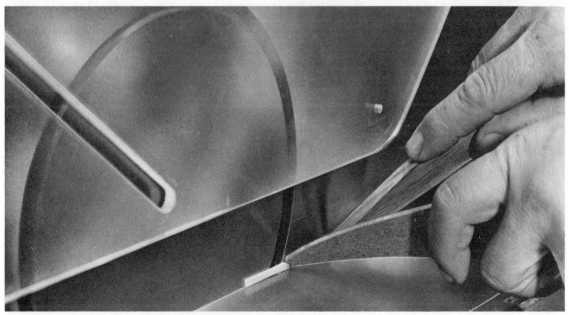

Fig. 23-21. Uniplane with tiny stock (courtesy Rockwell International).

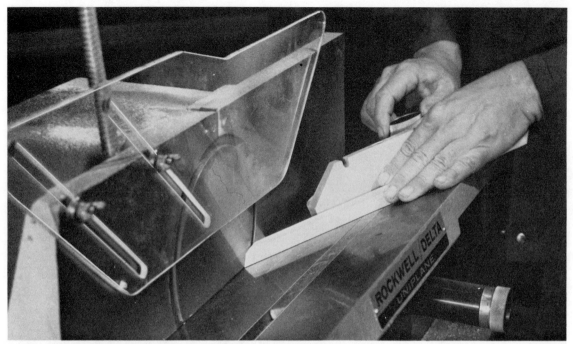

Fig. 23-22. Uniplane with angled stock (courtesy Rockwell International).

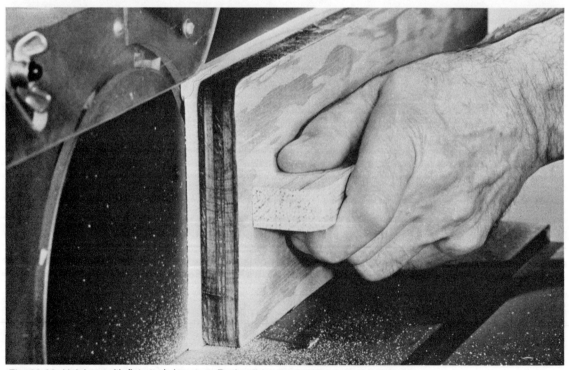

Fig. 23-23. Uniplane with flat stock (courtesy Rockwell International).

Fig. 23-24. Uniplane with heavy stock (courtesy Rockwell International).

Fig. 23-25. Small Uniplane (courtesy Rockwell International).

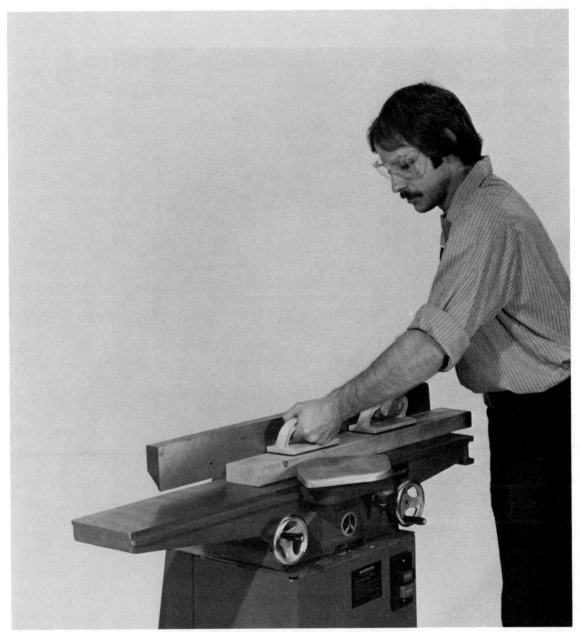

Fig. 23-26. Standard small planer (courtesy Rockwell International).

is a heavy-base table with a wood top. It has an erect arm extending up at its rear much like the radial-arm saw. Out from that extends the actual router arm that moves up and down on the post. A quill feed handle moves the bit into the work and it can be locked in position with little more than a twist of the wrist. A depth-stop rod keeps the bit from cutting any more deeply than you want for a particular pattern.

Fig. 23-27. A table shaper with an open-grid table allows chips to fall with less worry about waste buildup (courtesy Sears, Roebuck and Co.).

Fig. 23-28. The Rockwell Wood Shaper.

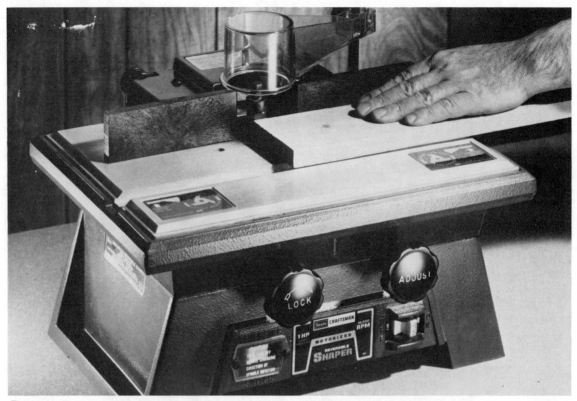

Fig. 23-29. For the small shop, table-top shapers are available, such as this Craftsman model (courtesy Sears, Roebuck and Co.).

Like some of the Sears' Craftsman router accessories, this Shopsmith router arm adds another dimension to router use. It makes duplication simple, mortising easier, edging easier, and depth control for inlay work far, far easier.

With its welded steel base (slotted for easy mounting on a bench top) and a birch veneer plywood base top—along with a center ground steel pole and an I-beam arm ending in a dovetail assembly with a steel rack-and-pinion gear mechanism for moving the arm up and down on the post—the quality of this relatively new Shopsmith tool is extremely high. It is another tool intended for the serious woodworker. It would be especially good for anyone contemplating the need for a number of units.

Duplication starts with the original design being routed into a piece of plastic laminate (carbide-tipped cutters must be used). This provides a fixture (as Shopsmith calls it). A workpiece is mounted on the opposite side of the fixture and the groove is guided over the pin to provide a perfect duplicate of the original design. The process is simply repeated as often as need be until the number of pieces needed are done.

In addition, the router arm simplifies the cutting of circles and curves. It gives great precision to virtually all kinds of wood joint forms whether it's a simple end rabbet or a dovetail dado or even a drop leaf form for a table. The tool is rather expensive, but commercial pin routers start at about three times its price, and go up rapidly.

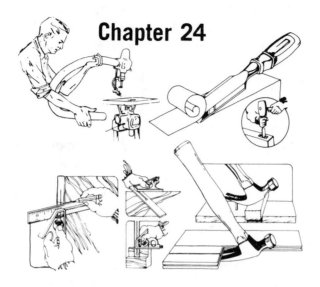

Chapter 24

Chain Saws

I N THE PAST DECADE AND A HALF, THERE has been an explosion in the sale of consumer-oriented chain saws. Sizes range from tiny trimming units with 10-inch bars to immense professional units carrying bars 5 feet or more in length. Often both types of saws are produced by the same manufacturer.

At one point, chain saw selection was simple. You bought the model you could afford and then used it. There were few brands around. Most manufacturers made two or three models, if that many. The saws were bulky, heavy, and hard to start. Then along came the developing two-stroke engine that borrowed much from motorcycle racing-engine technology and kicked out amazing amounts of horsepower.

In 1948, the first 50-pound chain saw was developed. By 1949, the weight had been halved and an all-position carburetor was added. In 1965, the real homeowner's saw came into being with the development of a 10-pound chain saw. Three years later the small chain saw had gone down to 6-pounds. Today, some small electric models might well be under that mark, but such saws are suitable only for very light trimming. For average use, a larger chain saw is needed. For anyone who plans to use a chain saw a great deal, much thought should be given to whether or not it is wisest to buy the top end of the consumer line or near the bottom end of the professional line—no matter the brand you select.

First you need to at least outline the work you must have done. Then select the saw in the size and price range that will fit the job. Consideration must be given to guide-bar length and engine size. Too short a guide bar greatly limits cutting capabilities. Too long a guide bar adds too much weight to the saw, is more expensive, and adds to chain-replacement expense. Too small a saw won't handle all the work you might want to do and it will wear out rather rapidly if too much is demanded of it. In addition, more effort is needed to make large cuts with small saws. Too big a chain saw adds unnecessarily to the basic expense and it can be tiring to use in some operations if you're not used to slinging the thing around every day.

If you lead a particularly sedentary life and then go out to cut firewood with a 22-pound chain saw, I can promise, at the very least, an ache on the inside of your right elbow joint, a very sore right forearm, a very tired upper and lower back area, and a rather short day's cutting. If you use a middle-weight saw, tipping the scales at something on the order of 13 or 14 pounds, you'll probably get more work done, with less effort, and spend half as much, or even less, for the chain saw itself (not to mention the future costs of chains and guide bars).

As a good example, Sears offers a Craftsman professional model chain saw with a 16-inch guide bar and a 2.3-cubic-inch engine. The saw weighs about 13 pounds. At the top of the Craftsman line is another Craftsman professional chain saw with a 30-inch guide bar and a 5.2 cubic-inch engine. The saw weighs about 22½ pounds. It also has a 31-ounce fuel capacity and an 18-ounce chain oil capacity, as compared to the 11-ounce fuel capacity and 6-ounce-chain-oil capacity of the smaller saw. All that liquid adds more weight. The larger saw is going to burn more fuel and need more chain oil (it will have twice as many teeth, or nearly so, to keep lubricated along nearly double the chain length and double the groove length on the guide bar). In addition to the extra weight, the larger chain saw is almost $300 more costly than the smaller unit. Your wallet will definitely be lighter.

In addition to the nearly $300 additional cost, when you need an extra chain for the 30-inch guide bar, expect to spend about $35 for it. The 16-inch guide takes a chain costing around $19. The replacement guide bar for the large saw is over $60; the 16-inch guide bar costs little over $30. Add that to doubled or worse fuel consumption, and unless you have a real need for a pro-style chain saw, you can see you're just defeating yourself by buying the most expensive and thinking it's the best.

Too small a chain saw is as big a waste of money as getting too big a chain saw. You won't get done what you need to get done or you'll be so bone tired you won't be able to move at day's end from pushing a job that a larger saw could have completed with ease hours earlier. Smaller chains have fewer teeth. That means they contact the wood being cut more frequently and, therefore, get duller more quickly. Small saws down on power can take a minute to cut through a log a more powerful saw would zip through in a few seconds.

If your work varies a lot, from tree trimming jobs to cutting a dozen cords of firewood in two or three days, you are going to have to face the fact that you'll either have to use a hand bow saw for the tree trimming or own two chain saws. One of my saws is a small Homelite with a 14-inch guide bar. I use it when I have to clamber around in trees or do light work such as limbing trees under 18 inches diameter. I try to avoid clambering around in trees because heights don't scare me quite so much as terrify me. Still, that small saw is far easier to haul up on a rope than is the larger Homelite 360 with its 2-foot guide bar. And it's also easier to start a small

Fig. 24-1. Homelite 410 in use (courtesy Homelite).

saw when you're standing on a limb. The small saw would be almost useless when felling trees 30 inches or so in diameter, getting a winter's firewood down, and bucked to length for the stoves.

The Homelite 410 is their newest professional saw. It offers a 4.1-cubic-inch engine and a 9000-rpm cutting speed. The cylinder is vertical and the muffler is set at the front of the saw to keep the noise away from the saw's operator. This chain saw can carry guide bars up to 31 inches long. It retails for about $480 with a 16-inch bar. See Figs. 24-1 and 24-2.

Some thought should be given to the size of the trees in your locale. If many are over 16 inches, you might want to think seriously about a chain saw which will carry a 20-inch guide bar. Many people know you can fell a tree up to about twice the diameter of the guide bar's length, but that becomes a time-consuming process. It forces you to, in essence, make six cuts instead of three when felling most trees. As an occasional happening, it isn't all that bad. If 90 percent of your felling work has to be from both sides of a tree trunk, then you're going to be wasting a lot of time.

When you start to consider any chain saw, there are several important points to consider, but none of them is of more real importance than how the saw feels to you. There are certain brands, quite popular, that I cannot use because they simply don't feel comfortable in my hands. Maybe with practice the ease would come, but I've walked right up to Echo, Homelite, McCulloch, Poulan and Skil gas-powered chain saws and found they fit my hands and feel right. Some Craftsman models feel fine and others don't. This is probably because, over the years, Sears has had several different companies manufacture saws for them.

How do the controls fall to hand? Is the manual oiler easy to depress when the saw is at full throttle? Does the front handle feel comfortable in use? Is it easy to keep the throttle depressed while keeping proper grip on the rear handle? How is the saw's balance? Ask yourself all these questions when checking out a chain saw to buy.

If the saw is the size you need, in your price range, and feels right, then is the time to start looking for features and overall quality of manufacture. How easy is the chain to adjust? Most saws have a chain adjustment

Fig. 24-2. Homelite 410 (courtesy Homelite).

screw on the inside of the case close to the guide bar. Virtually all of these are easy to adjust. Chains are reasonably easy to change.

I like virtually everything about the Homelite 360, but I feel there is a design problem. The side plate that comes off to change the chain also includes the chain adjuster. Getting the whole works back together—you have to fit the adjusting tip in the adjusting slot blind—takes too much time and causes extreme frustration. It is the only chain saw I've ever had on which I preferred to sharpen chains in the field rather than just slipping on a fresh, sharp chain. Quality is excellent for a small professional model. Power is just fine whether I use a 16-, 20-, or 24-inch bar (the maximum recommended for the 360).

Durability is always a question with any product that has moving parts (and some that don't). Almost all of the chain saws available today have cast aluminum cylinders. Heads are often cast as a part of the engine block. Of course, aluminum wears far too rapidly to be a good cylinder material so the aluminum cylinders have chrome-plated bores to cut down on wear. Check for chrome plating on the bore; you won't be able to see it, but the manufacturers' literature will surely mention it.

An all-position carburetor is standard today. You probably don't need to check, but you can check the weight of the saw compared to the engine size. The main reason for aluminum cylinder blocks is the weight savings. Homelite's new 410 weighs 15.5 pounds even with a 4.1-cubic-inch engine. Look for reasonable care in finishing. The saw will almost certainly look fairly bedraggled after a couple years' use, but starting out with a nice-looking saw means pretty much the same as it means with other tools.

Talk to at least two or three people, preferably more about their chain saws. If you're lucky enough to be in an area where a lot of heavy cutting, (pulpwood or timber) is done, you've got a good shot at finding what loggers think are best for them. Smaller saws in the same manufacturer's line should approach the quality of the top-of-the-line models.

After looking for quality, check over features. There are a couple of antikickback features on the market. Cutting down on kickback is a good idea, but I'm not overwhelmingly impressed by any of the present-day designs. The Homelite design is good, but it must be removed from the saw to make cuts longer than the guide bar. I've yet to see a chain brake that works rapidly enough to really prevent slicing someone up under severe kickback.

The best kickback prevention with any chain saw is operator control and sensibility. Many chain saws today come with automatic chain oilers. The best of these allow you to adjust the amount of oil going to the chain. I would suggest, if possible, that you select a chain saw that offers both automatic and manual chain oiling. Under extreme cutting conditions, you can add oil to the flow yourself, as needed, or select an automatic oiling chain saw that has a wide adjustment range to allow the same heavy flow. In hard cutting, there is virtually no such thing as too much chain oil. See Fig. 24-3.

Some time ago, the chain saw industry as a whole got off the horsepower wagon and began simply stating the size, in cubic inches, of their engine. Most of today's small, two-stroke engines produce over 1 horsepower per cubic inch, but how much more it is impossible to say. A rough guess might be at least 1.5 horsepower per cubic inch. Very few chain-saw engines are larger

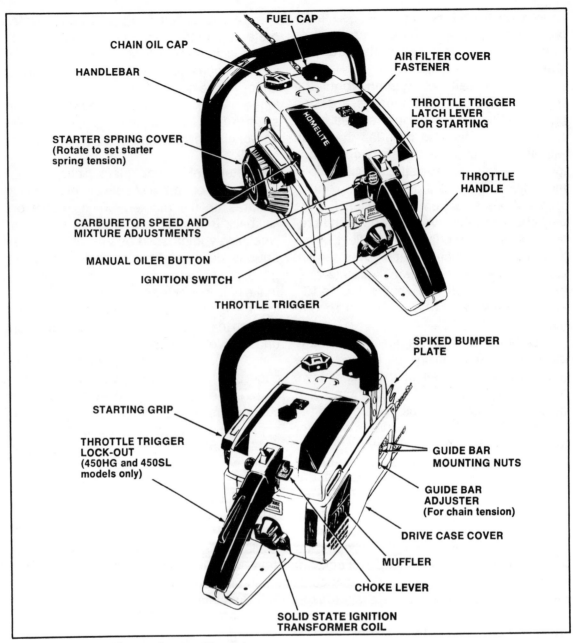

FUEL CAP

CHAIN OIL CAP

HANDLEBAR

AIR FILTER COVER
FASTENER

THROTTLE TRIGGER
LATCH LEVER
FOR STARTING

STARTER SPRING COVER
(Rotate to set starter
spring tension)

THROTTLE
HANDLE

CARBURETOR SPEED AND
MIXTURE ADJUSTMENTS

MANUAL OILER BUTTON

IGNITION SWITCH

THROTTLE TRIGGER

SPIKED BUMPER
PLATE

STARTING GRIP

THROTTLE TRIGGER
LOCK-OUT
(450HG and 450SL
models only)

GUIDE BAR
MOUNTING NUTS

GUIDE BAR
ADJUSTER
(For chain tension)

DRIVE CASE COVER

MUFFLER

CHOKE LEVER

SOLID STATE IGNITION
TRANSFORMER COIL

Fig. 24-3. Power head features (courtesy Homelite).

than 75 cubic centimeters. Most of the homeowner styles are 50cc or less. There is less rotating mass to draw off power and smaller surfaces to create horesepower re- ducing friction. By most standards, these engines are a bit understressed. That is probably why durability is pretty darned good for the top-quality brand names.

The way to find out anything about saws with comparable engine sizes is to try them out. Many dealers have samples you can use for cutting. Remember that, even with a lot of use as samples, these saws are seldom really broken in. The demonstrator models get sold each season in most cases and each tester gives the saw only a few minutes use. It takes several hours to properly break in a chrome-ringed engine with chromed cylinder walls.

Vibration levels are important in chain saw use. There is a logger's syndrome known as *white tip* that is caused by chain saw vibration. Basically, the vibration of the saw in constant use tends to interfere with, and eventually stop, blood circulation to the finger tips. Most of today's chain saws offer vibration isolation; some do a better job than others. Noise level is another point to consider. The more noise the saw makes the more tiring it is to use. In some cases, such as Homelite's 410, the muffler is front mounted so that any noise produced is directed away from the operator. No matter where the muffler is mounted on a chain saw, the exterior baffles on that muffler must be pointed away from the operator.

Depending on the type of cutting you intend to do, the capability of a chain saw to cut close to the ground might or might not be of importance. If you don't want to leave stumps, then the capability to lay a saw on its side and cut possibly an inch or less above ground level can be important. Stumps make as good firewood as the rest of the tree. The capability to cut low to the ground will often allow you to work around other obstructions and makes it easier to trim away brush around the tree before felling it.

Whenever possible, select a guide bar with a roller or sprocket nose. The roller nose guide bar cuts down on friction as the chain travels over the most difficult part of its trip, where it must change direction sharply, so that both chain and guide-bar life tend to be longer. You'll find it easier to maintain cutting speed in heavy wood. Most sprocket- and roller-nose guide bars have replaceable sprockets. The old rivets must be drilled out, a new sprocket inserted, and the new rivets set. Then you're ready to go again.

Summarizing the features you should look for in any chain-saw purchase, you should have a saw that fits your needs as to power, weight, and guide-bar size. From that point, you'll want an all-position carburetor, a roller-nose guide bar, ease of handling, adjustable automatic oiling, backup manual oiling (if possible), low noise, good vibration isolation, and, probably, the capability to cut low to the ground.

USING A CHAIN SAW

The chain saw is probably the single most dangerous tool you will ever use. It is the only power tool I have ever injured myself with, and I've worked with virtually every power tool imaginable at one time or another. It bit me when I let my attention lapse for little more than a second. I took the saw from a cut with my right hand and used my left leg to kick at some brush. The chain was dropping to idle and, zip, I was sliced on the kneecap, right down to the bone. The cut wasn't really serious. Don't work when you're tired!

Most chain saws will eventually be used to fell trees. Once a tree starts falling, you don't want to be around the point of impact. Tree felling, no matter how much experience a person gains, is never a safe occupation because of the wide range of variables that can affect the direction of fall.

The first safety step concerns fueling the chain saw. Chain saws should be fueled

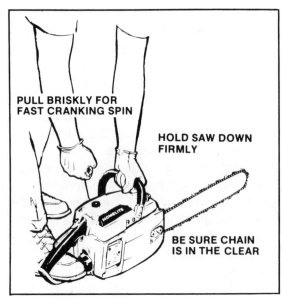

PULL BRISKLY FOR
FAST CRANKING SPIN

HOLD SAW DOWN
FIRMLY

BE SURE CHAIN
IS IN THE CLEAR

Fig. 24-4. Proper starting grip (courtesy Homelite).

through a funnel—for two reasons. Fuel spilled on a hot chain saw can ignite. Fuel spilled on a forest floor can prevent growth of just about any plant you can name. I prefer, when possible, to do my refueling on a stump or large rock. Any spillage of fuel must be wiped from the chain saw before it is started. You should also wipe any dirt and sawdust from the chain saw before removing the fuel or chain oil caps. Do your fueling at least 25 feet from the point where you'll be starting the chain saw. Make sure the gas can is well out of the way of any work. Most chain saws have spark arresting mufflers, but if you do get a spill all it takes is the smallest spark to set it off.

After switching the saw on place your foot through the back loop. Open the choke. Make sure the chain is well away from you. Place your left hand on the top handle and pull the starter cord with your right hand (Fig. 24-4). Many experienced loggers will hold even the largest chain saw in one hand, with the chain pointing away from the body, and

simply yank the starter cord. Unless you've got wrists like a gorrila, this is not at all safe.

Let the saw idle while you check the felling area for other people. Never allow children in a felling area. They are extremely difficult to keep track of and they have no true conception of danger. Your concentration when felling trees must be on yourself and your job or you will end up injured.

When you operate a chain saw, whether for limbing, bucking or felling operations, your footing should always be firm, with body weight well balanced. Make all cuts at or below chest level to keep control of the saw and hold your balance.

Use a proper grip on the saw to reduce the chance of kickback. Your right hand should have a firm grip on the throttle handle while your left hand is wrapped around the top handle, with the thumb underneath. The thumb must be *around* the top handle to provide sure control and cut down on any chance of your hand slipping into the moving chain (Fig. 24-5).

When you start to cut, and as you continue to cut, do your best to keep your body out of line with the chain while the chain is in motion. In something like 93 out of 100 cases when a chain breaks, it will simply run off the saw and onto the ground. In a few

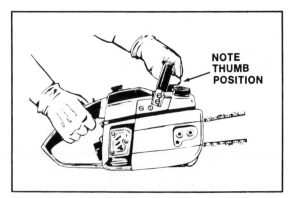

NOTE
THUMB
POSITION

Fig. 24-5. Proper hold during the cut (courtesy Homelite).

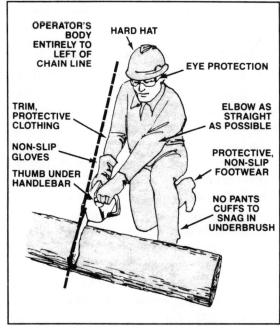

OPERATOR'S BODY ENTIRELY TO LEFT OF CHAIN LINE

HARD HAT

EYE PROTECTION

TRIM, PROTECTIVE CLOTHING

ELBOW AS STRAIGHT AS POSSIBLE

NON-SLIP GLOVES

PROTECTIVE, NON-SLIP FOOTWEAR

THUMB UNDER HANDLEBAR

NO PANTS CUFFS TO SNAG IN UNDERBRUSH

Fig. 24-6. Correct cut position (courtesy Homelite).

always possible. When you have to make a boring cut, for example, you must use the nose of the bar. At such times, as odd as it sounds, you should make sure the saw is operating at full throttle and the engine has had time to reach its maximum operating speed. This, along with a proper and strong grip, will cut down on kickback quite a lot. See Fig. 24-7 through 24-10.

Boring cuts are usually needed only when some obstruction keeps you from continuing through a log with a top cut or keeps you from getting underneath a log to relieve stresses. The best way to make a boring cut is to make the first contact with the wood as far back from the nose of the bar as possible. Make an angular cut until the cut becomes deep enough to serve as a guide. Then exert slight downward pressure to bring the bar slowly into line for boring on through the log.

cases it will not and you don't want to be in its way as it goes by.

There's also the chance the wood you're cutting might contain nails or other junk harder than the chain. There's also some chance you might touch the chain to a rock. This could rip off one or more teeth that could fly every which way. With your body out of line with the chain, should the saw kick back, you won't get slapped in the face with the saw and, possibly, the moving chain (Fig. 24-6).

Kickback becomes more dangerous as saw power increases. Also increased are the normal push and pull forces involved in cutting. Kickback is the reaction of the chain saw when the nose of the guide bar and chain contact an object. The nose of the guide bar recoils back toward the operator. The simplest way to prevent kickback is to make sure the nose of the guide bar doesn't make contact with anything, but that isn't

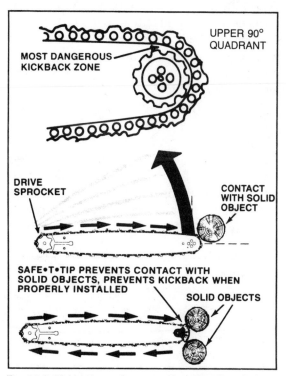

UPPER 90° QUADRANT

MOST DANGEROUS KICKBACK ZONE

DRIVE SPROCKET

CONTACT WITH SOLID OBJECT

SAFE•T•TIP PREVENTS CONTACT WITH SOLID OBJECTS, PREVENTS KICKBACK WHEN PROPERLY INSTALLED

SOLID OBJECTS

Fig. 24-7. Kickback reaction zones (courtesy Homelite).

Fig. 24-8. A potential kickback situation (courtesy Homelite).

KICKBACK PATH

(Fig. 24-11). Resisting push and pull forces should be carried out, but with as relaxed a body as possible.

Wear no loose clothing when operating a chain saw, but don't wear so many clothes, or clothing so tight, you find it hard to move. Wear no scarves, mufflers, or jewelry. Shoes need to be sturdy and have nonslip soles. Good work gloves are a help and those with nonslip palms are even better. Many people hate to work with gloves on even in cold weather, but there are two good reasons for wearing them while using a chain saw. First, when doing heavy cutting in hard wood, you might have to sharpen the chain, or at least touch it up, every half hour or so. That chain can cut your bare hands to ribbons. Second, even chain saws with vibration isolation do pass on vibration enough to cause a fair to middlilng crop of blisters. A pair of gloves does much to prevent those blisters from forming (Fig. 24-12).

Eye protection is needed. If you wear eyeglasses, make certain that they have safety lenses. If you don't wear safety glasses, wear safety goggles.

Wear a hard hat when working under large trees whether or not you can actually see loose branches above you. A *widow-maker*, a loose, dead branch high up in a tree, can live up to its name.

Wearing ear protectors, whether plugs or headsets, is a good idea as precaution against hearing loss.

When the bar is through the log, or as far in as it will go, you can continue the cut upward or downward as needed. Boring cuts, by the way, cause rapid bar and chain wear because of the small area in touch with the wood during cutting.

Pull is the effect you'll notice when you're making a cut with the bottom portion of the guide bar (the most common type of cutting). You and your saw will be pulled toward the log being cut. *Push* occurs when you're using the top part of the bar to make a cut. Keeping your balance and a good grip is the way to overcome both of these forces

KICKBACK

WHEN INCORRECTLY STARTING TO BORE

KICKBACK

WHEN NOSE STRIKES ANY SOLID OBJECT

KICKBACK

IF NOSE OF SAW HITS BOTTOM OF SAW CUT WHEN REINSERTED INTO PREVIOUS CUT

Fig. 24-9. Situations known to cause kickback toward the operator (courtesy Homelite).

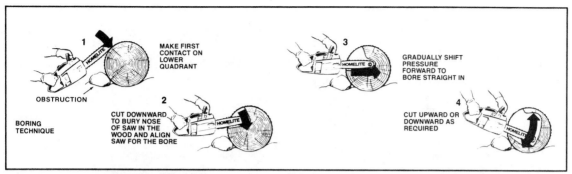

Fig. 24-10. Boring cuts (courtesy Homelite).

Work only as much as your physical condition allows. Many of us spend too much desk time to put in a full 8 or 10 hours with a chain saw. The amount of muscle and the muscle tone needed to control a chain saw after a couple of hours can be a surprise to those not used to them. You must be relaxed, but alert, to maintain safe working conditions. Getting over tired is one of the worst things you can do. Take frequent breaks.

Don't drink when working with a chain saw, and make sure any drugs your doctor prescribes are not the sort that will cause drowsiness. Make the same check on non-prescription medications.

Any heavy work with a moderate- to large-size chain saw is just that—heavy work. If you have physical ailments, or fear you might have, get a doctor's checkup before setting out into the woods. The exercise might be good for you, but in some cases it could be the final straw.

Use a chain cover when carrying a chain saw or a case for the entire saw. When you expect to be working with a chain saw in the woods, you'll need to tote along more than one or two accessories (Fig. 24-13). As a start, extra fuel, extra chain oil, and a funnel will be needed. Use the proper container for the fuel—a metal safety can—with the fuel premixed at home so it's ready to go.

Chain oil can be carried in its original container: you should carry at least a quart with you. This depends on the size of the reservoir on your chain saw. Most cutting will use a tank of fuel to a reservoir of fuel oil. If your saw has an 18-ounce-or-so chain-oil reservoir, and you go through four tanks of fuel, you're going to come up short with only a quart. Chain oil usually comes in plastic bottles in 1-quart, ½-gallon, and 1-gallon sizes. Many people use low-grade, 30-weight motor oil. That will usually mean that you need another container once the can is opened.

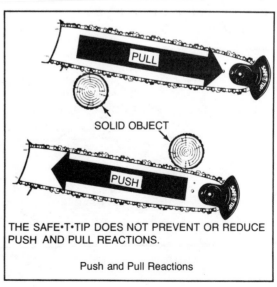

THE SAFE•T•TIP DOES NOT PREVENT OR REDUCE PUSH AND PULL REACTIONS.

Push and Pull Reactions

Fig. 24-11. Push-pull effects (courtesy Homelite).

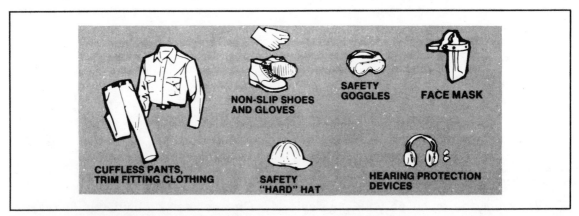

Fig. 24-12. Clothing and gear (courtesy Homelite).

Plastic or aluminum felling wedges can be extremely handy if you misjudge stresses when bucking a tree. They are also good for redirecting a tree that doesn't seem to want to fall where it must for safety. They'll keep a cut from clamping down on your guide bar if you misjudge things while felling. Never use a hard metal wedge to free a guide bar or help fell a tree. Last year I was taking down an old, dead tree (punk wood) and the thing settled back on the saw. I used Homelite plastic wedges to free the saw and ended up having to cut through one of the wedges, finally, to fell the tree.

A sprocket-nose guide bar makes it a good idea to take along a grease gun. An extra sparkplug and sparkplug wrench are handy. And you'll need the wrench to loosen the guide bar and a screwdriver to adjust the chain.

A fire extinguisher (on dry days) is a good idea, but an even better idea is to not cut in the woods when the weather is very dry.

Optional accessories can include extra-sharp chains, chain sharpening files, extra air filters, and a sharp, single-bit axe. Actually, the axe isn't really optional. You

Fig. 24-13. Supplies (courtesy Homelite).

342

might need the poll to drive wedges. A hatchet is usually too light for such work. Other optional tools include log-handling equipment such as log lifters and peaveys, but saplings can often be cut off and substituted for these.

CUTTING TECHNIQUES

In most cases, felling a tree will involve making more than a single cut. Some trees, up to a possible tops of 6 inches in diameter, can be felled with a single cut slanting in the direction you want it to fall. In other cases, you'll need to make what amounts to three cuts. The first two cuts form the notch. This should be just about one-third the diameter of the tree. The center of the notch should be aimed directly where you want the tree to fall. The wide area or edge of the notch should be about one-fifth the diameter of the tree. Once you've completed the notch, and removed the wood chunk, start the backcut. Normally, the backcut will come in at least 2 inches above the lower cut of the notch. For large trees, you can open up that distance a bit more (Fig. 24-14).

As you make the back cut, keep one eye on how the tree is behaving. If the tree settles back and starts to bind the chain saw's guide bar, you can almost bet the tree isn't going to fall in the notch direction. This is where plastic wedges come in handy. They are driven into the backcut to free the guide bar and tilt the tree in the intended fall direction. If you must use wedges, keep an even more careful eye on the tree. Keep the wedges driven in the cut. Stay only an inch or so behind the guide bar with the wedge tips.

Stop your back cut when there is a hinge of about two inches left between it and the notch. The hinge of uncut wood serves to keep the tree on line as it falls, giving more directional control. If there is no hinge or too little hinge left, the tree's fall will be almost uncontrolled (Fig. 24-15).

Before beginning felling plan and clear a line of retreat at a 45-degree angle to the predicted line of fall. Once the tree begins to go, drop the chain saw, or sit it down gently if the start of the fall is slow, and take off along that line. In most cases, you'll have to walk only a few yards to be safe. Getting rid of the

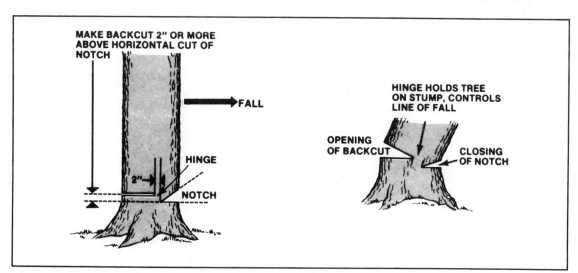

Fig. 24-14. Normal cut (courtesy Homelite).

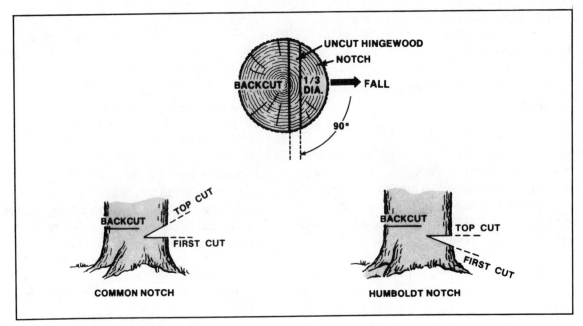

Fig. 24-15. Hinge wood (courtesy Homelite).

saw is essential. Chain saws, even with engines not running, are not ideal carry-along items when you have to rush. Taking time to be too gentle with the saw or turning off the engine could get you slapped with the tree butt ripping free of its hinge wood and kicking back. The larger the tree the more likely it is to kick back. And the larger the tree the further it is likely to kick back. Some large trees will kick back a dozen feet and some giants will kick back two dozen feet. That kick-back area is no place to be when the butt comes traveling through. See Fig. 24-16.

If you're felling a tree on a hill, always make your escape path on the uphill side of the tree. There's not much point in felling a tree, well clear of you, only to have it roll downhill and over you. Don't believe branches will keep it from rolling. About three years ago, I dropped a huge white oak on a steep hill. The tree used up most of a 2-foot bar cutting from both sides. When it hit

it really shook the ground. It rolled downhill a good 10 or 12 feet before coming to rest. There were plenty of branches.

Felling trees against their natural fall lines can be quite a job. It isn't really something (especially on large trees) anyone inexperienced in using a chain saw should try. Leaners are probably the worst. If the lean is bad enough, no technique will bring it down against its natural line of fall. If at all possible, drop leaners in the direction they lean. Even the straight-line fall with a leaner can present problems such as barber-chaired stumps when a standard hinge and a normal backcut are used.

For such trees, start with a normal notch on the downhill face of the tree. Follow with a smaller side notch. Cut number three is a third notch in the opposite side of the tree, after which you come in with the backcut. In such cases, the first notch is deeper than normal. Bring in the undercut for the notch to the point where you feel the tree might start to settle and bind the guide bar. Make sure it doesn't because a saw bound in such an undercut poses a real problem. It usually requires a second saw to cut it loose (with damage result to one or both). See Fig. 24-16.

To drop a more normally situated tree away from its natural line of fall, you need a couple of plastic wedges. Once the notch is cut, begin the back cut. As you cut, leave the end of the hinge closest to the desired fall line thicker than the hinge on the other side. Drive the wedges into the backcut in line with the preferred direction of fall (that is, with the narrow end of the wedges pointing at where you want the tree to drop). Keep them driven as tightly as possible until the tree starts to go. See Fig. 24-17.

In more extreme cases, a block and tackle or a single-pulley arrangement will be needed. The block and tackle allows the person doing the hauling on the line to apply much more power, but it is a more complicated setup. Usually, this sort of arrangement is only needed when you have to make sure a tree will miss power lines, houses,

FELLING LEANERS

This variation is designed to prevent splitting and "barber chair" of leaners.

All standard felling techniques apply to leaning trees except as follows:

1. Make the directional control face notch shallower than usual.
2. Make shallow notches on both sides of the tree to cut through the outer layer (sapwood).
3. Now make your back cut to leave a parallel hinge.

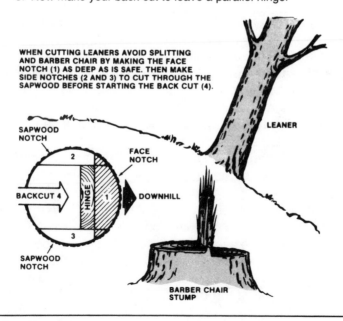

WHEN CUTTING LEANERS AVOID SPLITTING AND BARBER CHAIR BY MAKING THE FACE NOTCH (1) AS DEEP AS IS SAFE. THEN MAKE SIDE NOTCHES (2 AND 3) TO CUT THROUGH THE SAPWOOD BEFORE STARTING THE BACK CUT (4).

SAPWOOD NOTCH

FACE NOTCH

BACKCUT 4

HINGE

DOWNHILL

SAPWOOD NOTCH

LEANER

BARBER CHAIR STUMP

Fig. 24-16. Leaners (courtesy Homelite).

345

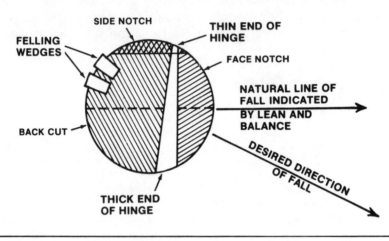

CHANGING THE DIRECTION OF FALL
(from the natural line of fall)

1. Where you would leave a parallel hinge (hingewood of equal thickness on both sides) the hinge is left thicker on the side *toward* which you want the tree to swing (away from the natural line of fall). The thicker hinge on that side will hold up the fall so that the tree will fall to that side.

2. Place your wedges in the back cut *between the back-center and the narrow side* of the hinge. Drive in the wedges to force the tree over in the direction desired.

SIDE NOTCH

THIN END OF HINGE

FELLING WEDGES

FACE NOTCH

NATURAL LINE OF FALL INDICATED BY LEAN AND BALANCE

BACK CUT

DESIRED DIRECTION OF FALL

THICK END OF HINGE

Fig. 24-17. Using felling wedges (courtesy Homelite).

and other expensive items. The rope handler must always be at least twice the tree height away from the tree because the tree will be falling in his direction and will have some additional impetus. Tree height is easy to misjudge. Remember that it's far better to be safe than crushed. The further up the tree being felled you can get the rope, the more pressure can be applied. See Fig. 24-18.

Trees too large to be cut with a single pass of the chain saw require some special techniques. A series of cuts will be needed to get the extra depth of cut needed (Fig. 24-19). Make the first cut by pivoting the bar into the cut (on what ever side of the trunk you select). The same technique is used on both notch cuts. The saw can usually then be

drawn through the centers of the cuts because it is seldom as deeply cut as the back. As you start the final cut, it's a good idea to use a wedge or two (even though they may not seem essential). The hinge wood is left as with any back cut. Remove the saw and turn it over for the second cut. Insert it carefully to keep it from touching the tip and kicking back. Keep the throttle wide open just in case. Now draw the saw forward and complete the felling.

Once you've got the tree on the ground, your job becomes one of trimming the limbs off and cutting the tree into usable sizes. Start by checking for *spring poles*. A spring pole is a sapling that has been caught and held by the falling tree. If at all possible, work

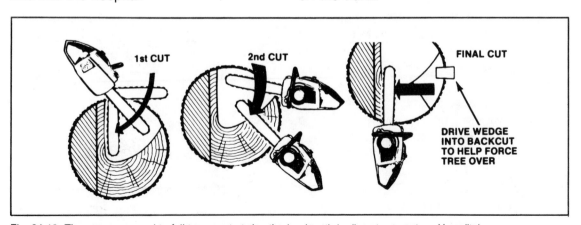

TECHNIQUES OF FELLING TREES

1. Consider the factors of wind direction and velocity, the natural lean and balance of the tree, and the location of large limbs. All these factors influence the direction in which the tree will fall. Do not try to fell a tree along a line different from its natural line of fall until you have had considerable experience in felling trees which present little problem as to where they will fall.

2. In tight situations, where a mistake in the direction of fall could be harmful, attach a tether line to the tree as illustrated.

HELPING TREE TO FALL IN DIRECTION PLANNED

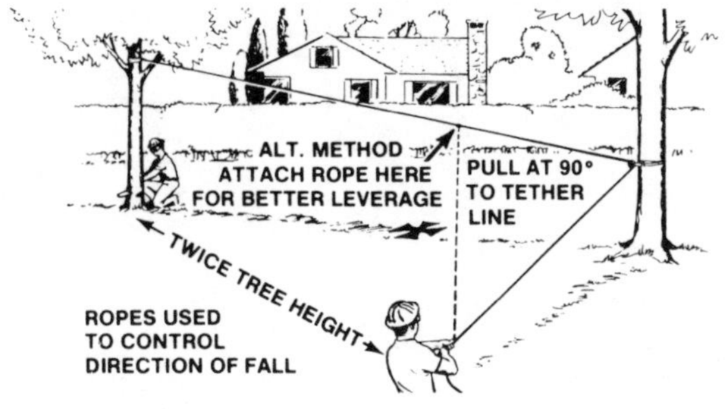

ALT. METHOD ATTACH ROPE HERE FOR BETTER LEVERAGE

PULL AT 90° TO TETHER LINE

TWICE TREE HEIGHT

ROPES USED TO CONTROL DIRECTION OF FALL

Fig. 24-18. Use ropes to control fall (courtesy Homelite).

around such spring poles when limbing and bucking. When the tree is in small enough sections, the spring poles will automatically be released as the weight on them decreases or when you roll the bucked log off of them. Try never to have to cut one. With careful study you can usually find a way to cut the spring pole so that it won't slap anyone into the hospital.

Bucking a log to usable lengths doesn't begin until the log is first limbed. It is best to use a chain saw for limbing from the opposite side. In other words, whenever possible, stand on the side opposite the branches being cut off. Always limb from the uphill side of a tree. Unless the tree is a real monster, you shouldn't limb it while standing on the trunk.

1st CUT   2nd CUT   FINAL CUT

DRIVE WEDGE INTO BACKCUT TO HELP FORCE TREE OVER

Fig. 24-19. The sequence used to fell trees up to twice the bar length in diameter (courtesy Homelite).

347

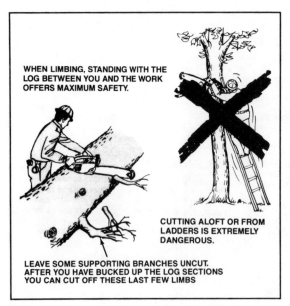

WHEN LIMBING, STANDING WITH THE LOG BETWEEN YOU AND THE WORK OFFERS MAXIMUM SAFETY.

CUTTING ALOFT OR FROM LADDERS IS EXTREMELY DANGEROUS.

LEAVE SOME SUPPORTING BRANCHES UNCUT. AFTER YOU HAVE BUCKED UP THE LOG SECTIONS YOU CAN CUT OFF THESE LAST FEW LIMBS

Fig. 24-20. The working area (courtesy Homelite).

1. Position yourself and the saw for cutting. Hold the saw near the log and throttle up to full speed just before letting the chain touch the wood. Then exert moderate feed pressure to help the chain cut the wood. The chain must always be running at full throttle speed when it is contacting the wood, or you will burn out the clutch.
2. If desired you can pivot the saw blade back and forth during cutting. This often helps to speed up the cutting a bit.

Fig. 24-21. Bucking on through (courtesy Homelite).

If you leave a few limbs on the underside of the tree, it will usually be easier to buck. When bucking a log, the selection of length is up to you. For firewood, lengths from 16 inches to 30 inches are common (the shorter lengths are more easily split).

Anyone selling to a sawmill will cut to 10-foot or greater lengths. Various pulpwood companies require different lengths (Fig. 24-20). Small-diameter logs can be bucked right on through even when the bumper can't be placed directly against the log. Larger logs are more easily bucked if you can bring the bumper right up to it and pivot the saw on through the log (Figs. 24-21 and 24-22).

Keep the chain at its top and nose section from making contact with the wood being bucked. Also keep it all from contact with the ground or any object other than the log being cut. Touching the chain to the ground will, at best, speed dulling and contact with the nose could cause kickback.

When you're bucking wood, two cuts are used (Fig. 24-23). *Overbucking* is the cut used when you are coming down onto the log with the bottom part of the guide bar. With an *underbuck*, you cut into the log from the underside using the top of the guide bar. Some logs can be cut just an overbuck or just an underbuck, but in many cases you'll have to use a combination of the two to keep the guide bar and chain from getting bound up (and a bound-up chain saw can be a pain. I can recall having to use a truck to pull a log end far enough to free a hung-up saw).

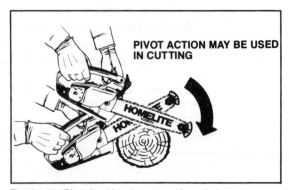

PIVOT ACTION MAY BE USED IN CUTTING

Fig. 24-22. Pivot bucking (courtesy Homelite).

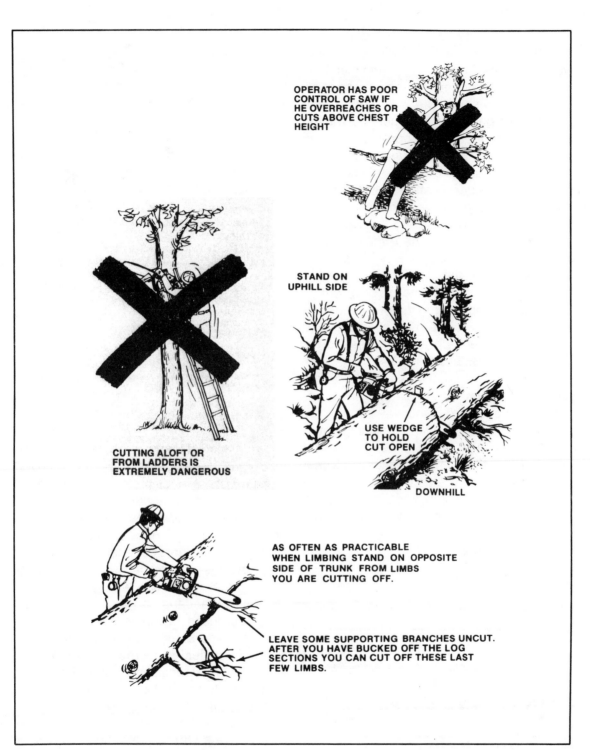

Fig. 24-23. Work area precautions (courtesy Homelite).

Wood is quite heavy and it does bend and flex. As you cut through a log and weaken it, it will bend at that point unless it is lying flat on the ground under no stress at all. To avoid stressing the cut closed and pinching the guide bar, you must cut the log in such a way that the cut opens up instead of closing down. For logs supported at both ends, an overbuck through the middle would pinch the guide bar. Therefore, two cuts are needed. First use an overbuck going about one-third of the way through the log. Then bring an underbuck up the remaining two-thirds of the log to meet the overbuck. The overbuck relieves the top of the log stresses and prevents pinching at the top of the cut. In cases where end support is not so extreme, you can sometimes overbuck at an angle so that the cut opens up as the stress is relieved. See Figs. 24-24 and 24-25.

Limbing live trees works on the same principals, but the first cut made is an underbuck about one-third of the way through the limb. This is then met with a finishing cut to keep from splitting off sections of bark and wood and possibly harming the tree. It's best to begin the cutting some distance from the main trunk, drop the limb, and then lop off the stub close to the trunk. After that it must receive a coating of sealer to keep insects out. See Fig. 24-26.

BASIC CARE

Like most other woodworking tools, chain

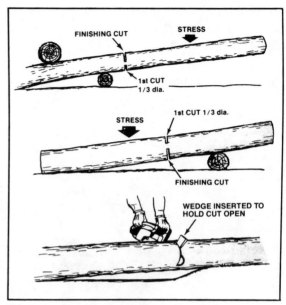

Fig. 24-25. Stress factors (courtesy Homelite).

saws cost a good deal of money. Unlike many shop tools, however, a chain saw requires more than cleaning after use and possible annual lubrication. Care and feeding of chain saws can, over the years, save a great deal of money. This is true even though improved metallurgy and improved lubricants have made most of the jobs easier (as well as less frequently necessary).

As a start, the proper fuel mixture is of great importance. You start by selecting a clean fuel container. Your best, even though most expensive, bet here is to go with a heavy metal safety can with good venting. Unvented fuel cans can provide some unhappy surprises. Gasoline is so volatile that a slight temperature change causes it to expand a great deal in volume. Unvented cans, no matter how well made, will often leak; light unvented cans can easily rupture.

After the can is selected, you'll need to choose a gasoline. Today's regular gasolines have an 89 octane rating. It's best to use fresh gasoline. You should seldom mix

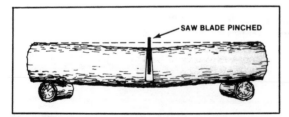

Fig. 24-24. Cutting variation according to stress (courtesy Homelite).

more than a gallon at a time. Gasoline loses many of its higher, more volatile fractions fairly rapidly. Gasoline kept mixed from year to year should never be used in a chain saw. This is one of the primary reasons why people have so much trouble starting chain saws that are otherwise in fine shape.

The oil added to the fuel mix for your chain saw must be of a type designed for use in two-stroke engines. Avoid all motor oils for 4-stroke engines as they do not mix properly with the gasoline and don't have the correct additives for protection of the engine's internal parts. Regular motor oil will cause a great deal more carbon formation and spark plug fouling. Gasoline and oil must be mixed in the amounts recommended by the manufacturer of the oil. If the oil container states

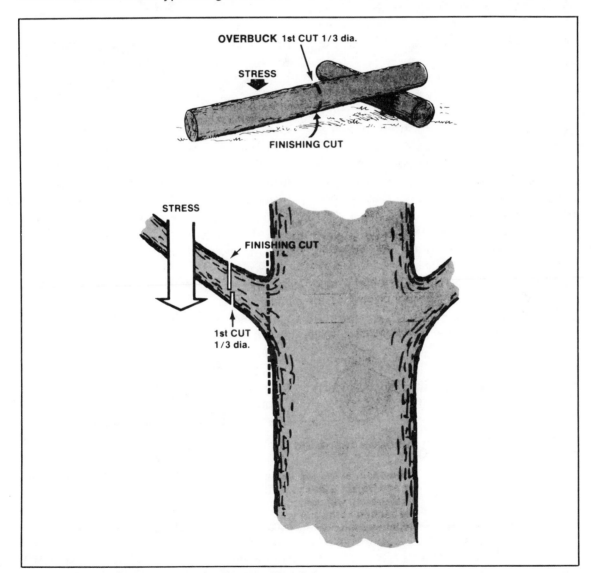

Fig. 24-26. Stressed log and limb situations (courtesy Homelite).

that you must mix the oil at a 32-to-1 ratio, that is what is required—not 16-to-1 or 50-to-1. In cases where you use a borderline product, such as outboard engine oil, you'll want to add a bit more oil than the manufacturer may recommend.

There is really no excuse for using anything but the best quality two-stroke oils. With a gasoline-to-oil ratio—in most cases, 32-to-1—a single quart will provide you with 32 quarts of fuel mix (8 gallons). And 8 gallons of fuel will run any chain saw for quite a long time.

Don't pour unmixed gasoline and then oil, or vice versa, directly into the chain saw fuel tank. Precise measurement is nearly impossible in such cases and mixing is almost sure to be poor.

Air filtration is often the last thing many chain saw owners worry about. Yet a clogged air filter causes hard starting, poor running, and general loss of power. In addition, virtually all modern chain saws have a readily reached air filter—usually one knob or screw—that can be cleaned repeatedly by tapping it on a hard surface. Some need to be washed with gasoline and then have a light bit of oil squeezed into them. The oil-soaked air filter is the most efficient. But because it sits over the carburetor feeding fuel, always make sure the oil in which you soak it is compatible with the oil mixed with your fuel. For air filters that aren't oil soaked, you might consider getting some white grease and putting a light coating of this on the interior surfaces of the air filter box to trap dust particles. Keep the coating light and wipe it off and replace it every time the air filter is cleaned.

Spark plug and ignition maintenance on chain saws is quite simple in these days of electronic ignition systems. About all you need to do, ever, is clean and gap the spark plug and replace it when that doesn't do the job. It pays even to check the spark-plug gap on new chain saws. Use only a round wire spark plug gapping tool and an electrode blender when the gap must be changed. Never tap the spark plug electrode to change the gap. If the plug must be cleaned, use a thin, flat spark plug or ignition file.

CHAINS

Chain tension and chain sharpness are the hallmarks of good handling on a chain saw. New operators tend to overlook, especially on new saws, the correct tensioning of the chain. It's a farily simple job. Start by making sure your hands are protected. A few years ago, I went to Charlotte, North Carolina to watch Homelite's Tournament of Champions. I watched some of the competitors filing their speed contest chains. The filing here is extreme. Those without gloves ended up with very bloody hands. If you don't want to wear gloves, use a rag to hold and move the chain.

Get ready to adjust the chain by loosening the bare mounting nuts, bolts, or screws while holding the nose of the bar up. Now, move the chain along the guide bar until it reaches a point of maximum tension. If you tighten a chain at a spot where it tends to run loosely along the guide bar, the final tightening will prove to be too taut and the chain will not run freely. During normal operation, a freshly tightened chain will tend to loosen up a bit. An overtightened chain creates drag, reducing cutting efficiency, and causing heat build-up. See Figs. 24-27 and 24-28.

With the chain-mounting nuts, just finger tight, lift the nose of the guide bar and set the chain tension—with a cold bar and chain—so the chain tie straps on the lower chain span don't quite touch the guide bar

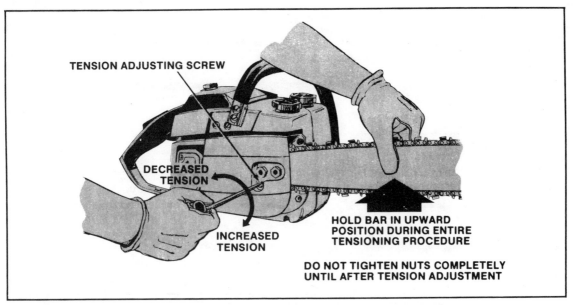

TENSION ADJUSTING SCREW

DECREASED
TENSION

INCREASED
TENSION

HOLD BAR IN UPWARD
POSITION DURING ENTIRE
TENSIONING PROCEDURE

DO NOT TIGHTEN NUTS COMPLETELY
UNTIL AFTER TENSION ADJUSTMENT

Fig. 24-27. Tensioning the chain (courtesy Homelite).

rails. This is for a hard-nose guide bar. Make sure the tie straps are no more than a dime's width away from the guide bar. If the chain is warm, set the chain tension to the point where the drive tangs hang about halfway out of the bar's groove at the center of the lower chain span. A warm chain does not need adjustment until the tangs hang all the way out of the guide bar groove. Even then, if the bar is overheated, you should wait to adjust the chain. If you grasp the nose of the guide bar with your fingers, bare, and have to pull them away, the guide bar is too warm for chain adjustment. See Fig. 24-30.

A sprocket-nose guide bar requires you to bring in enough tension so that the chain is snug against the guide bar rails. If the chain is snug against the rails, and still moves freely on the guide bar, then the adjustment is correct.

For all types of guide bars, you'll need to tighten the guide-bar holding nuts and then move the chain by hand to ensure that it moves freely. Always hold the nose of the

guide bar up while tightening the nuts.

There's no need to be over sensitive about chain adjustment, but most will need adjusting at least during a full day's cutting. New chains will have to be adjusted almost hourly until all the stretch is removed.

You might want to consider some auxiliary sharpening tools. Sears carries a powered chain sharpener that comes with several different-size grinding stones and a

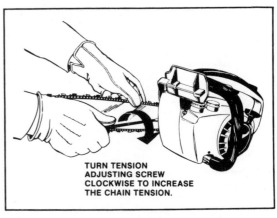

TURN TENSION
ADJUSTING SCREW
CLOCKWISE TO INCREASE
THE CHAIN TENSION.

Fig. 24-28. Tensioning chain (courtesy Homelite).

353

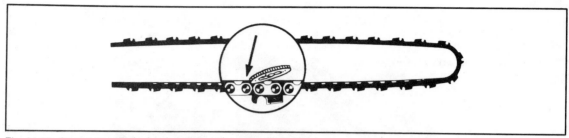

Fig. 24-29. Correct tension for hard nose bars (courtesy Homelite).

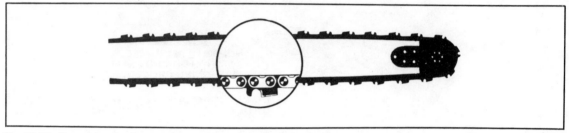

Fig. 24-30. Correct tension for sprocket nose bars (courtesy Homelite).

guide with the correct angles marked on it. It is available in 120-volt ac models and 12-volt dc models. The latter costs about $20 more than the ac models. If power sharpening isn't what you want or need, there are clamp-on hand sharpeners that help you hold the correct angle while keeping the file level. In my experience, such clamp-style holders tend to slow the sharpening down a bit. They do make it more accurate than most of us are able to by hand. For those who want to do sharpening by hand, there is a file holder that provides a handle to keep you from stabbing yourself with the file tang (most professionals don't bother with the handle).

Chain saw files cost about $1.50 or more each, but for some reason they wear rapidly. Don't expect to get more than about three sharpenings out of any of them.

The modern chain saw can provide years of almost worry-free use if you attend to safety and general care features. It is the fastest firewood getter in history and a logger's aid supreme.

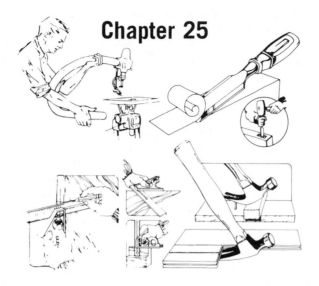

Chapter 25

Driven Fasteners

THERE ARE PRIMARILY FOUR METHODS OF fastening wood. Nailing is the least expensive and the oldest of the modern styles. Screws take longer and cost more and adhesives are generally more expensive. Glue can be neater and screws are stronger than nails. All wood joints, whether dovetail or mortise and tenon, take a great deal more time. For most large-scale projects such as residential construction, nails are the least expensive and most efficient method of wood joinery.

The variety of nails on the market allows a wide choice for most jobs. Sizes and shapes vary greatly and proper selection is almost as important as properly driving the nail.

Nails work by displacing wood fibers as the nail shaft is driven. The fibers provide a pressure on the nail shank to give holding power. Holding power will vary according to nail shank size and design. The slimmer, smoother shanks give you the least holding power and the annular, or ring, shanks giving the greatest holding power.

In addition to different shank styles, nails have different styles of heads and points. Even the shank of the nail can vary in shape from the most common round styles used in smooth- and ring-shanked styles.

Screws for working with wood come in a wide variety of styles, sizes, and materials. Round heads, flat heads for countersinking, machine screws with nuts, and screws made of brass, aluminum, and steel are readily available today. As with nails, certain techniques can aid in adding to the holding power of screws.

NAILS

Modern nails are of wire, cut pointed and headed by machine. Nails made by our ancestors were cut nails made individually. At one time, the cost of nails to build an entire house was more or less insignificant. Today that's no longer true. The proportion of the overall cost probably remains about the same, but the actual price is way, way up. Still, I can remember feeling contractors had a great deal of nerve to ask $19,500 for some houses built in Westchester, New York less than 20 years ago. Those same houses now sell in the $95,000 range. It really shouldn't be a shock to find that nails that once sold for a dime a pound now cost nearly a dollar a pound.

Nails should be carefully selected for the job at hand. Consider the size, type of head, type of point, shank finish, the nail material and the finish on the nail, if any. See Fig. 25-1. The lengths of nails in most common use are stated in inches, but nail size is listed in pennies (abbreviated d). The penny designation comes from the number of pennies it once took to buy a hundred of the particular size nails. The designation has remained in use over the years regardless of the cost of the nails. When a job calls for 10d nails, that means you need 10-penny nails (which are 3 inches long). Finishing nails are the same length as other nails of the same penny size, but they have narrower shanks and, of course, the smaller head typical of finishing nails.

When a nail grows beyond 20d, it is commonly called a *spike* (20d nails are 4 inches long). Penny designations continue on through to 60d (which is 6 inches long). Nails under 2d-size drop out of the penny

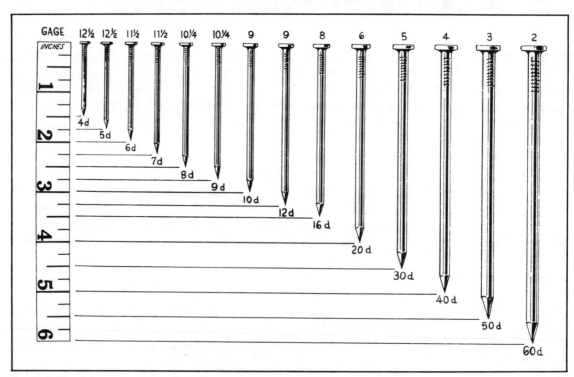

Fig. 25-1. Sizes of some common wire nails.

designation system and are size listed in inches (fractions of an inch actually, because a 2d nail is 1 inch long). Nail diameter increases with length in most nails. The minimum diameter of any nail will be the size that allows the nail to be driven in normal materials without buckling or bending. That means the stronger the material the thinner the shank can be. Hardened-steel nails can be quite a lot thinner for use in wood than can the same length aluminum or mild-steel nails. In most cases, woodworking is done with mild-steel and aluminum nails. Hardened-steel nails are used only with masonry.

Nail diameter also strongly affects the holding power of the nail. Holding power increases just about in line with the increase in diameter. Doubling the nail's diameter assures twice the holding power for the same length of nail (and also doubles the difficulty of withdrawing the nail should it be in the wrong spot or otherwise need removal). Size increases such as this are only sensible up to the point where the nail might too readily split the wood as it is driven.

When you must choose nail size (when it isn't specified for a particular job), there is a rule of thumb for face-nailing softwoods: the penetration of the nail into the bottom, or larger, piece of wood should be at least two-thirds that piece of wood's thickness. For hardwood, the nail should penetrate at least halfway through the wood. In other words, for most softwood nailing, the nail must be three times as long as the thinner of the two pieces being nailed—if possible. Hardwoods require a nail twice as long as the piece being nailed. Edge nailing of any kind of wood requires that two-thirds of the nail penetrate. Therefore, the nail must be three times as long as the wood being nailed (Table 25-1).

Nail heads come in many styles and each head has a specific purpose. Common nails with large, flat heads give the greatest holding power. Casing and finishing nails have smaller heads tapering into the shank for easy below-surface setting with a nail set so that the holes can be filled with wood putty.

Roofing nails come in various styles. Most of them have wide, flat heads. Roofing nails meant for use with large sheet roofing of metal or fiberglass will sometimes have neoprene washers under them to seal the hole made when the nail is driven.

Double-headed nails, with one head down the shank, come in two styles. The first style has double heads of about the same size. The nails are meant for temporary work such as concrete forms. The first head stops the nails and the second head makes withdrawal of the nail easier when the forms are ready to be taken down after the concrete has cured. The second type of double-headed nail is used to install insulators for electric fencing wire on posts or on trees. The lower head on the shank is smaller than the top head so that the insulator can be slipped on the nail. The top head keeps the insulator on the nail and the bottom head stops the nail before the insulator is cracked.

As an incidental point, if you do use this type of fencing and use trees as fence posts, your wisest course is to first nail a foot-long strip of 1×2 or 1×3 to the tree and nail the insulator to that. If you nail the insulator directly to the tree trunk, the tree will eventually grow right out around it (Fig. 25-2).

Nail points vary almost as much as do commonly available nail heads. The selection of point type depends on the type of wood and the holding power needed. Most common and casing nails have diamond points that allow the nail to drive easily and hold reasonably well without splitting less

Table 25-1. Recommended Schedule for Nailing Framing and Sheathing of a Wood-Frame House.

Joining	Nailing method	Nails Number	Nails Size	Nails Placement
Header to joist	End-nail	3	16d	
Joist to sill or girder	Toenail	2	10d or	
		3	8d	
Header and stringer joist to sill	Toenail		10d	16 in. on center
Bridging to joist	Toenail each end	2	8d	
Ledger strip to beam, 2 in. thick		3	16d	At each joist
Subfloor, boards:				
1 by 6 in. and smaller		2	8d	To each joist
1 by 8 in.		3	8d	To each joist
Subfloor, plywood:				
At edges			8d	6 in. on center
At intermediate joists			8d	8 in. on center
Subfloor (2 by 6 in., T&G) to joist or girder	Blind-nail (casing) and face-nail	2	16d	
Soleplate to stud, horizontal assembly	End-nail	2	16d	At each stud
Top plate to stud	End-nail	2	16d	
Stud to soleplate	Toenail	4	8d	
Soleplate to joist or blocking	Face-nail		16d	16 in. on center
Doubled studs	Face-nail, stagger		10d	16 in. on center
End stud of intersecting wall to exterior wall stud	Face-nail		16d	16 in. on center
Upper top plate to lower top plate	Face-nail		16d	16 in. on center
Upper top plate, laps and intersections	Face-nail	2	16d	
Continuous header, two pieces, each edge			12d	12 in. on center
Ceiling joist to top wall plates	Toenail	3	8d	
Ceiling joist laps at partition	Face-nail	4	16d	
Rafter to top plate	Toenail	2	8d	
Rafter to ceiling joist	Face-nail	5	10d	
Rafter to valley or hip rafter	Toenail	3	10d	
Ridge board to rafter	End-nail	3	10d	
Rafter to rafter through ridge board	Toenail	4	8d	
	Edge-nail	1	10d	
Collar beam to rafter:				
2 in. member	Face-nail	2	12d	
1 in. member	Face-nail	3	8d	
1-in. diagonal let-in brace to each stud and plate (4 nails at top)		2	8d	
Built-up corner studs:				
Studs to blocking	Face-nail	2	10d	Each side
Intersecting stud to corner studs	Face-nail		16d	12 in. on center
Built-up girders and beams, three or more members	Face-nail		20d	32 in. on center, each side
Wall sheathing:				
1 by 8 in. or less, horizontal	Face-nail	2	8d	At each stud
1 by 6 in. or greater, diagonal	Face-nail	3	8d	At each stud
Wall sheathing, vertically applied plywood:				
3/8 in. and less thick	Face-nail		6d	6 in. edge
1/2 in. and over thick	Face-nail		8d	12 in. intermediate
Wall sheathing, vertically applied fiberboard:				
1/2 in. thick	Face-nail.		1 1/2 in. roofing nail	3 in. edge and
25/32 in. thick	Face-nail		1 3/4 in. roofing nail	6 in. intermediate
Roof sheathing, boards, 4-, 6-, 8-in. width	Face-nail	2	8d	At each rafter
Roof sheathing, plywood:				
3/8 in. and less thick	Face-nail		6d	6 in. edge and 12 in. intermediate
1/2 in. and over thick	Face-nail		8d	

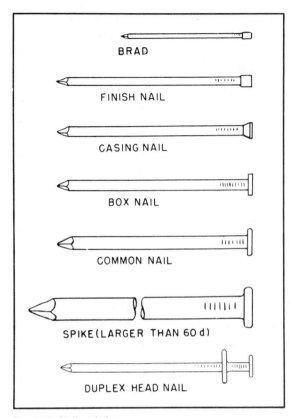

BRAD

FINISH NAIL

CASING NAIL

BOX NAIL

COMMON NAIL

SPIKE (LARGER THAN 60 d)

DUPLEX HEAD NAIL

Fig. 25-2. Nail varieties.

working, round needle-point nails are useful if you are putting up wall paneling of composition board. Such paneling might split apart too far with diamond points. Wedge-shaped points are more easily driven in hardwoods such as white oak and locust. This makes them good nails to use for plank fencing.

There are six types of round-nail shanks and a couple of cut nails with near rectangular shanks that are of importance to woodworking. Common nails come with smooth, round shanks. They give the least holding power of all shank types. More holding power is to be gained from the barbed shank nail. The spiral-threaded shank gives even more holding power.

Annular-shank (nonspiral) rings are also readily found and sometimes you'll be able to locate knurled-threaded shanks. Spiral-threaded shanks cause the nail to turn, much like a screw, as it is driven. The increase in holding power over smooth and barbed shanks is very high.

The ringed nail has closely spaced grooves all up the shank and it looks much like the spiral-threaded nail—except that the rings do not spiral. Wood fibers get forced over the shoulders of the rings and act much like wedges. Such nails are particularly good for cutting down or eliminating squeaks in floors and stairs. Knurled-thread nails don't have the same holding power as do spiral-threaded nails, but they are generally available galvanized and are thus good for outdoor work such as building decks.

You'll find the cost of threaded shank nails about double that of common smooth shanked nails, but the increase in holding power can be as much as 10 times over that smooth-shanked nail. For permanent work that requires a lot of strength, this can prove to be a bargain. At somewhat lower cost, you

dense woods such as most fir or pines. Long diamond points are found on nails meant for use with gypsum wallboard. They drive easily without causing the inner layer of the wallboard to crumble a lot.

Blunt diamond points are often available for use with denser woods. But any time you're nailing and have trouble with splitting, and can't locate blunt pointed nails, you can just hold the nail head against a solid surface and tap the nail point with a hammer to make your own. If you end up framing with a material such as yellow pine, you'll probably find this necessary. Blunt-pointed nails increase holding power and they are good for use when nailing close to a board's edges or ends—even with the less dense woods.

Of less general importance in wood-still get more holding power from nails that have their shanks coated (usually with cement). The coating doesn't last long enough, under extreme conditions, to make these ideal nails for building outdoors.

Rectangular (or flat) shank nails are used when increased holding power must be gained. Generally, they are used today for flooring purposes. Flooring nails are almost triangular in appearance, from head to point, and they do an excellent job of blind nailing hardwood flooring surfaces when tongue-and-groove flooring is put down (without splitting the tongues).

Nail materials and finishes vary quite a lot and some materials and finishes are not all that readily available. Most nails used today are made of mild-steel wire, but manufacturers of aluminum nails are trying hard to get into and act on a larger basis. You might also, at times, need nails of stainless steel, copper, or brass. Such nails are used generally only when you're nailing through copper, stainless steel, or brass. Materials must always be matched in this manner. For example, if you install aluminum gutters with steel nails, eventually corrosion will result and ruin the job.

Mild-steel nails are not suitable for use where exposure to moisture is heavy because they will rust and discolor the surface. It's at this point where nail finish becomes really important. There's nothing quite like laying out a lot of money for wood on the order of Koppers Company's Outdoor brand of pressure-treated lumber to build a deck only to have rust streaks running down the wood before it even has a chance to turn silvery gray. At the very least, galvanized (zinc plated) nails are required for such work.

There are three types of "galvanizing" used and only one of those is truly suitable for outdoor use. *Electroplating* a nail with a very thin coating of zinc is fine for indoor moisture problem areas. The nails are coated by a process called *tumbler galvanizing*. The second process produces a heavier coating of rust-resistant material, but it is still too thin for outdoor applications. What you need will be *hot-dipped galvanized nails* that have a much thicker coating of zinc.

Cement coating is another way of finishing a nail. A resin coating is used on a roughened shank surface. The coating is generally too light for long-term outdoor use (as is *bluing*, much like what you see on rifles and pistols).

For indoor uses, you'll also find finishing nails in colors to match various kinds of wall paneling. This is nothing more than paint. If a standard hammer is used to drive these nails, you've wasted your money because the paint will come off the head. Use a plastic-tipped hammer.

NAIL TYPES

The type of nail you need is determined by the kind of job you have to do. The four most common types are common nails, box nails, finishing nails, and casing nails. For building a house, you will also need flooring, roofing, and drywall nails. Most houses are built without the use of box nails or casing nails (either casing or finishing nails are used, seldom both).

Common nails and box nails both have flat heads and diamond points, but the box nail is about 15 percent smaller in diameter. Most general framing jobs are done with common nails in the appropriate size. If you're having trouble with wood splitting, you might get your lumberyard to order you some box nails. Generally, though, blunting the point of common nails will stop most splitting problems.

Finishing and casing nails do pretty much the same job, but the finishing nail, with its cupped head, is designed to be set below the wood's surface with a nail set. This will leave only a small hole to putty over. The casing nail has a flatter, countersink style of head that allows you to drive the nail flush with the wood surface and leave it be. Both casing and finishing nails have lighter shanks—and much smaller heads—than common nails and box nails. The casing nail is a bit heavier in the shank than the finishing nail.

Drywall nails are ring-shanked nails for installing gypsum wallboard. The heads are flat and slightly countersunk in style. The nails are driven just below the surface of the wallboard to form a slight dimple to take the covering of joint compound that provides a smooth, plaster-like finish after the wall is painted.

Roofing nails come in several types. For asphalt and asphalt-fiberglass shingles, you would normally use galvanized, round-shanked nails with broad, flat heads. Use a length that penetrates well into the roof sheathing boards. If you are reroofing without tearing off the old shingles, nails should be at least 1½ inches long so as to fully penetrate the old roofing material and stick well into the sheathing. Roofing nails for other types of projects will have a gasket that flattens out when the nail is driven in (thus covering the hole made with a watertight seal). This type of nail is used with metal roofing and fiberglass roofing panels.

Methods of nailing vary with the work and the material being nailed. Consider first how wet the wood is. I've helped put up some fences that should have been erected six months later. It takes them about that long for the undried wood to lose moisture content to the air.

Toenailing is a technique that is used to nail studs to sole plates, and joists to sill boards and beams. This gives good holding power, but you will usually need a slightly longer nail. Most 2-×-4 studs will need 10-penny nails. Larger materials such as joists will need 16- or 20-penny nails. Toenailing is a bit of a problem unless you do a lot of it because the frame member will tend to dance about a bit until you learn exactly how to hold things. TECO makes framing anchors of metal that are supplied with nails that cut out entirely the need for toenailing. I believe they add to the strength and overall rigidity of a structure by making sure the load force on the nails is in the direction of least pull.

Load forces must be considered when nailing. Never nail with the shank of the nail in the direction of the load force. In other words, don't nail up into a ceiling joist or other frame member and expect the lower member to support much, if any, load. Staggering nails so they are not directly in line over short distances is a good idea. Nails only a few inches apart along the grain can easily split the wood. Staggering them a half inch or so would prevent splitting.

SCREWS AND BOLTS

For wood fastening, screws and bolts offer several advantages. The primary one is added holding power when compared to nails. There are also disadvantages. Better holding power when stresses are to be fairly continual, such as on door hinges, is one advantage. Screws also make later disassembly of the work simpler (assuming you don't countersink the screw and plug the holes). Screws can also be used to pull the joints of the work more tightly together (as can clamping and gluing).

The primary disadvantage of wood screws and bolts is the additional cost in both labor and the fasteners. It takes more time to drill pilot holes and drive screws than it does to drive nails. If the work is on a piece not to be decorative or subject to special stresses, you are usually best off going with nails.

Wood screws and wood bolts differ essentially in that wood bolts go all the way through the work pieces being joined and take a nut on the opposite end to hold things together. Screws thread in to the wood without coming out the other side. Wood screws must thread their own way into the wood with the help of pilot holes (always smaller in diameter than the main part of the threaded portion of the screw shank and never as deep as the tip of the screw will penetrate), countersinking, and counterboring holes. See Fig. 25-3.

For most work, you'll almost certainly be

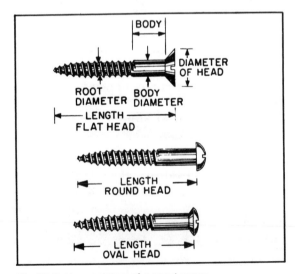

Fig. 25-3. Nomenclature of a wood screw.

using a standard slotted screw or a Phillips-head screw with a flat head (for counter-sinking), a round head, or an oval head. Phillips-head screws are preferred where you need to get a lot of pressure on the screwdriver as the crosses. Recessed slots do allow you to get more power behind driving the screw. See Fig. 25-4.

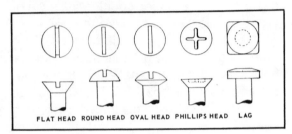

Fig. 25-4. Woodscrew heads.

Wood screws will usually be of mild steel, but in special instances—either as protection against corrosion or to give a decorative look—you will need other materials. Stainless-steel, chrome, aluminum-, brass-, and zinc-coated screws are readily found. If a screw goes through metal before entering the wood, it must be of the same type of metal or corrosion will result. Use only aluminum screws with aluminum—and so forth. For exposed applications, aluminum-, brass- and nickel-plated screws are good. Most other coatings are for decorative purposes.

When starting to drive a screw into wood, it is usually best to begin with a pilot hole. Pilot holes become especially important when you work near the edges or ends of a piece of wood. They reduce splitting to almost nothing. In softwoods, drill pilot holes no more than half as deep as the threaded shank of the screw. In hardwoods where driving a screw is especially difficult, you might want to drill the pilot hole the full depth of screw. Make sure that the hole is some-

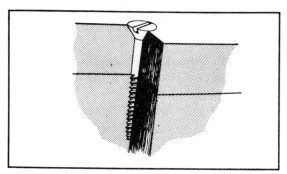

Fig. 25-5. Wood screw used to join two pieces of wood.

what smaller than the threaded portion of the screw's shank. See Fig. 25-5.

Special bits are available from Stanley Tools and elsewhere to drill pilot holes, countersink holes, and cut dowels for plugs in one, or at most, two operations. These can really speed up a job where you want to cover all screw heads or have all screw heads flush with the work surface. Start driving a screw, fairly gently, even with a pilot hole. Once the screw has a good bite in the wood, then you can apply more pressure without having to worry about the screw slipping out of the hole or the screwdriver slipping out of the slotted head.

Wood screws in woodworking don't stop with the common wood screws covered above. Lag screws are heavy wood screws with coarse threads. They come with heads meant for a wrench. The heads are either square-shaped or hexagonal. I prefer the hexagonal for longer lag screws because it is far easier to use a ratchet and socket wrench to drive them.

For example, when you are installing a 36-foot ledger board on a house you want some speed to drive the 36 or so lag screws you'll use. Lag screws, like regular wood screws, are more easily installed when pilot holes are drilled. You begin by drilling a larger hole that is the same diameter or a bit larger than the unthreaded portion of the shank. This hole goes to the depth of that unthreaded portion. You then drill a second, smaller hole, part of the way (no more than two-thirds) in to accept the threaded portion of the shank.

Bolts are only used in woodwork when extreme strength is needed. Nuts are fastened on the opposite side and usually with a flat washer to keep the nut from sinking into the wood. Carriage bolts come with square necks, finned necks, and ribbed necks. Threads only come a relatively short way up the shaft of the bolt; often this is as little as three times the bolt's diameter. The various head types are all designed to be pulled into the work as the nut is run down on the threaded portion of the carriage bolt. Holes bored for these bolts must be large enough to allow the shaft to go through, but small enough to allow the gripping device to work. I've always preferred to work to holes that are just enough larger than the bolt shank to allow the bolt to be tapped through the hole with a hammer when the shank is coated with soap or beeswax. Carriage bolts provide great strength. They are available in diameters from 1 inch down to a quarter of an inch, and in lengths up to about 2 feet. See Fig. 25-6.

Machine bolts are sometimes used in woodwork when there is metal on both sides of the wood. They also come with square

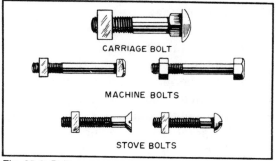

Fig. 25-6. Bolts.

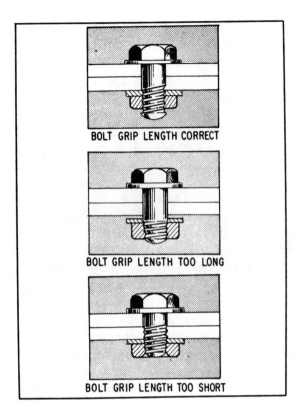

BOLT GRIP LENGTH CORRECT

BOLT GRIP LENGTH TOO LONG

BOLT GRIP LENGTH TOO SHORT

Fig. 25-7. Bolt lengths.

Table 25-2. Screw Threads per Inch.

Diameter			Threads Per Inch		
No.	Inch	Decimal Equivalent	NC	NF	EF
0	----	.0600	---	80	---
1	----	.0730	64	72	---
2	----	.0860	56	64	---
3	----	.0990	48	56	---
4	----	.1120	40	48	---
5	----	.1250	40	44	---
6	----	.1380	32	40	---
8	----	.1640	32	36	---
10	----	.1900	24	32	40
12	----	.2160	24	28	---
---	1/4	.2500	20	28	36
---	5/16	.3125	18	24	32
---	3/8	.3750	16	24	32
---	7/16	.4375	14	20	28
---	1/2	.5000	13	20	28
---	9/16	.5625	12	18	24
---	5/8	.6250	11	18	24
---	3/4	.7500	10	16	20
---	7/8	.8750	9	14	20
---	1	1.0000	8	14	20

and hexagonal heads. You are less likely to need them on wood. They are not as suitable as carriage bolts for wood-to-wood applications or wood-to-metal applications.

Stove bolts come with either round heads or flat heads and they are far from as precise in manufacture as regular wood screws or carriage bolts. They can be used in woodwork, but they seldom are. See Fig. 25-7 and Table 25-2.

Corrugated fasteners are often used these days in fastening miter joints in windows and doors. These simple devices have one square edge and one beveled edge. They are driven into the corners to fasten them fairly tightly and closely. Sizes vary with the metal usually being 18- or 22-gauge. Widths are from about half an inch to a little over an inch. Lengths are usually

about 1 inch. I'm not fond of corrugated fasteners. It has been my general experience that they are too often used to speed a job that should be done with brads. When the time comes to remove a door or window molding, the fasteners tend to split the wood more readily than would proper nails. See Fig. 25-8.

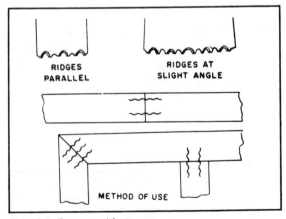

RIDGES PARALLEL

RIDGES AT SLIGHT ANGLE

METHOD OF USE

Fig. 25-8. Corrugated fasteners

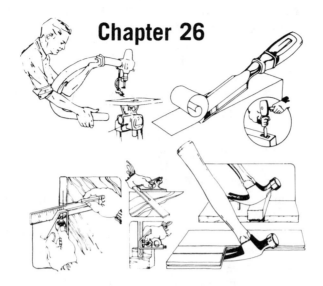

Chapter 26

Adhesives

SELECTING A PROPER ADHESIVE FOR A PAR-
ticular job is in some ways simple and in
other ways complex. Follow the manufacturers' application directions for *any* adhesive—no matter the job you're doing. In
general, when you are working with wood
you need an adhesive for a porous material.
The same is true when you are working with
paper, leather, or cloth (which is why some
white glues serve so many purposes).

You must consider the possible flexibility requirements of adhesive joints. Some
years back, I made the mistake of using a
two-part epoxy adhesive to repair a bunch of
old oak chairs with doweled backs. Within
about 2 years, the dowels at the seat holes
were starting to break or break loose because the epoxy had virtually no flexibility.
The wood needed to move a bit. The chairs,
fortunately, were not all that valuable. Over

the years, they became kindling in various
wood stoves. In essence, a joint needs to be
very little stronger and no more rigid than the
materials being joined. Too much strength
can destroy all your work of restoration or
basic construction.

You must also think of the possible
moisture-resistant qualities needed and
chances of strong heat application (such as
when a hot frying pan is set on a kitchen
counter). Can the object be clamped, if the
glue recommended requires it? Most can.
How important is the glue-setting time?
Contact cement sets at just about the time
you push the well, but thinly, coated pieces.
Most brands require about half an hour of
drying time after the surfaces are coated.
Almost none will allow you more than a two-
hour working time.

Adhesive color can be of importance on

pieces to receive a natural finish. Some adhesives give off rather nasty fumes and some can leave a not-so-healthy, after-coating. Such things would be important in finishing or refinishing such items as a crib or wooden toys. Most of today's adhesives have synthetic bases. A few natural-base glues are still to be found and they still have their uses.

Liquid hide glues are good at filling small gaps in joints. They provide a strong joint for interior furniture use. An advantage is ease of clean-up because warm water will do quite well. Most liquid hide glues will set in 2 to 3 hours, but they will need from 8 to 16 hours at 70 degrees Fahrenheit or warmer to attain full strength. You must use clamps for bonding with liquid hide glues, and you'll get, depending on the brand, a glue line that is a light brown to a brownish yellow. Liquid hide glues are water based; they have a very low resistance to moisture. They'd be fine for building a living or dining room cabinet, but they probably shouldn't be used in kitchen cabinets or bath cabinets, and certainly not in any outdoor applications.

White glues (actually polyvinyl acetates) are probably the most commonly used glues. It is not waterproof, but it is adaptable to wood, cloth, leather and almost any porous material. In addition, the glue is nontoxic and fairly fast bonding. Clamping is needed for a good bond. Work must be done at about 70 or 72 degrees Fahrenheit. White glues set in about an hour and they gain full strength after about 24 hours. Cleaning up with water is easily done. The glue line is translucent. It is useful for items under only moderate stress such as dovetailed drawers where the joint design takes most of the strain.

Creamy yellowish glues, called aliphatic resin adhesives, resemble white glues in many ways, but they offer greater strength and the need for only a half hour of clamping. They reach full strength after a 24-hour cure. Heat resistance is good (another advantage over white glues) and they are moisture resistant (not waterproof). It can be used on all the materials that white glue can. It would serve well for surfaces such as inlaid coffee table tops because aliphatic resin adhesives are not affected by varnish or lacquers.

Another "natural" glue is casein glue (made from milk protein). This comes as a light tan powder and it is mixed with water before use. Casein glue is moisture resistant (not waterproof). It can be used on exterior work where exposure is slight. Nevertheless, other glues are available that are much better for heavy outdoor exposure (the primary advantage in outdoor work with casein glue is low cost). Application can be made at any temperature above freezing with about 3 hours of clamping under medium pressure. Casein glue is also great when used on oily woods—such as teak—that many other glues will not hold at all. Disadvantages include that casein glues tend to stain dark woods and dry residue is rough on cutting edges of tools.

Resorcinol adhesives are two-part adhesives that are completely waterproof and exceptionally strong. Meant primarily for use with wood, resorcinols are excellent for items such as patio furniture. The product is packed in two cans. One can will contain a moderately bright red liquid (resin) and the other can has a tannish-colored powder for a catalyst. The resulting mix is a dark brown paste. You should never mix more than you're sure you can use within about 2 hours or so (check for manufacturers' directions for exact times).

Check manufacturers' directions with

any two-part glue even more carefully than with single-part glues. The powder catalyst of resorcinol adhesives tends to pack down when it is shipped and stored. Shaking the closed can will help to fluff the contents to the usable point. Always take care never to get any resin or catalyst in your eyes when working with adhesives.

Clamping is required until the adhesive is totally dry. This usually takes a dozen or so hours at about 70 degrees, (the time decreases as the temperature goes up). It still pays to leave the clamps in place for at least twice as long as drying takes to ensure full strength of the bond. Make sure cleaning up is done while the adhesive is still quite damp. Once the stuff hardens, it won't be removed without also removing some of the underlying surface. Gap filling in loose joints is quite good and resistance to extremes of moisture, heat, cold, and most chemicals is high. The long clamping time is a disadvantage if many pieces must be joined. You cannot, as with some glues, pull the clamps as soon as the adhesive takes its first set. Cost is also high in relation to other adhesives.

Acrylic resin adhesives continue the two-part resin-catalyst high-strength line. They have good gap-filling properties and total waterproofing. In the case of acrylic resins, the catalyst is again a powder. This glue is used where very fast work is possible (much faster than is usually required in working with wood). Glue lines are a light tan and you must use acetone for cleaning up spillage. In most cases, acrylic resin adhesives would be used, with wood, for repair work. For something like a dovetail joint, you'd have almost too little time to slip the pieces together. If you overmixed, the expense of gluing a couple of drawers together could be excessive. Clamping is not needed.

Epoxy adhesives are two-parters (with a resin and a catalyst or hardener). Proper proportions are essential for a good bond. As a result, you have an adhesive that can be used with most materials. This is provided that a bond is totally waterproof, highly heat-resistant, and almost completely nonflexible. Epoxies are among the most expensive in terms of the amount required to bond an area. They are nonflexible so they are not appropriate for most woodworking applications. The materials must be clamped until the adhesive bonds. It cannot be worked (depending on the manufacturers' instructions) under about 60 degrees Fahrenheit. It will not cure when cool.

Airplane glues (plastic cement) are highly flammable. Even a lighted cigarette a few feet away is dangerous around them. Uses are pretty well confined to model building and repairs on items that will receive little or no stress.

Super glues are highly overrated, but they can be useful in repairing some hardwoods that are not very porous. The so-called super glue, whatever the brand name, is a cyanoacrylate that bonds materials in little more than a minute. A full cure isn't reached for about 18 hours with most such products. Never work with any super glue without having some nail polish remover (acetone) at hand. The super glues have been known to bond flesh to flesh. An immediate flush with acetone will cut the bond. Keep your hands away from your eyes with this stuff. I use it mostly to repair glass or ceramic items and I always apply it with a toothpick.

Contact cements are interesting because the cement is let dry before the surfaces to be bonded are put together. After that they stay in place. They are meant to bond such dissimilar materials as a strip of Formica countertop or edging to a plywood countertop. No clamping is needed with contact cements. Both surfaces to be bonded are coated generously, but not sloppily, with the contact cement and allowed to air dry for about half an hour (with most brands you must finish the repair within two hours). No clamping is used, but when you place the two pieces together, you're not only not going to be able to pull them apart, you won't be able to budge them. Perfect alignment is needed.

When working with larger sheets of laminate on countertops, I've found that getting the perfect alignment is made simpler by placing heavy butcher's paper between the pieces. Then align them and gently draw the paper about 2 inches out. Use C-clamps to lightly hold one edge in alignment and then slowly slide the paper out of the way until all is clear. The temperature must be around 70 degrees Fahrenheit. You will probably get a slightly better bond if you take a small, hard rubber roller and run it back and forth and from side to side over the laminate several times afterward.

Construction adhesives include panel adhesives to cut out most nailing when installing wall paneling or gypsum wallboard and adhesives to aid in gaining rigidity when using plywood subflooring, roof sheathing, and sidewall sheathing during construction. Virtually all of these adhesives come in tubes to fit normal caulking guns. You clip off the indicated portion of the plastic nozzle and apply a heavy bead.

Make sure, on panels, it stays at least ¼ of an inch from the edges and that it is applied within an inch of any cutout openings (such as for switches, wall receptacles, etc.). Intermittent beads, 3 inches long and spaced 3 inches or so apart, are first used and then beads are run continuously, either down the panel or down the wall, at 16-inch centers. Set the panel in place. Use several small finishing nails driven about halfway in to hold it in place until the adhesive sets. These should be driven in the top edge of the panel. Make a paddle block of rug-covered 2×4 to press the panel against the wall once it is properly placed. Then drive the finishing nails all the way in and set them (if there is to be no molding).

Panel adhesive obviously is not going to provide a good bond if it goes on over flaking plaster, chipping or curling paint or wallpaper, or other poor surfaces. In such instances, you can either clean the wall or use nails to install the panel.

Construction adhesives are, essentially, just slightly stronger and more weatherproof versions of panel adhesives. Construction adhesives are used to bond plywood subflooring to joists, sheathing to walls and roofs, and foamed insulation panels to reducing the number of nails required and to cut labor time quite a bit. The American Plywood Association has developed a method of using construction adhesives called the glue/nail system. It gives a considerable labor savings and adds to overall building rigidity as well.

Hot-melt glues require an electric glue gun. The glue gun is plugged in and a stick of glue, or cartridge if you prefer, is inserted at the top of the gun. You wait a few minutes for the gun to heat and then use your thumb to press the top of the stick, pressing the melted glue out a small hole in the tip. Some guns have triggers. The glue supplied is waterproof and reasonably strong, but it seems to me that every time I try to reglue a chair dowel, the glue has set before my assembly is completed. No clamping is needed and even today the glue sticks aren't unreasonably priced (about $8 for 40 of them at Sears).

APPLICATION

Start by checking the manufacturers' directions and the fit of the parts. If the work is to be clamped after gluing, make sure of all clamp positions without causing a mess which could prove impossible to clean up later.

Check the application of the glue. If you're gluing oily woods, don't use a glue that won't hold. If the adhesive is the quick-setting variety, make sure it will allow you enough time to put all the pieces together or that the work can be taken in steps to allow proper assembly and bonding.

Check the temperature. Virtually all glues do better if used at 70 degrees Fahrenheit or better. If you must work at lower temperatures, make certain the adhesive will bond at those temperatures (or that you have a heat lamp or other appliance nearby and ready to go to bring the glue and the work up to the right temperature). If you work indoors in winter weather, any wood brought in should be allowed to warm up for a few hours.

Make sure the surfaces to be joined are clean, free of dirt, grease, and any old glue. Removing old glue is particularly important because new adhesives aren't likely to bond to it. It prevents the new adhesive from penetrating the wood fibers to make a bond.

Get as tight a joint fit as you can because even glues with good gap-filling capabilities work better with tight joints. If the wood you're working is tight pored and very smooth, it would be wise to use a bit of fine sandpaper to rough it up enough to allow the adhesive a better bite.

If you're working with end-grain wood (as on chair legs and chair dowels), you'll get a stronger bond by applying a light first coat of glue a few minutes before you glue the entire joint and assemble the piece. Apply adhesive evenly, smoothly, and cover all areas that will be in touch in the joint. Don't slop on glue just to be adding glue. Use only as much as is needed and not enough to have glue running out of the joint.

Don't start counting drying time until the joints have all been glued and the work is properly clamped. When you clamp work, use just enough pressure to bring the parts of the joint together firmly. Too much pressure is as bad as too little because the excess pressure will warp the piece and twist it out of alignment.

Wipe the excess glue off as soon as you finish clamping. Use water for those adhesives allowing water clean up and the manufacturer recommended solvent for all others.

With contact cements, the bond is immediate. Don't let the pieces touch until they are aligned. When rolling it after the original bond is formed, don't worry about applying too much pressure. The more the better. If you can't find a laminate roller, use a basic kitchen rolling pin for the job. Any bubbles that form between thin plastic laminates and the plywood undersurface can be removed by covering the plastic with newspaper, setting an iron on low (or silk), and pressing the bubble out, or rolling it out, once the cement is heated enough.

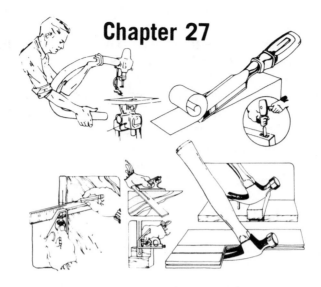

Chapter 27

Abrasives

IF YOU DON'T SELECT THE CORRECT ABRA-sives the finishes on your woodworking projects will not be nearly as fine as they might be. Coarser abrasives can be used to shape woods, especially with power sanders, but in most instances you will use them to smooth and finish raw wood, to smooth between coats, and after the final coat. Woodworking in the finer styles commonly involves not only finish sanding of the bare wood surface, but sanding between coats of finish and sanding the finish coat.

Use a light-duty abrasive for edge rounding on decks and other places that might be too sharp.

Garnet is a natural material called al-mandite. Garnet is a lot harder than flint. It has narrow, wedge-shaped grains of a reddish brown color. Garnet is fine for finish sanding.

Aluminum oxide is far harder than garnet and it has a wider grain shape. Bauxite (aluminum ore) is processed to a crystal form and small amounts of alloy material are added to toughen the relatively soft aluminum. Aluminum oxide is brown, and is fine for sanding even the harder woods.

Silicon carbide has sharply wedge-shaped grains. Greenish black silicon carbide is the hardest of these abrasives and also the sharpest of synthetic abrasives. It is more brittle than aluminum oxide. Not generally used for woodworking, the very fine grits are sometimes used for between coat sanding of finishes.

GRADING

In essence, all abrasives are graded in the same manner. After crushing, they are sifted through a series of very, very accurately woven silk screens. The mesh of the screens is rated in number of openings per linear inch of screen material. Presumably, the mesh numbers are used to designate grit size on the finished product. If you bought an 80-grit paper, that would be a grit size that would pass through a mesh with 80 openings per linear arch. Silk screening will designate grits down to 220 size. Any finer grits are graded by air floatation or sedimentation methods.

A 600-grit is far, far finer than a 60-grit abrasive. When you run into something like a 2½-grit or an 8/0. Well, the first is a 30 grit and the latter is a 280. As a not so incidental point, seldom in the silk screen/air floatation methods will you find a single number: 200/220. Not too bad. But the older system is still around, and it is still confusing.

To make things easier manufacturers some time ago began marking abrasive sheets and belts as coarse, medium, and so on to "simplify" matters. To add to your selection fun, letters after the grit number tell you the weight of the backing used and, if you have the key, the material. Sometimes! In the case of fiber backings, you won't know what's in them. Most are made from heavy ragstock paper and are used for sanding discs and drums. Combination backings are laminates of either paper and cloth or fiber and cloth. The combinations, or laminates, are used mainly for high-speed drum sanders (paper and cloth), with the second type used on heavy-duty sanding discs.

High-quality paper backings are designated as follows: A is light paper stock, for hand sanding; B doesn't appear for some reason; both C and D are of stiffer paper, often called cabinet paper and are used for pad (finishing) sanders; and E is a heavy paper backing used for drum and belt sanding. With cloth backings, J is lightweight and flexible. It is meant for sanding curves and other contours, while X is a lot heavier and is suitable only for flat or almost flat work.

The addition of adhesive to the process makes the job of picking your abrasive material even more fun. First, coated abrasives use both a bond and size coat of adhesive. Some adhesives can only do one job or the other. In most cases, fortunately, you don't have to worry whether we're using animal hide glue or resin over glue or resin over resin. All you need do is select an abrasive of the type needed. If your application is going to require resistance to a great deal of heat, use heat-resistant abrasive belts, discs, or sheets. If you need moisture resistance as well (not often with woodworking), look for a wet and dry abrasive.

The next abrasive selection quality is, fortunately, a simple one. Abrasives come with both closed and open coats and the selection depends on the surface to be smoothed. With the closed-coat abrasive, you need to consider only finish and near finish operations because in other work the coating clogs too rapidly to be economical of either time or abrasive material. Open-coat abrasives have spaces between the abrasive chunks or grain. They are best for rough sanding almost any kind of wood and taking off paint, varnish, other finishes, and any relatively soft material that would quickly clog closed-coat abrasives.

If you have a drum sander, select the drum sanding style that fits the size of your drum sander. Do the same for any other power sander. There's no sense in buying sanding discs for belt sanders, and so forth.

When sanding, you start with the coarsest abrasive and move in steps to the finest abrasive you expect to require. Roughing and removal of general material requires the coarsest grits, while blending with some material to be removed requires a medium grit. Fine finishing is done to remove the scratch marks laid down by the previous sanding operations. Very little material is removed. Polishing and rubbing blend in any scratches left by earlier finish operations. This is done with the finest grits and, often, some form of lubricant.

When you use a series of abrasives, don't make giant steps from coarse grits to very fine ones. Start coarse, go to a medium grit, and then move to a finer grit until you reach the desired level of finish. Begin with an abrasive just coarse enough to make the surface level. Cut out excessive roughness of the material and go from there to a final finish.

Final finishing with certain types of woods will require many steps after so-called final sanding. Begin with a sealer or filler and move from there to a wood stain or a varnish over the natural wood. Most people use a lacquer, rather than varnish, for several reasons. First, varnish dries very slowly and that increases dust pick up. Second, varnish doesn't retain color all that well over a long period of time. Oleoresinous varnishes, such as tung oil, are easier to use and they are less costly than lacquers. Tung oils can just be wiped on.

For really fine finishes, you'll want to use wet and dry abrasive papers, pumice and rottenstone, with oil of some sort of water as a lubricant. Water tends to raise the grain of most woods and mess up the job.

Most varnishes require a week of drying time before being rubbed out and polished. ZAR Tung Oil can be done in 12 to 24 hours (and most lacquers even sooner). A slightly different effect is had by using the finest available (#0000) steel wool for final rubbing out.

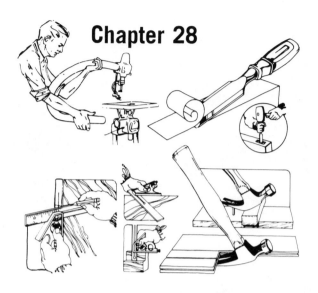

Chapter 28

Hardware

ABINET AND GENERAL HOME HARDWARE pieces, whether hinges, latches or other parts, have a lot in common. The major differences are in size, weight and strength. There is some difference in the ways, for example, decorative H-strap hinges for a cabinet door and an exterior house-door hinge can safely be installed. After all, part of the job of any door hinge is to help aid home security. Placing such a hinge on the face of the door—where it can be easily removed with only a few tools—counters overall security.

Decorative hinges are available and quite reasonable for interior doors of any kind. That is just fine, but not for exterior doors of any kind. Mortise hinges, with the hinge pins either nonremovable (not a good idea in residential construction) or installed on the inside of the door, are essential.

Today, the latchstring isn't out, though, and in almost all areas shouldn't be.

HINGES

For most residential uses, a standard-weight hinge is perfectly fine. See Fig. 28-1. Hinges such as Stanley's LifeSpan models offer four screws on each hinge plate, use stainless steel pins, and a material Stanley calls Stanite (I assume some sort of modern high durability plastic) as a bearing surface inside the hinge, as shaft liner for the hinge pin, and to take the vertical loads at the hinge joints in the pin tube. These are far preferable for exterior door use to many lightweight models. Even then Stanley's Hardware Division recommends the use of three hinges.

Raised-barrel hinges are for use in applications where the hinge is to be set deep and the jamb is very wide. Pivot-reinforced

Fig. 28-1. Door hinges (courtesy the Hardware Division of Stanley Tools).

hinges can add many years to a door's life. Stresses are transferred to the specially constructed top hinge. Damage from abusing the door should be cut back substantially, if it happens at all.

For other special applications, Paumelle hinges and olive knuckle hinges can be used to fit modern decors. They are designed to fit standard-thickness doors—1⅜-inch to 1¾-inch interior doors—and use a chrome alloy ball bearing in a hardened steel raceway with a nylon bushing over the pin to hold up under normal residential use. Several other special hinge types are available.

Use a totally concealed door hinge for medium-weight doors to 3 feet wide and 1¼ inch or more thickness. For thinner doors, if you want concealed hinges, use concealed casework hinges that will fit doors from ¾ to ⅞ of an inch thick. They shouldn't be used on doors over 2 feet wide. Stanley recommends two hinges for doors to 20 pounds. For doors 20 to 40 pounds you would use three hinges. For doors up to 60 pounds, use four hinges.

Cabinet hinges (Fig. 28-2) include those used for lipped cabinet doors and for overlay doors, pivots or pivot hinges. An overlay door in a cabinet is simply a door that overlaps the actual cabinet face. Spring-action hinges provide self-closing cabinet door action.

Ornamental cabinet hinges are fancier designs for all kinds of cabinetry. See Fig. 28-3. Ornamental hinges can be cabinet-size hinges or full-size hinges for interior and exterior uses.

When nothing fancy is needed, in the way of a hinge, for such items as shed doors, fence gates, barn doors and so on, the variety is still quite wide. Such hinges are surface mount hinges and they are quite simple to install. No mortising is needed for any of the strap or similar style hinges. See Fig. 28-4. Piano hinges are excellent for mounting tops on blanket chests.

For that Old West effect, hinges for swinging doors are readily available and easily installed. You must use care in mounting the hinge baseplate to get the exact height on any particular job. After mounting that and the pin mounts on each door, you simply place the bottom pin in the mounted baseplate hole and mark the spot where the top plate must be mounted (the process can readily be reversed, but it's usually easier to hold in the baseplate).

LATCHES

Cabinetry requires all kinds of latches and knobs. The mounting processes are usually complex. Virtually all cabinetry latch and knob mounting is begun while the wood is in the unfinished state.

Measurements are taken, the holes drilled, and the knobs and latches are checked for fit. Then all the hardware is removed and the cabinets are finished. Figures 28-5 and 28-6 give only an indication of the types of cabinet knobs and latches to be found. It is important, extremely important, in any cabinet work to keep measurements as accurate as you can when mounting such hardware. Whether the latch is magnetic or mechanical, the two parts must mate exactly for things to hold together well.

Latches for full-size doors, whether in a shed, barn or house, retain that same need for accuracy in measurement. When locksets are being installed, if the striker plate doesn't meet the door striker, you can bet that the door will pop open a lot (if it remains closed at all). This might only be an inconvenience for an interior door, but a poorly fitted striker plate is a lessening in any protection your exterior doors might give. Fig-

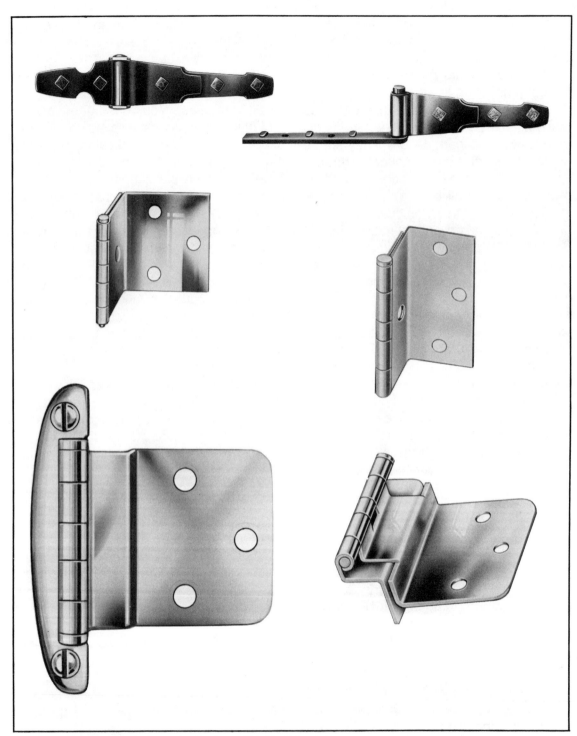

Fig. 28-2. Cabinet hinges (courtesy the Hardware Division of Stanley Tools).

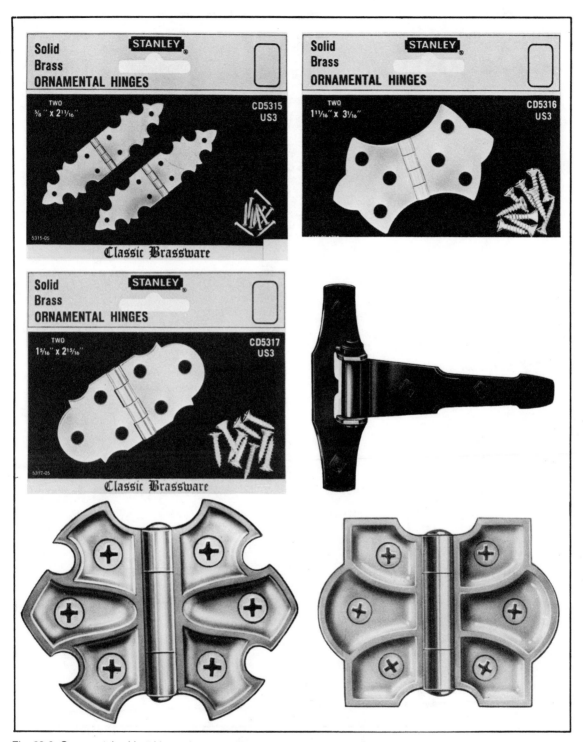

Fig. 28-3. Ornamental cabinet hinges (courtesy the Hardware Division of Stanley Tools).

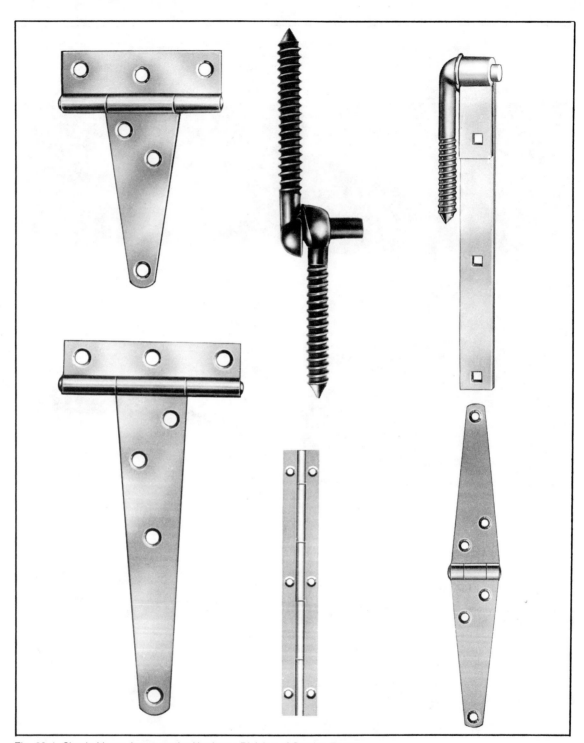

Fig. 28-4. Simple hinges (courtesy the Hardware Division of Stanley Tools).

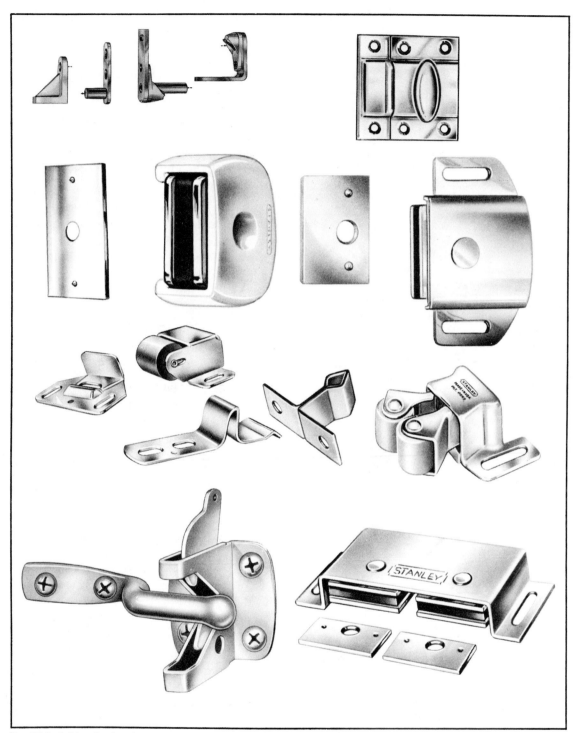

Fig. 28-5. Cabinet latches (courtesy the Hardware Division of Stanley Tools).

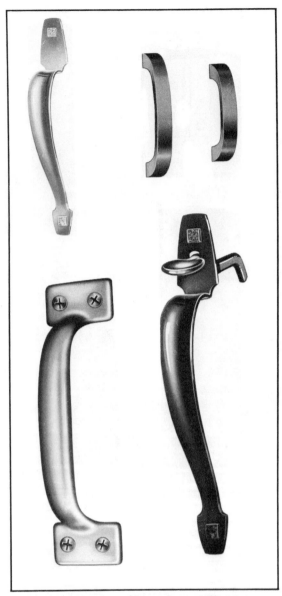

Fig. 28-6. Cabinet handles (courtesy the Hardware Division of Stanley Tools).

ure 28-7 provides some examples of the variety of latches, striker plates and pulls for full-size doors.

SLIDING DOORS

Sliding doors can be either the bypass or bifold type. You should look for, in the case of bypass sliding doors, an easy way to align the door with the jamb as well as sturdy tracks and ease of mounting. You'd need only 1¼ inches of clearance between the top of the door and the header to fit track, wheels and adjuster in place in openings 4, 5, 6, or 8 feet wide.

Bifold doors are, in a sense, also sliding doors. Instead of bypassing each other, the units fold. Because the doors fold, it is a simpler job to get nearly the full width of the opening. Depending on the number of doors and the door thickness, these will accept doors to 75 pounds, and 1¾ inches thick. For the louvered doors, total opening width is up to 6 feet and door thicknesses from 1⅛ to 1⅜ inches will fit (with each door weighing up to 30 pounds). See Fig. 28-8.

MISCELLANEOUS

The list of miscellaneous hardware items available includes adjustable closet poles, closet-pole hangers, shelf brackets, corner-braces, triple corner braces, and decorative solid brass corners for chests. Decorative wrought-metal shelf hangers are also readily available and so are differently shaped brass corner protectors. Brass box latches for small chests are easily found and you'll find it easy to order kits that employ decorative hardware. See Fig. 28-9.

KITS

The door kit is one of the larger, and often more important, kits available to the home-owner. Installing entry doors can be a forbidding experience for those who have never hung a door. The new kits do take much of the difficulty from the job. Most entryway doors do not come prehung, as do interior doors, and even those that did before

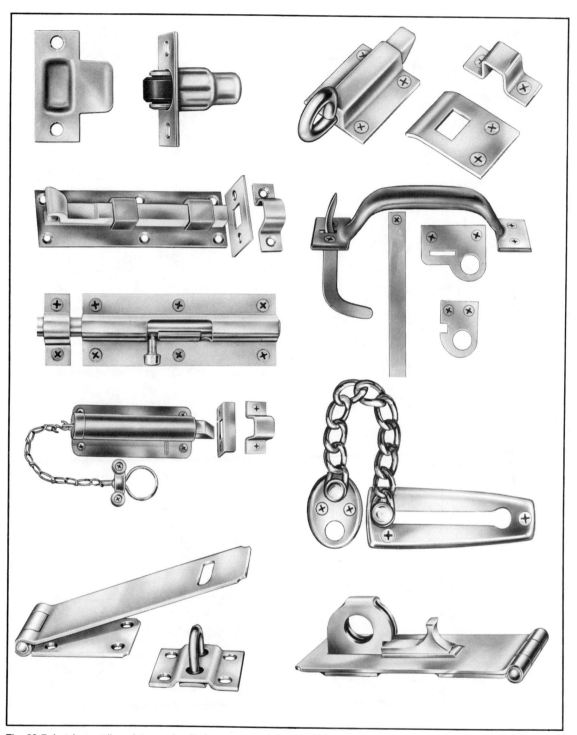

Fig. 28-7. Latches, striker plates and pulls (courtesy the Hardware Division Stanley Tools).

Fig. 28-8. Door hardware (courtesy the Hardware Division of Stanley Tools).

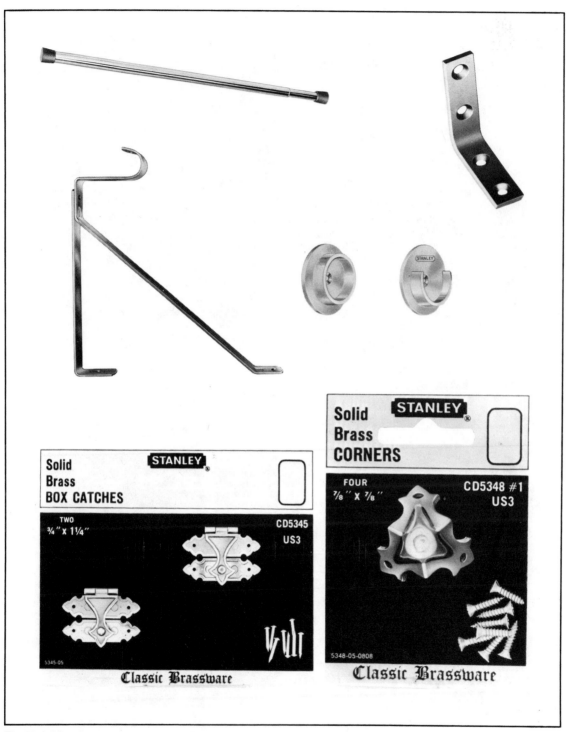

Fig. 28-9. Miscellaneous hardware (courtesy the Hardware Division of Stanley Tools).

Fig. 28-10. Door installation techniques (courtesy the Hardware Division of Stanley Tools).

Fig. 28-11. Door installation techniques (courtesy the Hardware Division of Stanley Tools).

recent times required a great deal of figuring and fooling around. Stanley calls their door unit the U-install. It is specially designed for easy installation and has a special steel adapter frame that attaches to your existing door opening. The present wood frame can remain in place. If you've never tried to replace an existing wood frame around an entryway door without tearing up interior and exterior walls, my advice is to avoid the job. According to Stanley, the average person can have a new door in place in about three hours.

The doors and door frames are made of steel, adding to security, and they are spe-cially insulated. The R-value of the door is 15.49 and it almost eliminates any need for a storm door. It has magnetic weather strip-ping and an adjustable aluminum sill. Air infiltration is almost zero. Air infiltration, or leakage, is the major source of heat—and cooling—loss in most homes.

Sizes available range from 30 inches wide to 3 feet wide; both are 80 inches tall. The job starts with the removal of the old door and trim. Then you simply proceed as shown in Figs. 28-10 and 28-11. Install your old, or a new, lockset—there's a 12-inch block to allow this installation—and you're ready to go.

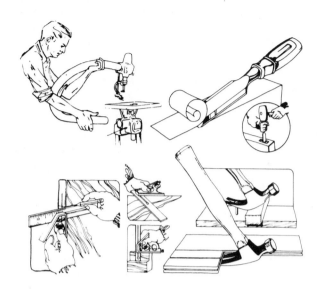

Suppliers

THE CATALOG SALES GIANTS OFFER LINES of tools made specially for them. In addition, tools, materials, plans and other details can be obtained from a number of companies.

All of the following companies advertise for mail inquiries and should respond with reasonable speed. Some will be faster than others, but don't count on catalog prices remaining firm.

Bob Morgan Wood, 1123 Barberstown Road, Louisville, KY 40204. Wood veneers and tools. The current catalog is listed at $.50.

Constantine, 2059 Eastchester Road, Bronx, NY 10461. Exotic woods, tools, veneers. Current catalog is $1.00.

D.R.I. Industries, Inc., 11100 Hampshire Avenue, Bloomington, MN 55438. Fasteners. Catalog is $1.00.

Easco Tools, Inc., 6721 Baymeadow Drive, Glen Burnie, MD 21601. A new line of curved handle hammers at around $20 each.

Edmund Scientific Co., Edscorp Building, Barrington, NJ 08007. Many tools of odd and useful natures. Free catalog.

Equality Screw Co., Inc., Box 1296, El Cajon, CA 92022. Fasteners. Free guide and price list.

The Fine Tool Shops, Inc., 20 Backus Avenue, Danbury, CT 06810. Fine and unusual tools. Catalog is $5.00.

Garrett Wade Co., 161 Avenue of the Americas, New York, NY 10013. Fine tools from around the world. Catalog is $3.00.

Hirsch Co., 8051 Central Park Avenue, Skokie, IL 60076. Special workbenches and saw horses.

Hyde Tools, Southbridge, MA 01550. A how-to book on their tool line: cost $1.50.

Liechtung, Inc., 4944 Commerce Building, Cleveland, OH 44128. Woodworking tools. Catalog is $2.00.

Markita Power Tools, 12930 East Alondra Boulevard, Cerritos, CA 90701. Heavy-duty small power tools. Free catalog.

Red Devil, Inc., 2400 Vauxhall Road, Union, NJ 07083. Painting and finishing tools.

Shopsmith, Inc., 750 Center Drive, Vandalia, OH 45377. The major multi-shop tool manufacturer. Also carries a line of high-quality hand tools and accessories. Free material on the Shopsmith Mark V. Catalog information.

Standish Co., Box 20400, Dallas, TX 75220. Unusual tools. Free catalog.

Stanley Tools, P.O. Box 3000, New Britain, CT 06050. One of the widest single manufacturer lines of hand tools in the world. Catalog: $1.00.

The Stanley Works, Ad Services Dept., Box 1800, New Britain, CT 06050. Project plans. Write for current list.

Woodcraft Supply Corp., 313 Montvale Avenue, Woburn, MA 01888. Woodworking supplies. Free catalog.

Woodline, The Japanese Woodworker, 1731 Clement Avenue, Alameda, CA 94501. Japanese tools. Inquire about the current catalog price.

The Woodworker's Store, 21801 Industrial Boulevard, Rogers, MN 55374. Tools and other supplies. Catalog: $1.00.

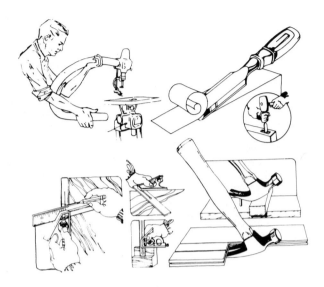

Index

Edited by Steven Bolt